Learning Boost C++ Libraries

Solve practical programming problems using powerful, portable, and expressive libraries from Boost

Arindam Mukherjee

BIRMINGHAM - MUMBAI

Learning Boost C++ Libraries

First published: July 2015

Production reference: 1280715

Published by Packt Publishing Ltd.
Livery Place
35 Livery Street
Birmingham B3 2PB, UK.

ISBN 978-1-78355-121-7

www.packtpub.com

Credits

Author
Arindam Mukherjee

Reviewers
Michael Medin
Anthony Shoumikhin
Drew Tennenbaum
Sergey Zubkov

Commissioning Editor
Usha Iyer

Acquisition Editor
Nikhil Karkal

Content Development Editors
Natasha DSouza
Sweny Sukumaran

Technical Editors
Pramod Kumavat
Saurabh Malhotra
Mitali Somaiya

Copy Editor
Rashmi Sawant

Project Coordinator
Vijay Kushlani

Proofreaders
Stephen Copestake
Safis Editing

Indexer
Hemangini Bari

Graphics
Sheetal Aute

Production Coordinator
Komal Ramchandani

Cover Work
Komal Ramchandani

About the Author

Arindam Mukherjee is a senior principal software engineer at Symantec, Pune, India, where he is involved in the research and development of business continuity solutions for enterprises. He has used C++ extensively for developing large-scale distributed systems. He was a speaker at Dr. Dobb's Journal India Conference 2014 and is the organizer of regular meets for the Pune C++ and Boost Meetup. He believes that writing books and articles, speaking for interest groups, and engaging with the programming community are the best ways to develop a critical understanding of technology. He is also an amateur musician, dabbles in food photography, and loves profound discussions with his 4-year-old daughter, especially about dinosaurs and their diets.

I would like to express my sincerest gratitude to Sergey Zubkov for helping me refine the content of this book with his critical reviews and observations. Special thanks to Anthony Shoumikhin, Drew Tennenbaum, and Michael Medin for their thoughtful reviews and feedback. A special word of thanks to Nikhil Karkal, Natasha DSouza, Pramod Kumavat, and Sweny Sukumaran at Packt Publishing for their tremendous support and helping me manage all the missed deadlines. Last but not least, I thank my father for making me believe as a child that writing books could be fun, my mother for far more than words can ever express, my wife for believing in my dream, and my daughter for making it all worthwhile.

About the Reviewers

Michael Medin is a senior developer and lead architect of the NSClient++ project. He is an avid C++ developer and has been developing open source software using C++ and the Boost library for longer than he cares to remember.

> As always, I would like to thank my beloved, Xiqun, for putting up with me when I spend countless hours working on NSClient++ and my two daughters for always bringing a smile to my face.

Anthony Shoumikhin is yet another geek who loves hacking, cycling, swimming, and occasional work at Microsoft.

He grew up in Ukraine and spent his early years in a city of rocket science and secret technologies—Dnipropetrovsk. These days, he works in Redmond, WA, on an upcoming release of Microsoft Office for Mac and iOS.

In his spare time, he creates full-stack mobile apps and funny low-level system hacks on Mac OS X and Linux (mostly in his beloved C++ empowered with Boost).

Drew Tennenbaum was introduced to programming at the age of 12. As a present, his parents gave him his first computer, a Commodore 64. A family friend purchased a book titled, *Assembly Language for Kids: Commodore 64*. Bored one night, he began reading the book and instantly found attraction in learning how to make a machine perform specific tasks. He quickly took to assembly language, which is now the foundation for much of what he works on today.

He attended the University of Arizona, where he received a BS degree in Computer Science and Math.

Since graduating from university in 1997, he has worked on a vast array of technologies, ranging from video games to embedded devices. He spent many years working on massively multiplayer online video games. In 2011, he was a Technical Director at BioWare, helping launch *Star Wars: The Old Republic*. More recently, he managed the development of the Appstore for Amazon's line of hardware devices, including the Kindle and Fire TV. In early 2015, he founded Titan Labs. Titan Labs is a small boutique consulting firm based in sunny Southern California.

In his spare time, he enjoys riding one of his many motorcycles and also holds an amateur motorcycle racing license.

I want to thank my parents for giving me the room to explore my passions in life. Without their patience, I would not have been where I am today, and more importantly, I would not have been the person I've become. I would also like to thank Dawn, my partner in life who supports me in anything I do and puts up with those late night programming sessions. Finally, I would like to thank all of my family members, including my grandmother, brother, and sister.

Sergey Zubkov is a former biochemistry researcher who became a C++ programmer. He is currently working at Morgan Stanley and spends his free time updating `http://cppreference.com`.

www.PacktPub.com

Support files, eBooks, discount offers, and more

For support files and downloads related to your book, please visit www.PacktPub.com.

Did you know that Packt offers eBook versions of every book published, with PDF and ePub files available? You can upgrade to the eBook version at www.PacktPub.com and as a print book customer, you are entitled to a discount on the eBook copy. Get in touch with us at service@packtpub.com for more details.

At www.PacktPub.com, you can also read a collection of free technical articles, sign up for a range of free newsletters and receive exclusive discounts and offers on Packt books and eBooks.

https://www2.packtpub.com/books/subscription/packtlib

Do you need instant solutions to your IT questions? PacktLib is Packt's online digital book library. Here, you can search, access, and read Packt's entire library of books.

Why subscribe?

- Fully searchable across every book published by Packt
- Copy and paste, print, and bookmark content
- On demand and accessible via a web browser

Free access for Packt account holders

If you have an account with Packt at www.PacktPub.com, you can use this to access PacktLib today and view 9 entirely free books. Simply use your login credentials for immediate access.

Table of Contents

Preface

Boost is not just a collection of useful, portable, generic C++ libraries. It is an important incubator for ideas and concepts that make their way to the ISO C++ Standard itself. If you are involved in the development of software written in C++, then learning to use the Boost libraries would save you from reinventing the wheel, improve the quality of your software, and very likely push up your productivity.

I first came across the Boost libraries a decade ago, while looking for a portable C++ regular expressions library. Over the next couple of days, porting Perl and Korn Shell text-processing code to C++ became a breeze, and I took an instant liking to Boost. In using many more Boost libraries to write software since then, I often found myself digging deep into the documentation, or asking questions on the mailing list and online forums to understand library semantics and nuances. As effective as that was, I always sorely missed a book that would get me started on the most useful Boost libraries and help me become productive faster. *This is that book.*

Boost has a wide array of libraries for solving various kinds of programming tasks. This book is a tutorial introduction to a selection of over of the most useful libraries from Boost to solve programming problems effectively. The chosen libraries represent the breadth of cross-cutting concerns from software development, including data structures and algorithms, text processing, memory management, exception safety, date and time calculations, file and directory management, concurrency, and file and network I/O, among others. You will learn about each library by understanding the kind of problems it helps solve, learning the fundamental concepts associated with it, and looking at a series of code examples to understand how the library is used. Libraries introduced earlier in this book are freely used in later examples, exposing you to the frequent synergies that occur in practice between the Boost libraries.

As a collection of peer-reviewed, open source libraries, Boost draws heavily from community expertise. I firmly believe that this book will give you a strong practical foundation in using the Boost libraries. This foundation will reflect in the quality of the software you write, and also give you the leverage to engage with the Boost community and make valuable contributions to it.

What this book covers

Chapter 1, Introducing Boost, discusses how to set up a development environment to use the Boost libraries. We cover different ways of obtaining Boost library binary packages, building them from source for different configurations, and using them in a development environment.

Chapter 2, The First Brush with Boost's Utilities, explores a handful of Boost libraries for common programming tasks that include dealing with variant data types, handling command-line arguments, and detecting the configuration parameters of the development environment.

Chapter 3, Memory Management and Exception Safety, explains what is meant by exception safety, and shows how to write exception-safe code using the different smart pointer types provided by Boost and C++11.

Chapter 4, Working with Strings, explores the Boost String Algorithms library for performing various computations with character strings, the Boost Range library for elegantly defining subsequences, the Boost Tokenizer library to split strings into tokens using different strategies, and the Boost Regex library to search for complex patterns in text.

Chapter 5, Effective Data Structures beyond STL, deals with the Boost Container library focusing on containers not available in the C++ Standard Library. We see the Pointer Container library for storing dynamically-allocated objects in action, and use the Boost Iterator library to generate various value sequences from underlying containers.

Chapter 6, Bimap and Multi-index Containers, looks at bidirectional maps and multi-index containers — two nifty container templates from Boost.

Chapter 7, Higher Order and Compile-time Programming, delves into compile-time programming using Boost Type Traits and Template Metaprogramming libraries. We take a first look at Domain Specific Embedded Languages and use Boost Phoenix to build basic expression templates. We use Boost Spirit to build simple parsers using the Spirit Qi DSEL.

Chapter 8, Date and Time Libraries, introduces the Boost Date Time and Boost Chrono libraries to represent dates, time points, intervals, and periods.

Chapter 9, Files, Directories, and IOStreams, features the Boost Filesystem library for manipulating filesystem entries, and the Boost IOStreams library for performing type-safe I/O with rich semantics.

Chapter 10, Concurrency with Boost, uses the Boost Thread library and Boost Coroutine library to write concurrent logic, and shows various synchronization techniques in action.

Chapter 11, Network Programming Using Boost Asio, shows techniques for writing scalable TCP and UDP servers and clients using the Asio library.

Appendix, C++11 Language Features Emulation, summarizes C++11 move semantics and Boost's emulation of several C++11 features in C++03.

What you need for this book

You will need a computer capable of running an operating system that supports a C++ compiler toolchain supported by Boost. You can find more details at http://www. boost.org/doc/libs/release/libs/log/doc/html/log/installation.html.

To compile and run the code from this book, you will need to install the Boost libraries version 1.56 or later. See *Chapter 1, Introducing Boost*, for more details.

Many code examples in this book require C++11 support, and thus, you should choose versions of your compiler that have good support for C++11. You can find more details at http://en.cppreference.com/w/cpp/compiler_support.

A CMake project is provided with the downloadable source code to help you quickly build all the examples using your preferred build system (gmake or Microsoft Visual Studio). In order to use this, you need to install CMake version 2.8 or later. See *Chapter 1, Introducing Boost*, for more details.

This book tries not to repeat content from the online reference manual. You should use the Boost library's online reference manuals liberally in conjunction with this book to discover additional properties, functions, and techniques. You can find the documentation at http://www.boost.org/doc/libs/.

Finally, the code listings in this book are sometimes abridged for brevity and focus. The code examples accompanying this book are complete versions of these listings, and you should use them when trying to build the examples.

Who this book is for

This book is for every C++ programmer who is interested in learning about Boost. In particular, if you have never used the Boost libraries before, *Learning Boost C++Libraries* will get you up to speed with understanding, building, deploying, and using the Boost libraries. If you are familiar with the Boost libraries, but were looking for a springboard to dive deeper and take your expertise to the next level, this book will give you a comprehensive round-up of the most useful Boost libraries and the ways to use them in practical code.

Boost is a collection of C++ libraries, and naturally, C++ is the sole language used in this book. You need to have a good working knowledge of C++. In particular, you should be able to read code that uses C++ templates, understand the C++ compilation model, and be able to use a C++ development environment on Linux, Windows, or Mac OS.

This book does not cover general C++ concepts as a rule, but some useful C++ books and articles, listed at the end of some chapters, should serve as excellent references.

Conventions

In this book, you will find a number of text styles that distinguish between different kinds of information. Here are some examples of these styles and an explanation of their meaning.

Code words and C++ language keywords *in text* are shown as follows: "We pass the number of bytes returned by `async_receive` to the handler."

Folder names, filenames, file extensions, pathnames, include file names in text are shown as follows: "The header file `boost/asio.hpp` includes most of the types and functions required for using the Asio library".

A block of code is set as follows:

```
46 int main() {
47    asio::io_service service;
48    UDPAsyncServer server(service, 55000);
49
50    boost::thread_group pool;
51    pool.create_thread([&service] { service.run(); });
52    pool.create_thread([&service] { service.run(); });
53    pool.join_all();
54 }
```

Except in smaller code snippets, each line of code is numbered for ease of reference from within the text. Important lines of code in a block are highlighted as shown above, and referred to from text using line numbers in parentheses (lines 51-52).

Any command-line input is written as follows:

```
$ g++ -g listing1.cpp -o listing1 -lboost_system -lboost_coroutine
-lboost_date_time -std=c++11
```

Important new **programming terms** are shown in bold. *Conceptual terms* are shown in italics.

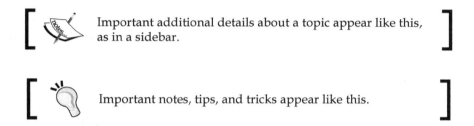

> Important additional details about a topic appear like this, as in a sidebar.

> Important notes, tips, and tricks appear like this.

Reader feedback

Feedback from our readers is always welcome. Let us know what you think about this book—what you liked or disliked. Reader feedback is important for us as it helps us develop titles that you will really get the most out of.

To send us general feedback, simply e-mail feedback@packtpub.com, and mention the book's title in the subject of your message.

If there is a topic that you have expertise in and you are interested in either writing or contributing to a book, see our author guide at www.packtpub.com/authors.

Customer support

Now that you are the proud owner of a Packt book, we have a number of things to help you to get the most from your purchase.

Downloading the example code

You can download the example code files from your account at http://www.packtpub.com for all the Packt Publishing books you have purchased. If you purchased this book elsewhere, you can visit http://www.packtpub.com/support and register to have the files e-mailed directly to you.

Errata

Although we have taken every care to ensure the accuracy of our content, mistakes do happen. If you find a mistake in one of our books—maybe a mistake in the text or the code—we would be grateful if you could report this to us. By doing so, you can save other readers from frustration and help us improve subsequent versions of this book. If you find any errata, please report them by visiting http://www.packtpub.com/submit-errata, selecting your book, clicking on the **Errata Submission Form** link, and entering the details of your errata. Once your errata are verified, your submission will be accepted and the errata will be uploaded to our website or added to any list of existing errata under the Errata section of that title.

To view the previously submitted errata, go to https://www.packtpub.com/books/content/support and enter the name of the book in the search field. The required information will appear under the **Errata** section.

Piracy

Piracy of copyrighted material on the Internet is an ongoing problem across all media. At Packt, we take the protection of our copyright and licenses very seriously. If you come across any illegal copies of our works in any form on the Internet, please provide us with the location address or website name immediately so that we can pursue a remedy.

Please contact us at copyright@packtpub.com with a link to the suspected pirated material.

We appreciate your help in protecting our authors and our ability to bring you valuable content.

Questions

If you have a problem with any aspect of this book, you can contact us at questions@packtpub.com, and we will do our best to address the problem.

1
Introducing Boost

Welcome to learning about the richest collection of C++ libraries around, that is, Boost. In this introductory chapter, we will take a look at:

- The history and evolution of Boost
- What is Boost?
- Getting started with Boost libraries

Like all the chapters in the book, this is a hands-on chapter that will require you to type in commands, write and test your code. Therefore, you should have access to a computer with a reasonably modern C++ compiler and an internet connection to download free software, including Boost libraries.

How it all started

Sometime around 1997-98, when the draft of the first C++ Standard was being finalized for publication as an ISO/IEC Standard, Robert Klarer from the IBM Labs conceived the idea of a programming language that would be called BOOSE (pronounced "booz"), and which would compete with Java in the area of high-performance embedded software development, which the latter had been aimed at. In a 1998 article for the now defunct *C++ Report* magazine, C++ guru Herb Sutter wrote a tongue-in-cheek spoof on this new language, whose name ostensibly expanded to Bjarne's Object Oriented Software Environment. In this article, he claimed that portability and *potability* were, among other things, key advantages of this language, which also supposedly promoted extraordinary camaraderie in team environments and made developers excessively happy, communicative, and passionate.

While this was an April Fools' Day article in 1998, the fact remained that the first C++ Standard was going to have a fairly basic standard library consisting of a memory allocation subsystem, type-generic containers and algorithms, a string class, basic abstractions for input and output devices, and sundry utilities. Now around the same time, a few folks from the C++ Standards Committee formed a group that worked on producing a collection of high-quality, peer-reviewed, free, and open source libraries in C++ that would have wide applicability and complement the features in standard C++. Inspired by BOOSE, perhaps for its stated competition with Java, which was a newer language but with a much richer library, they named this initiative Boost, a working title that stuck (source: FAQ on the Boost website, http://www.boost.org).

What is Boost?

Boost is a collection of free, peer-reviewed, portable, open source libraries in C++. Over the last decade and a half, there have been, as of this writing, 57 releases of the Boost libraries. In this span, Boost has released libraries of compelling usefulness that promote correct, portable, efficient, and readable C++ code. A number of prominent Standards Committee members are also the most active participants in Boost and subsequent directions of C++ standardization have been heavily influenced by the work done at Boost. Boost has provided the Standards Committee with the laboratory they need to perfect their ideas for the best new features that C++ should have. Several Boost libraries were included in the *Technical Report 1* of the C++ Standards Committee, which considerably enhanced the functionality defined in the C++ 2003 revised standard; these included both language and library features. Most of these libraries made it to the C++11 Standard published in 2011. A couple more library features that originated in Boost have been added to the latest revision of the C++ Standard known as C++14 (published in 2014).

Over the years, Boost has added libraries for string and text processing, including regular expression handling, generic containers compatible with the Standard Library, smart pointers for efficient exception-safe memory management, concurrent programming, network programming, interprocess communication, filesystem handling, template metaprogramming, and many others. The following table lists some of the prominent Boost libraries grouped by category. This is by no means exhaustive:

Category	Libraries
Memory management	Smart Ptr, Align, Pool
Data structures	Container, Array, Multi-Index, Bimap, Pointer Container, Optional, Variant, Any, Tuple, Assign
Algorithms	Algorithm, Range

Category	Libraries
String and text	Conversion, String Algo, Regex, Tokenizer, Spirit, Xpressive
Systems programming	System, Filesystem, Chrono, Date Time, Thread, Asio, Interprocess
I/O	IOStreams, Locale, Serialization, Format
Higher-order programming	Function, Bind, Phoenix, Signals2
Generic programming	Enable If, Type Traits, MPL, Fusion, Proto
Language features emulation	Foreach, Move, Exception, Parameter
Correctness and testing	Test, Static Assert
Miscellaneous	Utility, Log, Uuid, Program Options, CRC

Boost libraries have found varied use in the industry because of some very high-performance libraries (such as Boost.Asio and Boost.Intrusive), and because of a very permissive and uncomplicated Boost license, which allows source redistribution, distribution of derivative work, and distribution in a binary form for noncommercial as well as commercial purposes with minimal constraints. In the next section, we will set up a development environment that enables us to use any Boost library in our C++ code using consistent conventions. This should serve us well for the rest of the book.

Getting started with Boost libraries

We shall now set up a development sandbox for you to write code using the Boost libraries. We can either install a binary distribution of the Boost libraries, or build them from source. If we build them from source, we have a whole range of concerns to take care of from choosing a suitable naming convention for the library files and building the libraries, to making sure that we are linking them to the correct versions of the library. There are platform-specific differences too that need to be handled; we shall take a look at both the Linux and Windows environments.

Necessary software

On Linux, we will only consider the C++ compiler (g++) version 4.8.1 or later, distributed with the **GNU Compiler Collection (GCC)**. On Windows, we will use Visual Studio 2013. You can get more elaborate software support matrices for each Boost release on the Boost website.

Linux toolchain

You should be able to build Boost on most major Linux distributions. I use a Lubuntu 14.04 32-bit installation with GCC 4.8.1 and Clang 3.4. You can possibly build on much older distributions, as the Boost website lists GCC 3.3 as the minimum supported version. If you also want good C++11 support, use GCC 4.8 or higher.

Required software	Minimum version	Recommended version	Ubuntu package	Fedora/ CentOS package
GNU C++ compiler	4.8.x	4.8.4	g++	gcc-c++
GNU Standard C++ Library	4.8.x	4.8.4	libstdc++-dev	libstdc++-devel
GNU Standard C++ runtime	4.8.x	4.8.4	libstdc++	libstdc++

If you want to use Clang instead of GCC, the recommended version is 3.4 or higher. Here are the required packages on Ubuntu:

Required software	Minimum version	Recommended version	Ubuntu package
LLVM compiler toolchain	3.2	3.4	llvm
LLVM C, C++, and Objective-C compiler	3.2	3.4	clang
LLVM C++ Standard Library	3.2	3.4	libc++-dev

Windows toolchain

You should be able to build Boost on Visual Studio 7.1 upwards. I use Visual Studio 2013 on a Windows 7 64-bit installation:

Required software	Minimum version	Recommended version
Visual Studio with Visual C++	7.1	12 (2013)

I would also recommend installing 7-Zip on Windows to extract Boost sources from the `.7z` or `.tar.bz2` archives, which offer much better compression than the `.zip` archives.

Obtaining and building Boost libraries

You can build the Boost libraries from source or install them as an operating system package on platforms where such as package is available. All examples in this book use Boost version 1.57. You may choose to download a more recent version of the sources and most of the discussion here should still hold. However, few details may change from one release to the next, so you should be prepared to dig into the online documentation.

Planning your Boost sandbox

As part of our day-to-day development work using Boost, we would need access to Boost's header files and Boost's libraries. A vast number of Boost libraries are *header-only*, which means that you just need to include the appropriate headers and build your sources. Some others have to be built into binary libraries that can be *linked statically or dynamically* to your application.

If we build from source, we will first identify a directory on our development machine, where we would like to install these files. The choice is arbitrary, but we can follow conventions if they exist. So on Linux, we can choose to install the library headers and binaries under /opt/boost. On Windows, this could be f:\code\libraries\Boost. You are free to choose different paths, just avoid spaces within them for less hassle.

Library naming conventions

Boost library binaries can have names that are difficult to decipher at first. So, we shall learn about what goes into naming the libraries. Library names have different layouts. Depending on the layout, different components are added to the base name in order to identify different facets of the library's binary compatibility and functionality.

Library name components

Each library, whether static or shared, is named according to a well-defined scheme. The name of a library can be split into several components, not all of which are mandatory:

- **Prefix**: Libraries may have a prefix, typically `lib`. On Windows, only static libraries have this prefix while on Unix, all libraries have this prefix.

- **Toolset identifier**: Library names may be tagged with the string, identifying the toolset with which it was built. Roughly speaking, a toolset or toolchain is the set of system utilities, including compiler, linker, archiver, and so on, that are used to build libraries and programs. For example, `vc120` identifies the Microsoft Visual C++ 12.0 toolchain.

- **Threading model**: If a library is thread-safe, that is, it can be used in multithreaded programs without additional synchronization, then its name may be tagged with mt, which stands for multithreaded.

- **ABI**: ABI stands for **application binary interface**. This component captures details, such as whether the library is a debug library (d) or not, whether it is linked to a debug version of the runtime (g) or not, and whether the link to the runtime is static (s) or not. Thus, a debug library that is statically linked to a release version of the runtime would be marked with only sd, while one that is dynamically linked to a debug version would be marked with gd. A release version of the library dynamically linked to a release version of the runtime will have a blank ABI marker.

- **Version**: This is the version string of the Boost library. For example, 1_57 would be the version marker for the Boost 1.57 libraries.

- **Extension**: Library extensions identify the file types. On Windows, dynamic libraries have the extension .dll, while static libraries and import libraries have the extension .lib. On Linux and some other Unix systems, dynamic libraries have the extension .so, while static libraries or archives have the extension .a. Dynamic library extensions often have a version suffix, for example, .so.1.57.0.

Library name layouts

How a library name is made up of its components determines its name layout. There are three kinds of name layouts supported by Boost: versioned, system, and tagged.

Versioned layout

It is the most elaborate layout and is the default layout on Windows. The general structure of the versioned layout name is libboost_<name>-<toolset>-<threading>-<ABI>-<version>.<ext>. For example, here is the Boost.Filesystem library debug DLL for Windows: boost_filesystem-vc100-mt-gd-1_57.dll. The tokens in the filename tell the complete story. This DLL was built using Visual C++ 10.0 compiler (-vc100), is thread-safe (-mt), and is a debug DLL (d) linked dynamically to the debug version of the runtime (g). The version of Boost is 1.57 (1_57).

System layout

The default layout on Unix is the system layout that removes all the name decorations. The general structure of library names in this layout is `libboost_<name>.<ext>`. For example, here is the `Boost.System` shared library on Linux: `libboost_filesystem.so.1.57.0`. Looking at it, there is no way to tell whether it supports multithreading, whether it is a debug library, or any other detail that you could wean from a filename in the versioned layout. The `1.57.0` suffix of the extension indicates the version of the shared library. This is the Unix convention for versioning shared libraries and is not affected by the Boost name layout.

Tagged layout

There is a third layout called the tagged layout, which is midway between the versioned and system layouts in terms of detail. It removes all the version information but retains other information. Its general structure is `libboost_<name>-<threading>-<ABI>.<ext>`.

Here is the `Boost.Exception` static library from Windows built using the non-default tagged layout: `libboost_filesystem-mt.lib`. This is a static library as indicated by its `lib-` prefix. Also, `-mt` indicates that this library is thread-safe, and the lack of an ABI indicator means that this is not a debug library (`d`), nor does it link to the static runtime (`s`). Also, it does not link to the debug version of the runtime (`g`).

The versioned layout is a bit unwieldy. On systems where you need to manually specify names of libraries to link against, moving from one version of Boost to the next would require some effort to fix the build scripts. The system layout is a bit minimalistic and is great for environments where you need only one variant of a given library. However, you cannot have both debug and release versions of the library, or thread-safe and thread-unsafe ones side by side, with system layout. For this reason, in the rest of this book, we will only use tagged layout for the libraries. We will also only build thread-safe libraries (`-mt`) and shared libraries (`.dll` or `.so`). Some libraries can only be built as static libraries and, as such, would be automatically created by the Boost build system. So now, we finally get to the point where we have enough information to start creating our Boost sandbox.

Installing a Boost binary distribution

On Microsoft Windows and several distributions of Linux, you can install a binary distribution of the Boost libraries. The following table lists the methods of installing Boost on some of the popular operating systems:

Operating system	Package name	Install method
Microsoft Windows	`boost_1_57_0-msvc-12.0-64.exe` (64-bit) `boost_1_57_0-msvc-12.0-32.exe` (32-bit)	Download executable from `http://sourceforge.net/projects/boost/files/boost-binaries/` and install it by running the executable
Ubuntu	`libboost-all-dev`	`sudo apt-get install libboost-all-dev`
Fedora/ CentOS	`boost-devel`	`sudo yum install boost-devel`

Installing a binary distribution is convenient because it is the fastest way to be up and running.

Installing on Windows

Starting with Boost 1.54, you can download a binary distribution of the Boost libraries, built using Microsoft Visual Studio, from SourceForge. The download is available as a 64-bit or 32-bit installable executable that contains header files, libraries, sources, documentation, and tools. There are separate distributions for different versions of Visual Studio, from version 12 (VS 2013) backward through version 8 (VS 2005). The name of the executable is of the form `boost_ver-msvc-vcver-W.exe`, where `ver` is the Boost version (for example, 1_57_0), `vcver` is the version of Visual C++ (for example, 12.0 for Visual Studio 2013), and `W` is the native word size of your operating system (for example, 64 or 32).

As part of the installation, you can choose the directory where you want to install the Boost libraries. Let us consider that you choose to install it under `boost-dir`. Then, the following directories contain the necessary headers and libraries:

Directory	Files
`boost-dir`	This is the base directory of the Boost installation. All the header files are present in a hierarchy under the `boost` subdirectory.

Directory	Files

`boost-dir/`
`libW-msvc-`
`vcver`
	This directory contains all variants of the Boost libraries, static and shared (DLLs), debug and release. The library filenames follow the versioned layout.
	
	W: 32 or 64 depending on whether you installed a 32-bit version or 64-bit version.
	
	vcver: Visual Studio version.

`boost-dir/` `doc`	This directory contains the library documentation in the HTML format and contains scripts to build PDF docs.

Installing on Linux

On Ubuntu, you need to install the `libboost-all-dev` package. You need to perform the installation using superuser privileges, so run the following command:

```
$ sudo apt-get install libboost-all-dev
```

This installs the necessary headers and libraries in the following directories:

Directory	Files
`/usr/include`	This contains all the header files present in a hierarchy under the `boost` subdirectory.
`/usr/lib/arch-` `linux-gnu`	This contains all the Boost libraries, static and shared (DSOs). The library filenames follow the system layout. Replace arch with `x86_64` for 64-bit operating systems and with `i386` for 32-bit operating systems.

On CentOS/Fedora, you need to install the `boost-devel` package. You need to perform the installation using superuser privileges, so this is the command to run:

```
$ sudo yum install boost-devel
```

This installs the necessary headers and libraries in the following directories:

Directory	Files
`/usr/include`	This contains all the header files present in a hierarchy under the boost directory.
`/usr/lib`	This contains all the Boost libraries, static and shared (DSOs). The library filenames follow the system layout.

Building and installing the Boost libraries from source

Building the Boost libraries from source offers more flexibility, as it is easy to customize the build, use alternative compilers/toolchains, and change the default name layout like we plan to. We shall build the Boost libraries from a source archive downloaded from the Boost website http://www.boost.org or http://sourceforge.net/projects/boost. I prefer the 7-Zip or the bzip2 archives, as they have the best compression ratios. We will use Boost libraries Version 1.57, and we will look at building them only on Linux and Windows operating systems.

Optional packages

There are several *optional* packages that are used to provide additional functionality by certain Boost libraries when present. These include:

- The zlib and bzip2 development libraries, used by Boost.IOStream to read and write compressed archives in gzip and bzip2 formats

- The ICU i18n development libraries, which are heavily used by Boost. Locale and also by Boost.Regex to support Unicode regular expressions

- The expat XML parser library, used by the Boost.Graph library to support the GraphML XML vocabulary for describing graphs

Some of these libraries may be made available through your native package management systems, particularly on Linux. When installed from such packages, the Boost build system may find these libraries automatically and link them by default. If you chose to build these libraries from source and installed them at non-standard locations instead, then you should use specific environment variables to point to the installation directory of these libraries or to the include and library directories. The following table summarizes these optional libraries, their source websites, Ubuntu package names, and the environment variables needed by Boost to identify them when installed from source:

Library	Details
Zlib library (http://www.zlib.net)	Environment variable: ZLIB_SOURCE (extracted source directory)
	Ubuntu packages: zlib1g, zlib1g-dev, and zlib1c
Bzip2 library (http://www.bzip.org/downloads.html)	Environment variable: BZIP2_SOURCE (extracted source directory)
	Ubuntu packages: libbz2 and libbz2-dev

Library	Details
ICU library (`http://www.icu-project.org/download`)	Environment variables:
	`HAVE_ICU=1`
	`ICU_PATH` (installation root)
	Ubuntu package: `libicu-dev`
Expat library (`http://sourceforge.net/projects/expat`)	Environment variables: `EXPAT_INCLUDE` (expat include dir) and `EXPAT_LIBPATH` (expat library dir)
	Ubuntu packages: `libexpat1` and `libexpat1-dev`

We will be using the `gzip` and `bzip2` libraries in *Chapter 9, Files, Directories, and IOStreams*, to compress data, while we will not be using the ICU and Expat libraries for the code examples in this book.

Building the Boost libraries on Linux

If you choose not to install a binary distribution of Boost or if such a distribution is not available for your platform, then you must build the Boost libraries from source. Download the source archives for the Boost libraries, `zlib` and `bzip2`. Assuming that you want to install Boost in the `/opt/boost` directory, perform the following steps from a shell command prompt to build Boost with the GNU toolchain:

1. Create a directory and extract the Boost source archive in it:

   ```
   $ mkdir boost-src
   $ cd boost-src
   $ tar xfj /path/to/archive/boost_1_57_0.tar.bz2
   $ cd boost_1_57_0
   ```

2. Generate the Boost build system for your toolset. The following should work if you are building with **g++**:

   ```
   $ ./bootstrap.sh
   ```

   If you are using Clang instead, run the following:

   ```
   $ ./bootstrap.sh toolset=clang cxxflags="-stdlib=libc++
   -std=c++11" linkflags="-stdlib=libc++"
   ```

3. Extract the `bzip2` and `zlib` source archives and make a note of the directories they have been extracted to.

4. Build the libraries and install them. For GCC, run the following command:

```
$ ./b2 install --prefix=/opt/boost --build-dir=../boost-build
--layout=tagged variant=debug,release link=shared runtime-
link=shared threading=multi cxxflags="-std=c++11" -sZLIB_
SOURCE=<zlib-source-dir> -sBZIP2_SOURCE=<bzip2-source-dir>
```

For Clang, run the following command instead:

```
$ ./b2 install toolset=clang --prefix=/opt/boost --build-dir=../
boost-build --layout=tagged variant=debug,release link=shared
runtime-link=shared threading=multi cxxflags="-stdlib=libc++
-std=c++11" linkflags="-stdlib=libc++" -sZLIB_SOURCE=<zlib-source-
dir> -sBZIP2_SOURCE=<bzip2-source-dir>
```

The last step should build all the Boost libraries and install them under the `/opt/boost` directory, as identified by the `--prefix` option. All the libraries will be installed under `/opt/boost/lib` and all include files under `/opt/boost/include`. In addition to the Boost libraries, you should also see `libboost_zlib-mt.so` and `libboost_bzip2-mt.so`—the dynamic shared objects for `zlib` and `bzip2`, which `libboost_iostreams-mt.so` depends on.

- The `--build-dir` option would identify the directory in which the intermediate products of the build are created.

- The `--layout=tagged` option chooses the tagged layout for library names.

- We will build only thread-safe (`threading=multi`) shared libraries (`link=shared`) if possible, linked them to the dynamic runtime (`runtime-link=shared`). We would need both debug and release versions of the library (`variant=debug,release`).

- The `-sZLIB_SOURCE=<zlib-source-dir>` option is used to point the build to the directory under which the `zlib` sources were extracted in step 3; likewise, for the `bzip2` source directory, using `-sBZIP2_SOURCE=<bzip2-source-dir>`.

- If you want to build Boost libraries using support for C++11, then you should use the `cxxflags="-std=c++11"` option. Throughout the rest of the book, many of the code examples use features from C++11. Enabling a C++11 build of Boost at this point might be a good idea. Make sure that your compiler has good support for C++11. For g++, it would be version 4.8.1 or later. Also, make sure that you compile all your own code using the Boost libraries with C++11 as well.

Most of the examples in this book use C++11 features, and so you should keep the C++11 option on while compiling Boost. Appendix provides a short introduction to the important C++11 features used in this book, and also describes how you can emulate them in C++03 using Boost if you are still using an older compiler.

Building the Boost libraries on Windows

Once you have downloaded the Boost source archive, from a Windows Explorer session, create a directory called boost-src and extract the source archive inside this directory. Assuming that you want to install Boost in the boost-dir directory and boost-build is the directory in which the intermediate products of the build are kept, perform the following steps from a command prompt:

1. Initialize the 32-bit Visual C++ build environment to build the Boost build system (even if you want to build 64-bit):

   ```
   "C:\Program Files\Microsoft Visual Studio 12.0\VC\vcvarsall.bat"
   x86
   ```

2. On a 64-bit system with a 32-bit Visual Studio installation, Visual Studio is typically installed under C:\Program Files (x86), so you will have to run this command instead:

   ```
   "C:\Program Files (x86)\Microsoft Visual Studio 12.0\VC\vcvarsall.
   bat" x86
   ```

3. Generate the Boost build system for your toolset:

   ```
   cd /d drive:\path\to\boost-src
   ```

   ```
   bootstrap.bat
   ```

4. If you want to build 64-bit Boost libraries, initialize the 64-bit Visual C++ build environment:

   ```
   "C:\Program Files\Microsoft Visual Studio 12.0\VC\vcvarsall.bat"
   x86_amd64
   ```

5. On a 64-bit system with 32-bit Visual Studio installation, you will have to run this command instead:

   ```
   "C:\Program Files (x86)\Microsoft Visual Studio 12.0\VC\vcvarsall.
   bat" x86_amd64
   ```

6. Extract the bzip2 and zlib source archives, and make a note of the directories they have been extracted to.

7. Build the libraries and install them. If you want to build 32-bit libraries, use the following command line:

```
b2 install --libdir=boost-dir\libs --includedir= boost-dir\include
--build-dir= boost-build --layout=tagged variant=debug,release
threading=multi link=shared runtime-link=shared -sZLIB_
SOURCE=<zlib-src-dir> -sBZIP2_SOURCE=<bzip2-src-dir>
```

8. If you want to build 64-bit libraries, use the following command line:

```
b2 install --libdir=boost-dir\libs64 --includedir= boost-
dir\include --build-dir= boost-build64 --layout=tagged
variant=debug,release threading=multi link=shared runtime-
link=shared address-model=64 -sZLIB_SOURCE=<zlib-src-dir> -sBZIP2_
SOURCE=<bzip2-src-dir>
```

This last step builds and installs the necessary headers and libraries in the following directories:

Directory	Files
`boost-dir/ include`	All header files present in a hierarchy under the `boost` directory.
`boost-dir/libs`	All 32-bit Boost libraries, static and shared libraries (DLLs), debug and release.
`boost-dir/libs64`	All 64-bit Boost libraries, static and shared libraries (DLLs), debug and release

In addition to the Boost libraries, you should also see `boost_zlib-mt.dll` and `boost_bzip2-mt.dll` — the DLLs for `zlib` and `bzip2`, which `boost_iostreams-mt.dll` depends on.

Let us take a look at the various options we have used in the preceding commands:

- The `--build-dir` option will identify the directory in which the intermediate products of the build are created.

- The `--layout=tagged` option chooses the tagged layout for the library names, as explained earlier.

- We will build only the shared libraries (`link=shared`). If possible, link them to the dynamic runtime (`runtime-link=shared`), and create thread-safe libraries (`threading=multi`).

- We will want both debug and release versions of the library (variant=debug,release).

- The 32- and 64-bit builds will take place in separate intermediate directories identified by the --build-dir option and will be copied to separate library directories identified by the --libdir option.

- The address-model=64 option would trigger the 64-bit build.

Under Visual Studio 2013, C++11 support is automatically enabled, and you do not need to use any specific switches for the purpose.

Using Boost libraries in your projects

We shall now write our first small C++ program that uses the Boost Filesystem library to check for the existence of a file whose name is passed to on the command line and then build on Linux and Windows.

Here is the listing for chkfile.cpp:

```
1 #include <iostream>
2 #include <boost/filesystem.hpp>
3 // define a short alias for the namespace
4 namespace boostfs = boost::filesystem;
5
6 int main(int argc, char *argv[])
7 {
8   if (argc <= 1) {
9     std::cerr << "Usage: " << argv[0] << " <filename>"
10               << std::endl;
11     return 1;
12   }
13
14   boostfs::path p(argv[1]);
15
16   if (boostfs::exists(p)) {
17     std::cout << "File " << p << " exists." << std::endl;
18   } else {
19     std::cout << "File " << p << " does not exist." << '\n';
20   }
21
22   return 0;
23 }
```

Linking against Boost libraries on Linux

If you have installed Boost in a nonstandard location (which is typically the case if you have not installed it from a native package), then you will need to make sure that your preprocessor can find the Boost header files you have included using the -I option in the compiler:

```
$ g++ -c chkfile.cpp -I/opt/boost/include -std=c++11
```

This step will create an object file called chkfile.o, which we will link to the binary. You can specify which library to link to using the -l option. In case of a nonstandard installation, you will need to ensure that the linker can find the path to the library you want to link against using the -L option:

```
$ g++ chkfile.o -o chkfile -L/opt/boost/lib -lboost_filesystem-mt
-lboost_system-mt -std=c++11
```

 Use the -std=c++11 option only if you built your Boost libraries using C++11.

The preceding command line will work for either a static or a shared library. However, if both types of library are found, it will use the shared version. You can override this with appropriate linker options:

```
$ g++ chkfile.o -o chkfile -L/opt/boost/lib -Wl,-Bstatic -lboost_
filesystem-mt -Wl,-Bdynamic -lboost_system-mt -std=c++11
```

In the preceding case, the filesystem library is linked statically while others are linked dynamically. The -Wl switch is used to pass its arguments to the linker. In this case, it passes the -Bstatic and -Bdynamic switches.

If it is a shared library that you link against, then at runtime the dynamic linker needs to locate the shared library and load it too. The way to ensure this varies from one version of Unix to the other. One way to ensure this is to embed a search path in your executable using the rpath linker directive:

```
$ g++ -o chkfile chkfile.o -L/opt/boost/lib -lboost_filesystem-mt
-lboost_system-mt -Wl,-rpath,/opt/boost/lib:/usr/lib/boost -std=c++11
```

On the target system, where the binary mytest is run, the dynamic linker would look for the filesystem and system shared libraries under /opt/boost/lib and /usr/lib/boost.

Other ways besides using the `rpath` mechanism also exist. Linux uses a utility called `ldconfig` to locate shared libraries and update search paths. For more details, look at the man pages for `ldconfig (8)`. On Solaris, the `crle` utility performs a similar action.

Linking against Boost libraries on Windows

Using the Visual Studio IDE, we will have to tweak certain project settings in order to link against the Boost libraries.

First, ensure that your compiler is able to find the necessary header files:

1. Open your C++ project in Visual Studio. From the menu, select **Project | Project Properties**.

2. In the **Property Pages** dialog that comes up, expand **Configuration Properties** and select **C/C++**.

3. Edit the value of **Additional Include Directories** by adding the path to your Boost, include directories. Separate it from other entries in the field using a semicolon:

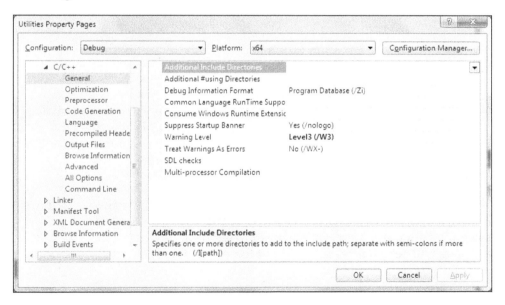

4. Next, ensure that your linker is able to find the shared or static libraries. In the **Project Properties** dialog, under **Configuration Properties**, choose **Linker**.

5. Edit the **Additional Library Directories** field to add the path to the Boost libraries, separated by a semicolon from any other entries:

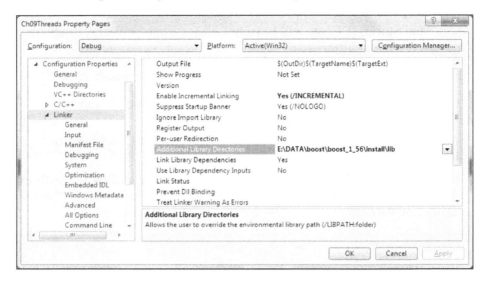

6. Now you can leverage Boost's *auto-linking* feature on Windows to automatically link to the correct libraries. To enable this, you have to define the BOOST_ALL_DYN_LINK preprocessor symbol. To do this, in the **Project Properties** dialog, navigate to **Configuration Properties | C/C++ | Preprocessor**, and add BOOST_ALL_DYN_LINK to the **Preprocessor Definitions** field, separating it from other entries with a semicolon.

If you built your Boost libraries on Windows with the default layout (versioned), this is all you will need to do for linking correctly. If we use the tagged layout, we must also define a second preprocessor symbol BOOST_AUTO_LINK_TAGGED. If we use system layout for naming, we will need to define BOOST_AUTO_LINK_NOMANGLE instead. You will get a linker error without these definitions:

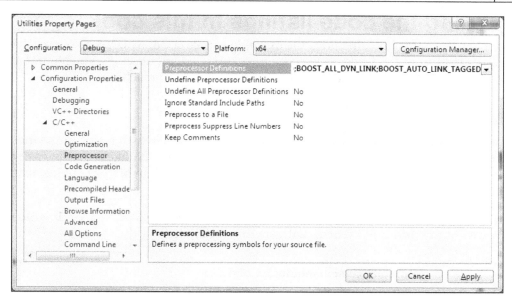

You should now be able to build your project from your IDE without any problems. In order to run your program, the dynamic linker must be able to locate the dynamic library. To take care of this, on Windows, you can add the path of your Boost libraries to the PATH environment variable. For running your programs from within the IDE, you can add the path of your Boost libraries to the PATH variable by navigating to **Debugging | Environment**, as shown in the following screenshot:

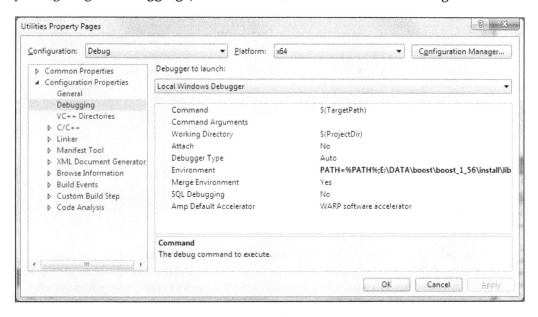

Building the code listings in this book

Each chapter in this book includes the example source code, which is also available for download from the Packt website (http://www.packtpub.com). You should download and build these examples on your development machines.

CMake

In order to build the examples, you need to install CMake, which is one of the most popular cross-platform build tools for C++ programs. With CMake, you can easily generate a build system of your choice on an operating system of your choice, using a single set of CMake specifications.

You can download a binary package for CMake from www.cmake.org, or download a source archive and build it on a platform of your choice.

Minimum version required: CMake 2.8.

Windows: A 32-bit exe-installer is available for Windows that works for both 32-bit and 64-bit builds.

Linux: CMake is usually bundled with all major Linux distributions and is available as an optional package. Consult your distribution's package repository.

Code examples

Download the source code archive and extract it to a directory on your development machine. The layout of the extracted directory would look like this:

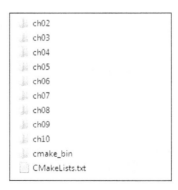

The source code archive available for download contains separate directories for each chapter. Within each chapter directory, you will find the complete source code for each example. The source code files are named based on the listing identifier.

A listing identifier is a unique tag used for examples in this book, as shown in the following screenshot:

```
Listing 11.18 Asynchronous UDP server
  1 #include <boost/asio.hpp>
  2 #include <iostream>
  3 namespace asio = boost::asio;
  4 namespace sys = boost::system;
  5
  6 const size_t MAXBUF = 256;
  7
  8 class UDPAsyncServer {
  9 public:
 10    UDPAsyncServer(asio::io_service& service,
 11                        unsigned short port)
```

Here, the listing identifier is **Listing 11.18** and indicates that this is the eighteenth example in *Chapter 11, Network Programming Using Boost Asio*. Therefore, in the ch11 folder, you will find listing11_18.cpp, which contains the asynchronous UDP server example that appears in *Chapter 11, Network Programming Using Boost Asio*. In some cases, a big example is broken down into multiple listings in the text, but they all form part of the same source file. In such cases the listings are tagged with letters; for example, listing 7.22a, 7.22b, 7.22c, and so on. You can still expect a file called listing7_22.cpp, which combines the code from these listings.

In order to build all the examples in this book, you need to follow these steps:

1. Make sure that CMake 2.8 or higher is installed.

2. Extract the source archive for the book to a directory, say srcdir.

3. Change to the cmake_bin directory under the source directory:

   ```
   $ cd srcdir/lbcpp-src/cmake_bin
   ```

4. Export the BOOST_DIR environment variable to point to the Boost installation directory.

   For example, if it is /opt/boost on Linux, you can run the following command:

   ```
   $ export BOOST_DIR=/opt/boost
   ```

   If you have installed Boost from a standard package in the package repository of your distribution, then you can skip this step.

   On Windows, if you have installed it under f:\boost, you can run this command:

   ```
   set BOOST_DIR=f:\boost
   ```

5. If the Boost include directory and the Boost library directory do not share a common parent, as may be the case if you installed a binary distribution of Boost, then you should skip setting BOOST_DIR and instead set the following two environment variables:

   ° BOOST_INCDIR should be set to the directory that contains the Boost header files, for example, /usr/include on Ubuntu.

   ° BOOST_LIBDIR should be set to the directory that contains the Boost library files, for example, /usr/lib/x86_64-linux-gnu on Ubuntu.

6. Generate the build system of your choice using CMake.

   On Linux, run the following command:

   ```
   $ cmake
   ```

   This generates a Makefile-based build system using GNU g++. If you want to use clang++ instead, export the environment variables CC and CXX, as shown here:

   ```
   export CC=`which clang`
   export CXX=`which clang++`
   ```

   On Windows, run the following command:

   ```
   $ cmake .. -G "Visual Studio 12"
   ```

   This generates a Visual C++ 2013 solution file and project files. The string passed with the -G option is called the generator string and identifies the toolchain for which you want to generate the build system. The CMake documentation lists all the supported generator strings. For our purposes, we will use **Visual Studio 12** or **Visual Studio 12 Win64**.

7. Build the sources using the generated build system.

   On Linux, you can build it by simply running the following command:

   ```
   $ gmake
   ```

   On Windows, it is best to build by opening the generated solution file in Visual C++ IDE and then building all the sources or a single source at a time. You can run the examples by running the executables formed under srcdir/lbcpp-src/bin.

We do not cover CMake in this book. It is worth exploring CMake further on your own, and a great place to get started is the CMake Wiki (http://www.cmake.org/Wiki/CMake).

Self-test questions

1. What are the different types of name layouts supported by Boost libraries?

   a. Tagged, native, and mangled

   b. Tagged, mangled, and versioned

   c. Tagged, versioned, and system

   d. Versioned, systems, and decorated

2. Boost allows you to automatically link to necessary Boost libraries on Windows.

   a. True

   b. False

3. What does the following filename tell you about the library?
   `boost_date_time-vc100-mt-gd-1_57.dll`
   Tick all that apply.

   a. It is the DateTime library.

   b. It is a thread-safe library.

   c. It was built using g++.

   d. It is not a debug library.

4. What is the name layout of the following library?
   `libboost_exception-mt-gd.lib`

   a. Tagged

   b. System

   c. Versioned

   d. Default

Summary

In this chapter, we got an overview of the Boost C++ libraries and set up a development environment for us, which should help us to easily build and run C++ programs, using Boost libraries that we will learn in the rest of the book.

In the next chapter, we will learn a variety of techniques using different Boost libraries, which simplify some common day-to-day programming tasks and set us up for the heavy lifting to be done in the later chapters.

2
The First Brush with Boost's Utilities

Over the course of this book, we will focus on a number of Boost libraries that deal with different subsystems, such as filesystems, threads, network I/O, and a variety of containers, among others. In each chapter, we will delve into the details of a few such libraries. This chapter is different, in the sense that we will pick up a set of useful and varied tricks that will help you in almost all programming situations. To that end we have the following topics lined up for us:

- Simple data structures
- Working with heterogeneous values
- Handling command-line arguments
- Other utilities and compile-time checks

This is the kitchen-sink chapter that you can keep coming back to and scour for an interesting technique that would seem to apply to a problem at hand.

Simple data structures

In this section, we will look at two different libraries that will help you create simple data structures of immediate usefulness: Boost.Optional and Boost.Tuple. Boost. Optional can be used to represent optional values; objects that may or may not be there. Boost.Tuple is used to create ordered sets of heterogeneous values.

Boost.Optional

Let us consider that you need to maintain about musicians in a data store. Among other things, you can look up the latest album released by an artiste. You have written a simple API in C++ for doing this:

```
std::string find_latest_album_of(const std::string& artisteName);
```

For simplicity we will ignore the possibility that two or more artistes could share the same name. Here is a simple implementation of this function:

```
 1 #include <string>
 2 #include <map>
 3
 4 typedef std::map<std::string, std::string> artiste_album_map;
 5
 6 extern artiste_album_map latest_albums;
 7
 8 std::string find_latest_album_of(
 9                    const std::string& artiste_name) {
10    auto iter = latest_albums.find(artiste_name);
11
12    if (iter != latest_albums.end()) {
13      return iter->second;
14    } else {
15      return "";
16    }
17 }
```

We store the names of artistes and their latest albums in a map called `latest_albums`. The `find_latest_album_of` function takes the name of an artiste and uses the `find` member function of `std::map` to look up the latest album. If it does not find an entry, it returns an empty string. Now, it is possible that some artistes have not released an album yet. Returning an empty string seems legit for such cases until you realize that musicians have their unique whims and sometimes, they release an album without a name. So, how do you distinguish between the cases where the musician is yet to release an album, versus where the musician's latest album was untitled? In one case, there is no value to return while in the other case, it is an empty string.

The `boost::optional<T>` template can be used to represent an optional value; one that may or may not be present. In this case, it is tailor-made for our problem. To represent a `std::string` value that may or may not be present, you use `boost::optional<std::string>`. We can rewrite the `find_latest_album_of` function using `boost::optional`, as shown in the following code listing:

Listing 2.1: Using Boost.Optional

```
1  #include <string>
2  #include <map>
3  #include <boost/optional.hpp>
4
5  typedef std::map<std::string, std::string> artiste_album_map;
6
7  extern artiste_album_map latest_albums;
8
9  boost::optional<std::string> find_latest_album_of(
10                           const std::string& artiste_name) {
11   auto iter = latest_albums.find(artiste_name);
12
13   if (iter != latest_albums.end()) {
14     return iter->second;
15   } else {
16     return boost::none;
17   }
18 }
```

We simply return the value found (line 14), which is automatically wrapped in a `boost::optional` container. If there is no value to return, we return a special object, `boost::none` (line 16). This causes an empty `boost::optional` object to be returned. The code using `boost::optional` does exactly what we need; it checks whether a key is present in the container and returns the value or indicates that it is absent without any ambiguity (that is, empty versus untitled).

A default-initialized instance of `boost::optional` is always empty. If the value stored in `boost::optional` is movable (see *Appendix, C++11 Language Features Emulation*), the wrapper `optional` object is also movable. If the stored value is copyable, the wrapper `optional` object is also copyable.

We can generalize the lookup function in listing 2.1 to any container with a map-like or dictionary interface as follows:

Listing 2.2: Generic lookup using optional

```
 1 #include <boost/optional.hpp>
 2
 3 template <typename C>
 4 boost::optional<typename C::mapped_type>
 5 lookup(const C& dict, const typename C::key_type& key)
 6 {
 7   typename C::const_iterator it = dict.find(key);
 8   if (it != dict.end()) {
 9     return it->second;
10   } else {
11     return boost::none;
12   }
13 }
```

In the preceding code, we have converted `lookup` to a function template that can be called on any `map`, `multimap`, their unordered variants, or any other nonstandard container, exposing a similar interface. It is parameterized on the container type `C`. The container type `C` must have nested type definitions: `key_type` and `mapped_type` corresponding to the types of keys and values the map stores; a constraint satisfied by `std:map` and other associative containers from the Standard Library.

The use of the `typename` keyword (lines 4, 5, 7) may need some explanation. If we omit the `typename` keyword from these lines, the compiler will fail to identify `C::mapped_type`, `C::key_type`, and `C::const_iterator` as names of types. Because `mapped_type`, `key_type`, and `const_iterator` are names that are dependent on the type template parameter `C`, the compiler needs to be told that they identify types. We use the `typename` keyword to do this.

Accessing values stored in boost::optional

You can check whether an `optional` object contains a value or is empty, and extract the value stored in a non-empty `optional` object:

```
1 std::string artiste("Korn");
2 boost::optional<std::string> album =
3                           find_latest_album_of(artiste);
4 if (album) {
```

```
5    std::cout << "The last album from " << artiste;
6
7    if (album->empty()) {
8      std::cout << " is untitled\n";
9    } else {
10     std::cout << " is named " << *album << '\n';
11   }
12 } else {
13   std::cout << "No information on albums from "
14             << artiste << '\n';
15 }
```

In the code that calls find_latest_album_of, to test whether the returned value is empty, we invoke the object in a Boolean context (line 4). If it evaluates to true, it means that album is not empty. If it has a value, we can obtain a reference to the contained value using the overloaded operator* (line 10). We can access members of the underlying object using an overloaded operator->; in this case we call the empty member function of std::string (line 7). We could also use get member function of a nonempty boost::optional object instead of the overloaded operator* to access the value stored. Dereferencing an empty optional value by calling the operator*, get, or operator-> causes a runtime error, which is why we first check whether the optional object is empty before trying to dereference it.

get_value_or

Using optional, we indicate that there may or may not be a value present for albums. But we would sometimes need to use APIs that should have taken optional values but do not. In such cases, we may want to return empty values with some default value. Imagine residents of Paris being asked about their favorite city and for those who do not name one, Paris being used as the default favorite:

```
1 void printFavoriteCity(const std::string& name,
2                        const std::string& city)
3 {
4   std::cout << name "'s favorite city is " << city << '\n';
5 }
6
7 boost::optional<std::string> getFavoriteCity(
8                        const std::string& resident_id);
9 ...
```

```
10 std::string resident = "Serge";
11 boost::optional<std::string> fav_city =
12                              getFavoriteCity(resident);
13
14 printFavoriteCity(fav_city.get_value_or("Paris"));
```

If the imaginary `getFavoriteCity` function returns an empty value, we want `Paris` to be passed to the `printFavoriteCity` function. We do this using the `get_value_or` member function (line 14).

Boost.Optional versus pointers

If we did not use `optional`, what would the functions `find_last_album_of` or `lookup` return in order to indicate that there was no value found? They would either need to return a pointer to a dynamically-allocated object or `nullptr` if there was no value found. Besides using dynamic memory, it requires that the caller function manage the lifetime of the dynamically-allocated object that is returned. This condition can be mitigated using smart pointers (*Chapter 3, Memory Management and Exception Safety*), but it does not eliminate free store allocations that are costly. The `boost::optional` class eliminates free store allocations and stores the encapsulated object in its layout. In addition, it stores a Boolean flag to keep track of whether it is initialized or not.

Boost.Tuple

Boost Tuples are a cool way to group disparate types of data together into ordered tuples and pass them around. Structures do the same thing but a couple of things set tuples apart:

- You can write generic code to manipulate tuples of all kinds, for example, to print all their members and comparing two tuples for similarity in structure and types.

- Each new structure or class defines a new type in your software. Types should represent interfaces and behaviors. Representing every ad hoc clumping of data with a type results in proliferation of types that have no meaning in the problem space or its abstraction.

A Boost Tuple is an incredibly useful library that helps you conveniently create schemas for moving related data around together, such as exchanging data between functions. Boost Tuples are a generalization of `std::pair`, which is used to create 2-element tuples.

If you are using a C++ compiler with good C++11 support, you should use the std::tuple facility from the Standard Library—one of the Boost libraries that made it to the C++11 standard. The header to be included is <tuple>. Most of what we discuss here is applicable to std::tuple.

Creating tuples

Let us look at an example. Given a series of stock prices at different points in time, we want to find out the best two points in time to buy and sell the stock to maximize the profit. We can assume that there is no option to short-sell, that is, you must buy before you sell. For simplicity, the input can be assumed to be a vector of doubles. In this vector, we are interested in the pair of indices that represent the best time to buy and sell the stock to maximize profit:

Listing 2.3: Using tuples

```
1 #include <boost/tuple/tuple.hpp>
2 #include <vector>
3
4 boost::tuple<size_t, size_t, double>
5      getBestTransactDays(std::vector<double> prices)
6 {
7   double min = std::numeric_limits<double>::max();
8   double gain = 0.0, max_gain = 0.0;
9   size_t min_day, max_day;
10  size_t buy_day;
11  for (size_t i = 0, days = prices.size(); i < days; ++i) {
12    if (prices[i] < min) {
13      min = prices[i];
14      min_day = i;
15    } else if ((gain = prices[i] - min) > max_gain) {
16      max_gain = gain;
17      buy_day = min_day;
18      max_day = i;
19    }
20  }
21
22  return boost::make_tuple(buy_day, max_day, max_gain);
23 }
```

The function `getBestTransactDays` returns a tuple of two unsigned integers (`size_t`) and a double (line 4) that represent the two indices at which buying and selling the stock would maximize profit, and the maximum profit possible. The return type of the function is `boost::tuple<size_t, size_t, double>`. The header `boost/tuple/tuple.hpp` provides the necessary functions and types for working with tuples (line 1).

The function `getBestTransactDays` implements a simple linear algorithm that runs through the vector, keeping track of the lowest stock price seen so far. If the current element has a lesser value than the lowest stock price so far, then this is set as the new lowest, and its index is noted (lines 12-14). The function also keeps track of the maximum gain, that is, the maximum difference in prices noted so far. If we encounter an element whose difference from the lowest price is higher than the maximum gain, then we note this difference as the new maximum gain (line 15), and also note the days of transaction required to achieve this gain (lines 16-18).

We create the tuple using `boost::make_tuple` (line 22), which is a convenience function for creating tuples from its elements without explicit template instantiations. You could have also created and returned a tuple like this in place of line 22:

```
22 boost::tuple<size_t, size_t, double> best_buy(buy_day, max_day,
23                                                max_gain);
24 return best_buy;
```

As you can see, `boost::make_tuple` is more compact and, being a function template, resolves the types of its arguments automatically to create the tuple of correct types. This is a frequently seen pattern where you use a factory function template to instantiate a class template, thus automating type detection.

Accessing tuple elements

There are several ways in which we can access the elements in a tuple. Look at the following example of calling the `getBestTransactDays` function:

```
1 std::vector<double> stockPrices;
2 ...
3 boost::tuple<size_t, size_t, double> best_buy =
4                            getBestTransactDays(stockPrices);
5
6 size_t buyDay = boost::get<0>(best_buy);  // Access 0th element
7 size_t sellDay = boost::get<1>(best_buy); // Access 1st element
8 double profit = boost::get<2>(best_buy);  // Access 2nd element
```

We can also unpack the elements in the tuple into individual variables using
`boost::tie`:

```
1 size_t buyDay, sellDay;
2 double profit;
3 boost::tie(buyDay, sellDay, profit) =
4                    getBestTransactDays(stockPrices);
```

The preceding line of code will assign the first element of the tuple to `buyDay`, the
second to `sellDay`, and the third to `profit`. If we are interested in only a subset of
the elements in the tuple, we can ignore the others using `boost::tuples::ignore`.
Here is the same example, but we have ignored `sellDay` this time using
`boost::tuples::ignore`:

```
1 size_t buyDay, sellDay;
2 boost::tie(buyDay, sellDay, boost::tuples::ignore) =
3                       getBestTransactDays(stockPrices);
```

Comparing tuples

Tuples of the same length can be compared to relational operators, such as ==, <, >,
<=, and >=. In any such comparison, the corresponding elements at each position
are compared. The types of elements at the corresponding positions need not be
identical; they just need to be comparable using the relational operator in question:

```
1 boost::tuple<int, int, std::string> t1 =
2                       boost::make_tuple(1, 2, "Hello");
3 boost::tuple<double, double, const char*> t2 =
4                       boost::make_tuple(1, 2, "Hi");
5 assert(t1 < t2);   // because Hello < Hi
```

Note that the actual types in tuples `t1` and `t2` are different, but both have the same
length, and the elements at corresponding positions are comparable with each other.
In general, comparison stops at the first pair of elements that determines the outcome
of the comparison. In this example, all three elements are compared because the first
two elements compare equal.

```
1 boost::tuple<int, int, std::string> t1 =
2                       boost::make_tuple(1, 20, "Hello");
3 boost::tuple<double, double, const char*> t2 =
4                       boost::make_tuple(1, 2, "Hi");
5 assert(t1 > t2);   // because 20 > 2
```

The following code is used to define relational operators for structs with very little code:

```
 1 struct my_type {
 2    int a;
 3    double b;
 4    char c;
 5 };
 6
 7 bool operator<(const my_type& left, const my_type& right) {
 8    return boost::make_tuple(left.a, left.b, left.c) <
 9                 boost::make_tuple(right.a, right.b, right.c);
10 }
```

Writing generic code using tuples

We will now write a generic function to find the number of elements in a tuple:

```
 1 template <typename T>
 2 size_t tuple_length(const T&) {
 3    return boost::tuples::length<T>::value;
 4 }
```

This function simply uses the `boost::tuples::length<T>` metafunction to compute the number of elements in the tuple. This computation takes place at compile time. A **metafunction** is just a class template that has an accessible static member or a nested type computed at compile time from its template arguments (see *Chapter 7, Higher Order and Compile-time Programming,* for a more rigorous definition). In this case, the `boost::tuples::length<T>` metafunction has a public static member called `value`, which is computed as the number of elements in the tuple T. If you use tuples from the Standard Library, you should use `std::tuple_size<T>` instead of `boost::tuples::length<T>`. This is just a small illustration of generic programming using metafunctions and type computation.

Working with heterogeneous values

The need to have a value that can hold different types of data at different times during the lifetime of a program is not new. C++ supports the `union` construct of C, which essentially allows you to have a single type that can, at different times, assume values of different underlying POD types. **POD** or **Plain Old Data** types, roughly speaking, are types that do not require any special initialization, destruction, and copying steps and whose semantic equivalents may be created by copying their memory layouts byte for byte.

These restrictions mean that most C++ classes, including a majority of those from the Standard Library, can never be part of a union. Starting with C++11, these restrictions on a union have been relaxed somewhat, and you can now store objects of types with nontrivial construction, destruction, and copy semantics (that is, non-POD types) in a union. However, the life cycle management of such objects stored in a union is not automatic and can be a pain in the neck, hence it is best avoided.

Two libraries from Boost, Variant, and Any, provide useful variant types that provide the same functionality as unions without many of the restrictions. Using Variants and Any, storing heterogeneous data in the Standard Library containers becomes remarkably easy and error-free. These libraries represent discriminated union types. Values of a range of types can be stored in discriminated unions, and the type information is stored along with the value.

In addition to storing data of heterogeneous types, we frequently need to convert between different representations of the same data, for example, text to numeric and vice versa. Boost Conversion provides, among other things, a way to seamlessly convert between types using a uniform syntax. We look at Any, Variant, and Conversion libraries in the following sections.

Boost.Variant

Boost Variant avoids all that is wrong with C++ unions and provides a union-like construct defined over a fixed set of arbitrary types, not just POD types. We can define a variant datatype using the Boost Variant header-only library by instantiating the `boost::variant` template with a list of types. The list of types identifies the different types of values that the variant object can assume at different points in time. The different types in the list can be varied and unrelated, conforming to only one binding condition—that each of the types be copyable or at least movable. You may even create variants that contain other variants.

In our first example, we create a variant of an integer, a `std::string`, and two user-defined types `Foo` and `Bar`. With this, we illustrate the constraints on creating variant types and on operations that can be performed on such variant values:

Listing 2.4: Creating and using variants

```cpp
 1 #include <boost/variant.hpp>
 2 #include <string>
 3
 4 struct Foo {
 5   Foo(int n = 0) : id_(n) {} // int convertible to Foo
 6 private:
 7   int id_;
 8 };
 9
10 struct Bar {
11   Bar(int n = 0) : id_(n) {} // int convertible to Bar
12 private:
13   int id_;
14 };
15
16 int main()
17 {
18   boost::variant<Foo, int, std::string> value; // error if Foo
19                                 // not be default constructible
20   boost::variant<std::string, Foo, Bar> value2;
21
22   value = 1;                   // sets int, not Foo
23   int *pi = boost::get<int>(&value);
24   assert(pi != 0);
25   value = "foo";               // sets std::string
26   value = Foo(42);             // sets Foo
27
28   // value2 = 1;               // ERROR: ambiguous - Foo or Bar?
29   // std::cout << value << ' ' << value2 << '\n'; // ERROR:
30               // Foo, Bar cannot be streamed to ostream
31 }
```

We create two bare bones types: Foo (line 4) and Bar (line 10); we can initialize both implicitly from int. We define a variant called value (line 18) over three types, Foo, int, and std::string. A second variant, value2 (line 20) is defined over std::string, Foo, and Bar.

By default, each variant instance is value-initialized to an object of its first type. Thus, value is default-constructed to a Foo instance—the first type in the list of type parameters to the variant. Similarly, value2 is default-constructed to std::string—the first type in its list of type parameters. If the first type is a POD type, it is zero-initialized. Thus, the first type must be default constructible for the variant to be default constructible.

We assign an integer to `value` (line 22). This sets it to be an `int` and not `Foo`, which an integer is implicitly convertible to. We confirm this using the `boost::get<T>` function template on the address of `value` with `T=int` (line 23), and we confirm that it is not null (line 24).

We assign a `const char*` to `value` (line 25), which implicitly converts to `std::string` that gets stored in `value`, overwriting the integer value stored earlier. Next, we assign an object of `Foo` (line 26), which overwrites the earlier `std::string` value.

If we try to assign an integer to `value2` (line 28, commented), it will cause a compilation error. The variable `value2` being a variant defined over `std::string`, `Foo`, and `Bar`, an integer can implicitly be converted to either `Foo` or `Bar` and neither is a better choice—hence, it causes ambiguity and the compiler throws an error. In general, variant initialization and assignment should not result in an ambiguity over which type to instantiate within the variant.

If we try to stream the contents of `value` to `std::cout` (line 29, commented), then again, we would encounter a compilation error. This would be because one of the types (`Foo`) supported by the variant is not *streamable*, which means it cannot be written to `ostreams` using the insertion operator (`<<`).

Accessing values in a variant

We use the `boost::get<T>` function template to access the value of type `T` in a variant, where `T` is the concrete type of the value we want. This function, when called on a variant reference, returns a reference to the stored value or throws a `boost::bad_get` exception if the stored value is not of the type specified. When called on a pointer to a variant, it returns the address of the stored value or a null pointer if the stored value is not of the specified type. The latter behavior can be used to test whether a variant stores a particular type of value or not, the way it was used in listing 2.4 (line 23). This behavior of `get<>` closely mirrors that of `dynamic_cast`:

Listing 2.5: Accessing values in a variant

```
 1 #include <boost/variant.hpp>
 2 #include <string>
 3 #include <cassert>
 4
 5 int main() {
 6   boost::variant<std::string, int> v1;
 7   v1 = "19937";                      // sets string
 8   int i1;
 9
10   try {
```

```
11      i1 = boost::get<int>(v1);      // will fail, throw
12    } catch (std::exception& e) {
13      std::cerr << e.what() << '\n';
14    }
15
16    int *pi = boost::get<int>(&v1);  // will return null
17    assert(pi == 0);
18
19    size_t index = v1.which();       // returns 0
20  }
```

In the preceding code, we create a variant v1 that can store a std::string or an int value (line 6). We set v1 to the character string "19937" (line 7). We use the boost::get<int> function to try and get an integer from v1 (line 11) but, since v1 stores a string at this point, this results in an exception being thrown. Next, we use the pointer overload of boost::get<int> that takes the address of the variant v1. This returns the pointer to the stored value if its type matches the one requested via get function's template parameter. If it does not, as in this case, a null pointer is returned (lines 16 and 17). Finally, we can get the zero-based index of the type of the value that is currently stored in the variant by calling the which member function. Since v1 contains std::string and the declared type of v1 is boost::variant<std::string, int>, therefore v1.which() should return the index of std::string in the variant's declaration—0 in this case (line 19).

Compile-time visitation

How the value stored in a variant is consumed usually depends on the type of the value. Checking a variant for each possible type using an if-else ladder can quickly aggravate the readability and maintainability of your code. Of course, we can find out the zero-based index of the type of the current value using the which member method of the variant, but it would be of little immediate use. Instead, we will look at a very elegant and versatile compile-time visitation mechanism provided by the Boost Variant library without which handling variants would be quite a drag.

The idea is to create a visitor class that contains an overloaded function call operator (operator()) to handle each type that may be stored in the variant. Using the function boost::apply_visitor, we can invoke the appropriate overload in the visitor class on a variant object, based on the type of value it contains.

The visitor class should publicly inherit from the `boost::static_visitor<T>` template, where `T` is the return type of the overloaded function call operator. By default, `T` is `void`. Let us look at an example:

Listing 2.6: Compile-time visitation of variants

```
 1 #include <boost/variant.hpp>
 2
 3 struct SimpleVariantVisitor :public boost::static_visitor<void>
 4 {
 5   void operator() (const std::string& s) const
 6   { std::cout << "String: " << s << '\n'; }
 7
 8   void operator() (long n) const
 9   { std::cout << "long: " << n << '\n'; }
10 };
11
12 int main()
13 {
14   boost::variant<std::string, long, double> v1;
15   v1 = 993.3773;
16
17   boost::apply_visitor(SimpleVariantVisitor(), v1);
18 }
```

We create a variant over the types `std::string`, `long`, and `double` called `v1` (line 14). We set it to a value of type `double` (line 15). Finally, we invoke a visitor of type `SimpleVariantVistor` on `v1` (line 17). The `SimpleVariantVisitor` inherits from `boost::apply_visitor<void>` (line 3) and contains overloads of `operator()` for `std::string` (line 5) and `long` (line 8) but not `double`. Each overload prints its argument to the standard output.

The resolution of overloads happens at compile time rather than at runtime. Thus, an overload must be available for every type of value that the variant may contain. A particular overload is invoked if its parameter type is the best match for the type of the value stored in the variant. Moreover, a single overload may handle multiple types if all the types are convertible to the type of the argument of the overload.

Interestingly, in the preceding example, there is no overload available for `double`. However, narrowing conversions are allowed and the overload for `long` is invoked with potential narrowing. In this case, the overload for `long` handles both `long` and `double` types. On the other hand, if we had separate overloads available for `double` and `long` but none for `std::string`, we would have had a compilation error. This would happen because not even a narrowing conversion would be available from `std::string` to either `long` or `double`, and the overload resolution would fail. Being a compile-time mechanism, this is independent of the type of the actual value stored in a variant object at any time.

Generic visitors

You may create a member function template that handles a family of types. In cases where the code for handling different types does not significantly differ, it may make sense to have such member templates. Here is an example of a visitor which prints the contents of the variant:

Listing 2.7: Generic compile-time visitation

```
1 #include <boost/variant.hpp>
2
3 struct PrintVisitor : boost::static_visitor<>
4 {
5    template <typename T>
6    void operator() (const T& t) const {
7      std::cout << t << '\n';
8    }
9 };
10
11 boost::variant<std::string, double, long, Foo> v1;
12 boost::apply_visitor(PrintVisitor(), v1);
```

In the preceding code, we define a variant over the types `std::string`, `double`, `long`, and `Foo`. The visitor class `PrintVisitor` contains a generic `operator()`. As long as all the types in the variant are *streamable*, this code will compile and print the value of the variant to the standard output.

Applying visitors to variants in a container

Often, we have an STL container of variant objects, and we want to visit each object using our visitor. We can utilize the `std::for_each` STL algorithm and a single-argument overload of `boost::apply_visitor` for the purpose. The single-argument overload of `boost::apply_visitor` takes a visitor instance and returns a functor that applies the visitor to a passed element. The following example best illustrates the usage:

```
1 #include <boost/variant.hpp>
2
3 std::vector<boost::variant<std::string, double, long> > vvec;
4 ...
5 std::for_each(vvec.begin(), vvec.end(),
6                   boost::apply_visitor(SimpleVariantVisitor()));
```

Defining recursive variants

The last few years have seen a phenomenal growth in the popularity of one particular data interchange format—JavaScript Object Notation or JSON. It is a simple text-based format that is often less verbose XML. Originally used as object literals in JavaScript, the format is more readable than XML. It is also a relatively simple format that is easy to understand and parse. In this section, we will represent well-formed JSON content using `boost::variants` and see how variants can handle recursive definitions.

The JSON format

To start with, we will look at an example of people records in the JSON notation:

```
{
    "Name": "Lucas",
    "Age": 38,
    "PhoneNumbers" : ["1123654798", "3121548967"],
    "Address" : { "Street": "27 Riverdale", "City": "Newtown",
                       "PostCode": "902739"}
}
```

The preceding code is an example of a JSON object—it contains key-value pairs identifying the attributes of an unnamed object. The attribute names are quoted strings, such as `"Name"`, `"Age"`, `"PhoneNumbers"` (of which you can have more than one), and `"Address"`. Their values could be simple strings (`"Name"`) or numeric values (`"Age"`), or arrays of such values (`"PhoneNumbers"`) or other objects (`"Address"`). A single colon (`:`) separates keys from values. The key-value pairs are separated by commas. The list of key-value pairs in an object are enclosed in curly braces. This format allows arbitrary levels of nesting as seen in the case of the `"Address"` attribute whose value itself is an object. You can create more nested objects that are values of attributes of other nested objects.

You may combine many such records together in an array, which are enclosed in square brackets and separated by commas:

```
[
    {
        "Name": "Lucas",
        "Age": 38,
        "PhoneNumbers" : ["1123654798", "3121548967"],
        "Address" : { "Street": "27 Riverdale", "City": "Newtown",
                        "PostCode": "902739"}
    },
    {
        "Name": "Damien",
        "Age": 52,
        "PhoneNumbers" : ["6427851391", "3927151648"],
        "Address": {"Street": "11 North Ave.", "City" : "Rockport",
                    "PostCode": "389203"}
    },
    ...
]
```

A well-formed JSON text contains an object or an array of zero or more objects, numeric values, strings, Booleans, or null values. An object itself contains zero or more unique attributes each represented by a unique string. The value of each attribute can be a string, numeric value, Boolean value, null value, another object, or an array of such values. Thus, the basic tokens in JSON content are numeric values, strings, Booleans, and nulls. The aggregates are objects and arrays.

Representing JSON content with recursive variants

If we were to declare a variant to represent a basic token in a JSON, it would look like this:

```
1 struct JSONNullType {};
2 boost::variant<std::string, double, bool, JSONNullType> jsonToken;
```

The type JSONNullType is an empty type that may be used to represent a null element in JSON.

To extend this variant to represent more complex JSON content, we will try to represent a JSON object—a key-value pair as a type. The keys are always strings, but the values can be any of the types listed above or another nested object. So, the definition of a JSON object is essentially recursive, and this is why we need a recursive variant definition to model it.

To include the definition of a JSON object in the preceding variant type, we use a metafunction called boost::make_recursive_variant. It takes a list of types and defines the resultant recursive variant type as a nested type called type. So, here is how we write a recursive definition of the variant:

```
1  #define BOOST_VARIANT_NO_FULL_RECURSIVE_VARIANT_SUPPORT
2  #include <boost/variant.hpp>
3
4  struct JSONNullType {};
5
6  typedef boost::make_recursive_variant<
7                      std::string,
8                      double,
9                      bool,
10                     JSONNullType,
11                     std::map<std::string,
12                                 boost::recursive_variant_>
13                     >::type JSONValue;
```

The #define statement on line 1 may be necessary for many compilers where the support for recursive variants, especially using make_recursive_variant, is limited.

We define the recursive variant using the `boost::make_recursive_variant`
metafunction (line 6). In the list of types, we add a new type `std::map` with keys
of type `std::string` (line 11) and values of type `boost::recursive_variant_`
(line 12). The special type `boost::recursive_variant_` is used to indicate that the
outer variant type can occur as a value in the map itself. Thus, we have captured the
recursive nature of a JSON object in the variant definition.

This definition is still not complete. A well-formed JSON content may contain arrays
of elements of all these different kinds. Such arrays may also be the values of an
object's attributes or be nested inside other arrays. If we choose to represent an array
by a vector, then an extension of the preceding definition is easy:

Listing 2.8a: Recursive variant for JSON

```
 1 #define BOOST_VARIANT_NO_FULL_RECURSIVE_VARIANT_SUPPORT
 2 #include <boost/variant.hpp>
 3
 4 struct JSONNullType {};
 5
 6 typedef boost::make_recursive_variant<
 7                   std::string,
 8                   double,
 9                   bool,
10                   JSONNullType,
11                   std::map<std::string,
12                             boost::recursive_variant_>,
13                   std::vector<boost::recursive_variant_>
14                   >::type JSONValue;
15
16 typedef std::vector<JSONValue> JSONArray;
17 typedef std::map<std::string, JSONValue> JSONObject;
```

We add one more type — `std::vector<boost::recursive_variant_>`
(line 13) — which represents an array of `JSONValue` objects. By virtue of this
one additional line, we now support several more possibilities:

- A top-level array consisting of JSON objects, other JSON arrays, and the
  basic types of tokens

- An array-valued attribute of an object

- An array-valued element in another JSON array

This is the complete definition of `JSONValue`. In addition, we create typedefs for
the recursive aggregate types — JSON arrays and JSON objects (line 16 and 17).

Visiting recursive variants

We shall now write a visitor to print JSON data stored in a variant in its standard notation. Visiting a recursive variant is not different from visiting a nonrecursive one. We still need to define overloads that can handle all types of values that the variant may store. In addition, in the overloads for the recursive aggregate types (in this case, `JSONArray` and `JSONObject`), we may need to recursively visit each of its elements:

Listing 2.8b: Visiting recursive variants

```
1  void printArrElem(const JSONValue& val);
2  void printObjAttr(const JSONObject::value_type& val);
3
4  struct JSONPrintVisitor : public boost::static_visitor<void>
5  {
6    void operator() (const std::string& str) const
7    {
8      std::cout << '"' << escapeStr(str) << '"';
9    }
10
11   void operator() (const JSONNullType&) const
12   {
13     std::cout << "null";
14   }
15
16   template <typename T>
17   void operator()(const T& value) const
18   {
19     std::cout << std::boolalpha << value;
20   }
21
22   void operator()(const JSONArray& arr) const
23   {
24     std::cout << '[';
25
26     if (!arr.empty()) {
27       boost::apply_visitor(*this, arr[0]);
28       std::for_each(arr.begin() + 1, arr.end(), printArrElem);
29     }
30
```

```
31        std::cout << "\n";
32    }
33
34    void operator()(const JSONObject& object) const
35    {
36        std::cout << '{';
37
38        if (!object.empty()) {
39            const auto& kv_pair = *(object.begin());
40            std::cout << '"' << escapeStr(kv_pair.first) << '"';
41            std::cout << ':';
42            boost::apply_visitor(*this, kv_pair.second);
43
44            auto it = object.begin();
45            std::for_each(++it, object.end(), printObjAttr);
46        }
47        std::cout << '}';
48    }
49
50 };
51
52 void printArrElem(const JSONValue& val) {
53    std::cout << ',';
54    boost::apply_visitor(JSONPrintVisitor(), val);
55 }
56
57 void printObjAttr(const JSONObject::value_type& val) {
58    std::cout << ',';
59    std::cout << '"' << escapeStr(val.first) << '"';
60    std::cout << ':';
61    boost::apply_visitor(JSONPrintVisitor(), val.second);
62 }
```

The visitor JSONPrintVisitor inherits publicly from boost::static_visitor<void> and provides overloads of operator() for the different possible types of JSON values. There is an overload for std::string (line 6), which prints strings in double quotes (line 8) after escaping any embedded quotes and other characters that need escaping. For this, we assume the availability of a function called escapeStr. We have a second overload for the JSONNullType (line 11), which just prints the string null without quotes. Other types of values, such as double or bool are handled by the member template (line 17). For bool values, it prints the unquoted strings true and false using the std::boolalpha ostream manipulator (line 19).

The main work is done by the two overloads for JSONArray (line 22) and JSONObject (line 34). The JSONArray overload prints the elements of the array enclosed in square brackets and separated by commas. It prints the first element of the vector of JSONValues (line 27) and then, applies the std::for_each generic algorithm on this vector, starting with its second element to print the subsequent elements separated by commas (line 28). For this purpose, it passes as the third argument to std::for_each, a pointer to the function printArrElem. The printArrElem (line 52) function prints each element by applying JSONPrintVisitor (line 54).

The JSONObject overload prints the elements of the map as a comma-separated list of key-value pairs. The first pair is printed as a quoted, escaped key (line 40), then a colon (line 41) followed by a call to boost::apply_visitor (line 42). Subsequent pairs are printed separated by commas from the preceding ones by iterating over the remaining elements of the map using the std::for_each and printObjAttr function pointers (line 45). The logic is analogous to that in the JSONArray overload. The printObjAttr function (line 57) prints each key-value pair passed to it, prefixing a comma (line 58), printing the escaped, quoted key (line 59), prints a colon (line 60), and invoking the visitor on the variant value (line 61).

Boost.Any

The Boost Any library takes a different route to store heterogeneous data than Boost Variant. Unlike Variant, Any allows you to store almost any type of data not limited to a fixed set and maintains the runtime type information of the stored data. Thus, it does not use templates at all and requires that **Runtime Type Identification (RTTI)** be enabled, while compiling the code using Boost Any (most modern compilers keep this enabled by default).

 For the Boost Any library to work correctly, you must not disable the generation of RTTI for your programs.

In the following example, we create instances of boost::any to store numeric data, character arrays, and non-POD type objects:

Listing 2.9: Using Boost Any

```
1 #include <boost/any.hpp>
2 #include <vector>
3 #include <iostream>
4 #include <string>
```

```
 5 #include <cassert>
 6 using boost::any_cast;
 7
 8 struct MyValue {
 9   MyValue(int n) : value(n) {}
10
11   int get() const { return value; }
12
13   int value;
14 };
15
16 int main() {
17   boost::any v1, v2, v3, v4;
18
19   assert(v1.empty());
20   const char *hello = "Hello";
21   v1 = hello;
22   v2 = 42;
23   v3 = std::string("Hola");
24   MyValue m1(10);
25   v4 = m1;
26
27   try {
28     std::cout << any_cast<const char*>(v1) << '\n';
29     std::cout << any_cast<int>(v2) << '\n';
30     std::cout << any_cast<std::string>(v3) << '\n';
31     auto x = any_cast<MyValue>(v4);
32     std::cout << x.get() << '\n';
33   } catch (std::exception& e) {
34     std::cout << e.what() << '\n';
35   }
36 }
```

You can also use a nonthrowing version of any_cast by passing the address of an any object instead of a reference. This returns a null pointer, instead of throwing an exception if the stored type does not match the type it is cast to. The following snippet illustrates this:

```
1 boost::any v1 = 42;
2 boost::any v2 = std::string("Hello");
3 std::string *str = boost::any_cast<std::string>(&v1);
4 assert(str == nullptr);
```

```
 5 int *num = boost::any_cast<int>(&v2);
 6 assert(num == nullptr);
 7
 8 num = boost::any_cast<int>(&v1);
 9 str = boost::any_cast<std::string>(&v2);
10 assert(num != nullptr);
11 assert(str != nullptr);
```

We pass the address of `any` objects to `any_cast` (lines 3, 5, 8, and 9), and it returns null unless the type parameter to `any_cast` matches the type of the value stored in the `any` object. Using the pointer overload of `any_cast`, we can write a generic predicate to check whether an `any` variable stores a value of a given type:

```
template <typename T>
bool is_type(boost::any& any) {
  return ( !any.empty() && boost::any_cast<T>(&any) );
}
```

This is how you would use it:

```
boost::any v1 = std::string("Hello");
assert( is_type<std::string>(v1) );
```

This behavior of `boost::any_cast` emulates how `dynamic_cast` works.

In listing 2.9, we used different instances of the type `boost::any` to store different types of values. But the same instance of `boost::any` can store different types of values at different times. The following snippet illustrates this using the `swap` member function of `any`:

```
 1 boost::any v1 = 19937;
 2 boost::any v2 = std::string("Hello");
 3
 4 assert(boost::any_cast<int>(&v1) != nullptr);
 5 assert(boost::any_cast<std::string>(&v2) != nullptr);
 6
 7 v1 = 22.36;
 8 v1.swap(v2);
 9 assert(boost::any_cast<std::string>(&v1) != nullptr);
10 assert(boost::any_cast<double>(&v2) != nullptr);
```

We first assign a value of type double to v1 (line 7), which was carrying a value of type int (line 1). Next, we swap the contents of v1 with v2 (line 8), which was carrying a value of type std::string (line 2). We can now expect v1 to contain a std::string value (line 9) and v2 to contain a double value (line 10).

Besides using the pointer overload of any_cast, we can also use the type member function of any to access the type of the stored value:

Listing 2.10: Accessing type information in Any

```cpp
boost::any value;
value = 20;
if (value.type().hash_code() == typeid(int).hash_code()) {
  std::cout << boost::any_cast<int>(value) << '\n';
}
```

The type member function of any returns an object of std::type_info (defined in the Standard Library header <typeinfo>). To check whether this type is the same as a given type, we compare it with the type_info object obtained by applying the typeid operator on the given type (in this case, it is int). Instead of directly comparing the two type_info objects, we compare their hash codes obtained using the hash_code member function of type_info.

Boost.Conversion

If you have ever tried parsing a text input (from a file, standard input, network, and so on) and tried a semantic translation of the data in it, you would have possibly felt the need for an easy way to convert text to numeric values. The opposite problem is to write text output based on values of numeric and textual program variables. The basic_istream and basic_ostream classes provide facilities for reading and writing specific types of values. However, the programming model for such uses is not very intuitive or robust. The C++ Standard Library and its extensions offer various conversion functions with various degrees of control, flexibility, and a general lack of usability. For example, there exists a whole slew of functions that convert between numeric and character formats or the other way round (for example, atoi, strtol, strtod, itoa, ecvt, fcvt, and so on). If we were trying to write generic code for converting between types, we would not even have the option of using any of these functions, which only work for conversions between specific types. How can we define a generic conversion syntax that can be extended to arbitrary types?

The Boost Conversion library introduces a couple of function templates that provide a very intuitive and uniform conversion syntax, which can also be extended through user-defined specializations. We will look at the conversion templates one by one.

lexical_cast

The `lexical_cast` function template can be used to convert a source type to a target type. Its syntax resembles the syntax of various C++ casts:

```
#include <boost/lexical_cast.hpp>
namespace boost {
template <typename T, typename S>
T lexical_cast (const S& source);
}
```

The following example shows how we can use `lexical_cast` to convert a string to an integer:

Listing 2.11: Using lexical_cast

```
1 std::string str = "1234";
2
3 try {
4   int n = boost::lexical_cast<int>(str);
5   assert(n == 1234);
6 } catch (std::exception& e) {
7   std::cout << e.what() << '\n';
8 }
```

We apply `lexical_cast` (line 4) to convert a value of type `std::string` to a value of `int`. The beauty of this approach is that it can provide a uniform syntax to all conversions and can be extended to new types. If the string does not contain a valid numeric string, then the `lexical_cast` invocation will throw an exception of type `bad_lexical_cast`.

Overloads of the `lexical_cast` function template are provided to allow the conversion of a part of a character array:

```
#include <boost/lexical_cast.hpp>
namespace boost {
template <typename T >
T lexical_cast (const char* str, size_t size);
}
```

We can use the preceding function in the following way:

```
1 std::string str = "abc1234";
2
3 try {
4   int n = boost::lexical_cast<int>(str.c_str() + 3, 4);
5   assert(n == 1234);
```

```
6 } catch (std::exception& e) {
7   std::cout << e.what() << '\n';
8 }
```

When converting objects of types that are streamable, `lexical_cast` streams the objects to an `ostream` object, such as an instance of `stringstream`, and reads it back as the target type.

 A streamable object can be converted to a stream of characters and inserted into an `ostream` object, such as an instance of `stringstream`. In other words, a type T, such that `ostream& operator<<(ostream&, const T&)`, is defined is said to be streamable.

Setting up and tearing down stream objects for each such operation incurs some overhead. As a result, in some cases, the default version of `lexical_cast` may not give you the best possible performance. In such cases, you may specialize the `lexical_cast` template for the set of types involved, and use a fast library function or provide your own fast implementation. The `Conversion` library already takes care of optimizing `lexical_cast` for all common type pairs.

Besides the `lexical_cast` template, there are other templates available for conversion between different numeric types (`boost::numeric_cast`), downcasts and cross-casts in class hierarchies (`polymorphic_downcast`, `polymorphic_cast`). You can refer to the online documentation for more information on these features.

Handling command-line arguments

Command-line arguments, like API parameters, are the remote control buttons that help you tune the behavior of commands to your advantage. A well-designed set of command-line options is behind much of the power of a command. In this section, we will see how the Boost.Program_Options library helps you add support for a rich and standardized set of command-line options to your own programs.

Designing command-line options

C provides the most primitive abstraction for the command line of your program. Using the two arguments passed to the main function—the number of arguments (`argc`) and the list of arguments (`argv`)—you can find out about each and every argument passed to the program and their relative ordering. The following program prints `argv[0]`, which is the path to the program itself with which the program was invoked. When run with a set of command-line arguments, the program also prints each argument on a separate line.

Most programs need to add more logic and validation to verify and interpret command-line arguments and hence, a more elaborate framework is needed to handle command-line arguments:

```
1 int main(int argc, char *argv[])
2 {
3   std::cout << "Program name: " << argv[0] << '\n';
4
5   for (int i = 1; i < argc; ++i) {
6     std::cout << "argv[" << i << "]: " << argv[i] << '\n';
7   }
8 }
```

The diff command – a case study

Programs usually document a set of command-line options and switches that modify their behavior. Let us take a look at the example of the `diff` command in Unix. The `diff` command is run like this:

$ diff file1 file2

It prints the difference between the content of the two files. There are several ways in which you can choose to print the differences. For each different chunk found, you may choose to print a few additional lines surrounding the difference to get a better understanding of the context in which the differing part appears. These surrounding lines or "context" do not differ between the two files. To do this, you can use one of the following alternatives:

$ diff -U 5 file1 file2

$ diff --unified=5 file1 file2

Here, you choose to print five additional lines of context. You can also choose the default of three by specifying:

$ diff --unified file1 file2

In the preceding examples, `-U` or `--unified` are examples of command-line options. The former is a short option consisting of a single leading hyphen and a single letter (`-U`). The latter is a long option with two leading hyphens and a multi-character option name (`--unified`).

The number 5 is an option value; an argument to the option (-U or --unified) preceding it. The option value is separated from a preceding short option by space, but from a preceding long option by an equals sign (=).

If you are "diffing" two C or C++ source files, you can get more useful information using a command-line switch or flag -p. A switch is an option that does not take an option value as an argument. Using this switch, you can print the name of the C or C++ function in the context of which a particular difference is detected. There is no long option corresponding to it.

The diff command is a very powerful tool with which you can find differences in the content of files in full directories. When diffing two directories, if a file exists in one but not the other, diff ignores this file by default. However, you may want to instead see the contents of the new file. To do this, you will use the -N or --new-file switch. If we want to now run our diff command on two directories of C++ source code to identify changes, we can do it in this way:

```
$ diff -pN –unified=5 old_source_dir new_source_dir
```

You don't have to be eagle-eyed to notice that we used an option called -pN. This is actually not a single option but two switches, (-p) and (-N), collapsed together.

Certain patterns or conventions should be evident from this case-study:

- Starting short options with single hyphens
- Starting long options with double hyphens
- Separating short options and option-values with space
- Separating long options and option-value with equals
- Collapsing short switches together

These are *de facto* standardized conventions on highly POSIX-compliant systems, such as Linux. It is, however, by no means the only convention followed. Windows command lines often use a leading forward slash (/) in place of a hyphen. They often do not distinguish between short and long options, and sometimes use a colon (:) in place of an equals sign to separate an option and its option value. Java commands as well as commands in several older Unix systems use a single leading hyphen for both short and long options. Some of them use a space for separating an option and option-value irrespective of whether it is a short option or a long one. How can you take care of so many complex rules that vary from platform to platform while parsing your command line? This is where Boost Program Options library makes a big difference.

Using Boost.Program_Options

The Boost Program Options library provides you with a declarative way of parsing command lines. You can specify the set of options and switches and the type of option-values for each option that your program supports. You can also specify which set of conventions you want to support for your command line. You can then feed all of this information to the library functions that parse and validate the command line and extract all the command-line data into a dictionary-like structure from which you can access individual bits of data. We will now write some code to model the previously mentioned options for the `diff` command:

Listing 2.12a: Using Boost Program Options

```
 1 #include <boost/program_options.hpp>
 2
 3 namespace po = boost::program_options;
 4 namespace postyle = boost::program_options::command_line_style;
 5
 6 int main(int argc, char *argv[])
 7 {
 8   po::options_description desc("Options");
 9   desc.add_options()
10     ("unified,U", po::value<unsigned int>()->default_value(3),
11             "Print in unified form with specified number of "
12             "lines from the surrounding context")
13     (",p", "Print names of C functions "
14             " containing the difference")
15     (",N", "When comparing two directories, if a file exists in"
16             " only one directory, assume it to be present but "
17             " blank in the other directory")
18     ("help,h", "Print this help message");
```

In the preceding code snippet, we declare the structure of the command line using an `options_description` object. Successive options are declared using an overloaded function call `operator()` in the object returned by the `add_options`. You can cascade calls to this operator in the same way that you can print multiple values by cascading calls to the insertion operator (`<<`) on `std::cout`. This makes for a highly readable specification of the options.

We declare the `--unified` or `-U` option specifying both the long and short options in a single string, separated by a comma (line 10). The second argument indicates that we expect a numeric argument, and the default value will be taken as 3 if the argument is not specified on the command line. The third field is the description of the option and will be used to generate a documentation string.

We declare the short options -p and -N (lines 13 and 15), but as they do not have corresponding long options, they are introduced with a comma followed by a short option ("‚p" and "‚N"). They also do not take an option value, so we just provide their description.

So far so good. We will now complete the code example by parsing the command line and fetching the values. First, we will specify the styles to follow in Windows and Unix:

Listing 2.12b: Using Boost Program Options

```
19    int unix_style      = postyle::unix_style
20                          |postyle::short_allow_next;
21
22    int windows_style = postyle::allow_long
23                          |postyle::allow_short
24                          |postyle::allow_slash_for_short
25                          |postyle::allow_slash_for_long
26                          |postyle::case_insensitive
27                          |postyle::short_allow_next
28                          |postyle::long_allow_next;
```

The preceding code highlights some important differences between Windows and Unix conventions:

- A more or less standardized Unix style is available precanned and called, unix_style. However, we have to build the Windows style ourselves.
- The short_allow_next flag allows you to separate a short option and its option value with a space; this is used on both Windows and Unix.
- The allows_slash_for_short and allow_slash_for_long flags allow the options to be preceded by forward slashes; a common practice on Windows.
- The case_insensitive flag is appropriate for Windows where the usual practice is to have case insensitive commands and options.
- The long_allow_next flag on Windows allows long options and option values to be separated by a space instead of equals.

Now, let us see how we can parse a conforming command line using all of this information. To do this, we will declare an object of type variables_map to read all the data and then parse the command line:

Listing 2.12c: Using Boost Program Options

```
29    po::variables_map vm;
30    try {
31      po::store(
32        po::command_line_parser(argc, argv)
33            .options(desc)
34            .style(unix_style)   // or windows_style
35            .run(), vm);
36
37      po::notify(vm);
38
39      if (argc == 1 || vm.count("help")) {
40        std::cout << "USAGE: " << argv[0] << '\n'
41                  << desc << '\n';
42        return 0;
43      }
44    } catch (po::error& poe) {
45      std::cerr << poe.what() << '\n'
46                << "USAGE: " << argv[0] << '\n' << desc << '\n';
47      return EXIT_FAILURE;
48    }
```

We create a command-line parser using the `command_line_parser` function (line 32). We call the `options` member function on the returned parser to specify the parsing rules encoded in `desc` (line 33). We chain further member function calls, to the `style` member function of the parser for specifying the expected style (line 34), and to the `run` member function to actually perform the parsing. The call to `run` returns a data structure containing the data parsed from the command-line. The call to `boost::program_options::store` stores the parsed data from this data structure inside the `variables_map` object `vm` (lines 31-35). Finally, we check whether the program was invoked without arguments or with the `help` option, and print the help string (line 39). Streaming the `option_description` instance `desc` to an `ostream` prints a help string, that is automatically generated based on the command-line rules encoded in `desc` (line 41). All this is encapsulated in a try-catch block to trap any command line parsing errors thrown by the call to `run` (line 35). In the event of such an error, the error details are printed (line 45) along with the usage details (line 46).

If you notice, we call a function called `notify(...)` on line 37. In more advanced uses, we may choose to use values that are read from the command line to set variables or object members, or perform other post-processing actions. Such actions can be specified for each option while declaring option descriptions, but these actions are only initiated by the call to `notify`. As a matter of consistency, do not drop the call to `notify`.

We can now extract the values passed via the command line:

Listing 2.12d: Using Boost Program Options

```
49   unsigned int context = 0;
50   if (vm.count("unified")) {
51     context = vm["unified"].as<unsigned int>();
52   }
53
54   bool print_cfunc = (vm.count("p") > 0);
```

Parsing positional parameters

If you were observant, you would have noticed that we did nothing to read the two file names; the two main operands of the `diff` command. We did this for simplicity, and we will fix this now. We run the `diff` command like this:

$ diff -pN --unified=5 old_source_dir new_source_dir

The `old_source_dir` and `new_source_dir` arguments are called positional parameters. They are not options or switches, nor are they arguments to any options. In order to handle them, we will have to use a couple of new tricks. First of all, we must tell the parser the number and type of these parameters that we expect. Second, we must tell the parser that these are positional parameters. Here is the code snippet:

```
 1 std::string file1, file2;
 2 po::options_description posparams("Positional params");
 3 posparams.add_options()
 4         ("file1", po::value<std::string>(&file1)->required(), "")
 5         ("file2", po::value<std::string>(&file2)->required(), "");
 6 desc.add(posparams);
 7
 8
 9 po::positional_options_description posOpts;
10 posOpts.add("file1", 1);  // second param == 1 indicates that
11 posOpts.add("file2", 1);  //  we expect only one arg each
12
13 po::store(po::command_line_parser(argc, argv)
14                 .options(desc)
15                 .positional(posOpts)
16                 .style(windows_style)
17                 .run(), vm);
```

In the preceding code, we set up a second options description object called `posparams` to identify the positional parameters. We add options with names `"file1"` and `"file2"`, and indicate that these parameters are mandatory, using the `required()` member function of the `value` parameter (lines 4 and 5). We also specify two string variables `file1` and `file2` to store the positional parameters. All of this is added to the main options description object `desc` (line 6). For the parser to not look for actual options called `"--file1"` and `"--file2"`, we must tell the parser that these are positional parameters. This is done by defining a `positional_options_description` object (line 9) and adding the options that should be treated as positional options (lines 10 and 11). The second parameter in the call to `add(...)` specifies how many positional parameters should be considered for that option. Since we want one file name, each for options `file1` and `file2`, we specify `1` in both the calls. Positional parameters on the command line are interpreted according to the order in which they are added to the positional options description. Thus, in this case, the first positional parameter will be treated as `file1`, and the second parameter will be treated as `file2`.

Multiple option values

In some cases, a single option may take multiple option values. For example, during compilation, you will use the `-I` option multiple times to specify multiple directories. To parse such options and their option values, you can specify the target type as a vector, as shown in the following snippet:

```
1 po::options_description desc("Options");
2 desc.add_option()
3     ("include,I", po::value<std::vector<std::string> >(),
4      "Include files.")
5     (...);
```

This will work on an invocation like this:

```
$ c++ source.cpp -o target -I path1 -I path2 -I path3
```

In some cases, however, you might want to specify multiple option values, but you specify the option itself only once. Let us say that you are running a command to discover assets (local storage, NICs, HBAs, and so on) connected to each of a set of servers. You can have a command like this:

```
$ discover_assets --servers svr1 svr2 svr3 --uid user
```

In this case, to model the `--server` option, you would need to use the `multitoken()` directive as shown here:

```
1 po::options_description desc("Options");
2 desc.add_option()
3     ("servers,S",
4      po::value<std::vector<std::string> >()->multitoken(),
5      "List of hosts or IPs.")
6     ("uid,U", po::value<std::string>, "User name");
```

You can retrieve vector-valued parameters through the variable map like this:

```
1 std::vector<std::string> servers = vm["servers"];
```

Alternatively, you can use variable hooks at the time of option definition like this:

```
1 std::vector<std::string> servers;
2 desc.add_option()
3     ("servers,S",
4      po::value<std::vector<std::string> >(&servers
5          ->multitoken(),
6      "List of hosts or IPs.")...;
```

Make sure that you don't forget to call `notify` after parsing the command line.

> Trying to support positional parameters and options with
> multi-tokens together in the same command can confuse the
> parser and should be generally avoided.

The Program Options library uses Boost Any for its implementation. For the Program Options library to work correctly, you must not disable the generation of RTTI for your programs.

Other utilities and compile-time checks

Boost includes a number of micro-libraries that provide small but useful functionalities. Most of them are not elaborate enough to be separate libraries. Instead, they are grouped under `Boost.Utility` and `Boost.Core`. We will look at two such libraries here.

We will also look at some useful ways to detect errors as early as possible, at compile time, and glean information about the program's compilation environment and tool chains using different facilities from Boost.

BOOST_CURRENT_FUNCTION

When writing debug logs, it is incredibly useful to be able to write function names and some qualifying information about functions from where logging is invoked. This information is (obviously) available to compilers during the compilation of sources. However, the way to print it is different for different compilers. Even for a given compiler, there may be more than one ways to do it. If you want to write portable code, this is one wart you have to take care to hide. The best tool for this is the macro BOOST_CURRENT_FUNCTION, formally a part of Boost.Utility, shown in action in the following example:

Listing 2.13: Pretty printing current function name

```
 1 #include <boost/current_function.hpp>
 2 #include <iostream>
 3
 4 namespace FoFum {
 5 class Foo
 6 {
 7 public:
 8   void bar() {
 9     std::cout << BOOST_CURRENT_FUNCTION << '\n';
10     bar_private(5);
11   }
12
13   static void bar_static() {
14     std::cout << BOOST_CURRENT_FUNCTION << '\n';
15   }
16
17 private:
18   float bar_private(int x) const {
19     std::cout << BOOST_CURRENT_FUNCTION << '\n';
20   return 0.0;
21   }
22 };
23 } // end namespace FoFum
24
25 namespace {
26 template <typename T>
27 void baz(const T& x)
28 {
29   std::cout << BOOST_CURRENT_FUNCTION << '\n';
30 }
```

```
32 } // end unnamed namespace
33
34 int main()
35 {
36   std::cout << BOOST_CURRENT_FUNCTION << '\n';
37   FoFum::Foo f;
38   f.bar();
39   FoFum::Foo::bar_static();
40   baz(f);
41 }
```

Depending on your compiler, the output you see would vary in format. GNU compilers tend to have a more readable output, while on Microsoft Visual Studio you will see some very elaborate output including details such as calling conventions. In particular, the output for template instantiations is much more elaborate on Visual Studio. Here is a sample output I see on my systems.

With GNU g++:

```
int main()
void FoFum::Foo::bar()
float FoFum::Foo::bar1(int) const
static void FoFum::Foo::bar_static()
void {anonymous}::baz(const T&) [with T = FoFum::Foo]
```

With Visual Studio:

```
int __cdecl main(void)
void __thiscall FoFum::Foo::bar(void)
float __thiscall FoFum::Foo::bar1(int) const
void __cdecl FoFum::Foo::bar_static(void)
void __cdecl 'anonymous-namespace'::baz<class FoFum::Foo>(const class
FoFum::Foo &)
```

You can immediately see some differences. GNU compilers call out static methods from nonstatic ones. On Visual Studio, you have to differentiate based on calling conventions (__cdecl for static member methods as well as global methods, __thiscall for instance methods). You might want to take a look at the current_function.hpp header file to figure out which macros are used behind the scenes. On GNU compilers, for example, it is __PRETTY_FUNCTION__, while on Visual Studio, it is __FUNCSIG__.

Boost.Swap

The Boost Swap library is yet another useful micro library and is part of Boost Core:

```
#include <boost/core/swap.hpp>
namespace boost {
  template<typename T1, typename T2>
  void swap(T1& left, T2& right);
}
```

It wraps a well-known idiom around swapping objects. Let us first look at the problem itself to understand what is going on.

There is one global `swap` function in the `std` namespace. In many cases, for a type defined in a particular namespace, a specialized `swap` overload may be provided in the same namespace. When writing generic code, this can pose some challenges. Imagine a generic function that calls `swap` on its arguments:

```
1 template <typename T>
2 void process_values(T& arg1, T& arg2, …)
3 {
4     …
5     std::swap(arg1, arg2);
```

In the preceding snippet, we call `std::swap` on line 5 to perform the swapping. While this is well-formed, this may not do what is desired in some cases. Consider the following types and functions in the namespace `X`:

```
1 namespace X {
2   struct Foo {};
3
4   void swap(Foo& left, Foo& right) {
5     std::cout << BOOST_CURRENT_FUNCTION << '\n';
6   }
7 }
```

Of course, `X::Foo` is a trivial type and `X::swap` is a no-op, but they can be replaced with a meaningful implementation and the points we make here would still hold.

So, what happens if you call the function `process_values` on two arguments of type `X::Foo`?

```
1 X::Foo f1, f2;
2 process_values(f1, f2, …); // calls process_values<X::Foo>
```

The call to `process_values` (line 2) will call `std::swap` on the passed instances of `X::Foo`, that is, `f1` and `f2`. Yet, we would likely have wanted `X::swap` be called on `f1` and `f2` because it is a more appropriate overload. There is a way to do this; you call `boost::swap` instead. Here is the rewrite of the `process_values` template snippet:

```
1 #include <boost/core/swap.hpp>
2
3 template <typename T>
4 void process_values(T& arg1, T& arg2, …)
5 {
6    …
7    boost::swap(arg1, arg2);
```

If you now run this code, you will see the `X::swap` overload printing its name to the console. To understand how `boost::swap` manages to call the appropriate overload, we need to understand how we could have solved this without `boost::swap`:

```
1 template <typename T>
2 void process_values(T& arg1, T& arg2, …)
3 {
4    …
5    using std::swap;
6    swap(arg1, arg2);
```

If we did not have the `using` declaration (line 5), the call to `swap` (line 6) would still have succeeded for a type `T` that was defined in a namespace, which had a `swap` overload defined for `T` — thanks to **Argument Dependent Lookup (ADL)** — `X::Foo`, accompanied by `X::swap`, is such a type. However, it would have failed for types defined in the global namespace (assuming you didn't define a generic `swap` in the global namespace). With the `using` declaration (line 5), we create the fallback for the unqualified call to `swap` (line 6). When ADL succeeds in finding a namespace level `swap` overload, the call to `swap` gets resolved to this overload. When ADL fails to find such an overload, then `std::swap` is used, as dictated, by the `using` declaration. The problem is that this is a nonobvious trick, and you have to know it to use it. Not every engineer in your team will come equipped with all the name lookup rules in C++. In the meantime, he can always use `boost::swap`, which essentially wraps this piece of code in a function. You can now use just one version of `swap` and expect the most appropriate overload to be invoked each time.

Compile-time asserts

Compile-time asserts require certain conditions to hold true at some point in the code. Any violation of the condition causes the compilation to fail at the point. It is an effective way to find errors at compile time, which otherwise would cause serious grief at runtime. It may also help reduce the volume and verbosity of compiler error messages of the sort generated due to template instantiation failures.

Runtime asserts are meant to corroborate the invariance of certain conditions that must hold true at some point in the code. Such a condition might be the result of the logic or algorithm used or could be based on some documented convention. For example, if you are writing a function to raise a number to some power, how do you handle the mathematically undefined case of both the number and the power being zero? You can use an assert to express this explicitly, as shown in the following snippet (line 6):

```
1 #include <cassert>
2
3 double power(double base, double exponent)
4 {
5   // no negative powers of zero
6   assert(base != 0 || exponent > 0);
7   ...
8 }
```

Any violation of such invariants indicates a bug or a flaw, which needs to be fixed, and causes a catastrophic failure of the program in debug builds. Boost provides a macro called BOOST_STATIC_ASSERT that takes an expression, which can be evaluated at compile time and triggers a compilation failure if this expression evaluates to false.

For example, you may have designed a memory allocator class template that is meant to be used only with "small" objects. Of course, smallness is arbitrary, but you can design your allocator to be optimized for objects of size 16 bytes or smaller. If you want to enforce correct usage of your class, you should simply prevent its instantiation for any class of size greater than 16 bytes. Here is our first example of BOOST_STATIC_ASSERT that helps you enforce the small object semantics of your allocator:

Listing 2.16a: Using compile-time asserts

```
1 #include <boost/static_assert.hpp>
2
3 template <typename T>
```

```
 4 class SmallObjectAllocator
 5 {
 6   BOOST_STATIC_ASSERT(sizeof(T) <= 16);
 7
 8 public:
 9   SmallObjectAllocator() {}
10 };
```

We define our dummy allocator template called `SmallObjectAllocator` (lines 3 and 4) and call the `BOOST_STATIC_ASSERT` macro in the class scope (line 6). We pass an expression to the macro that must be possible to evaluate at compile time. Now, `sizeof` expressions are always evaluated by the compiler and 16 is an integer literal, so the expression `sizeof(T) <= 16` can be entirely evaluated at compile time and can be passed to `BOOST_STATIC_ASSERT`. If we now instantiate the `SmallObjectAllocator` with a type `Foo`, whose size is 32 bytes, we will get a compiler error due to the static assert on line 6. Here is the code that can trigger the assertion:

Listing 2.16b: Using compile-time asserts

```
11 struct Foo
12 {
13   char data[32];
14 };
15
16 int main()
17 {
18   SmallObjectAllocator<int> intAlloc;
19   SmallObjectAllocator<Foo> fooAlloc; // ERROR: sizeof(Foo) > 16
20 }
```

We define a type `Foo` whose size is 32 bytes, which is larger than the maximum supported by `SmallObjectAllocator` (line 13). We instantiate the `SmallObjectAllocator` template with the types `int` (line 18) and `Foo` (line 19) . The compilation fails for `SmallObjectAllocator<Foo>`, and we get an error message.

C++11 supports compile-time asserts using the new `static_assert` keyword. If you are using a C++11 compiler, `BOOST_STATIC_ASSERT` internally uses `static_assert`.

The actual error message naturally varies from compiler to compiler, especially on C++03 compilers. On C++11 compilers, because this internally uses the `static_assert` keyword, the error message tends to be more uniform and meaningful. However, on pre-C++11 compilers too, you get a fairly accurate idea of the offending line. On my system, using the GNU g++ compiler in C++03 mode, I get the following errors:

```
StaticAssertTest.cpp: In instantiation of 'class
SmallObjectAllocator<Foo>':
StaticAssertTest.cpp:19:29:   required from here
StaticAssertTest.cpp:6:3: error: invalid application of 'sizeof' to
incomplete type 'boost::STATIC_ASSERTION_FAILURE<false>'
```

The last line of the compiler error refers to an incomplete type `boost::STATIC_ASSERTION_FAILURE<false>`, which comes from the innards of the `BOOST_STATIC_ASSERT` macro. It is clear that there was an error on line 6, and the static assertion failed. If I switch to C++11 mode, the error messages are a lot saner:

```
StaticAssertTest.cpp: In instantiation of 'class
SmallObjectAllocator<Foo>':
StaticAssertTest.cpp:19:29:   required from here
StaticAssertTest.cpp:6:3: error: static assertion failed: sizeof(T) <=
16
```

There is another variant of the static assert macro called `BOOST_STATIC_ASSERT`, which takes a message string as the second parameter. With C++11 compilers, it simply prints this message for the error message. Under pre-C++11 compilers, this message may or may not make it to the compiler error content. You use it this way:

```
1 BOOST_STATIC_ASSERT_MSG(sizeof(T) <= 16, "Objects of size more"
2                         " than 16 bytes not supported.");
```

Not all expressions can be evaluated at compile time. Mostly, expressions involving constant integers, sizes of types, and general type computations can be evaluated at compile time. The Boost TypeTraits library and the Boost **Metaprogramming Library (MPL)** offer several metafunctions using which many sophisticated conditions can be checked on types at compile time. We illustrate such use with a small example. We will see more examples of such use in later chapters.

We may use static assertions not only in class scope but also in function and namespace scope. Here is an example of a library of function templates that allow bitwise operations on different POD types. When instantiating these functions, we assert at compile time that the types passed are POD types:

Listing 2.17: Using compile-time asserts

```
 1 #include <boost/static_assert.hpp>
 2 #include <boost/type_traits.hpp>
 3
 4 template <typename T, typename U>
 5 T bitwise_or (const T& left, const U& right)
 6 {
 7   BOOST_STATIC_ASSERT(boost::is_pod<T>::value &&
 8                       boost::is_pod<U>::value);
 9   BOOST_STATIC_ASSERT(sizeof(T) >= sizeof(U));
10
11   T result = left;
12   unsigned char *right_array =
13           reinterpret_cast<unsigned char*>(&right);
14   unsigned char *left_array =
15           reinterpret_cast<unsigned char*>(&result);
16   for (size_t i = 0; i < sizeof(U); ++i) {
17     left_array[i] |= right_array[i];
18   }
19
20   return result;
21 }
```

Here, we define a function `bitwise_or` (lines 4 and 5) , which takes two objects, potentially of different types and sizes, and returns the bitwise-or of their content. Inside this function, we use the metafunction `boost::is_pod<T>` to assert that both the objects passed are of POD types (line 7). Also, because the return type of the function is `T`, the type of the left argument, we assert that the function must always be called with the larger argument first (line 9) so that there is no data loss.

Diagnostics using preprocessor macros

A number of times in my career as a software engineer, I have worked on products with a single code base that were built on five different flavors of Unix and on Windows, often in parallel. Often these build servers would be big iron servers with hundreds of gigs of attached storage that would be used by multiple products for the purpose of building. There would be myriad environments, tool chains, and configurations cohabiting on the same server. It must have taken ages to stabilize these systems to a point where everything built perfectly. One day, all hell broke loose when, overnight, without any significant check-ins having gone in, our software started acting weird. It took us almost a day to figure out that someone had tinkered with the environment variables, as a result of which we were linking using a different version of the compiler and linking with a different runtime from the one with which our third-party libraries were built. I don't need to tell you that this was not ideal for a build system even at the time that it existed. Unfortunately, you may still find such messed up environments that take a long time to set up and then get undone by a flippant change. What saved us that day after half a day's fruitless toil was the good sense of using preprocessor macros to dump information about the build system, including compiler names, versions, architecture, and their likes at program startup. We could soon glean enough information from this data dumped by the program, before it inevitably crashed and we spotted the compiler mismatch.

Such information is doubly useful for library writers who might be able to provide the most optimal implementation of a library on each compiler or platform by leveraging specific interfaces and doing conditional compilation of code based on preprocessor macro definitions. The bane of working with such macros is, however, the absolute disparity between different compilers, platforms, and environments on how they are named and what their function is. Boost provides a much more uniform set of preprocessor macros for gleaning information about the software build environment through its `Config` and `Predef` libraries. We will look at a handful of useful macros from these libraries.

The `Predef` library is a header-only library that provides all sorts of macros for getting useful information about the build environment at compile time. The information available can fall into different categories. Rather than providing a long list of options and explaining what they do — a job that the online documentation does adequately — we will look at the following code to illustrate how this information is accessed and used:

Listing 2.18a: Using diagnostic macros from Predef

```
 1 #include <boost/predef.h>
 2 #include <iostream>
 3
 4 void checkOs()
 5 {
 6   // identify OS
 7 #if defined(BOOST_OS_WINDOWS)
 8   std::cout << "Windows" << '\n';
 9 #elif defined(BOOST_OS_LINUX)
10   std::cout << "Linux" << '\n';
11 #elif defined(BOOST_OS_MACOS)
12   std::cout << "MacOS" << '\n';
13 #elif defined(BOOST_OS_UNIX)
14   std::cout << Another UNIX" << '\n'; // *_AIX, *_HPUX, etc.
15 #endif
16 }
```

The preceding function uses the `BOOST_OS_*` macros from the `Predef` library to identify the OS on which the code is built. We have only shown macros for three different OSes. The online documentation provides a full list of macros for identifying different OSes.

Listing 2.18b: Using diagnostic macros from Predef

```
 1 #include <boost/predef.h>
 2 #include <iostream>
 3
 4 void checkArch()
 5 {
 6   // identify architecture
 7 #if defined(BOOST_ARCH_X86)
 8  #if defined(BOOST_ARCH_X86_64)
 9   std::cout << "x86-64 bit" << '\n';
10  #else
11   std::cout << "x86-32 bit" << '\n';
12  #endif
```

```
13 #elif defined(BOOST_ARCH_ARM)
14   std::cout << "ARM" << '\n';
15 #else
16   std::cout << "Other architecture" << '\n';
17 #endif
18 }
```

The preceding function uses the BOOST_ARCH_* macros from the Predef library to identify the architecture of the platform on which the code is built. We have only shown macros for x86 and ARM architectures; the online documentation provides a complete list of macros for identifying different architectures.

Listing 2.18c: Using diagnostic macros from Predef

```
1 #include <boost/predef.h>
2 #include <iostream>
3
4 void checkCompiler()
5 {
6   // identify compiler
7 #if defined(BOOST_COMP_GNUC)
8   std::cout << "GCC, Version: " << BOOST_COMP_GNUC << '\n';
9 #elif defined(BOOST_COMP_MSVC)
10   std::cout << "MSVC, Version: " << BOOST_COMP_MSVC << '\n';
11 #else
12   std::cout << "Other compiler" << '\n';
13 #endif
14 }
```

The preceding function uses the BOOST_COMP_* macros from the Predef library to identify the compiler that was used to build the code. We have only shown macros for GNU and Microsoft Visual C++ compilers. The online documentation provides a complete list of macros for identifying different compilers. When defined, the BOOST_COMP_* macro for a particular compiler evaluates to its numeric version. For example, on Visual Studio 2010, BOOST_COMP_MSVC evaluates to 100030319. This could be translated as version 10.0.30319:

Listing 2.18d: Using diagnostic macros from Predef

```
1 #include <boost/predef.h>
2 #include <iostream>
3
4 void checkCpp11()
5 {
6   // Do version checks
```

```
 7 #if defined(BOOST_COMP_GNUC)
 8 #if BOOST_COMP_GNUC < BOOST_VERSION_NUMBER(4, 8, 1)
 9   std::cout << "Incomplete C++ 11 support" << '\n';
10 #else
11   std::cout << "Most C++ 11 features supported" << '\n';
12 #endif
13 #elif defined(BOOST_COMP_MSVC)
14 #if BOOST_COMP_MSVC < BOOST_VERSION_NUMBER(12, 0, 0)
15   std::cout << "Incomplete C++ 11 support" << '\n';
16 #else
17   std::cout << "Most C++ 11 features supported" << '\n';
18 #endif
19 #endif
20 }
```

In the preceding code, we use the BOOST_VERSION_NUMBER macro to construct versions against which we compare the current version of the GNU or Microsoft Visual C++ compilers. If the GNU compiler version is less than 4.8.1 or the Microsoft Visual Studio C++ compiler version is less than 12.0, we print that the support for C++11 might be incomplete.

In the final example of this section, we use macros from boost/config.hpp to print compiler, platform, and runtime library names (lines 6, 7, and 8). We also use two macros defined in boost/version.hpp to print the version of Boost used, as a string (line 10) and as a numeric value (line 11):

Listing 2.19: Using configuration information macros

```
 1 #include <boost/config.hpp>
 2 #include <boost/version.hpp>
 3 #include <iostream>
 4
 5 void buildEnvInfo() {
 6   std::cout << "Compiler: " << BOOST_COMPILER << '\n'
 7             << "Platform: " << BOOST_PLATFORM << '\n'
 8             << "Library: " << BOOST_STDLIB << '\n';
 9
10   std::cout << "Boost version: " << BOOST_LIB_VERSION << '['
11                          << BOOST_VERSION << ']' << '\n';
12 }
```

Self-test questions

For multiple choice questions, choose all the options that apply:

1. What are the advantages of using `boost::swap` over `std::swap`?

   a. There is no real advantage

   b. `boost::swap` invokes swap overloads supplied with the passed type, if any

   c. `boost::swap` is faster than `std::swap`

   d. `boost::swap` does not throw exceptions

2. Can you apply a visitor to multiple variant arguments in a single call? (*Hint:* you may want to look up the online documentation)

   a. Yes. A visitor can only be applied to one or two variant arguments

   b. Yes. A visitor can be applied to one or more arguments

   c. No. The member operators take only one variant argument

   d. None of the above

3. Is the following a valid compile-time assert?
   ```
   BOOST_STATIC_ASSERT(x == 0);  // x is some variable
   ```

   a. Yes, provided x is of an integral type

   b. Yes, provided x is declared as a `const static` numeric variable

   c. No, x is a variable, and its value cannot be known at compile time

   d. Only expressions involving `sizeof` are valid in a `BOOST_STATIC_ASSERT`

4. What do we mean when we say that a type x is a POD type?

   a. x does not have a user-defined constructor or destructor

   b. x can be copied by copying its memory layout bit-wise

   c. x does not have a user-defined copy constructor or copy assignment operator

   d. All of the above

5. What is the type and value stored in a default-constructed object of type `boost::variant<std::string, double>`?

   a. The type is `const char*` and value is `NULL`

   b. The type is `double` and value is `0.0`

   c. The type is `std::string` and value is the default constructed `std::string`

   d. The type is `boost::optional<double>` and value is empty

6. Check the reference on Boost.Optional in the online documentation for the latest Boost libraries. What happens if you call the `get` and `get_ptr` methods on an empty `optional` object?

   a. Both throw the `boost::empty_optional` exception

   b. `get` throws an exception, while `get_ptr` returns a null pointer

   c. `get` asserts, while `get_ptr` returns a null pointer

   d. Both `get` and `get_ptr` assert

Summary

This chapter was a quick tour of several Boost libraries that help you do important programming chores, such as parsing command lines, creating type-safe variant types, handling empty values, and performing compile-time checks.

Hopefully, you have appreciated the diversity of libraries in Boost and the expressive power they lend to your code. In the process, you would have also become more familiar with compiling code that uses the Boost libraries and linking to the appropriate libraries as needed.

In the next chapter, we will look at how you can deterministically manage heap memory and other resources in exception-safe ways using various flavors of Boost's smart pointers.

References

Curiously Recurring Template Pattern: https://en.wikibooks.org/wiki/More_C%2B%2B_Idioms/Curiously_Recurring_Template_Pattern

3
Memory Management and Exception Safety

C++ has a great deal of compatibility with the C programming language. C++ retains pointers for representing and accessing specific memory addresses and provides manual memory management primitives via the new and delete operators. You can also seamlessly access from C++, the C Standard Library functions and C system calls or platform APIs of most major operating systems. Naturally, C++ code often deals with *handles* to various OS resources, like heap memory, open files, sockets, threads, and shared memory. Acquiring such resources and failing to release them could have undesirable consequences for your programs, showing up as insidious bugs, including memory leaks and deadlocks.

In this chapter, we look at ways of encapsulating pointers to dynamically-allocated objects using **smart pointers** to ensure that they are automatically deallocated when they are no longer needed. We then extend these techniques to non-memory resources. In the process, we develop an understanding of what is meant by exception-safe code and use smart pointers to write such code.

These topics are divided into the following sections:

- Dynamic memory allocation and exception safety
- Smart pointers
- Unique ownership semantics
- Shared ownership semantics

For some sections of this chapter, you will need access to a compiler with C++11 support. This will be called out with additional instructions in individual sections.

Dynamic memory allocation and exception safety

Imagine that you have to write a program to rotate images. Your program takes the name of the file and the angle of rotation as input, reads the contents of the file, performs the processing, and returns the output. Here is some sample code.

```
 1 #include <istream>
 2 #include <fstream>
 3 typedef unsigned char byte;
 4
 5 byte *rotateImage(std::string imgFile, double angle,
 6                   size_t& sz) {
 7   // open the file for reading
 8   std::ifstream imgStrm(imgFile.c_str(), std::ios::binary);
 9
10   if (imgStrm) {
11     // determine file size
12     imgStrm.seekg(0, std::ios::end);
13     sz = imgStrm.tellg();
14     imsStrm.seekg(0);          // seek back to start of stream
15
16     byte *img = new byte[sz]; // allocate buffer and read
17     // read the image contents
18     imgStrm.read(reinterpret_cast<char*>(img), sz);
19     // process it
20     byte *rotated = img_rotate(img, sz, angle);
21     // deallocate buffer
22     delete [] img;
23
24     return rotated;
25   }
26
27   sz = 0;
28   return 0;
29 }
```

The actual work of rotating the image is done by an imaginary C++ API called img_rotate (line 20). The img_rotate function takes three parameters: the contents of the image as an array of bytes, the size of the array in a non-const reference, and the angle of rotation. It returns the contents of the rotated image as a dynamically-allocated byte array. The size of this array is returned via the reference passed as the third parameter. This is an imperfect code, more reminiscent of C. Code like this is surprisingly common "in the wild" and that's why it is important to know its pitfalls. So, let us dissect the problem.

In order to read the contents of the image file, we first determine the size of the file (lines 12-13), and then allocate a byte array img just big enough to hold the entire data in the file (line 16). We read the image contents (line 18), and after performing rotation of the image through a call to img_rotate, we delete the buffer img containing the original image (line 22). Finally, we return the byte array with the rotated image (line 24). For simplicity, we do not check for read errors (line 18).

There are two glaring issues in the preceding code. If the rotation of the image failed (line 19) and img_rotate threw an exception, then the function rotateImage would return without deallocating the byte buffer img, which would thus be *leaked*. This is a definitive example of code that is not well-behaved in the face of exceptions, that is, it is not *exception-safe*. Moreover, even if everything went right, the function would return the rotated buffer (line 24), which itself was dynamically-allocated. So we leave its deallocation entirely at the caller's mercy with no guarantees whatsoever. We ought to do better.

There is a third less obvious problem. The img_rotate function ought to have documented how it allocates memory for us to know how to free it—by calling the array delete (delete []) operator (line 22). But what if there was a more efficient custom memory management scheme that the developers of img_rotate found and wanted to use in the next version? They would avoid doing so; otherwise all of their client code would break as the delete [] operator may no longer be the correct way to deallocate that memory. Ideally, this is one detail that the clients of the img_rotate API should never have had to bother about.

Exception safety and RAII

In the previous example, we looked informally at the concept of exception safety. We saw that a potential exception thrown from the `img_rotate` API could leak resources in the `rotateImage` function. It turns out that you can reason about the behavior of your code in the face of exceptions in terms of a set of criteria called **The Abrahams Exception Safety Guarantees**. They are named after Dave Abrahams, the Boost cofounder and an eminent C++ Standards Committee member, who formalized these guarantees in 1996. They have since been refined further by others, including notably Herb Sutter, and are listed below:

- **Basic guarantee**: An operation terminated midway preserves invariants and does not leak resources
- **Strong guarantee**: An operation terminated midway will not have any effect, that is, the operation is atomic
- **No-throw guarantee**: An operation that cannot fail

An operation that does not satisfy any of these criteria is said to be "not exception-safe" or more colloquially, exception-unsafe. The appropriate level of exception safety for an operation is the programmer's prerogative but exception-unsafe code is rarely acceptable.

The most fundamental and effective C++ technique for making code exception-safe goes by the curious name **Resource Acquisition is Initialization (RAII)**. The RAII idiom proposes the following model for encapsulating resources that require manual management:

1. Encapsulate resource acquisition in the constructor of a wrapper object.
2. Encapsulate resource release in the destructor of the wrapper object.
3. Additionally, define consistent copy and move semantics for the wrapper object or disable them.

If the wrapper object is created on the stack, its destructor is called for normal scope exit as well as exit due to exceptions. Otherwise, the wrapper object itself should be managed by the RAII idiom. Loosely speaking, you either create your objects on the stack or manage them using RAII. At this point, some examples are in order, and we can go straight back to the image rotation example and fix it using RAII:

```
1 struct ScopeGuard
2 {
3   ScopeGuard(byte *buffer) : data_(buffer) {}
```

```
 4    ~ScopeGuard() { delete [] data_; }
 5
 6    byte *get() { return data_; }
 7  private:
 8    byte *data_;
 9  };
10
11  byte *rotateImage(std::string imgFile, double angle, size_t& sz)
12  {
13    // open the file for reading
14    std::ifstream imgStrm(imgFile.c_str(), std::ios::binary);
15
16    if (imgStrm) {
17      // determine file size
18      imgStrm.seekg(0, std::ios::end);
19      sz = imgStrm.tellg();
20      imgStrm.seekg(0);
21
22      // allocate buffer and read
23      ScopeGuard img(new byte[sz]);
24      // read the image contents
25      imgStrm.read(reinterpret_cast<char*>(img.get()), sz);
26      // process it
27      return img_rotate(img.get(), sz, angle);
28    } // ScopeGuard destructor
29
30    sz = 0;
31    return 0;
32  }
```

The preceding code is a modest attempt that makes the rotateImage function exception-safe, provided the img_rotate function itself is exception-safe. First up we define a struct called ScopeGuard (lines 1-9) for encapsulating character arrays allocated by the array new operator. It takes a pointer to an allocated array as its constructor argument and sets the data member data_ to this pointer (line 3). Its destructor deallocates the array pointed to by its data_ member using the array delete operator (line 4). The get member function (line 6) provides a way to get the underlying pointer from a ScopeGuard object.

Inside the `rotateImage` function, we instantiate a `ScopeGuard` object called `img`, wrapping the byte array allocated using array `new` operator (line 23). We call `read` on the open file stream and pass to it the raw byte array obtained by calling the `get` method on `img` (line 25). We assume read always succeeds but, in production code, we should always have proper error checks in place. Finally, we call the `img_rotate` API and return the rotated image it returns (line 27). As we exit the scope, the `ScopeGuard` destructor is called and automatically deallocates the encapsulated byte array (line 28). Even if `img_rotate` threw an exception, the `ScopeGuard` destructor would still be called as part of stack unwinding. Through the use of RAII via the `ScopeGuard` class, we are able to claim that the `rotateImage` function can never leak the buffer containing the image data.

On the other hand, the buffer containing the rotated image returned by `rotateImage` *could* be leaked, unless the caller takes care to assign it to a pointer and then duly release it in an exception-safe way. The `ScopeGuard` class in its current form is no good there. It turns out that Boost ships different kinds of smart pointer templates to address various use cases like these, and it is worthwhile to understand these smart pointers and the patterns of resource acquisition, and the exception safety problems they help solve.

Smart pointers

A smart pointer, definitively, is a class that encapsulates access to a pointer and often manages memory associated with the pointer. If you paid attention, you would have noticed the similarity smart pointers have with pineapples — smart pointers are classes, not pointers, just as pineapples aren't really apples. Moving away from fruit analogies, different types of smart pointers often have additional features like bounds-checking, null-checking, and access control, among others. In C++, smart pointers usually overload the dereference operator (`operator->`), which allows any method calls invoked on the smart pointer using `operator->` to be bound to the underlying pointer.

Boost includes a set of four different smart pointers with differing semantics. Also, because C++ often uses pointers to identify and manipulate arrays of objects, Boost provides two different smart array templates that encapsulate array access via pointers. In the following sections, we study the different classes of smart pointers from Boost and their semantics. We will also look at `std::unique_ptr`, a C++11 smart pointer class that supersedes one of the Boost smart pointers and supports semantics not readily available from Boost.

Unique ownership semantics

Consider the following code snippet for instantiating an object and calling a method on it:

```
 1 class Widget;
 2
 3 // …
 4
 5 void useWidget()
 6 {
 7   Widget *wgt = new Widget;
 8   wgt->setTitle(...);
 9   wgt->setSize(...);
10   wgt->display(...);
11   delete wgt;
12 }
```

As we saw in the previous section, the preceding code is not exception-safe. Exceptions thrown from operations after the Widget object is constructed on dynamic memory (line 7) and before the Widget object is destroyed (line 11), can cause the dynamically-allocated memory for the Widget object to leak. To fix this, we need something akin to the ScopeGuard class we wrote in the previous section, and Boost obliges with the boost::scoped_ptr template.

boost::scoped_ptr

Here is the preceding example fixed using scoped_ptr. The scoped_ptr template is available from the header file boost/scoped_ptr.hpp. It is a header-only library, and you don't need to link your program against any other libraries:

Listing 3.1: Using scoped_ptr

```
 1 #include <boost/scoped_ptr.hpp>
 2 #include "Widget.h"  // contains the definition of Widget
 3
 4 // …
 5
 6 void useWidget()
 7 {
 8   boost::scoped_ptr<Widget> wgt(new Widget);
 9   wgt->setTitle(...);
10   wgt->setSize(...);
11   wgt->display(...);
12 }
```

In the preceding code, `wgt` is an object of type `scoped_ptr<Widget>`, which is a drop-in replacement for the `Widget*` pointer. We initialize it with a dynamically-allocated `Widget` object (line 8) and drop the call to `delete`. These are the only two changes needed to make this code exception-safe.

Smart pointers like `scoped_ptr` and others from Boost, take care of calling `delete` on the encapsulated pointer in their destructor. When `useWidget` completes or if an exception terminates it midway, the destructor of the `scoped_ptr` instance `wgt` will be invoked and will destroy the `Widget` object and release its memory. The overloaded dereference operator (`operator->`) in `scoped_ptr` allows `Widget` members to be accessed via the `wgt` smart pointer (lines 9-11).

The destructor of `boost::scoped_ptr` template uses `boost::checked_delete` to release the dynamically-allocated memory that the encapsulated pointer points to. Thus, the type of the object pointed to by the encapsulated pointer must be completely defined at the point the `boost::scoped_ptr` instance goes out of scope; otherwise, the code will fail to compile.

The `boost::scoped_ptr` is the simplest of Boost's smart pointers. It takes ownership of the dynamically-allocated pointer passed and calls `delete` on it inside its own destructor. This binds the life of the underlying object to the scope in which the encapsulating `scoped_ptr` operates—hence, the name `scoped_ptr`. Essentially, it implements RAII on the encapsulated pointer. Moreover, `scoped_ptr` cannot be copied. This means that a dynamically-allocated object can only be wrapped by one `scoped_ptr` instance at any given point in time. Thus, `scoped_ptr` is said to exhibit *unique ownership semantics*. Note that `scoped_ptr` instances cannot be stored in Standard Library containers because they can neither be copied nor moved from in the C++11 sense.

In the following example, we explore some more features of `scoped_ptr`:

Listing 3.2: scoped_ptr in detail

```
 1 #include <boost/scoped_ptr.hpp>
 2 #include <cassert>
 3 #include "Widget.h" // Widget definition
 4 // …
 5
 6 void useTwoWidgets()
 7 {
 8   // default constructed scoped_ptr
 9   boost::scoped_ptr<Widget> wgt;
10   assert(!wgt);          // null test - Boolean context
```

```
11
12    wgt.reset(new Widget); // create first widget
13    assert(wgt);           // non-null test - Boolean context
14    wgt->display();        // display first widget
15    wgt.reset(new Widget); // destroy first, create second widget
16    wgt->display();        // display second widget
17
18    Widget *w1 = wgt.get();  // get the raw pointer
19    Widget& rw1 = *wgt;      // 'dereference' the smart pointer
20    assert(w1 == &rw1);      // same object, so same address
21
22    boost::scoped_ptr<Widget> wgt2(new Widget);
23    Widget *w2 = wgt2.get();
24    wgt.swap(wgt2);
25    assert(wgt.get() == w2);  // effect of swap
26    assert(wgt2.get() == w1); // effect of swap
27 }
```

In this example, we first construct an object of type scoped_ptr<Widget> using its default constructor (line 9). This creates a scoped_ptr containing a null pointer. Any attempts to dereference such a smart pointer will result in undefined behavior typically leading to a crash. scoped_ptr supports implicit conversion to a Boolean value; so we can use a scoped_ptr object like wgt in Boolean contexts to check whether the encapsulated pointer is null or not. In this case, we know that it should be null because it is default-constructed; hence, we assert on wgt being null (line 10).

There are two ways to change the pointer contained inside a scoped_ptr and one of them is to use the reset member method of scoped_ptr. When we call reset on a scoped_ptr, the encapsulated pointer is deallocated and scoped_ptr takes ownership of the newly passed pointer in its place. Thus, we can use reset to change the pointer owned by a scoped_ptr instance (line 12). Following this, scoped_ptr contains a non-null pointer, and we assert as much using the ability to implicitly convert scoped_ptr to a Boolean value (line 13). Next, we call reset again to store a new pointer in wgt (line 15). In this case, the earlier stored pointer is deallocated, and the underlying object is destroyed before the new pointer is stored.

We can get at the underlying pointer by calling the get member function of scoped_ptr (line 18). We can also get a reference to the object pointed to by the smart pointer by dereferencing the smart pointer (line 19). We assert the fact that this reference and the pointer returned by get both point to the same object (line 20).

There is of course a second way to change the pointer contained inside a scoped_ptr. By swapping two scoped_ptr objects, their encapsulated pointers are swapped (lines 24-26). This is the only way to change the owning scoped_ptr of a dynamically-allocated object.

In summary, we can say that once you have wrapped an object in a scoped_ptr, it can never be detached from a scoped_ptr. The scoped_ptr could destroy the object and take on a new object (using the reset member function), or it could swap its pointer with that in another scoped_ptr. In that sense, scoped_ptr exhibits unique, transferrable ownership semantics.

Uses of scoped_ptr

scoped_ptr is a lightweight and versatile smart pointer that is capable of more than just acting as a scope guard. Here is a look at how it can be used in code.

Creating exception-safe scopes

scoped_ptr is useful in creating exception-safe scopes, when objects are dynamically-allocated in some scope. C++ allows objects to be created on the stack and often that is the route you would take to create objects instead of allocating them dynamically. But, in some cases, you would need to instantiate an object by calling factory functions that return pointers to the dynamically-allocated objects. This could be from some legacy library and scoped_ptr can be a handy wrapper for such pointers. In the following example, makeWidget is one such factory function that returns a dynamically-allocated Widget:

```
 1 class Widget { ... };
 2
 3 Widget *makeWidget() // Legacy function
 4 {
 5   return new Widget;
 6 }
 7
 8 void useWidget()
 9 {
10   boost::scoped_ptr<Widget> wgt(makeWidget());
11   wgt->display();              // widget displayed
12 }   // Widget destroyed on scope exit
```

In general, useWidget in the preceding form would be exception-safe, provided the function makeWidget called from within useWidget also is exception-safe.

Transferring object ownership across functions

As non-copyable objects, scoped_ptr objects cannot be passed or returned by value from functions. One may pass a non-const reference to a scoped_ptr as an argument to a function, which resets its contents and puts a new pointer into the scoped_ptr object.

Listing 3.3: Ownership transfer using scoped_ptr

```
 1 class Widget { ... };
 2
 3 void makeNewWidget(boost::scoped_ptr<Widget>& result)
 4 {
 5   result.reset(new Widget);
 6   result->setProperties(...);
 7 }
 8
 9 void makeAndUseWidget()
10 {
11   boost::scoped_ptr<Widget> wgt;  // null wgt
12   makeNewWidget(wgt);             // wgt set to some Widget object.
13   wgt->display();                 // widget #1 displayed
14
15   makeNewWidget(wgt);             // wgt reset to some other Widget.
16                                   // Older wgt released.
17   wgt->display();                 // widget #2 displayed
18 }
```

The makeNewWidget function uses the scoped_ptr<Widget> reference passed to it as an out parameter using it to return the dynamically-allocated object (line 5). Each call to makeNewWidget (line 12, 15) replaces its previous content with a new Widget object allocated dynamically and deletes the previous object. This is one way to transfer ownership of an object allocated dynamically inside a function to a scope outside the function. It is not frequently used, and there are more idiomatic ways of achieving the same effect in C++11 using std::unique_ptr, as discussed in the next section.

As a class member

Among the smart pointers from Boost, scoped_ptr is often used only as a local scope guard in functions, when in fact, it can be a useful tool for ensuring exception safety as a class member as well.

Consider the following code in which the class DatabaseHandler creates two dynamically-allocated objects of the imaginary types FileLogger and DBConnection for logging to a file and connecting to a database. FileLogger and DBConnection as well as their constructor parameters are imaginary classes that are used for illustrative purposes.

```
// DatabaseHandler.h
 1 #ifndef DATABASEHANDLER_H
 2 #define DATABASEHANDLER_H
 3
 4 class FileLogger;
 5 class DBConnection;
 6
 7 class DatabaseHandler
 8 {
 9 public:
10    DatabaseHandler();
11    ~DatabaseHandler();
12    // other methods here
13
14 private:
15    FileLogger *logger_;
16    DBConnection *dbconn_;
17 };
18
19 #endif /* DATABASEHANDLER_H */
```

The preceding code is the listing for the DatabaseHandler class definition in the header file DatabaseHandler.h. FileLogger and DBConnection are incomplete types having only been forward-declared. We only declare pointers to them, and since the size of pointers is not dependent on the size of the underlying types, the compiler does not need to know the definitions of FileHandler and DBConnection to determine the total size of the DatabaseHandler class in terms of its pointer constituents.

There is an advantage to designing classes like this. The clients of DatabaseHandler include the DatabaseHandler.h file listed earlier but do not depend on the actual definitions of FileLogger or DBConnection. If their definitions change, the clients remain unaffected and do not need to recompile. This, in essence, is the idiom that Herb Sutter popularized as the **Pimpl Idiom**. The actual implementation of the class is abstracted in a separate source file:

```
// DatabaseHandler.cpp
 1 #include "DatabaseHandler.h"
 2
```

```
 3 // Dummy concrete implementations
 4 class FileLogger
 5 {
 6 public:
 7   FileLogger(const std::string& logfile) {...}
 8 private:
 9   ...
10 };
11
12 class DBConnection
13 {
14 public:
15   DBConnection(const std::string& dbhost,
16                const std::string& username,
17                const std::string& passwd) {...}
18 private:
19   ...
20 };
21
22 // class methods implementation
23 DatabaseHandler::DatabaseHandler(const std::string& logFile,
24          const std::string& dbHost,
25          const std::string& user, const std::string& passwd)
26        : logger_(new FileLogger(logFile)),
27          dbconn_(new DBConnection(dbHost, user, passwd))
28 {}
29
30 ~DatabaseHandler()
31 {
32   delete logger_;
33   delete dbconn_;
34 }
35
36 // Other methods
```

In this source file, we have access to the concrete definitions of `FileLogger` and `DBConnection`. Even if these definitions and other parts of our implementation change, the clients of `DatabaseHandler` need not change or recompile as long as `DatabaseHandler`'s public methods and the class layout do not change.

But this code is very brittle and can potentially leak memory and other resources. Consider what happens if the FileLogger constructor throws an exception (line 26). The memory allocated for the logger_ pointer is freed automatically and no further damage is done. The exception propagates from the DatabaseHandler constructor to the calling context and no object of DatabaseHandler is instantiated; so far so good.

Now consider if the FileLogger object was constructed successfully and then the DBConnection constructor threw an exception (line 27). In this case, upon the exception the memory allocated for the dbconn_ pointer would be automatically freed, but not the memory allocated for the logger_ pointer. When an exception occurs destructors of any fully constructed members of non-POD types would be called. But logger_ is a raw pointer, which is a POD-type and therefore it does not have a destructor. Thus, the memory pointed to by logger_ is leaked.

In general, if your class has multiple pointers pointing to dynamically-allocated objects, ensuring exception safety becomes a challenge, and most procedural solutions around using try/catch blocks scale quite badly. A smart pointer is the perfect ingredient to fix these kinds of problems with very little code that scales. We use a scoped_ptr below to fix the preceding example. Here is the header file:

Listing 3.4: Using scoped_ptr as class members

```
// DatabaseHandler.h
 1 #ifndef DATABASEHANDLER_H
 2 #define DATABASEHANDLER_H
 3
 4 #include <boost/scoped_ptr.hpp>
 5
 6 class FileLogger;
 7 class DBConnection;
 8
 9 class DatabaseHandler
10 {
11 public:
12   DatabaseHandler(const std::string& logFile,
13       const std::string& dbHost, const std::string& user,
14       const std::string& passwd);
15   ~DatabaseHandler();
16   // other methods here
17
18 private:
```

```
19    boost::scoped_ptr<FileLogger> logger_;
20    boost::scoped_ptr<DBConnection> dbconn_;
21
22    DatabaseHandler(const DatabaseHandler&);
23    DatabaseHandler& operator=(const DatabaseHandler&);
24 };
25 #endif /* DATABASEHANDLER_H */
```

The logger_ and dbconn_ are now scoped_ptr instances rather than raw pointers (lines 19 and 20). On the flip side, scoped_ptr being non-copyable, the compiler cannot generate the default copy constructor and copy assignment operator. We could either disable them like we have done here (line 22 and 23) or define them ourselves. In general, defining copy semantics for scoped_ptr would make sense only when the encapsulated type is copyable. On the other hand, move semantics might be easier to define using the swap member function of scoped_ptr. Let us now look at the changes to the source file:

```
// DatabaseHandler.cpp
 1 #include "DatabaseHandler.h"
 2
 3 // Dummy concrete implementations
 4 class FileLogger
 5 {
 6 public:
 7   FileLogger(const std::string& logfile) {...}
 8 private:
 9   ...
10 };
11
12 class DBConnection
13 {
14 public:
15   DBConnection(const std::string& dbhost,
16                const std::string& username,
17                const std::string& passwd) {...}
18 private:
19   ...
20 };
21
22 // class methods implementation
23 DatabaseHandler::DatabaseHandler(const std::string& logFile,
```

```
24                  const std::string& dbHost, const std::string& user,
25                  const std::string& passwd)
26          : logger_(new FileLogger(logFileName)),
27            dbconn_(new DBConnection(dbsys, user, passwd))
28 {}
29
30 ~DatabaseHandler()
31 {}
32
33 // Other methods
```

We initialize the two scoped_ptr instances in the constructor initializer lists (lines 26 and 27). If the DBConnection constructor throws (line 27), the destructor of logger_, which is a scoped_ptr, is invoked, and it cleanly deallocates the dynamically-allocated FileLogger object it encapsulated.

The DatabaseHandler destructor is empty (line 31) because there are no POD-type members, and the destructors of the scoped_ptr members are automatically invoked. But we still have to define the destructor. Can you guess why? If we left it to the compiler to generate a definition, it would have generated the destructor definition in the scope of the class definition in the header file. In that scope, FileLogger and DBConnection were not completely defined, and the scoped_ptr destructors would have failed to compile, as they use boost::checked_delete (*Chapter 2, The First Brush with Boost's Utilities*)

boost::scoped_array

The scoped_ptr class template works great for single, dynamically-allocated objects. Now if you remember our motivating example of writing an image rotation utility, we needed to wrap a dynamic array in our custom ScopeGuard class to make the rotateImage function exception-safe. Boost provides the boost::scoped_array template as an array analogue for boost::scoped_ptr. The semantics of boost::scoped_array are identical to those of boost::scoped_ptr, except that this one has an overloaded subscript operator (operator[]) to access individual elements of the wrapped array and does not provide overloaded operators for other forms of indirection (operator* and operator->). Rewriting the rotateImage function using scoped_array will be instructive at this point.

Listing 3.5: Using scoped_array

```
1 #include <boost/scoped_array.hpp>
2
3 typedef unsigned char byte;
```

```
 4
 5  byte *rotateImage(const std::string &imgFile, double angle,
 6                    size_t& sz) {
 7    // open the file for reading
 8    std::ifstream imgStrm(imgFile, std::ios::binary);
 9
10    if (imgStrm) {
11      imgStrm.seekg(0, std::ios::end);
12      sz = imgStrm.tellg();            // determine file size
13      imgStrm.seekg(0);
14
15      // allocate buffer and read
16      boost::scoped_array<byte> img(new byte[sz]);
17      // read the image contents
18      imgStrm.read(reinterpret_cast<char*>(img.get()), sz);
19
20      byte first = img[0];  // indexed access
21      return img_rotate(img.get(), sz, angle);
22    }
23
24    sz = 0;
25    return 0;
26  }
```

We now use `boost::scoped_array` template in place of our `ScopeGuard` class to wrap the dynamically-allocated array (line 16). Upon scope exit, due to normal execution or exception, the destructor of `scoped_array` will invoke the array delete operator (`delete[]`) on the contained dynamic array and deallocate it in an exception-safe way. To highlight the ability to access array elements from the `scoped_array` interface, we access the first byte using the overloaded `operator[]` of `scoped_array` (line 20).

The `scoped_array` template is mainly useful while dealing with legacy code with lots of dynamic arrays. Thanks to the overloaded subscript operator, `scoped_arrays` are a drop-in replacement for dynamically-allocated arrays. Boxing up the dynamic arrays in `scoped_arrays` is thus a fast path to exception safety. C++ advocates using `std::vectors` over dynamic arrays and that might be your eventual goal. Yet as wrappers with hardly any space overhead compared to vectors, `scoped_arrays` could help transition faster to exception-safe code.

std::unique_ptr

C++ 11 introduces the std::unique_ptr smart pointer template, which supersedes the deprecated std::auto_ptr, supports the functionality of boost::scoped_ptr and boost::scoped_array, and can be stored in Standard Library containers. It is defined in the standard header file memory along with other smart pointers introduced in C++11.

The member functions of std::unique_ptr are easily mapped to those of boost::scoped_ptr:

- A default-constructed unique_ptr contains a null pointer (nullptr) just like a default-constructed scoped_ptr.

- You can call the get member function to access the contained pointer.

- The reset member function frees the older pointer and takes ownership of a new pointer (which could be null).

- The swap member function swaps contents of two unique_ptr instances and always succeeds.

- You can dereference non-null unique_ptr instances with operator* and access members using operator->.

- You can use unique_ptr instances in Boolean contexts to check for nullness just like scoped_ptr instances.

- However, std::unique_ptr is more versatile than boost::scoped_ptr in certain matters.

- A unique_ptr is movable, unlike scoped_ptr. Thus, it can be stored in C++11 Standard Library containers and returned from functions.

- You can detach the pointer owned by a std::unique_ptr and manage it manually if you have to.

- There is a unique_ptr partial specialization available for dynamically-allocated arrays. scoped_ptr does not support arrays, and you have to use the boost::scoped_array template for this purpose.

Ownership transfer using unique_ptr

The std::unique_ptr smart pointer can be used as a scope guard just like the boost::scoped_ptr. Like boost::scoped_ptr, the type of the object pointed to by the encapsulated pointer must be completely known at the point where unique_ptr goes out of scope. However, unlike boost::scoped_ptr, a unique_ptr instance need not be bound to a single scope and can be moved from one scope to another.

The `std::unique_ptr` smart pointer template cannot be copied but does support move semantics. Support for move semantics makes it possible to use `std::unique_ptr` as a function return value that transfers ownership of dynamically-allocated objects across functions. Here is such an example:

Listing 3.6a: Using unique_ptr

```
// Logger.h
1 #include <memory>
2
3 class Logger
4 {
5 public:
6   Logger(const std::string& filename) { ... }
7   ~Logger() {...}
8   void log(const std::string& message, ...) { ... }
9   // other methods
10 };
11
12 std::unique_ptr<Logger> make_logger(
13                         const std::string& filename) {
14   std::unique_ptr<Logger> logger(new Logger(filename));
15   return logger;

16 }
```

The `make_logger` function is a factory function that returns a new instance of `Logger`, wrapped in a `unique_ptr` (line 14). A function could use `make_logger` this way:

Listing 3.6b: Using unique_ptr

```
1 #include "Logger.h"
2
3 void doLogging(const std::string& msg, ...)
4 {
5   std::string logfile = "/var/MyApp/log/app.log";
6   std::unique_ptr<Logger> logger = make_logger(logfile);
7   logger->log(msg, ...);
8 }
```

In function `doLogging`, the local variable `logger` is move-initialized by the `unique_ptr` returned from `make_logger` (line 6). So the contents of the `unique_ptr` instance created inside `make_logger` are moved into the variable `logger`. When `logger` goes out of scope as `doLogging` returns (line 8), its destructor destroys the underlying `Logger` instance and deallocates its memory.

Wrapping arrays in unique_ptr

To illustrate the use of `unique_ptr` for wrapping dynamic arrays, we will rewrite the image rotation example (listing 3.5) yet again, replacing `scoped_ptr` with `unique_ptr`:

Listing 3.7: Using unique_ptr to wrap arrays

```
 1 #include <memory>
 2
 3 typedef unsigned char byte;
 4
 5 byte *rotateImage(std::string imgFile, double angle, size_t& sz)
 6 {
 7   // open the file for reading
 8   std::ifstream imgStrm(imgFile, std::ios::binary);
 9
10   if (imgStrm) {
11     imgStrm.seekg(0, std::ios::end);
12     sz = imgStrm.tellg();      // determine file size
13     imgStrm.seekg(0);
14
15     // allocate buffer and read
16     std::unique_ptr<byte[]> img(new byte[sz]);
17     // read the image contents
18     imgStrm.read(reinterpret_cast<char*>(img.get()),sz);
19     // process it
20     byte first = img[0];  // access first byte
21     return img_rotate(img.get(), sz, angle);
22   }
23
24   sz = 0;
25   return 0;
26 }
```

Apart from including a different header file (memory in place of boost/scoped_ptr.hpp), there is only one other line of code that needed an edit. In place of boost::scoped_array<byte>, the declared type of img is changed to std::unique_ptr<byte[]> (line 16)—a definitive drop-in replacement. The overloaded operator[] is available only for the array-specialization of unique_ptr and is used to refer to elements of the array.

make_unique in C++14

The C++14 Standard Library contains a function template std::make_unique, which is a factory function for creating an instance of an object on dynamic memory and wrap it in std::unique_ptr. The following example is a rewrite of listing 3.6b that illustrates the use of make_unique:

Listing 3.8: Using make unique

```
1 #include "Logger.h"   // Listing 3.6a
2
3 void doLogging(const std::string& msg, ...)
4 {
5   std::string filename = "/var/MyApp/log/app.log";
6   std::unique_ptr<Logger> logger =
7                 std::make_unique<Logger>(filename);
8   logger->log(msg, ...);
9 }
```

The std::make_unique function template takes the type of the underlying object to construct as a template argument and the arguments to the object's constructor as function arguments. We directly pass to make_unique, the filename argument, which it forwards to the constructor of Logger (line 7). make_unique is a variadic template; it takes a variable number of arguments that match the constructor parameters of the type instantiated, in number and type. If there was a two-parameter constructor of Logger, say one that took a filename and a default log level, we would pass two arguments to make_unique:

```
// two argument constructor
Logger::Logger(const std::string& filename, loglevel_t level) {
  ...
}

std::unique_ptr<Logger> logger =
              std::make_unique<Logger>(filename, DEBUG);
```

Assuming `loglevel_t` describes the type used to represent log levels, and `DEBUG` describes a valid value for that type, the preceding snippet illustrates the use of `make_unique` with multiple constructor arguments.

If you have moved your codebase to C++11, you should prefer using `std::unique_ptr` to `boost::scoped_ptr`.

Shared ownership semantics

Unique ownership semantics with the ability to transfer ownership is good enough for most purposes that you would use a smart pointer for. But in some real-world applications, you will need to share resources across multiple contexts without any of these contexts being a clear owner. Such a resource can be released only when all of the contexts holding references to the shared resource release them. When and where this happens cannot be determined in advance.

Let us understand this with a concrete example. Two threads in a single process read data from different sections of the same dynamically-allocated region in memory. Each thread does some processing on the data and then reads more data. We need to ensure that the dynamically-allocated memory region is cleanly deallocated when the last thread terminates. Either thread could terminate before the other; so who deallocates the buffer?

By encapsulating the buffer in a smart wrapper that can keep a count of the number of contexts referring to it, and deallocating the buffer only when the count goes to zero, we can encapsulate the logic of deallocation completely. The users of the buffer should switch to using a smart wrapper, which they can freely copy, and when all copies go out of scope, the reference count goes to zero and the buffer is deallocated.

boost::shared_ptr and std::shared_ptr

The `boost::shared_ptr` smart pointer template provides reference-counted shared ownership semantics. It keeps track of the number of references to it using a shared reference count that it maintains alongside the wrapped, dynamically-allocated object. Like other smart pointer templates we have seen so far, it implements the RAII idiom, taking responsibility of destroying and deallocating the wrapped object in its destructor, but it does so only when all references to it are destroyed, that is, the reference count goes to zero. It is a header-only library made available by including `boost/shared_ptr.hpp`.

shared_ptr was included in C++ Standards Committee Technical Report in 2007 (colloquially TR1), which was a precursor to the C++11 standard and was made available as std::tr1::shared_ptr. It is now part of the C++11 Standard Library as std::shared_ptr available through the standard C++ header file memory. If you have moved your codebase to C++11, you should use std::shared_ptr. Much of the discussion in this section applies to both versions; differences, if any, are called out.

You create shared_ptr instances to take ownership of a dynamically-allocated object. Unlike boost::scoped_ptr and std::unique_ptr, you can copy shared_ptr instances. std::shared_ptr also supports move semantics. It stores the dynamically-allocated pointer and a shared reference count object. Each time shared_ptr is copied via copy construction, the pointer and the reference count object are shallow-copied. Copying shared_ptr instances causes reference counts to be bumped up. shared_ptr instances going out of scope causes reference counts to be decremented. The use_count member function can be used to get the current reference counts. Here is an example that shows shared_ptr in action:

Listing 3.9: shared_ptr in action

```
 1 #include <boost/shared_ptr.hpp>
 2 #include <iostream>
 3 #include <cassert>
 4
 5 class Foo {
 6 public:
 7   Foo() {}
 8   ~Foo() { std::cout << "~Foo() destructor invoked." << '\n';}
 9 };
10
11 typedef boost::shared_ptr<Foo> SPFoo;
12
13 int main()
14 {
15   SPFoo f1(new Foo);
16   // SPFoo f1 = new Foo; // Won't work, explicit ctor
17   assert(f1.use_count() == 1);
18
19   // copy construction
20   SPFoo f2(f1);
21   assert(f1.use_count() == f2.use_count() &&
```

```
22              f1.get() == f2.get() && f1.use_count() == 2);
23      std::cout << "f1 use_count: " << f1.use_count() << '\n';
24
25      SPFoo f3(new Foo);
26      SPFoo f4(f3);
27      assert(f3.use_count() == 2 && f3.get() == f4.get());
28      std::cout << "f3 use_count: " << f3.use_count() << '\n';
29
30      // copy assignment
31      f4 = f1;
32      assert(f4.use_count() == f1.use_count() &&
33              f1.use_count() == 3 && f1.get() == f4.get());
34      assert(f3.use_count() == 1);
35      std::cout << "f1 use_count: " << f1.use_count() << '\n';
36      std::cout << "f3 use_count: " << f3.use_count() << '\n';
37  }
```

In the preceding code, we define a class Foo with a default constructor and a destructor that prints some message (lines 5-9). We include boost/shared_ptr.hpp (line 1), which provides the boost::shared_ptr template.

In the main function, we define two shared_ptr<Foo> instances f1 (line 15) and f3 (line 25), initialized with two different dynamically-allocated instances of class Foo. Note that the shared_ptr constructor is explicit and thus, you cannot use an assignment expression to copy-initialize shared_ptr using implicit conversion (line 16). The reference count of each shared_ptr<Foo> instance after construction is 1 (lines 17 and 25). Next, we create f2 as a copy of f1 (line 20) and f4 as a copy of f3 (line 26). The copying causes the reference counts to bump up. The get member function of shared_ptr returns the encapsulated pointer, and the use_count member function of shared_ptr returns the current reference count. Using use_count, we assert that f1 and f2 have the same reference count, and using get, we assert that they contain the same pointer (lines 21-22). Similar assertions hold true for f3 and f4 (line 27).

Next, we copy-assign f1 to f4 (line 31). As a result, f4 now contains the same pointer as f1 and f2, and no longer shares a pointer with f3. Now f1, f2, and f4 are three shared_ptr<Foo> instances pointing to the same pointer and their shared reference count goes to 3 (lines 32-33). f3 no longer shares its pointer with another instance, so its reference count goes to 1 (line 34).

Running the preceding code, you can expect the following output:

```
f1 use_count: 2
f3 use_count: 2
f1 use_count: 3
f3 use_count: 1
~Foo() destructor invoked.
~Foo() destructor invoked.
```

The reference counts duly go to zero at the end of the `main` function, and both the dynamically created instances of `Foo` are destroyed by the `shared_ptr` destructors.

Uses of shared_ptr

In pre-C++11 code, `boost::shared_ptr` or `std::tr1::shared_ptr` tends to be the default choice for a smart pointer owing to its flexibility and ease of use, compared to `boost::scoped_ptr`. It is used for purposes beyond pure shared-ownership semantics and this makes it the best-known smart pointer template. In C++11, such pervasive use should be curbed in favor of `std::unique_ptr`, and `shared_ptr` should only be used to model true shared-ownership semantics.

As a class member

Consider a scenario where multiple components of an application may share a single database connection for better performance. Such a connection could be created the first time it is requested and cached as long as there is some component using it. When all components are done using it, the connection ought to be closed. This is definitive of shared-ownership semantics and `shared_ptr` is useful in this scenario. Let us see how an application component might use `shared_ptr` to encapsulate a shared database connection:

Listing 3.10: Using shared_ptr as class members

```
1 class AppComponent
2 {
3 public:
4   AppComponent() : spconn_(new DatabaseConnection(...))
5   {}
6
7   AppComponent(
8         const boost::shared_ptr<DatabaseConnection>& spc)
9     : spconn_(spc) {}
11
12  // Other public member
```

```
13  ...
14
15  boost::shared_ptr<DatabaseConnection> getConnection() {
16    return spconn_;
17  }
18
19 private:
20  boost::shared_ptr<DatabaseConnection> spconn_;
21  // other data members
22 };
```

The AppComponent is a component of the application that uses a database connection wrapped in a shared_ptr (line 20). The default-constructed AppComponent creates a new database connection (line 4), but you can always create an AppComponent instance by passing it an existing database connection wrapped in a shared_ptr (lines 7-9). The getConnection member function retrieves the shared pointer-wrapped DatabaseConnection object wrapped in a shared_ptr (line 16). Here is an example:

```
1 AppComponent c1;
2 AppComponent c2(a.getConnection());
```

In this example, we create two AppComponent instances c1 and c2 that share the same database connection. The second instance is created using the shared_ptr-wrapped database connection cached by the first instance, obtained using the getConnection method. Irrespective of the order in which c1 and c2 are destroyed, the shared connection is destroyed only when the last of the two is destroyed.

Storing dynamically-allocated objects in Standard Library containers

Objects stored by Standard Library containers are copied or moved into the container and are destroyed with the container. Objects are retrieved too by copying or moving. Prior to C++11, there was no support for move semantics and copying was the sole mechanism for storing objects in containers. Standard Library containers do not support reference semantics. You may store pointers to dynamically-allocated objects in containers but, at the end of its life cycle, the container not attempt to destroy and deallocate these objects via their pointers.

You can wrap dynamically-allocated objects in `shared_ptr` or `unique_ptr` and store them in containers. Assuming that you can use C++11, `std::unique_ptr` is good enough if storing them in a single container is all you are ever going to need. But if you need to store the same dynamically-allocated object across multiple containers, `shared_ptr` is the best choice for the wrapper. When the container is destroyed, the destructor of each `shared_ptr` instance is called and the reference count of that `shared_ptr` is decremented. If the reference count goes to zero for any `shared_ptr`, the underlying dynamic object stored in it is deallocated. The following example illustrates how objects wrapped in `shared_ptr` can be stored in multiple STL containers:

Listing 3.11: Storing shared_ptr in containers

```
1 class Person;
2 typedef boost::shared_ptr<Person> PersonPtr;
3 std::vector<PersonPtr> personList;
4 std::multimap<std::string, PersonPtr> personNameMap;
5 ...
6
7 for (auto it = personList.begin();
8       it != personList.end(); ++it) {
9   personNameMap.insert(std::make_pair((*it)->name(), *it));
10 }
```

In the preceding example, let us assume that there is a class called `Person` (line 1). Now, given a list of objects of type `Person`, we would like to create a mapping of names to `Person` objects. Assume that `Person` objects cannot be copied, and so they need to be stored in containers as pointers. We define a type alias called `PersonPtr` for `shared_ptr<Person>` (line 2). We also define the data structures for storing a list of `Person` objects, (`std::vector<PersonPtr>` (line 3)) and the mapping of `Person` names to `Person` objects (`std::multimap<std::string, PersonPtr>` (line 4)). Finally, we construct the mapping from the list (lines 7-9).

Each entry into the `personNameMap` container is created as a `std::pair` of the name of a person and the `PersonPtr` object (using `std::make_pair`). Each such entry is inserted into the `multimap` using its `insert` member function (line 9). We assume that there is a member function in `Person` called `name`. The `PersonPtr` object being a `shared_ptr` is shared across the `vector` and the `multimap` containers. The `Person` objects are destroyed when the last of the two containers is destroyed.

Besides `shared_ptr`, Boost's Pointer Containers provide an alternative means of storing dynamically-allocated objects in containers. We cover Pointer Containers in *Chapter 5, Effective Data Structures beyond STL.* In *Chapter 9, Files, Directories, and IOStreams,* which deals with Boost Threads, we will see how `shared_ptr` instances can be shared across threads.

Nonowning aliases – boost::weak_ptr and std::weak_ptr

In the last section, one of the examples we looked at was that of a database connection shared among multiple application components. This form of use has certain shortcomings. While instantiating application components that are meant to reuse the open database connection, you need to refer to another existing component that uses the connection and pass that connection to the constructor of the new object. A more scalable approach is to decouple the connection creation and application component creation so that application components are not even aware of whether they got a new connection or an existing reusable connection. But the requirement still remains that the connection must be shared across all clients, and it must be closed when the last reference to it has gone.

One approach to building such a mechanism is to use a database connection factory, which creates connections to a specific database instance based on connection parameters passed by the caller. It then passes the connection back to the caller wrapped in a `shared_ptr` and also stores it in a map that can be looked up. When a new client requests a connection to the same instance for the same database user, the factory can simply look up the existing connection from the map and return it wrapped in a `shared_ptr`. The following and illustrative code implements this logic. It assumes that all information needed to connect to a database instance is encapsulated in a `DBCredentials` object:

```
 1 typedef boost::shared_ptr<DatabaseConnection> DBConnectionPtr;
 2
 3 struct DBConnectionFactory
 4 {
 5   typedef std::map<DBCredentials, DBConnectionPtr>
 6                                        ConnectionMap;
 7
 8   static DBConnectionPtr connect(const DBCredentials& creds)
 9   {
10     auto iter = conn_map_.find(creds);
11
12     if (iter != conn_map_.end()) {
13       return iter->second;
```

```
14      } else {
15        DBConnectionPtr dbconn(new DatabaseConnection(creds));
16        conn_map_[creds] = dbconn;
17        return dbconn;
18      }
19   }
20
21   static ConnectionMap conn_map_;
22 };
23
24 DBConnectionFactory::ConnectionMap
25                                 DBConnectionFactory::conn_map_;
26 int main()
27 {
28   DBCredentials creds(...);
29   DBConnectionPtr dbconn = DBConnectionFactory::connect(creds);
30   DBConnectionPtr dbconn2 =DBConnectionFactory::connect(creds);
31   assert(dbconn.get() == dbconn2.get()
32          && dbconn.use_count() == 3);
33 }
```

In the preceding code, DBConnectionFactory provides a static method called connect that takes a DBCredentials object and returns a shared_ptr-wrapped DatabaseConnection (DBConnectionPtr) (lines 8-19). We call DBConnectionFactory::connect twice, passing the same credentials. The first call (line 28) should result in the creation of a new connection (line 15), while the second call should just look up and return the same connection (lines 10-13).

There is one major problem with this code: DBConnectionFactory stores the connection wrapped in a shared_ptr inside a static std::map called conn_map_ (line 21). As a result, its reference count goes to 0 only at the end of the program, when the conn_map_ is destroyed. Otherwise, even when there are no contexts using the connection, the reference count remains at 1. We require that, when all contexts using the shared connection exit or expire, the connection should be destroyed. This is clearly not met.

Storing the raw pointer (DatabaseConnection*) instead of the shared_ptr (DBConnectionPtr) in the map would be no good because, we need the first shared_ptr instance we gave out for the connection, to be able to create more shared_ptr instances for that connection. Even with ways to get around this problem (as we will see later with enable_shared_from_this), by just looking up the raw pointer in the connection map we would not know whether it is still in use or has already been deallocated.

The boost::weak_ptr template, also available in C++11 as std::weak_ptr, is the right tool to fix this problem. You can refer to a shared_ptr instance using one or more weak_ptr instances, without contributing to the reference count that determines its lifetime. Using the weak_ptr instances, you can safely determine whether the shared_ptr it refers to is still active or expired. If not expired, you can use the weak_ptr instance to also create another shared_ptr instance referring to the same object. We will now rewrite the preceding example using weak_ptr:

Listing 3.12: Using weak_ptr

```
 1 typedef boost::shared_ptr<DatabaseConnection> DBConnectionPtr;
 2 typedef boost::weak_ptr<DatabaseConnection> DBConnectionWkPtr;
 3
 4 struct DBConnectionFactory
 5 {
 6   typedef std::map<DBCredentials, DBConnectionWkPtr>
 7                                       ConnectionMap;
 8
 9   static DBConnectionPtr connect(const DBCredentials& creds) {
10     ConnectionIter it = conn_map_.find(creds);
11     DBConnectionPtr connptr;
12
13     if (it != conn_map_.end() &&
14         (connptr = it->second.lock())) {
15       return connptr;
16     } else {
17       DBConnectionPtr dbconn(new DatabaseConnection(creds));
18       conn_map_[creds] = dbconn;  // weak_ptr = shared_ptr;
19       return dbconn;
20     }
21   }
22
23   static ConnectionMap conn_map_;
24 };
25
26 DBConnectionFactory::ConnectionMap
27                               DBConnectionFactory::conn_map_;
28 int main()
29 {
30   DBCredentials creds(...);
31   DBConnectionPtr dbconn = DBConnectionFactory::connect(creds);
32   DBConnectionPtr dbconn2 =DBConnectionFactory::connect(creds);
33   assert(dbconn.get() == dbconn2.get()
```

```
34              && dbconn.use_count() == 2);
35 }
```

In this example, we alter the definition of `ConnectionMap` to store `weak_ptr<DatabaseConnection>` instead of `shared_ptr<DatabaseConnection>` (line 6-7). When the `DBConnectionFactory::connect` function is called with appropriate credentials, the code looks up the entry (line 10), and on failure, creates a new database connection, wraps it in a `shared_ptr` (line 17), and stores it as a `weak_ptr` in the map (line 18). Note that we assign a `shared_ptr` to a `weak_ptr` using the copy assignment operator. The newly constructed `shared_ptr` is returned (line 19). If the lookup succeeded, it calls the `lock` method on the retrieved `weak_ptr` in an attempt to construct a `shared_ptr` from it (line 12). If the retrieved `weak_ptr` represented by `it->second` refers to a valid `shared_ptr`, the `lock` call will automatically return another `shared_ptr` referring to the same object and this would be assigned to the `connptr` variable and returned (line 15). Otherwise, the `lock` call will return a null `shared_ptr`, and we will create a new connection in the `else` block, as described earlier.

If you just wanted to check whether the `weak_ptr` instance refers to a valid `shared_ptr` or not without creating a new `shared_ptr` referent, just call the `expired` method on the `weak_ptr`. It will return `false` only if at least one `shared_ptr` instance is still around.

How does the `weak_ptr` achieve this? Actually, `shared_ptr` and `weak_ptr` are designed to work with each other. Each `shared_ptr` instance has two pieces of memory: the dynamically-allocated object it encapsulates and a chunk of memory called the shared counter, which contains not one but two atomic reference counts. Both chunks of memory are shared between all related `shared_ptr` instances. The shared counter chunk is also shared with all `weak_ptr` instances that refer to these `shared_ptr` instances.

The first reference count in the shared counter, the *use count*, keeps a count of the number of references to the `shared_ptr`. When this count goes to zero, the encapsulated, dynamically-allocated object is deleted and the `shared_ptr` expires. The second reference count, the *weak count*, is the number of `weak_ptr` references, plus one if and only if there are `shared_ptr` instances around. The shared counter chunk is deleted only when the weak count goes to zero, that is, when all `shared_ptr` and `weak_ptr` instances have expired. Thus, any remaining `weak_ptr` instance is able to tell whether the `shared_ptr` has expired by checking the use count, which is still accessible to it, and seeing if it is 0. The `lock` method of `weak_ptr` atomically checks the use count and increments it only if it is non-zero, returning a valid `shared_ptr` wrapping the encapsulated pointer. If the use count was already zero, lock returns an empty `shared_ptr`.

A shared_ptr critique – make_shared and enable_shared_from_this

shared_ptr has been used widely, beyond its appropriate use case for shared-ownership semantics. This is partly due to its availability as part of the C++ **Technical Report 1 (TR1)** release in 2007, whereas other viable options like Boost's Pointer Containers (see *Chapter 5, Effective Data Structures beyond STL*) were not part of the TR1. But shared_ptr requires an extra allocation for the shared counter, because of which construction and destruction is slower than it is for unique_ptr and scoped_ptr. The shared counter itself is an object containing two atomic integers. If you never need shared-ownership semantics but use shared_ptr, you pay for one extra allocation of the shared counter and for the increment and decrement operations on atomic counters, which make copying shared_ptr slower. If you need shared-ownership semantics but don't care about weak_ptr observers, you pay for the extra space occupied by the weak reference counter that you would not need.

One way to mitigate this problem is to somehow coalesce the two allocations — one for the object and one for the shared counter — into one. The boost::make_shared function template (also std::make_shared in C++11) is a variadic function template that does exactly this. Here is how you would use it:

Listing 3.13: Using make_shared

```
 1 #include <boost/make_shared.hpp>
 2
 3 struct Foo {
 4    Foo(const std::string& name, int num);
 5    ...
 6 };
 7
 8 boost::shared_ptr<Foo> spfoo =
 9              boost::make_shared<Foo>("Foo", 10);
10
```

The boost::make_shared function template takes the type of object as a template argument and the arguments to the object's constructor as function arguments. We call make_shared<Foo>, passing it the arguments we want to construct the Foo object with (lines 8-9). The function then allocates a single block of memory in which it lays out the object and also appends the two atomic counts, in one fell swoop. Note that you need to include the header file boost/make_shared.hpp to use make_shared. This is not as perfect as it seems but might be a good enough trade-off. It is not perfect because now it is a single block of memory not two, and is shared between all shared_ptr and weak_ptr referents.

Even when all the shared_ptr referents are gone and the object destructed, its memory is reclaimed only when the last weak_ptr is gone. Again, this is a problem only if you use lingering weak_ptr instances and your object size is large enough to be a worry.

There is yet another problem with shared_ptr that we briefly looked at earlier. If we create two independent shared_ptr instances from the same raw pointer, then they have independent reference counts and both try to delete the encapsulated object in due course. The first will succeed, but the destructor of the second instance will most likely crash, trying to delete an already deleted entity. Also, any attempts to dereference the object through the second shared_ptr after the first goes out of scope would be equally disastrous. The general solution to this problem is to not use shared_ptr at all but rather use boost::intrusive_ptr—something that we explore in the next section. An alternate way to get around the problem is to equip an instance method of the wrapped class to return a shared_ptr using the this pointer. For this, your class must derive from the boost::enable_shared_from_this class template. Here is an example:

Listing 3.14: Using enable_shared_from_this

```
1 #include <boost/smart_ptr.hpp>
2 #include <boost/current_function.hpp>
3 #include <iostream>
4 #include <cassert>
5
6 class CanBeShared
7         : public boost::enable_shared_from_this<CanBeShared> {
8 public:
9   ~CanBeShared() {
10     std::cout << BOOST_CURRENT_FUNCTION << '\n';
11   }
12
13   boost::shared_ptr<CanBeShared> share()
14   {
15     return shared_from_this();
16   }
17 };
18
19 typedef boost::shared_ptr<CanBeShared> CanBeSharedPtr;
20
21 void doWork(CanBeShared& obj)
22 {
```

```
23    CanBeSharedPtr sp = obj.share();
24    std::cout << "Usage count in doWork "<<sp.use_count() <<'\n';
25    assert(sp.use_count() == 2);
26    assert(&obj == sp.get());
27 }
28
29 int main()
30 {
31    CanBeSharedPtr cbs = boost::make_shared<CanBeShared>();
32    doWork(*cbs.get());
33    std::cout << cbs.use_count() << '\n';
34    assert(cbs.use_count() == 1);
35 }
```

In the preceding code, the class CanBeShared derives from boost:: enable_
shared_from_this<CanBeShared> (line 7). If you are wondering how come
CanBeShared inherits from a class template instantiation, which takes CanBeShared
itself as a template argument, let me refer you to the Curiously Recurring Template
Pattern, a C++ idiom you can read more about on the Web. Now, CanBeShared
defines a member function called share that returns the this pointer wrapped in
a shared_ptr (line 13). It does so using the member function shared_from_this
(line 15), which it inherits from its base class.

In the main function, we create an instance cbs of CanBeSharedPtr (which is a
typedef for boost::shared_ptr<CanBeShared>) from a dynamically-allocated
object of type CanBeShared (line 31). Next, we call the function doWork passing it the
raw pointer inside cbs (line 32). The doWork function is passed a reference (obj) to
CanBeShared, and calls the share method on it to get a shared_ptr wrapper of the
same object (line 23). The reference count of this shared_ptr goes to 2 now (line 25),
and the pointer it contains points to obj (line 26). Once doWork returns, the usage
count on cbs goes back to 1 (line 34).

The shared_ptr instance that is returned from the call to shared_from_this is
constructed from a weak_ptr member instance in the enable_shared_from_this<>
base and is only constructed at the end of the constructor of the wrapped object.
Thus, if you called shared_from_this inside the constructor of your class, you
would encounter a runtime error. You should also avoid calling it on raw pointers
that are not already wrapped in a shared_ptr object or objects that are
not dynamically constructed to start with. The C++11 Standard standardizes
this facility as std::enable_shared_from_this available through the standard
header file memory. We use enable_shared_from_this extensively while writing
asynchronous TCP servers in *Chapter 11, Network Programming Using Boost Asio*.

If you are eagle-eyed, you would have noticed that we included just a single header file `boost/smart_ptr.hpp`. This is a convenient header file that brings together all the available smart pointer functionality into a single header file so that you don't have to remember to include multiple headers.

> If you can use C++11, then you should use `std::unique_ptr` in the majority of cases, and use `shared_ptr` only when you need shared ownership. If you are still on C++03 for some reason, you should look to leverage `boost::scoped_ptr` wherever possible, or use `boost::shared_ptr` with `boost::make_shared` for better performance.

Intrusive smart pointers – boost::intrusive_ptr

Consider what happens when you wrap the same pointer in two different `shared_ptr` instances that are not copies of each other.

```
 1 #include <boost/shared_ptr.hpp>
 2
 3 int main()
 4 {
 5   boost::shared_ptr<Foo> f1 = boost::make_shared<Foo>();
 6   boost::shared_ptr<Foo> f2(f1.get());  // don't try this
 7
 8   assert(f1.use_count() == 1 && f2.use_count() == 1);
 9   assert(f1.get() == f2.get());
10 } // boom!
```

In the preceding code, we created a `shared_ptr<Foo>` instance (line 5) and a second independent instance of `shared_ptr<Foo>`, using the same pointer as for the first one (line 6). The net effect is that two `shared_ptr<Foo>` instances both have a reference count of 1 (asserts on line 8) and both contain the same pointer (asserts on line 9). At the end of the scope, reference counts of both `f1` and `f2` go to zero and both try to call `delete` on the same pointer (line 10). The code almost certainly crashes as a result of the double delete. The code is well-formed in the sense that it compiles, but hardly well-behaved. You need to guard against such usage of `shared_ptr<Foo>` but it also points to a limitation of `shared_ptr`. The limitation is due to the fact that there is no mechanism, given just the raw pointer, to tell whether it is already referenced by some smart pointer. The shared reference count is outside the `Foo` object and not part of it. `shared_ptr` is said to be nonintrusive.

An alternative is to maintain the reference count as part of the object itself. This may not be feasible in some cases but will be perfectly acceptable in others. There may even be existing objects that actually maintain such reference counts. If you have ever used Microsoft's Component Object Model, you have used such objects. The `boost::intrusive_ptr` template is an intrusive alternative to `shared_ptr` that puts the onus of maintaining reference counts on the user, and uses user-provided hooks to increment and decrement the reference counts. If the user so wishes, the reference count could be part of the class layout. This has two advantages. The object and the reference count are located next to each other in memory, so there is better cache performance. Secondly, all instances of `boost::intrusive_ptr` use the same reference count to manage the life cycle of the object. Thus, independent `boost::intrusive_ptr` instances don't create any problems of double deletion. In fact, you can potentially use multiple different smart pointer wrappers for the same object at the same time as long as they use the same intrusive reference count.

Using intrusive_ptr

To manage dynamically-allocated instances of type X, you create `boost::intrusive_ptr<X>` instances just as you would create other smart pointer instances. You just need to make sure that two global functions `intrusive_ptr_add_ref(X*)` and `intrusive_ptr_release(X*)` are available that take care of incrementing and decrementing the reference counts, and calling `delete` on the dynamically-allocated object if the reference count goes to zero. If X be part of a namespace, the two global functions too should ideally be defined in the same namespace to facilitate Argument Dependent Lookup. Thus, the reference counting and deletion mechanisms are both in control of the user, and `boost::intrusive_ptr` provides an RAII framework, which they are hooked into. Do note how the reference count is maintained is the user's prerogative and incorrect implementations could cause leaks, crashes, or at the very least, inefficient code. Finally, here is some sample code that uses `boost::intrusive_ptr`:

Listing 3.15: Using intrusive_ptr

```
1 #include <boost/intrusive_ptr.hpp>
2 #include <iostream>
3
4 namespace NS {
5 class Bar {
6 public:
7   Bar() : refcount_(0) {}
```

```
 8    ~Bar() { std::cout << "~Bar invoked" << '\n'; }
 9
10    friend void intrusive_ptr_add_ref(Bar*);
11    friend void intrusive_ptr_release(Bar*);
12
13 private:
14    unsigned long refcount_;
15 };
16
17 void intrusive_ptr_add_ref(Bar* b) {
18    b->refcount_++;
19 }
20
21 void intrusive_ptr_release(Bar* b) {
22    if (--b->refcount_ == 0) {
23       delete b;
24    }
25 }
26 } // end NS
27
28
29 int main()
30 {
31    boost::intrusive_ptr<NS::Bar> pi(new NS::Bar, true);
32    boost::intrusive_ptr<NS::Bar> pi2(pi);
33    assert(pi.get() == pi2.get());
34    std::cout << "pi: " << pi.get() << '\n'
35              << "pi2: " << pi2.get() << '\n';
36 }
```

We use `boost::intrusive_ptr` to wrap dynamically-allocated objects of class `Bar` (line 31). We can also copy one `intrusive_ptr<NS::Bar>` instance into another (line 32). The class `Bar` maintains its reference count in a member variable `refcount_` of type `unsigned long` (line 14). The `intrusive_ptr_add_ref` and `intrusive_ptr_release` functions are declared as friends of the class `Bar` (lines 10 and 11) and are in the same namespace `NS` as `Bar` (lines 3-26). `intrusive_ptr_add_ref` increments `refcount_` each time it is called. `intrusive_ptr_release` decrements `refcount_` and calls `delete` on the pointer argument passed to it once `refcount_` goes to zero.

The class `Bar` initializes the variable `refcount_` to zero. We pass `true` for the Boolean second argument to the `intrusive_ptr` constructor so that the constructor increments `Bar`'s `refcount_` through a call to `intrusive_ptr_add_ref(NS::Bar*)` (line 31). This is the default behavior, and the Boolean second argument to the `intrusive_ptr` constructor defaults to `true`, so we did not really need to pass it explicitly. On the other hand, if we were dealing with a class that sets its reference count to 1 on initialization, not 0 as `Bar` does, then we would not like the constructor to increment the reference count again. In such cases, we should pass `false` for the second parameter to the `intrusive_ptr` constructor. The copy constructor always increments the reference count via a call to `intrusive_ptr_add_ref`. The destructor of each `intrusive_ptr` instance calls `intrusive_ptr_release`, passing it the encapsulated pointer.

While the preceding example illustrates how you can use the `boost::intrusive_ptr` template, Boost provides some conveniences if you are managing dynamically-allocated objects. The `boost::intrusive_ref_counter` wraps some generic boilerplate code so that you don't have to roll out so much of it yourself. The following example illustrates this use:

Listing 3.16: Lesser code with intrusive_ptr

```
 1 #include <boost/intrusive_ptr.hpp>
 2 #include <boost/smart_ptr/intrusive_ref_counter.hpp>
 3 #include <iostream>
 4 #include <cassert>
 5
 6 namespace NS {
 7 class Bar : public boost::intrusive_ref_counter<Bar> {
 8 public:
 9   Bar() {}
10   ~Bar() { std::cout << "~Bar invoked" << '\n'; }
11 };
12 } // end NS
13
14 int main() {
15   boost::intrusive_ptr<NS::Bar> pi(new NS::Bar);
16   boost::intrusive_ptr<NS::Bar> pi2(pi);
17   assert(pi.get() == pi2.get());
18   std::cout << "pi: " << pi.get() << '\n'
```

```
19                    << "pi2: " << pi2.get() << '\n';
20
21    assert(pi->use_count() == pi2->use_count()
22            && pi2->use_count() == 2);
23    std::cout << "pi->use_count() : " << pi->use_count() << '\n'
24            << "pi2->use_count() : " << pi2->use_count() << '\n';
25 }
```

Instead of maintaining reference counts and providing namespace level overloads for `intrusive_ptr_add_ref` and `intrusive_ptr_release`, we just publicly inherit the class `Bar` from `boost::intrusive_ref_counter<Bar>`. This is all we need to do. This also makes it easy to get the reference count at any point, using the `use_count()` public member inherited from `intrusive_ref_counter<>` into `Bar`. Note that `use_count()` is not a member function of `intrusive_ptr` itself, so we have to use the dereference operator (`operator->`) to invoke it (lines 21-24).

The reference counter used in the preceding example is not thread-safe. If you want to ensure reference count thread safety, edit the example to use the `boost::thread_safe_counter` policy class as the second type argument to `boost::intrusive_ref_counter`:

```
7 class Bar : public boost::intrusive_ref_counter<Bar,
8                              boost::thread_safe_counter>
```

Curiously, `Bar` inherits from an instantiation of the `boost::intrusive_ref_counter` template, which takes `Bar` itself as a template argument. This is once again the Curiously Recurring Template Pattern at work.

shared_array

Just like `boost::scoped_ptr` had a corresponding template for specifically managing dynamically-allocated arrays, there is a template called `boost::shared_array` that can be used to wrap dynamically-allocated arrays and manage them with shared ownership semantics. Like `scoped_array`, `boost::shared_array` has an overloaded subscript operator (`operator[]`). Like `boost::shared_ptr`, it uses a shared reference count to manage the lifetime of the encapsulated array. Unlike `boost::shared_ptr`, there is no `weak_array` for `shared_array`. It is a convenient abstraction that can be used as a reference counted vector. I leave it to you to explore this further.

Managing non-memory resources using smart pointers

All the smart pointer classes we have seen so far assume that their resource is dynamically-allocated using the C++ new operator and requires deletion using the delete operator. The scoped_array and shared_array classes as well as unique_ptr's array partial specialization assume that their resources are dynamically-allocated arrays and use the array delete operator (delete[]) to deallocate them. Dynamic memory is not the only resource that a program needs to manage in an exception-safe way, and smart pointers would be remiss to ignore this use case.

The shared_ptr and std::unique_ptr templates can work with alternative user-specified deletion policies. This makes them fit to manage not just dynamic memory but almost any resource with explicit APIs for creation and deletion, such as C-style heap memory allocation and deallocation using malloc and free, open file streams, Unix open file descriptors and sockets, platform-specific synchronization primitives, Win32 API handles to various resources, and even user-defined abstractions. Here is a short example to round off the chapter:

```
1  #include <boost/shared_ptr.hpp>
2  #include <stdio.h>
3  #include <time.h>
4
5  struct FILEDeleter
6  {
7    void operator () (FILE *fp) const {
8      fprintf(stderr, "Deleter invoked\n");
9      if (fp) {
10       ::fclose(fp);
11     }
12   }
13 };
14
15 int main()
16 {
18   boost::shared_ptr<FILE> spfile(::fopen("tmp.txt", "a+"),
19                                  FILEDeleter());
20   time_t t;
21   time(&t);
22
23   if (spfile) {
24     fprintf(spfile.get(), "tstamp: %s\n", ctime(&t));
25   }
26 }
```

We wrap the `FILE` pointer returned by `fopen` in a `shared_ptr<FILE>` object (line 18). However, the `shared_ptr` template knows nothing about `FILE` pointers, so we must also specify the deletion policy. For this, we define a function object called `FILEDeleter` (line 5), whose overloaded function call operator (`operator()`, line 7) takes a parameter of type `FILE` and calls `fclose` on it if it is not null (line 10). A temporary instance of `FILEDeleter` is passed to the constructor of `shared_ptr<FILE>` as a second, deleter argument (line 19). The destructor of `shared_ptr<FILE>` invokes the overloaded function call operator on the passed deleter object, passing the stored `FILE` pointer as argument. There is little use of the overloaded `operator->` in this case, so all operations on the wrapped pointer are performed by accessing the raw pointer using the `get` member function (line 24). We can also use a lambda expression in place of the `FILEDeleter` function object. We introduce lambda expressions in *Chapter 7, Higher Order and Compile-time Programming*.

If you have access to C++11, it is always better to use `std::unique_ptr` for such purposes. With `std::unique_ptr`, you have to specify a second template argument for the type of the deleter. The preceding example will use a `std::unique_ptr` with just the following edits:

```
 1 #include <memory>
...
18   std::unique_ptr<FILE, FILEDeleter> spfile(::fopen("tmp.txt",
19                                      "a+"), FILEDeleter());
```

We include the C++ standard header file `memory` instead of `boost/shared_ptr.hpp` (line 1), and wrap the `FILE` pointer returned by the call to `fopen` in a `unique_ptr` instance (line 18), passing it a temporary instance of `FILEDeleter` (line 19). The only additional detail is the second type argument to the `unique_ptr` template, specifying the type of the deleter. We can also use a C++ 11 Lambda expression in place of the FILEDeleter function object. We will look at such use in later chapters, after we have introduced Lambda expressions.

Self-test questions

For multiple choice questions, choose all options that apply:

1. What are the Abraham's Exception Safety Guarantees?

    a. Basic, weak, and strong

    b. Basic, strong, and no-throw

    c. Weak, strong, and no-throw

    d. None, basic, and strong

2. What are the main differences between `boost::scoped_ptr` and `std::unique_ptr`?

   a. `boost::scoped_ptr` does not support move semantics

   b. `std::scoped_ptr` has no partial specialization for arrays

   c. `std::unique_ptr` can be stored in STL containers

   d. `std::unique_ptr` supports custom deleters

3. Why is `boost::shared_ptr` heavier than other smart pointers?

   a. It uses a shared reference counter

   b. It supports both copy and move semantics

   c. It uses two allocations per encapsulated object

   d. It is not heavier than other smart pointers

4. What is the disadvantage of using `boost::make_shared` to create a `shared_ptr`?

   a. It is slower than directly instantiating `boost::shared_ptr`

   b. It is not thread safe

   c. It does not release object memory until all `weak_ptr` referents expire

   d. It is not available in C++11 Standard

5. What are the primary differences between `boost::shared_ptr` and `std::unique_ptr`?

   a. `std::unique_ptr` does not support copy semantics

   b. `std::unique_ptr` does not support move semantics

   c. `boost::shared_ptr` does not support custom deleters

   d. `boost::shared_ptr` cannot be used for arrays

6. If you want to return a `shared_ptr<X>` wrapping the `this` pointer from a member function of class `X`, which of the following would work?

   a. `return boost::shared_ptr<X>(this)`

   b. `boost::enable_shared_from_this`

   c. `boost::make_shared`

   d. `boost::enable_shared_from_raw`

Summary

This chapter formalized the requirements for exception safety of a piece of code, and then defined various means of managing dynamically-allocated objects in an exception-safe way using smart pointers. We looked at smart pointer templates both from Boost and ones that have been introduced by the new C++11 Standard, and understood the different ownership semantics and intrusive and nonintrusive reference counting. We also got a chance to look at ways of adapting some of the smart pointer templates for managing non-memory resources.

Hopefully, you have understood the various ownership semantics and would be able to judiciously apply the techniques in this chapter to such scenarios. There are facilities in the smart pointer library that we did not cover in any significant detail, like `boost::shared_array` and `boost::enable_shared_from_raw`. You should explore them further on your own, focusing on their applicability and their pitfalls. In the next chapter, we will learn about some nifty and useful techniques for dealing with text data using Boost's string algorithms.

References

- Rule of Zero: `http://en.cppreference.com/w/cpp/language/rule_of_three`

- *Designing C++ Interfaces - Exception Safety, Mark Radford*: `http://accu.org/index.php/journals/444`

- *Exception Safety Analysis, Andrei Alexandrescu and David B. Held*: `http://erdani.com/publications/cuj-2003-12.pdf`

4
Working with Strings

Text data is the most important and pervasive form of data that modern applications deal with. The ability to process text data efficiently through intuitive abstractions is a key marker of effectiveness in dealing with text data. Boost has a number of libraries dedicated toward effective text processing that enhance and extend the capabilities provided by the C++ Standard Library.

In this chapter, we will look at three key Boost libraries for processing text data. We will start with the Boost String Algorithms library, a library of general-purpose algorithms for text data that provides a host of easy text operations, often missed in the Standard Library. We will then look at the Boost Tokenizer library, an extensible framework for tokenizing string data based on various criteria. Thereafter, we will examine a regular expression library for searching and parsing strings, Boost.Regex, which has been included in the C++11 standard as well. The following topics appear in the following sections:

- Text processing with Boost String Algorithms library
- Splitting text using the Boost Tokenizer library
- Regular expressions with Boost.Regex

This chapter should help you get a good grasp of text processing techniques available in the Boost libraries. We do not deal with internationalization issues in this book, but most of the concepts discussed in this chapter will apply to text in languages with writing systems based on non-Latin character sets.

Text processing with Boost String Algorithms library

Text data is commonly represented as a sequence or *string* of characters laid out contiguously in memory and terminated by a special marker (the null terminator). While the actual data type used to represent a character can vary case by case, the C++ Standard Library abstracts the string concept in the class template `std::basic_string`, which takes the character data type as a parameter. The `std::basic_string` template takes three type parameters:

- The character type
- Some of the intrinsic properties and behaviors of the character type encapsulated in a traits class
- An allocator type that is used to allocate the internal data structures for `std::basic_string`

The traits and allocator parameters are defaulted, as shown in the following snippet:

```
template <typename charT,
          typename Traits = std::char_traits<chart>,
          typename Allocator = std::allocator<chart>>
std::basic_string;
```

The C++03 Standard Library also provides two specializations of `std::basic_string`:

- `std::string` for narrow characters (8-bit `char`)
- `std::wstring` for wide characters (16- or 32-bit `wchar_t`)

In C++11, we have two more:

- `std::u16string` (for `u16char_t`)
- `std::u32string` (for `u32char_t`)

In addition to these classes, plain old C-style strings, which are just arrays of `char` or `wchar_t` terminated by a null character, are also quite commonly used, especially in legacy C++ code.

There are two major shortcomings in the Standard Library, which makes dealing with text data types overly tedious at times. For one, there is only a limited set of readily available algorithms that can be applied to `string` and `wstring`. Moreover, most of these algorithms are member functions of `std::basic_string` and are not applicable to other string representations like character arrays. Even the algorithms available as non-member function templates deal in iterators rather than containers, making the code tedious and less flexible.

Consider how you would convert a string to its uppercase using the C++ Standard library:

Listing 4.1: Changing a string to uppercase using std::transform

```
 1 #include <string>
 2 #include <algorithm>
 3 #include <cassert>
 4 #include <cctype>
 5
 6 int main() {
 7   std::string song = "Green-tinted sixties mind";
 8   std::transform(song.begin(), song.end(), song.begin(),
 9                     ::toupper);
10
11   assert(song == "GREEN-TINTED SIXTIES MIND");
12 }
```

We use the `std::transform` algorithm to convert a sequence of characters to their uppercase forms, using the `toupper` function from the Standard Library applied to each character (lines 8-9). The sequence of characters to transform is specified by a pair of iterators to the first character of the string `song` (`song.begin()`) and one past its last character (`song.end()`)—passed as the first two arguments to `std::transform`. The transformed sequence is written back in-place starting at `song.begin()`, which is the third argument to `std::transform`. You may not see a lot amiss if you have programmed in C++ for a while, but the generality of the `transform` function somewhat obscures the expression of intent. This is where Boost String Algorithms library helps by providing a slew of useful string algorithm function templates that are intuitively named and work effectively, sometimes even on different string abstractions. Consider the following alternative to the preceding code:

Listing 4.2: Changing a string to uppercase using boost::to_upper

```
 1 #include <string>
 2 #include <boost/algorithm/string.hpp>
 3 #include <cassert>
 4
 5 int main()
 6 {
 7   std::string song = "Green-tinted sixties mind";
 8   boost::to_upper(song);
 9   assert(song == "GREEN-TINTED SIXTIES MIND");
10 }
```

To convert the string `song` to uppercase, you call `boost::to_upper(song)` (line 8). We include the header `boost/algorithm/string.hpp` (line 2) to access `boost::to_upper`, which is an algorithm function template from Boost String Algorithms library. It is named `to_upper`, not `transform`, and takes just one argument instead of four and no iterators — what's not to like? Also, you can run the same code on bare arrays:

Listing 4.3: Changing a character array to uppercase using boost::to_upper

```
 1 #include <string>
 2 #include <boost/algorithm/string.hpp>
 3 #include <cassert>
 4
 5 int main()
 6 {
 7   char song[17] = "Book of Taliesyn";
 8   boost::to_upper(song);
 9   assert(std::string(song) == "BOOK OF TALIESYN");
10 }
```

But iterators let you choose the range you want to transform to uppercase and here, we only seem to be able to apply anything to the whole string. Actually, that's not a problem either as we shall see.

Boost.Range

The algorithms from Boost String Algorithms library actually work on abstractions called ranges, not containers or iterators. A **range** is just a sequence of elements that can be completely traversed in some order. Loosely speaking, a container like `std::string` is a sequence of contiguous single-byte characters and a container like `std::list<Foo>` is a sequence of elements of type `Foo`. Thus, they qualify as valid ranges.

A simple range can be represented by a pair of iterators — one pointing to the first element in the range, and the other pointing to one past the last element in the range. A range can represent the entire sequence of elements in a container. Generalizing further, a range can be described as a subsequence of a container, that is, a subset of the elements in the container with their relative ordering preserved. For example, the subsequence of elements of a container with odd-numbered indexes is a valid range. A single iterator pair may not be sufficient to represent such a range; we need more constructs to represent them.

The Boost.Range library provides the necessary abstractions and functions needed to generate and deal with all kinds of ranges. The class template boost::iterator_range is used to represent different kinds of ranges using a pair of iterators. The algorithms in Boost String Algorithms take parameters that are ranges and also return them, enabling chaining of calls, something that is not possible with most STL algorithms. We will not venture into too many details of Boost.Range in this chapter but will develop an intuitive understanding needed to use ranges with the String Algorithms library.

If we want to transform the case of only a part of a string, we will need to construct a range representing that section. We can use the boost::iterator_range class template to generate arbitrary ranges. Here is how we do it:

Listing 4.4: Changing a section of a string to uppercase using to_upper

```
 1 #include <string>
 2 #include <boost/algorithm/string.hpp>
 3 #include <cassert>
 4
 5 int main()
 6 {
 7   std::string song = "Green-tinted sixties mind";
 8   typedef boost::iterator_range<std::string::iterator>
 9                                               RangeType;
10   RangeType range = boost::make_iterator_range(
11                       song.begin() + 13, song.begin() + 20);
12   boost::to_upper(range);
13   assert(song == "Green-tinted SIXTIES mind");
14 }
```

Specifically, we want to construct the range using two iterators to a string. So, the type of the range will be boost::iterator_range<std::string::iterator>. We create a typedef for this rather long type name (lines 8-9). We wish to change the word "sixties" in the string "Green-tinted sixties mind" to uppercase. This word starts at index 13 of the string song and is seven characters long. So, the iterators that define the range containing "sixties" are song.begin() + 13 and song.begin() + 13 + 7, that is, song.begin() + 20. The actual range (range) is constructed by passing these two iterators to the function template boost::make_iterator_range (lines 10-11). We pass this range to the boost::to_upper algorithm, which changes the case of the substring "sixties" (line 12), and we assert on the expected change (line 13).

This may look like a lot of code but remember that you don't have to construct an explicit range when you apply an algorithm to the whole string or container. Also, if you are using C++11, the auto keyword can help reduce verbosity; thus you can replace the highlighted lines (8-11) like this:

```
8 auto range = boost::make_iterator_range(song.begin() + 13,
9                                          song.begin() + 20);
```

You can learn more about the auto keyword in *Appendix, C++11 Language Features Emulation*.

Constructing iterator ranges from arrays is not all that different either:

Listing 4.5: Changing a section of a char array to uppercase using to_upper

```
1 #include <string>
2 #include <boost/algorithm/string.hpp>
3 #include <cassert>
4
5 int main()
6 {
7   char song[17] = "Book of Taliesyn";
8
9   typedef boost::iterator_range<char*> RangeType;
10   RangeType rng = boost::make_iterator_range(song + 8,
11                                              song + 16);
12   boost::to_upper(rng);
13   assert(std::string(song) == "Book of TALIESYN");
14 }
```

The range is defined to be of type boost::iterator_range<char*>, the type of the iterator for the array being char* (line 9). Once again, we can use auto to eliminate all the syntactic pain if we are on C++11. We create the iterator range using the appropriate offsets (8 and 16), bounding the word "Taliesyn" (lines 10-11) and transform the range using boost::to_upper (line 12).

Using Boost String Algorithms

In this section, we explore the various string algorithms available to us and understand the conditions under which they can be applied. Before we look at specific algorithms though, we will try to understand the general scheme of things first.

Consider the algorithm boost::contains. It checks whether the string passed, as its second argument, is a substring of the string passed as its first argument:

Listing 4.6: Using boost::contains

```
1 #include <boost/algorithm/string.hpp>
2 #include <string>
3 #include <cassert>
4
5 int main() {
6   std::string input = "linearize";
7   std::string test = "near";
8   assert(boost::contains(input, test));
9 }
```

The algorithm `boost::contains` should return true because `"linearize"` contains the substring `"near"` (line 8). While this call to `boost::contains` returns true, had we set `test` to `"Near"` instead of `"near"`, it would return false. If we want to check for substrings without caring about the case, we have to use `boost::icontains` instead as a drop-in replacement for `boost::contains`. Like `boost::contains`, most algorithms from Boost String Algorithms have a case insensitive version with an `i-` prefix.

Unlike `boost::contains`, some string algorithms generate a modified string content based on the string passed to it. For example, `boost::to_lower` converts the string content passed to it to lowercase. It does so by changing the string in-place thus, modifying its argument. A non-mutating version of the algorithm called `boost::to_lower_copy` copies the passed string, transforms the case of the copied string, and returns it, without modifying the original string. Such non-mutating variants have the `_copy` suffix in their names. Here is a short example:

Listing 4.7: Using _copy versions of Boost String Algorithms

```
1 #include <boost/algorithm/string.hpp>
2 #include <string>
3 #include <cassert>
4
5 int main() {
6   std::string str1 = "Find the Cost of Freedom";
7   std::string str2 = boost::to_lower_copy(str1);
8   assert(str1 != str2);
9   boost::to_lower(str1);
10  assert(str1 == str2);
11  assert(str1 == "find the cost of freedom");
12 }
```

The string `str1` is first copied and converted to lowercase using the non-mutating variant `boost::to_lower_copy`, and the result is assigned to `str2` (line 7). At this point, `str1` remains unchanged. Next, `str1` is converted to lowercase in-place, using `boost::to_lower` (line 9). At this point, both `str1` and `str2` have the same content (line 10). In most of what follows, we will work with case-sensitive variants and mutating variants where applicable, with the understanding that the case-insensitive and non-mutating (copy) versions of the algorithms also exist. We now start look at specific algorithms.

Find algorithms

There are several variants of *find algorithm* available from the Boost String Algorithms library, all of which search for a string or pattern in another input string. Each algorithm takes the input string and the search string as parameters, converts them to ranges, and then performs the search. Each find-variant returns the contiguous subsequence in the input, which matches the search string or pattern, as a range. An empty range is returned if no match was found.

find_first

We start by looking at `boost::find_first`, which looks for a string in another string:

Listing 4.8: Using boost::find_first

```
 1 #include <boost/algorithm/string.hpp>
 2 #include <string>
 3 #include <iostream>
 4
 5 int main()
 6 {
 7   const char *haystack = "Mary had a little lamb";
 8   const char *needles[] = {"little", "Little", 0};
 9
10   for (int i = 0; needles[i] != 0; ++i) {
11     auto ret = boost::find_first(haystack, needles[i]);
12
13     if (ret.begin() == ret.end()) {
14       std::cout << "String [" << needles[i] << "] not found in"
15               << " string [" << haystack << "\n";
16     } else {
17       std::cout << "String [" << needles[i] << "] found at "
18               << "offset " << ret.begin() - haystack
```

```
19                         << " in string [" << haystack << "\n";
20       }
21
22       std::cout << "'" << ret << "'" << '\n';
23    }
24 }
```

We have an array of strings we want to search for, called `needles` (line 8). We also have a C-style string called `haystack`, in which we want to look for the search strings which contains the text we want to search for (line 7). We loop through each string in `needles` and call the `boost::find_first` algorithm to look for it in `haystack` (line 11). We check whether the search failed to find a match (line 13). If a match was found, then we compute the offset in `haystack` where the match was found (line 18). The range `ret` defines a range of the input string `haystack`; hence, we can always perform offset computations like `ret.begin() - haystack`.

The first iteration would be able to find `"little"`, while the second iteration would fail to find `"Little"` because `boost::find_first` is case-sensitive. If we used `boost::ifind_first` which performs case-insensitive search, then both would match.

We use the C++11 `auto` keyword to escape writing an ungainly type for `ret` (line 11), but if we had to write, it would be `boost::iterator_range<char*>`. Note that we can actually stream the range `ret` returned from the algorithm to an output stream (line 22).

This example illustrates the technique on C-style character arrays but to apply it to `std::string` would require surprisingly little change. If `haystack` was a `std::string` instance, then the only change will be in the way we calculate offsets (line 18):

```
<< "offset " << ret.begin() - haystack.begin()
```

Since `haystack` is not a character array but an `std::string`, the iterator to its start is obtained via a call to its `begin()` member function.

If we want to find the last instance of the search string in `haystack` instead of the first, we can replace `boost::find_first` with `boost::find_last`. If there are potentially multiple matching tokens, we may ask for a specific match by index. For this, we would need to call `boost::find_nth`, passing it a third argument, which would be a zero-based index of the match. We may pass a negative index to ask for matches from the end. Thus, passing `-1` would give us the last match, `-2` the second-last match, and so on.

find_all

To find all matching substrings in an input string, we must use `boost::find_all` and pass it a sequence container to put all the matched substrings into. Here is a short example of how to do it:

Listing 4.9: Using boost::find_all to find all matching substrings

```
 1 #include <boost/algorithm/string.hpp>
 2 #include <string>
 3 #include <iostream>
 4 #include <vector>
 5
 6 int main()
 7 {
 8   typedef boost::iterator_range<std::string::const_iterator>
 9                                              string_range;
10   std::vector<string_range> matches;
11   std::string str = "He deserted the unit while they trudged "
12                     "through the desert one night.";
13
14   boost::find_all(matches, str, "desert");
15   for (auto match : matches) {
16     std::cout << "Found [" << "desert" << "] at offset "
17             << match.begin() - str.begin() << ".\n";
18   }
19 }
```

We first create a typedef `string_range` for the appropriate range type (lines 8-9). The `boost::find_all` algorithm copies all the matching ranges into the vector of ranges, `matches` (line 14). We iterate over the vector `matches` using C++11's new **range-based for-loop** syntax (line 15), and print the offsets at which each match was found (line 17). The nifty range-based for-loop declares a loop variable `match` to iterate over successive elements of the container `matches`. Using the `auto` keyword, the type of `match` is automatically deduced based on the type of values contained in `matches`. Using a vector of ranges rather than a vector of strings, we are able to calculate the exact offsets in `str` at which the matches occur.

find_token

One more interesting find algorithm is the `boost::find_token` algorithm. Using this algorithm, we can find substrings whose characters satisfy some predicate we specify. We can use a set of predefined predicates or define our own, although the latter approach requires a fair bit of work, and we will not attempt it in this book. In the next example, we search for hexadecimal numbers with four or more digits in a string. This will also illustrate how you can use functions to perform repeated searches.

For this purpose, we use the `boost::is_xdigit` predicate, which returns true if a particular character passed to it is a valid hexadecimal character. Here is the sample code:

Listing 4.10: Finding substrings using boost::find_token and predicates

```
 1  #include <boost/algorithm/string.hpp>
 2  #include <string>
 3  #include <iostream>
 4
 5  int main()
 6  {
 7    std::string str = "The application tried to read from an "
 8                      "invalid address at 0xbeeffed";
 9
10    auto token = boost::find_token(str, boost::is_xdigit(),
11                                  boost::token_compress_on);
12    while (token.begin() != token.end()) {
13      if (boost::size(token) > 3) {
14        std::cout << token << '\n';
15      }
16
17      auto remnant = boost::make_iterator_range(token.end(),
18                                                str.end());
19      token = boost::find_token(remnant, boost::is_xdigit(),
20                                boost::token_compress_on);
21    }
22  }
```

The string `str` contains an interesting hexadecimal token (`0xbeeffed`). We pass `str` to `boost::find_token` along with an instance of the predicate `boost::is_xdigit`, which identifies valid hexadecimal digits (line 10). We indicate, using `boost::token_compress_on`, that contiguous matching characters should be concatenated (line 11); this option is turned off by default. The returned range `token` represents the currently matched substring. We loop as long as the returned range `token` is not empty, that is, `token.begin() != token.end()` (line 12), and print its contents if it is longer than 3 in length (line 13). Note the use of the function `boost::size` on `token`. This is one of several functions that can be used to compute properties of a range like its beginning and end iterators, size, and so on. Also, note that we can directly stream a range object like a token to an `ostream` object, such as `std::cout`, to print all the characters in the range (line 14).

In each iteration, we search the remaining string after the match using find_token. The remaining string is constructed as a range called remnant (lines 17-18). The beginning of remnant is token.end(), which is the first position after the last matching token. The end of remnant is simply the end of the string str.end().

iter_find

Iterating through a string and finding all substrings matching some criterion is a common enough use case, and Boost provides an easier way to do this. By using boost::iter_find algorithm, passing it the input string, a finder functor, and a sequence container to hold the matched ranges, we can get the matching substrings back in the container passed. Here is the above example rewritten using boost:: iter_find:

Listing 4.11: Using boost::iter_find with boost::token_finder

```
 1 #include <boost/algorithm/string.hpp>
 2 #include <string>
 3 #include <iostream>
 4 #include <vector>
 5 #include <iterator>
 6 #include <algorithm>
 7
 8 struct MinLen
 9 {
10   bool operator()(const std::string& s) const
11   { return s.size() > 3; }
12 };
13
14 int main() {
15   std::string str = "The application tried to read from an "
16                     "invalid address at 0xbeeffed";
17
18   std::vector<std::string> v;
19   auto ret = boost::iter_find(v, str,
20                      boost::token_finder(boost::is_xdigit(),
21                                 boost::token_compress_on));
22
23   std::ostream_iterator<std::string> osit(std::cout, ", ");
24   std::copy_if(v.begin(), v.end(), osit, MinLen());
25 }
```

The boost::find_regex algorithm can search a string for substrings that match a regular expression pattern. We will cover this algorithm when we deal with regular expressions using Boost.Regex, later in this chapter.

find

There is a generic `boost::find` algorithm in terms of which most of the other find algorithms are implemented. Using the available finder-functor templates, as part of the string algorithms library, or writing our own, we can make the generic `boost::find` string algorithm do a variety of search tasks for us. Here is an example of using the `boost::last_finder` functor with `boost::find` algorithm to find the last matching substring—exactly what `boost::ifind_last` does. The `boost::last_finder` functor and others like it take an optional predicate and can be used to influence how character comparisons are done. To simulate the case-insensitive comparisons that `ifind_last` does, we need to pass a predicate that compares two characters in a case-insensitive way. For this, we use the `boost::is_iequal` predicate:

```
1 std::string haystack = "How little is too little";
2 std::string needle = "Little";
3
4 auto ret = boost::find(haystack,
5                        boost::last_finder(needle,
6                                           boost::is_iequal()));
```

We call `boost::find` on haystack passing it the `boost::last_finder` functor. Since we want `last_finder` to perform case insensitive comparisons, we pass it an instance of the `boost::is_iequal` predicate. This works like `boost::ifind_last` and is essentially the way it is implemented. You can even pass your own predicates for character comparisons. Say you received an encoded message, where each character is shifted by 4, and it wraps around so that a is e and z is d. You can use the `equalsShift` functor in the following code to check whether a particular real word exists in the encoded text:

Listing 4.12: Using custom predicates with Boost substring finders

```
 1 struct EqualsShift {
 2   EqualsShift(unsigned int n) : shift(n) {}
 3
 4   bool operator()(char input, char search) const
 5   {
 6     int disp = tolower(input) - 'a' - shift;
 7     return tolower(search) == (disp >= 0)?'a':'z' + disp;
 8   }
 9
10 private:
11   unsigned long shift;
12 };
13
```

```
14 // encoded ... How little is too little
15 std::string encoded = "Lsa pmxxpi mw xss pmxxpi";
16 std::string realWord = "little";
17 auto ret = boost::find(encoded,
18                       boost::first_finder(realWord,
19                                          EqualsShift(4)));
```

Without decoding the whole string contained in the variable encoded, we want to find a substring of encoded that, when decoded would match the string contained in the variable realWord. In order to do this, we call boost::find with two arguments, the encoded input string called encoded and a predicate that returns true only if a matching substring is found (line 17-19).

For the predicate, we construct a temporary class of type boost::first_finder, passing two arguments to its constructor: the word to look for is realWord and a binary predicate EqualShift(4). The EqualsShift functor performs a case-insensitive comparison of two characters: one from the encoded input and one from the word to look up. It returns true if the first character is an encoding of the second character, according to the scheme of shifting by a fixed integer N, as described earlier (N=4 in our case).

find_head and find_tail

There are a few more *find* algorithms like boost::find_head and boost::find_tail, which could well have been named prefix and suffix for that is exactly what they do — carve out a prefix or suffix of a specified length from a string:

```
1 std::string run = "Run Forrest run";
2 assert( boost::find_head(run, 3) == "Run");
3 assert( boost::find_head(run, -3) == "Run Forrest ");
4 assert( boost::find_tail(run, 3) == "run");
5 assert( boost::find_ tail(run, -3) == " Forrest run");
```

You call find_head with the input string and an offset. If the offset is a positive number N, find_head returns the first N characters in the input string or the whole string if N is larger than the size of the string. If the offset is a negative number -N, find_head returns the first size - N characters, where size represents the total number of characters in the string run.

You call find_tail with a string and an integer. When a positive integer N is passed, find_tail returns the last N characters of the input string or the whole string if N is larger than the size of the string. When a negative integer -N is passed, find_tail returns the last size - N characters in the string, where size represents the total number of characters in the string, an empty string if N > size.

Other algorithms for testing string properties

There exist several convenience functions, which make certain common operations very easy to code. Algorithms like `boost::starts_with` and `boost::ends_with` (and their case-insensitive variants), test whether a particular string is a prefix or suffix of another. To determine the dictionary order of two strings, you can use `boost::lexicographical_compare`. You can check for equality using `boost::equals`, and check whether a string is a substring of another using `boost::contains`. Corresponding case-insensitive variants exist for each of these functions, and the case-sensitive variants take an optional predicate for comparing characters. The Boost online documentation provides an adequately detailed listing of these functions and their behavior.

Case-conversion and trimming algorithms

Changing the case of a string or some part of it and trimming extra whitespace that is preceding or trailing a string are very common tasks, which take a bit of effort to be done using only the Standard Library. We have already seen `boost::to_upper`, `boost::to_lower`, and their copying versions for performing case changes in action. In this section, we will apply these algorithms to more interesting ranges and also look at trimming algorithms.

Case-conversion algorithms

How does one convert alternate characters in a string to uppercase leaving the rest untouched? Since the `boost::to_upper` function takes a range, we need to somehow generate the range that contains alternate elements from the string. The way to do this is to use **range adaptors**. Boost Range library provides a number of adaptors that allow the generation of newer patterns of ranges from existing ones. The adaptor that we are looking for is the `strided` adaptor that allows traversing the range by skipping a fixed number of elements at each step. We need to skip just one element per step:

Listing 4.13: Generating non-contiguous ranges with Boost.Range adaptors

```
1 #include <boost/range.hpp>
2 #include <boost/range/adaptors.hpp>
3 #include <string>
4 #include <iostream>
5 #include <boost/algorithm/string.hpp>
6 #include <cassert>
7
```

```
 8  int main()
 9  {
10    std::string str = "funny text";
11    auto range = str | boost::adaptors::strided(2);
12    boost::to_upper(range);
13    assert(str == "FuNnY TeXt");
14  }
```

In order to apply the `boost::to_upper` algorithm to the even-indexed characters, we first generate the correct range. The pipe operator (`operator |`) is overloaded to create an intuitive chaining syntax for adaptors, such as `strided`. Using the expression `str | strided(2)`, we are essentially applying the `strided` adaptor with an argument of 2 to the string `str` to get a range containing the even-indexed elements of `str` (line 11). Note that the `strided` adaptor always starts from the first character of the input.

The same effect can be achieved by writing:

```
auto range = boost::adaptors::stride(str, 2);
```

I prefer the piped notation, as it seems a lot more expressive, especially when more adaptors need to be chained. Following the generation of this `range`, we apply `to_upper` to it (line 12) and expectedly, the even-index characters of `str` are transformed to uppercase (line 13).

If we want to perform the same operation, but on all the odd indexes, there is one problem we need to solve. The `strided` adaptor takes the number to skip between two elements as an argument but always starts from the first character of the input. To start from the element at index 1 instead of 0, we have to take a slice of the container starting at the element we intend to start from (index 1 in this case), and then apply `strided` with an argument of 2.

To take the slice first, we use another adaptor, called `boost::adaptors::sliced`. It takes the indexes to the starting location and one past the ending location as arguments. In this case, we would like to start from index 1 and slice the rest of the container. So, we can write the entire expression like this:

```
auto range = str | boost::adaptors::sliced(1, str.size() - 1)
                 | boost::adaptors::strided(2);
```

Chaining adaptors in this way is a powerful way to generate ranges on the fly with a very readable syntax. The same techniques apply to C-style character arrays also.

Trimming algorithms

For trimming strings, there are three main algorithms: `boost::trim_left` for trimming leading whitespace in a string, `boost::trim_right` for trimming trailing whitespace in a string, and `boost::trim` for trimming both. Trimming algorithms potentially change the length of the output. Each algorithm has an `_if` variant that takes a predicate, which is used to identify what characters to trim. For example, if you want to drop only trailing newlines from a string read from the console (a frequent chore), you may write an appropriate predicate to identify only newlines. Finally, there are copy variants of all these algorithms. If we wrote an expanded list of the available algorithms, there would be twelve of them; four for `trim_left`: `trim_left`, `trim_left_copy`, `trim_left_if`, and `trim_left_if_copy`; and similarly four for `trim_right` and `trim` each. Here is an example of performing trims on strings:

Listing 4.14: Using boost::trim and its variants

```
 1 #include <boost/algorithm/string.hpp>
 2 #include <string>
 3 #include <iostream>
 4 #include <cassert>
 5
 6 bool isNewline(char c) {
 7   return c == '\n';
 8 }
 9
10 int main()
11 {
12   std::string input = "  Hello  ";
13   std::string input2 = "Hello   \n";
14
15   boost::trim(input);
16   boost::trim_right_if(input2, isNewline);
17
18   assert(*(input.end() - 1) != ' ');
19   assert(*(input2.end() - 1) != '\n' &&
20           *(input2.end() - 1) == ' ');
21 }
```

In listing 4.14, we have two strings: `input` with leading and trailing spaces (line 12), and `input2` with trailing spaces and a newline at the end (line 13). By applying `boost::trim` on the `input`, the leading and trailing spaces are trimmed (line 15). If we had applied `boost::trim_right` on `input2`, it would have removed all trailing whitespaces, including the spaces and the newline. We only wanted to drop the newline, not the spaces; so we wrote a predicate `isNewline` to help choose what needs to be trimmed. This technique can be used for non-whitespace characters too.

These functions do not work on C-style arrays and the non-copy versions expect a member function called `erase`. They work with the `basic_string` specializations in the Standard Library, and other classes that provide an `erase` member function with similar interface and semantics.

The replace and erase algorithms

The replace and erase algorithms are handy functions to perform search and replace operations on strings. The basic idea is to find one or more matches for a search string and replace the matches with a different string. Erase is a special case of replace, when we replace the matches with a null string.

These operations may change the length of the input when performed in-place because the matched content and its replacement may have different lengths. The core algorithm in the library is `boost::find_format` in terms of which all other algorithms are implemented. The algorithms `boost::replace_first`, `boost::replace_last`, `boost::replace_nth`, and `boost::replace_all` respectively replace the first, last, nth, or all matching occurrences of a search string in the input with an alternative string. The corresponding erase algorithms simply erase the matched sections. These algorithms do not work on C-style arrays:

Listing 4.15: Using boost::replace and boost::erase variants

```
 1 #include <boost/algorithm/string.hpp>
 2 #include <string>
 3 #include <iostream>
 4 #include <cassert>
 5
 6 int main()
 7 {
 8   std::string input = "Hello, World! Hello folks!";
 9   boost::replace_first(input, "Hello", "Hola");
10   assert(input == "Hola, World! Hello folks!");
11   boost::erase_first(input, "Hello");
12   assert(input == "Hola, World!  folks!");
13 }
```

In listing 4.15, we first use the `boost::replace_first` algorithm to replace the first instance of the string `"Hello"` with `"Hola"` (line 9). Had we used `boost::replace_all` instead, both instances of `"Hello"` would be replaced, and we would get `"Hola, World! Hola folks!"`. We then call `boost::erase_first` to remove the remaining `"Hello"` in the string (line 11). Each of these algorithms has a case-insensitive variant, which matches in a case-insensitive way. Predictably, they are named with an `i-` prefix: `ireplace_first`, `ierase_first`, and so on.

There is a _copy variant of each algorithm returning too, a new string rather than changing in place. Here is a short illustration:

```
std::string input = "Hello, World! Hello folks!";
auto output = boost::ireplace_last_copy(input, "hello", "Hola");
assert(input == "Hello, World! Hello folks!"); // input unchanged
assert(output == "Hello, World! Hola folks!"); // copy changed
```

Note how the boost::ireplace_last_copy variant worked here, matching "hello" in a case-insensitive manner and performing the replacement in a copy of the input.

You can replace or erase a prefix or suffix of a string using boost::replace_head or boost::replace_tail (and their erase variants). The boost::replace_regex and boost::replace_regex_all algorithms take a regular expression for finding matches, and replace them with a replacement string. The replacement string may contain a special syntax to refer back to parts of the matched string, the details of which we will defer till the section on Boost.Regex, later in this chapter.

The split and join algorithms

Boost provides an algorithm called boost::split, which is essentially used to split an input string into tokens based on some separators. The algorithm is passed an input string, a predicate for identifying separators, and a sequence container to store the parsed tokens. Here is an example:

Listing 4.16: Splitting a string on simple tokens using boost::split

```
 1 #include <boost/algorithm/string.hpp>
 2 #include <string>
 3 #include <iostream>
 4 #include <vector>
 5 #include <cassert>
 6
 7 int main()
 8 {
 9   std::string dogtypes = "mongrel, puppy, whelp, hound";
10   std::vector<std::string> dogs;
11   boost::split(dogs, dogtypes, boost::is_any_of(" ,"),
12               boost::token_compress_on);
13
14   assert(dogs.size() == 4);
15   assert(dogs[0] == "mongrel" && dogs[1] == "puppy" &&
16          dogs[2] == "whelp" && dogs[3] == "hound");
17 }
```

The listing 4.16 will list out the four types of dogs that appear in the string dogtypes separated by commas and spaces (line 9). It uses the boost::split algorithm to do so. The dogtypes string is tokenized using the predicate boost::is_any_of(" ,"), which identifies any space or comma as a separator (line 11). The boost::token_compress_on option ensures that the boost::split algorithm does not return an empty string for each adjacent pair of separator characters but clubs them together, treating it as a single separator (line 12). If we want to split a string at any punctuation mark, we will use boost::is_punct() instead of boost::is_any_of(...). However, it is a somewhat inflexible scheme of tokenizing with only a limited set of predicates available.

If you simply want to split a string using another string as a separator, you may use boost::iter_split instead:

Listing 4.17: Using boost::iter_split to tokenize strings

```
 1 #include <boost/algorithm/string.hpp>
 2 #include <string>
 3 #include <iostream>
 4 #include <vector>
 5
 6 int main()
 7 {
 8   std::string dogtypes =
 9             "mongrel and puppy and whelp and hound";
10   std::vector<std::string> dogs;
11   boost::iter_split(dogs, dogtypes,
12                     boost::first_finder(" and "));
13   assert(dogs.size() == 4);
14   assert(dogs[0] == "mongrel" && dogs[1] == "puppy" &&
15          dogs[2] == "whelp" && dogs[3] == "hound");
16 }
```

The main difference between boost::split and boost::iter_split is that in the latter, you use a finder to identify a separator, which can thus be a specific string. Both boost::iter_split and boost::iter_find take the same kind of arguments and use a finder to search for a matching substring, but boost::iter_split returns tokens that lie between two matching substrings, while its complement boost::iter_find returns the matching substring.

Finally, the boost::join and boost::join_if algorithms are pretty useful when you are trying to string together a sequence of values with some separator between successive values. While boost::join concatenates all the values in the sequence, boost::join_if concatenates only those values from the sequence that satisfy a passed predicate. Here is boost::join in action taking a vector of strings and a separator, and returning the joined string:

```
std::vector<std::string> vec{"mongrel", "puppy", "whelp", "hound"};
std::string joined = boost::join(vec, ", ");
assert(joined == "mongrel, puppy, whelp, hound");
```

In the preceding example, we see yet another useful C++11 feature in action: uniform initialization. We initialize the vector vec with a sequence of four strings enclosed in braces and separated by a comma. This initialization syntax works for all STL containers and can be used with regular classes with specific types of constructors. Now, if we wanted to pick and choose which strings were concatenated and which were not, we would use boost::join_if like this:

```
bool fiveOrLessChars(const std::string& s) { return s.size() <= 5; }

std::vector<std::string> vec{"mongrel", "puppy", "whelp", "hound"};
std::string joined = boost::join_if(vec, ", ", fiveOrLessChars);
assert(joined == "puppy, whelp, hound");
```

The fiveOrLessChars predicate checks whether the string passed to it is of length five or less. Thus, the string "mongrel" does not feature in the joined string as its length is more than five.

Splitting text using the Boost Tokenizer library

The boost::split algorithm, we saw in the last section, splits a string using a predicate and puts the tokens into a sequence container. It requires extra storage for storing all the tokens, and the user has limited choices for the tokenizing criteria used. Splitting a string into a series of tokens based on various criteria is a frequent programming requirement, and the Boost.Tokenizer library provides an extensible framework for accomplishing this. Also, this does not require extra storage for storing tokens. It provides a generic interface to retrieve successive tokens from a string. The criterion to split the string into successive tokens is passed as a parameter. The Tokenizer library itself provides a few reusable, commonly used tokenizing policies for splitting, but, most importantly, it defines an interface using which we can write our own splitting policies. It treats the input string like a container of tokens from which successive tokens may be parsed out.

Tokenizing based on separators

To begin with, let's see how we can split a string into its constituent words:

Listing 4.19: Using Boost Tokenizer to tokenize strings into words

```
 1 #include <iostream>
 2 #include <boost/tokenizer.hpp>
 3 #include <string>
 4
 5 int main()
 6 {
 7   std::string input =
 8       "God knows, I've never been a spiritual man!";
 9
10   boost::tokenizer<> tokenizer(input);
11
12   for (boost::tokenizer<>::iterator token = tokenizer.begin();
13        token != tokenizer.end(); ++token) {
14     std::cout << *token << '\n';
15   }
16 }
```

The `boost::tokenizer` class template abstracts the tokenization process. We create an instance of the default specialization of `boost::tokenizer`, passing it our input string `input` (line 10). Next, using the iterator interface of `boost::tokenizer`, we split `input` into successive tokens (lines 12-14). In general, you can customize how strings are split by passing appropriate tokenizing policies. As we did not pass one explicitly to the `boost::tokenizer` template, the default tokenizing policy splits the string using whitespace and punctuation as token delimiters or separators. The preceding code will print the following output to the standard output:

```
God
knows
I
ve
never
been
a
spiritual
man
```

Thus, it splits not only on spaces but also commas and apostrophes; `"I've"` is split into `"I"` and `"ve"` due to the apostrophe.

If we wanted to split the input based on spaces and punctuation but not split on an apostrophe, we would need to do more. Boost provides a few reusable templates for commonly used splitting policies. The `boost::char_delimiter` template splits the string using specified characters as delimiters. Here is the code:

Listing 4.20: Using Boost Tokenizer with boost::char_separator

```
 1 #include <boost/tokenizer.hpp>
 2 #include <string>
 3 #include <iostream>
 4
 5 int main()
 6 {
 7   std::string input =
 8             "God knows, I've never been a spiritual man!";
 9
10   boost::char_separator<char> sep(" \t,.!?;./\"(){}[]<>");
11   typedef boost::tokenizer<boost::char_separator<char> >
12                                             tokenizer;
13   tokenizer mytokenizer(input, sep);
14   for (auto& token: mytokenizer)
16   {
17     std::cout << token << '\n';
18   }
19 }
```

In this case, we first construct the splitting policy `sep` using the `boost::char_separator` template (line 10). Since we are splitting text of type `std::string` whose character type is `char`, we must pass `char` as argument to `boost::char_separator` to specify that the delimiters are of type `char`. We can also write `boost::char_separator<std::string::value_type>` instead of `boost::char_separator<char>` to better express the relationship. We construct the list of punctuation marks and whitespace characters we would like to use as delimiters and pass it as the constructor argument of `sep`. Finally, we construct the tokenizer, passing it the input string `input` and the splitting policy `sep`. We iterate through the successive tokens using a range-based for-loop, which makes for less verbose code than when using a token iterator.

Tokenizing records with fields containing metacharacters

The `boost::char_delimiter` policy is not the only available splitting policy. Consider a comma-separated data format, as shown in the following output:

```
Joe Reed,45,Bristol UK
Ophir Leibovitch,28,Netanya Israel
Raghav Moorthy,31,Mysore India
```

We have one record per line and three fields per record: the name, age, and city of residence of a person. We can parse such records with the `boost::char_separator` policy, passing it a comma as a separator character. Now, if we want to make the format a little richer, we may include full addresses of people instead of their current city. But addresses are longer fields, sometimes with embedded commas, and such addresses would break the parsing, which is based on using a comma as a separator. So, we decide to quote strings that may have embedded commas:

```
Joe Reed,45,"33 Victoria St., Bristol UK"
Ophir Leibovitch,28,"19 Smilanski Street, Netanya, Israel"
Raghav Moorthy,31,"156A Railway Gate Road, Mysore India"
```

Quoting itself may not be enough. Some addresses might have quoted strings, and we would like to preserve those. To fix this, we decide on using backslash (\) as an escape character. Here is a fourth record with quoted strings in the address:

```
Amit Gupta,70,"\"Nandanvan\", Ghole Road, Pune, India"
```

The trouble now is that it is no longer possible to parse the preceding records using the `boost::char_separator` policy. For such records, we should instead use `boost::escaped_list_char`. The `boost::escaped_list_char` policy is tailor-made for this kind of use. By default, it uses comma (,) as a field separator, double quotes (") as the quoting character, and backslash (\) as the escape character. To include commas in fields, quote the fields. To include quotes in the fields, escape the embedded quotes. We can now attempt to parse the most complex of the four persons' records, as discussed earlier:

Listing 4.21: Using boost::tokenizer with boost::escaped_list_separator

```
1 #include <iostream>
2 #include <boost/tokenizer.hpp>
3 #include <string>
4
5 int main()
6 {
```

```
 7    std::string input = "Amit Gupta,70,\"\\\"Nandanvan\\\", "
 8                        "Ghole Road, Pune, India\"";
 9
10    typedef boost::tokenizer<boost::escaped_list_separator<char> >
11                                            tokenizer;
12    tokenizer mytokenizer(input);
13
14    for (auto& tok: mytokenizer)
15    {
16      std::cout << tok << '\n';
17    }
18 }
```

An instance of boost::tokenizer<boost::escaped_list_separator<char> >
is created (line 12) using the typedef (lines 10-11). This is really the only operative
change to take care of for this new format. The record, hardcoded in the variable
input, needs some extra level of escaping to be made into a valid C++ string literal
(lines 7-8).

If the record had a different set of metacharacters, say hyphen (-) for field
separator, forward slash (/) for quotes, and tilde (~) for escaping, we would need
to specify these explicitly, as the default options for boost::escaped_list_
separator<<char> > would no longer work. Consider a person named Alon Ben-
Ari, aged 35, who lives at 11/5 Zamenhoff St., Tel Aviv. Using the specified quote,
field separators, and escape characters, this could be represented as:

```
/Alon Ben-Ari/-35-11~/5 Zamenhoff St., Tel Aviv
```

The name field has a hyphen in the last name Ben-Ari. As hyphen is also a field
separator, the name field must be quoted using forward slashes. The address field
has a forward slash and since a forward slash is the quote character, the address field
must be escaped with the escape character (~). Now it is our turn to tokenize it:

Listing 4.22: Using boost::escaped_list_separator with funky delimiters

```
1 #include <iostream>
2 #include <boost/tokenizer.hpp>
3 #include <string>
4
5 int main()
6 {
7   std::string input =
8       "/Alon Ben-Ari/-35-11~/5 Zamenhoff St., Tel Aviv";
9
```

```
10    typedef boost::tokenizer<boost::escaped_list_separator<char> >
11                                            tokenizer;
12    boost::escaped_list_separator<char> sep('~', '-', '/');
13    tokenizer mytokenizer(input, sep);
14
15    for (auto& tok: mytokenizer) {
16       std::cout << tok << '\n';
17    }
18 }
```

This is the output:

```
Alon Ben-Ari
35
11/5 Zamenhoff Str., Tel Aviv
```

Tokenizing records with fixed-length fields

One class of data formats that frequently occurs in financial transactions and several other domains consists of records at fixed offsets. Consider the following record format representing a payment instruction:

```
201408091403290000000188130361441 9ABNANL2AWSSDEUTDEMM720000000412000EUR...
```

Here, the record is barely human readable and is meant for consumption only by a program. It has fields at fixed offsets whose meanings must be known by the parsing program. The individual fields are described here:

```
Offset 0, length 8: date of record in YYYYMMDD format.
Offset 8, length 9: time of record in HHMMSSmmm format where mmm
represents milliseconds.
Offset 17, length 16: the transaction identifier for the transaction,
numeric format.
Offset 33, length 11: the Swift Bank Identifier Code for the bank from
which money is transferred.
Offset 44, length 11: the Swift Bank Identifier Code for the bank to
which money is transferred.
Offset 55, length 12: the transaction amount.
Offset 67, length 3: the ISO code for the currency of transaction.
```

In order to parse records like these, we use the `boost::offset_separator` splitting policy. This class (note that it isn't a template) takes lengths of successive tokens to parse in the form of a pair of iterators, bounding the sequence of lengths.

A code example to parse the preceding payment instruction should help illustrate the idea:

Listing 4.23: Tokenizing records with fixed-length fields

```
1 #include <boost/tokenizer.hpp>
2 #include <string>
3 #include <iostream>
4
5 int main()
6 {
7   std::string input =
8     "20140809140329000000018813036144419ABNANL2AWSSDEUTDEMM72"
9     "0000000412000EUR";
10    int lengths[] = {8, 9, 16, 11, 11, 12, 13};
11
12    boost::offset_separator ofs(lengths, lengths + 7);
13    typedef boost::tokenizer<boost::offset_separator> tokenizer;
14    tokenizer mytokenizer(input, ofs);
15
16    for (auto& token: mytokenizer) {
17      std::cout << token << '\n';
18    }
19 }
```

We first define an array containing the lengths of successive fields (line 10), and use it to initialize an object `ofs` of type `boost::offset_separator` (line 12). We could have also used a vector instead of an array and passed its `begin()` and `end()` iterators to the `offset_separator` constructor. We then create a tokenizer, which tokenizes a string based on offsets specified in `ofs` (lines 13-14), and print the successive tokens using a range-based for-loop (lines 16-18).

This program produces the following output:

```
20140809
140329000
0001881303614419
ABNANL2AWSS
DEUTDEMM720
000000412000
EUR
```

We see listed on successive lines, we see listed the values of the date, time, ID, sender SWIFT bank code (an identifier for the sender bank), receiver SWIFT bank code, amount, and currency of the transaction.

Now, what happens if all the fields have been parsed and there is still some input left? The default behavior is to start parsing afresh the remaining text, applying the length offsets to it from the start. This may make sense for some formats and may not make sense for some. If you want to turn this behavior off so that the parsing stops once all the length offsets have been used, you should pass a third argument to the constructor of `boost::offset_separator`, and its value should be `false`, as shown here:

```
boost::offset_separator ofs(lengths, lengths + nfields,
                            false);
```

Here, `lengths` is the array of length offsets and `nfields` is the number of fields we expect to parse.

Conversely, what happens if the input is shorter than the sum of the lengths? The default behavior is to return the last partially parsed field and stop. Suppose you have a format in which the payer's comments are appended to each transaction record. A comment is optional and need not be there. If it is there, it may or may not have a maximum size limit. The first behavior can be used to parse the last comment field by specifying the maximum size, or an arbitrarily large size that you don't expect the comments to reach, and thus leverage the partial parse of the last record. Again, if you want to turn this behavior off so that the first partial field encountered stops the parsing, you should pass a fourth argument of type `bool` to the `boost::offset_separator` constructor and its value should be `false`:

```
boost::offset_separator ofs(lengths, lengths + nfields, restart,
                            false);
```

Writing your own tokenizer functions

There are many instances when you will need to parse a string according to some criteria that are not available in a reusable class or template in Boost. While you could use alternative libraries like `boost::split`, you can use the `boost::tokenizer` facility by plugging in a custom **token generator**. A token generator class encapsulates the tokenizing strategy and is passed as a template argument to `boost::tokenizer`.

A token generator can be defined as a functor that conforms to the following requirements:

- Is copy-assignable.
- Is copy-constructible.

- Has an overloaded public function call operator (`operator()`) with the following signature:

```
template <typename InputIterator, typename StringType>
bool operator()(InputIterator& next,
                InputIterator end,
                StringType& token)
```

This operator is passed two iterators that define a section of a string in which it looks for the next token it is passed. If and only if a new token is found, it returns true. In such case, it sets its third parameter to the token and its first parameter to the first position in the string after the end of the token, from where parsing may continue. It returns false if no token is found. We must write the logic to identify successive tokens in this function.

- Has a public member function `void reset()`. This can be used to clear any member variables used to keep parsing state for a string. Then, the same instance of the object may be used to parse multiple inputs.

These functions are called by the `boost::tokenizer` implementation, never directly by the programmer.

We now write a token generator class to pick from some text, strings that are quoted or bracketed. For example, given the string `"I'm taking a train from Frankfurt (am Main) to Frankfurt (an der Oder)"`, we want to pick out the tokens `"am Main"` and `"an der Oder"`. To simplify our implementation, given strings with nested brackets or quotes, only the content of innermost quotes need be retrieved. Thus, given the string `"tokenizer<char_separator<char> >"`, it should return `"char"`, the innermost bracketed entity. Here is the code for such a class, named `qstring_token_generator`:

Listing 4.24a: The qstring_token_generator interface

```
 1 class qstring_token_generator
 2 {
 3 public:
 4   typedef std::string::const_iterator iterator;
 5
 6   qstring_token_generator(char open_q = '"',
 7             char close_q = '"', char esc_c = '\\',
 8             bool skip_empty = true);
 9
10   bool operator() (iterator& next, iterator end,
11                    std::string& token);
12
```

```
13    void reset();
14
15 private:
16    // helper functions to be defined
17
18    char start_marker;
19    char end_marker;
20    char escape_char;
21    bool skip_empty_tokens;
22    bool in_token;
23    bool in_escape;
24 };
```

The `qstring_token_generator` class has a constructor that takes the necessary inputs:

- The start and end marker characters, which are by default both double quotes (")

- The escape character, which is by default the backslash (\)

- A Boolean indicating whether to skip empty tokens, which is by default true (lines 6-8)

The corresponding private variables for storing these values are defined (lines 18-21). The class uses two additional state variables to keep track of parsing state: the `in_token` variable (line 22) which is true while parsing content inside quotes and false otherwise, and the `in_escape` variable (line 23) which is true if the current character is part of an escape sequence and false otherwise. Here is the implementation of the constructor:

Listing 4.24b: The qstring_token_generator constructor

```
1    qstring_token_generator::qstring_token_generator
2            (char open_q, char close_q, char esc_c,
3             bool skip_empty) :
4      start_marker(open_q), end_marker(close_q),
5      escape_char(esc_c), skip_empty_tokens(skip_empty),
6      in_token(false), in_escape(false)
7    {}
```

Note that `in_token` and `in_escape` are initialized to false. Each time we iterate through the successive tokens in the input using the tokenizer interface, the tokenizer implementation calls the token generator to parse the input again. To start parsing afresh, any internal parsing state must be reset. The `reset` function encapsulates these actions and is called by the tokenizer when new token iterators are created.

Here is the implementation of the reset function:

Listing 4.24c: The qstring_token_generator reset function

```
1    void qstring_token_generator::reset()
2    {
3      in_token = false;
4      in_escape = false;
5    }
```

The reset function makes sure that the internal variables used to maintain parsing state are reset appropriately for the parsing to restart.

Finally, the parsing algorithm is implemented in the overloaded function call operator member (`operator()`). To parse the string, we look for start and end markers to identify the start and end of tokens and count-escaped start and end markers as part of the tokens, and handle the case where the start and end markers are the same characters. We also handle cases where quoted tokens are nested. We will write the algorithms in terms of a few helper private functions in `qstring_token_generator` class.

Listing 4.24d: The parsing algorithm helpers

```
 1 iterator qstring_token_generator::start_token(iterator& next)
 2 {
 3   in_token = true;
 4   return ++next;
 5 }
 6
 7 std::string qstring_token_generator::end_token(iterator& next,
 8                                     iterator token_start)
 9 {
10   in_token = false;
11   auto token_end = next++;
12   return std::string(token_start, token_end);
13 }
```

The `start_token` function is meant to be called each time we identify the beginning of a new token (line 1). It sets the `in_token` flag to true, increments the iterator `next`, and returns its value.

The `end_token` function is meant to be called each time we identify the end of a token (line 7). It sets the `in_token` flag to false, increments the iterator `next`, and returns the complete token as a string.

We now need to write the logic to identify the start and end of tokens and call the preceding function appropriately. We do this directly in the overloaded operator():

Listing 4.24e: The parsing algorithm

```
 1 bool operator() (iterator& next, iterator end,
 2                  std::string& token)
 3 {
 4   iterator token_start;
 5
 6   while (next != end) {
 7     if (in_escape) {
 8       // unset in_escape after reading the next char
 9       in_escape = false;
10     } else if (*next == start_marker) { // found start marker
11       if (!in_token) { // potential new token
12         token_start = start_token(next);
13         continue;
14       } else { // already in a quoted string
15         if (start_marker == end_marker) {
16           // Found end_marker, is equal to start_marker
17           token = end_token(next, token_start);
18           if (!token.empty() || !skip_empty_tokens) {
19             return true;
20           }
21         } else {
22           // Multiple start markers without end marker.
23           // Discard previous start markers, consider
24           //  inner-most token only.
25           token_start = start_token(next);
26           continue;
27         }
28       }
29     } else if (*next == end_marker) {
30       // Found end_marker, is not equal to start_marker
31       if (in_token) {
32         token = end_token(next, token_start);
33         if (!token.empty() || !skip_empty_tokens) {
34           return true;
35         }
36       }
37     } else if (*next == escape_char) {
```

```
38        in_escape = !in_escape;   // toggle
39      }
40      ++next;
41    }
42
43    return false;
44  }
```

We loop through the successive characters of the input using a while loop (line 6). For each character, we check whether it is preceded by the escape character (line 7), or if it is the start marker (line 10), end marker (line 29), or the escape character (line 37).

If an unescaped start marker is found, and we are not already in the middle of parsing a token (line 11), then it potentially represents the start of a new token. So, we call start_token, note the starting position of the token, and continue to the next iteration (lines 12-13). But if we are already in the middle of parsing a token, and we find the start marker, then there are two possibilities. If the start and end markers happen to be the same, then this represents the end of the token (line 15). In this case, we call end_token to get the complete token and return it unless it is empty and skip_empty_ tokens is set (lines 16-20). If start and end markers are not the same, then a second start marker represents a nested token. Since we want to only extract the most nested token, we discard the previous token and call start_token to indicate that we have the start of a new token (lines 25-26).

If the end marker is distinct from the start marker, and we find it (line 29), then we call end_token generating and returning the complete token found, unless it is empty and skip_empty_tokens is set. Finally, if we find the escape character, we set the in_escape flag (lines 37-38).

We use the qstring_token_generator class to tokenize our input string:

Listing 4.25: Extracting bracketed strings using the custom tokenizer

```
1   std::string input = "I'm taking a train from Frankfurt "
2                       "(am Main) to Frankfurt (an der Oder)";
3   bool skipEmpty = true;
4   qstring_token_generator qsep('(', ')', '\\', skipEmpty);
5   typedef boost::tokenizer<qstring_token_generator> qtokenizer;
6   qtokenizer tokenizer(input, qsep);
7
8   unsigned int n = 0;
9   for (auto& token: tokenizer) {
10    std::cout << ++n << ':' << token << '\n';
11  }
```

The preceding highlighted code shows the key changes in our code. We define a `qstring_token_generator` object that takes a left and right quote character (in this case, left and right parentheses) and skips empty tokens (line 4). We then create a typedef for `boost::tokenizer<qstring_token_generator>` (line 4), create a tokenizer of that type to parse input (line 6), and print successive tokens (line 10).

Regular expressions using Boost.Regex

When we write a line of code like `boost::find_first("Where have all the flowers gone?", "flowers")`, we are asking for the string `"flowers"` (call it the **needle**) to be found in the larger string `"Where have all the flowers gone?"` (call it the **haystack**). The needle is the pattern; seven specific characters in a particular order whose presence must be looked up in the haystack. Sometimes, however, we don't know the exact string we are looking for; we only have an abstract idea or a pattern in mind. Regular expressions is a powerful language to express this abstract pattern.

Regular expression syntax

Regular expressions are strings that encode a pattern of text using a mix of regular characters and some characters with special interpretation, collectively called *metacharacters*. The Boost.Regex library provides functions that consume regular expression strings and generate the logic to search and verify text conforming to particular patterns. For example, to define the pattern, "a followed by zero or more b's", we use the regular expression `ab*`. This pattern will match text like `a`, `ab`, `abb`, `abbb`, and so on.

Atoms

At a very basic level, regular expressions consist of groups of one or more characters called **atoms**, each with an associated **quantifier** that trails the atom and optionally, **anchors** that define how some text is located relative to the surrounding text. The quantifier may be implicit. An atom can be a single character (or an escaped metacharacter), a **character class**, a string, or a **wildcard**. If it is a string, it must be enclosed in parentheses to indicate that it is an atom. A wildcard matches any character (other than a newline) and is written using the dot (.) metacharacter.

Quantifiers

A single atom without a trailing quantifier just matches a single occurrence of itself. When present, the trailing quantifier determines the minimum and maximum allowed occurrences of the preceding atom. The general quantifier looks like {m, M}, where m denotes minimum and M denotes maximum occurrence frequency. Omitting the maximum as in {m, } indicates that the maximum number of times the atom may be present is unbounded. One may also use a single number as {n} to match a fixed number of instances. More often, we use the following shortcut quantifiers:

- *: Equivalent to {0, }, called the **Kleene star**. Represents an atom that may not occur, or may occur any number of times.

- +: Equivalent to {1, }. Represents an atom that must occur at least once.

- ?: Equivalent to {0,1}. Represents an optional atom.

Using the above syntax rules, we construct summary examples in the following table:

Regular Expression	Atoms	Quantifier	Equivalent quantifier	Matching text
W	w	None (implicit)	{1}	w
a*	a	*	{0, }	(blank), a, aa, aaa, aaaa, …
(abba)+	abba	+	{1, }	abba, abbaabba, abbaabbaabba, …
a?b	a, b	?	{0,1}	b, ab
(ab){2,4}	(ab)	{2,4}	{2,4}	abab, ababab, abababab
.*x	. and x	* and None	{0, } and {1}	x and any string ending in x

By default, quantifiers are *greedy* and match as many characters as possible. Thus, given the string "abracadabra", the regular expression "a.*a" will match the entire string instead of the smaller substrings "abra", "abraca", or "abracada", all of which also start and end in 'a'. If we want to match only the smallest matching substring, we need to override the greedy semantics. To do this, we put the question mark (?) metacharacter after the quantifier "a.*?a".

Character classes

Characters can also be matched against character classes, which are shorthand representations of a group of functionally related characters. The following is a partial list of predefined character classes in the Boost libraries:

Character class	Short form	Meaning	Complement
[[:digit:]]	\d	Any decimal digit (0-9)	\D
[[:space:]]	\s	Any whitespace character	\S
[[:word:]]	\w	Any word character: letter, number, and underscore	\W
[[:lower:]]	\l	Any lowercase character	
[[:upper:]]	\u	Any uppercase character	
[[:punct:]]	None	Any punctuation character	

For example, \d is a character class that matches a single decimal digit. Its complement \D matches any single character, except decimal digits. \s matches a whitespace character and \S matches a non-whitespace character. Ad hoc character classes can be created with square brackets; [aeiouAEIOU] matches any character that is an English vowel, [1-5] matches a digit between 1 and 5 both inclusive. The expression [^2-4] matches any character except 2, 3, and 4, and the leading caret inside the square brackets having the effect of negating the characters following it. We can combine multiple character classes something like — [[:digit:][:lower:]] — to indicate the set of lowercase letters and decimal digits.

Anchors

Certain metacharacters, referred to as **anchors**, do not match characters but can be used to match specific locations in text. For example, a caret (^) in a regular expression (outside a character class) matches text at the start of a line (just after a newline). A dollar($) matches text before the end of a line (just before a newline). Also, \b represents a word boundary, while \B matches any location other than a word boundary.

Sub-expressions

In general, each character in a string of characters is interpreted as a distinct atom. In order to treat a string of characters as a single atom, we must parenthesize it. Parenthesized substrings of a regular expression are called **sub-expressions**. A quantifier following a sub-expression applies to the entire sub-expression:

```
([1-9][0-9]*)(\s+\w+)*
```

The preceding expression represents a number ([1-9][0-9]*) followed by zero or more words (\w+) separated from it and from each other by one or more whitespace characters (\s+). The second Kleene star applies to the entire sub-expression \s+\w+ due to the parentheses.

Regular expression libraries, including Boost.Regex keep track of substrings of a string that match the parenthesized sub-expressions. Matched sub-expressions can be referred back from within the regular expression using back-references, such as \1, \2, \3, and so on. For example, in the previous regular expression, the term \1 matches the leading number, while \2 matches the last matched word with leading spaces. It matches nothing if there are no trailing words. Sub-expressions can be nested and are numbered incrementally starting at 1 in the order that their left parentheses appear in the string from left to right.

If you want to use sub-expressions to be able to apply quantifiers and anchors to groups of characters, but do not need to capture them for later reference, you can use **non-capturing sub-expressions** of the form (?:expr), where the leading metacharacter sequence ?: inside the parentheses indicates that it is a non-capturing sub-expression, and expr is some valid regular expression. This will treat expr as an atom, but will not capture it. Sub-expressions without the leading ?: inside parentheses are thus called **capture groups** or **capturing sub-expressions**.

Disjunctions

You can create a regular expression that is a logical-or of one or more regular expressions. To do this, you use the | **disjunction operator**. For example, to match a word that contains a mix of lowercase and uppercase characters, you can use the expression (\l|\u)+.

You can use the disjunction operator to combine regular expressions and form more complex expressions. For example, to match either a word containing upper or lowercase characters, or a positive integer, we can use the expression (\l|\u)+|\d+.

Using Boost.Regex to parse regular expressions

Regular expressions are a rich topic that we have barely scratched the surface of in the preceding paragraphs. But this basic familiarity is sufficient for us to start using the Boost.Regex library. The Boost.Regex library was one of the libraries that was accepted into the C++ 11 Standard and is now part of the C++ 11 Standard Library, minus its ability to handle Unicode characters.

The Boost Regular Expressions library is *not* header-only and requires linking against the Boost.Regex shared or static library. It is available from the header file `boost/regex.hpp`. On my Linux desktop with Boost libraries installed via the native package manager, I use the following command line to build regex programs:

```
$ g++ source.cpp -o progname -lboost_regex
```

On Linux systems, where Boost has been installed from source, the header files could be under a nonstandard location like `/opt/boost/include` and libraries under `/opt/boost/lib`. On such systems, I have to use the following command line to build my programs:

```
$ g++ source.cpp -o progname -I/opt/boost/include -L/opt/boost/lib
-lboost_regex-mt -Wl,-rpath,/opt/boost/lib
```

The `-Wl,-rpath,/opt/boost/lib` directive tells the linker to hard-code the path from where shared libraries, like `libboost_regex-mt`, are loaded, and helps our program to run without additional settings. On Windows using Visual Studio, linking is automatic.

It uses the `boost::basic_regex` template to model regular expressions and provides its specializations `boost::regex` for type `char` and `boost::wregex` for type `wchar_t` as typedefs. Using this library, we can check whether a string conforms to a pattern or contains a substring conforming to a pattern, extract all substrings of a string conforming to a pattern, replace a substring matching a pattern with another formatted string, and split a string based on a matching expression to name the few most commonly used operations.

Matching text

Consider the string `"Alaska area"`. We want to match this against the regular expression `a.*a` to see whether the string fits the pattern. To do this, we need to call the `boost::regex_match` function, which returns a Boolean true to indicate a successful match and false otherwise. Here is the code for it:

Listing 4.26: Matching a string with a regular expression

```
1 #include <boost/regex.hpp>
2 #include <string>
3 #include <cassert>
4 int main()
5 {
6   std::string str1 = "Alaska area";
7   boost::regex r1("a.*a");
8   assert(!boost::regex_match(str1, r1));
9 }
```

The regular expression "a.*a" is encapsulated in an instance of `boost::regex`. When we match the string against this expression, the match fails (line 8) because the string starts with an uppercase `'A'`, while the regular expression expects a lowercase `'a'` at the start. We could have asked for a case insensitive regular expression by constructing and passing `boost::regex::icase` as a flag to the `boost::regex` constructor:

```
7    boost::regex r1("a.*a", boost::regex::icase);
8    assert(boost::regex_match(str1.begin(), str1.end(), r1));
```

Note that we called a different overload of `boost::regex_match`, which takes two iterators to a `std::string` (line 8) just to illustrate an alternative signature. You can also call `boost::regex_match` with a `const char*` or a `std::string` like in listing 4.25. The outcome of the function is not dependent on the variant.

Searching text

If we want to search for substrings of a string that matches a particular regular expression, we should use the `boost::regex_search` function instead of `boost::regex_match`. Consider the string `"An array of papers from the academia on Alaska area's fauna"`. We want to find all substrings that are part of the same word in this phrase and start and end with `'a'`. The regular expression to use would be a\w*a. Let us see how we can do this using `boost::regex_search`:

Listing 4.27: Searching for substrings matching a regular expression

```
1  #include <boost/regex.hpp>
2  #include <string>
3  #include <iostream>
4
5  int main() {
6    std::string str2 = "An array of papers from the academia "
7                       "on Alaska area's fauna";
8    boost::regex r2("a\\w*a");
9    boost::smatch matches;
10   std::string::const_iterator start = str2.begin(),
11                               end = str2.end();
12
13   while (boost::regex_search(start, end, matches, r2)) {
14     std::cout << "Matched substring " << matches.str()
15           << " at offset " << matches[0].first - str2.begin()
16           << " of length " << matches[0].length() << '\n';
17     start = matches[0].second;
18   }
19 }
```

This prints the following lines, each with a word or part of the word that begins and ends in `'a'`:

```
Matched substring arra at offset 3 of length 4.
Matched substring academia at offset 28 of length 8.
Matched substring aska at offset 42 of length 4.
Matched substring area at offset 47 of length 4.
Matched substring auna at offset 58 of length 4.
```

In the code example, we construct the string (line 6), the regular expression (line 8), and an instance of `boost::smatch` (line 9), which is a specialization of the template `boost::match_results` to be used when the input is of type `std::string`. We search for successive matching substrings in a loop, calling `boost::regex_search`. We pass to `boost::regex_search` two iterators to the input string, the `smatch` instance called `matches`, and the regular expression `r2` (line 13). You must pass `const` iterators to `boost::regex_search` (lines 10, 11), or the compilation will fail to resolve the function call with a ton of gratuitous messages.

The object `matches` of type `boost::smatch` stores information about the substring that matches a regular expression after a call to `regex_search`. Its `str` member returns the substring that was matched by the regular expression. `boost::smatch` is a sequence collection of `boost::ssub_match` objects. When a regular expression matches a substring, the pair of iterators to the start and one part to the end of that substring is stored in an object of type `boost::ssub_match`. This is stored at index 0 of `matches` and accessed as `matches[0]`. The members `first` and `second` of `ssub_match` are iterators to the start of the match (line 15) and one past the end of the match. The member function `length()` returns the length of the match (line 16). At the end of each iteration, we set the `start` iterator to the first location past the end of the last match (line 17) to begin looking for the next match. The `boost::ssub_match` is a specialization of the template `boost::sub_match` to be used when the input string is of type `std::string`.

Suppose that, for each match, we want to extract what lies between the two a's at the two ends. To do this, we can use capturing sub-expressions. The regular expression would be modified slightly to `a(\\w*)a`. To access what matches the parenthesized sub-expression, we again use the `boost::smatch` object. An additional `boost::ssub_match` object is constructed for each such sub-expression in the regular expression and added to successive indexes of the `boost::smatch` object passed. If the sub-expression matched anything in the string, then the start and end of the substring matching that sub-expression are stored in the `ssub_match` object.

This is how we would use it with the modified regular expression:

Listing 4.28: Parsing matching substrings and sub-expressions

```
1  #include <boost/regex.hpp>
2  #include <string>
3  #include <iostream>
4  int main()
5  {
6    std::string str2 = "An array of papers from the academia "
7                       "on Alaska area's fauna";
8  boost::regex r2("a(\\w*)a");
9  boost::smatch matches;
10   std::string::const_iterator start = str2.begin(),
11                               end = str2.end();
12
13   while (boost::regex_search(start, end, matches, r2)) {
14     std::cout << "Matched substring '" << matches.str()
15         << "' following '" << matches.prefix().str()
16         << " preceding '" << matches.suffix().str() << "'\n";
17     start = matches[0].second;
18     for (size_t s = 1; s < matches.size(); ++s) {
19       if (matches[s].matched) {
20         std::cout << "Matched substring " << matches[s].str()
21             << " at offset " << matches[s].first - str2.begin()
22             << " of length " << matches[s].length() << '\n';
23       }
24     }
25   }
26 }
```

In the inner loop (line 18), we iterate through all sub-expressions and for the ones that match any substring (line 19), we print that matching substring using the `str` member function of `boost::ssub_match` (line 20), the offset of the substring (line 21), and its length (line 22). The `prefix` and `suffix` methods of the `matches` object return respectively, the parts preceding and following the matched substring as `boost::ssub_match` objects (lines 15, 16).

The `boost::match_results` and `boost::sub_match` templates have different available specializations appropriate for different types of inputs, like an array of narrow or wide characters, or a specialization of `std::basic_string` (`std::string` or `std::wstring`).

The following table summarizes these specializations:

Input type	std::match_results specialization	std::sub_match specialization
std::string	std::smatch	std::ssub_match
std::wstring	std::wmatch	std::wsub_match
const char*	std::cmatch	std::csub_match
const wchar_t*	std::wcmatch	std::wcsub_match

Tokenizing text using regex

This is a lot of work to parse an input using a regular expression, and there ought to be better abstractions available for the application programmer. Indeed, this is the kind of job you can simplify using a boost::regex_iterator and boost::regex_token_iterator. Let us suppose we want to pick all words in the string that start and end in 'a'. Here is a relatively painless way to do it:

Listing 4.29: Parsing strings using boost::regex_iterator

```
 1 #include <boost/regex.hpp>
 2 #include <string>
 3 #include <iostream>
 4
 5 int main()
 6 {
 7   std::string str2 = "An array of papers from the academia "
 8                      "on Alaska area's fauna";
 9   boost::regex r1("\\ba\\w*a\\b", boost::regex::icase);
10   boost::sregex_iterator rit(str2.begin(), str2.end(), r1), rend;
11
12   while (rit != rend) {
13     std::cout << *rit++ << '\n';
14   }
15 }
```

This program prints the following text to the output, consisting of the three words that begin and end in 'a':

```
academia

Alaska

area
```

The `boost::sregex_iterator` is a specialization of the template `boost::regex_iterator` to be used when the input string is of type `std::string`. Its instance `rit` is initialized with the string iterators, defining the input string and the regular expression used to look for successive tokens (line 10). It is then used to iterate through successive tokens like any other iterator (line 12).

In the previous example, we didn't deal with sub-expressions. So, let us look at an example with sub-expressions. Consider a string `"animal=Llama lives_in=Llama and is related_to=vicuna"`. It consists of some key-value pairs separated by the equals sign, among other content. If we want to extract all such key-value pairs, we can use a regular expression like \w+=\w+. We assume that the keys and values are single words without embedded punctuation or spaces. If we also want to pick out the key and value separately, we can use capture-groups like (\w+)=(\w+) for sub-expression matching:.

By using the `boost::sregex_token_iterator`, we can actually pick out substrings matching individual sub-expressions relatively easily. The `boost::sregex_token_iterator` is a specialization of the template `boost::regex_token_iterator` for use with input string of type `std::string`. It takes the iterators to the input string, regular expression, and optional arguments specifying which sub-expressions to iterator over. Here is the code to boot:

Listing 4.30: Parsing input strings with boost::regex_token_iterator

```
 1 #include <boost/regex.hpp>
 2 #include <string>
 3 #include <iostream>
 4
 5 int main()
 6 {
 7   std::string str3 = "animal=Llama lives_in=Chile "
 8                      "and is related_to=vicuna";
 9   boost::regex r3("(\\w+)=(\\w+)");
10   int subindx[] = {2, 1};
11   boost::sregex_token_iterator tokit(str3.begin(), str3.end(),
12                                      r3, subindx), tokend;
13   while (tokit != tokend) {
14     std::cout << *tokit++ << '\n';
15   }
16   std::cout << '\n';
17 }
```

This code prints the following output:

```
Llama
animal
Chile
lives_in
vicuna
related_to
```

You may have noticed that we print the values followed by the keys. We initialize a `boost::sregex_token_iterator` using the iterators defining the input string, the regular expression, and the array `subindx` specifying the sub-expressions we are interested in (line 11). As `subindx` has value {2, 1} (line 10), the second field is printed before the first. Besides an array, we could have also passed a vector of integers identifying the sub-expression indexes, or a single integer identifying the index of the only sub-expression we are interested in. If we omit this argument, the behavior of `boost::regex_token_iterator` is identical to that of `boost::regex_iterator`. The size of the array does not need to be passed and is automatically deduced via template argument deduction.

Some algorithms in the Boost String Algorithms library provide convenient wrappers around the functionality in Boost.Regex. The `boost::find_all_regex` algorithm takes a sequence container, an input string, and a regular expression, and puts all substrings of the input string that match the regular expression into the sequence container with a single function call. The `boost::split_regex` container splits a string into tokens separated by text that matches some regular expression and puts the tokens into a sequence container. Here are both in action; `find_all_regex` splitting a sentence into words, and `split_regex` splitting a record with pipe character separators into fields:

Listing 4.31: Using find_all_regex and split_regex

```
 1 #include <boost/algorithm/string_regex.hpp>
 2 #include <boost/regex.hpp>
 3 #include <string>
 4 #include <iostream>
 5 #include <vector>
 6
 7 int main()
 8 {
 9   std::string line = "All that you touch";
10   std::vector<std::string> words;
11   boost::find_all_regex(words, line, boost::regex("\\w+"));
12
13   std::string record = "Pigs on the Wing|Dogs| Pigs| Sheep";
14   std::vector<std::string> fields;
```

```
15   boost::split_regex(fields, record, boost::regex("[\\|]"));
16
17   for (auto word: words) { std::cout << word << ","; }
18   std::cout << '\n';
19   for (auto field: fields) { std::cout << field << ","; }
20 }
```

This prints the following output:

```
All,ll,l,that,hat,at,t,you,ou,u,touch,ouch,ch,h,
Pigs on the Wing,Dogs, Pigs, Sheep,
```

Note that the first line prints all possible substrings that match the regular expression \w+ (line 11), not just the largest disjoint matching substrings. This is because find_all_regex finds every matching substring in the input.

Replacing text

One frequent use of regular expressions is to search for text and replace matching text by other text. For example, we may want to scan a particular paragraph for possessive phrases (England's Queen, India's culture, people's choice, and so on.) and convert them to an alternative form (Queen of England, culture of India, choice of people, and so on). The boost::regex_replace function template can come in handy for the purpose.

To begin with, we define the regular expression \w+'s\s+\w+. Since we have to reorder the phrase, we must capture parts of the match using sub-expressions. We use the regular expression (\w+)'s\s+(\w+) to match. We can use numbered back-references in the replacement string to refer to the submatches, so the replacement string is "\2 of \1". We pass these along with the input string to boost::regex_replace, which returns a string with the matched sections replaced appropriately. Here is the code:

Listing 4.32: Finding/Replacing strings with regular expressions

```
 1 #include <boost/regex.hpp>
 2 #include <cassert>
 3
 4 int main()
 5 {
 6   std::string str4 = "England's Queen, India's President, "
 7                      "people's choice";
 8   boost::regex r4("(\\w+)'s\\s+(\\w+)");
10   std::string rep = boost::regex_replace(str4, r4, "\\2 of \\1");
11
```

```
12    assert(rep == "Queen of England, President of India, "
13                   "choice of people");
14 }
```

By default, `regex_replace` replaces all matching substrings. If we want to replace only the first matching substring instead, then we need to pass `boost::regex_constants::format_first_only` as a fourth argument to `regex_replace`.

Self-test questions

For multiple choice questions, choose all options that apply:

1. How does Boost Range help Boost Algorithms provide a better interface?

   a. Any character range expressed as a single argument, not iterator pair

   b. It is faster than iterator pairs

   c. It supports C-style arrays, and is extensible to other abstractions

   d. It provides better exception safety

2. Which algorithm produces the shortest code for searching all substrings matching a search string or pattern?

   a. `boost::find_all`

   b. `boost::find_all_regex`

   c. `boost::find_first`

   d. `boost::regex_iterator`

3. Which of these are tokenizer functions provided by the Boost Tokenizer library?

   a. `boost::char_separator`

   b. `boost::split`

   c. `boost::escaped_list_separator`

   d. `boost::tokenizer`

4. The regular expression `"\ba.*a"` matches which part of the string `"two giant anacondas creeping around"`?

   a. `"ant anacondas creeping a"`

   b. `"anacondas creeping a"`

   c. `"ant anaconda"`

   d. `"anaconda"`

5. Which of the following is true of `boost::smatch`?

   a. It is a specialization of `boost:: match_results`

   b. It stores only matched sub-expressions

   c. It stores a `boost::ssub_match` object for each sub-expression

   d. Its `str` member returns the matched substring

Summary

In this chapter, we learned the use of miscellaneous functions from the Boost String Algorithms library for performing various operations on string data types. We then looked at the generic Boost String Tokenizer framework that provides an efficient and extensible way to tokenize strings based on criteria that the user can define. We finally looked at regular expressions, and the Boost.Regex library that provides the ability to match character data against regular expressions, search for patterns, tokenize, and replace patterns using regular expressions.

This chapter should have given you a broad perspective of basic text handling facilities available from the Boost libraries. Along the way, we also picked up some useful techniques from the Boost Range abstraction. In the next chapter, we turn our attention to various data structures available from the Boost libraries.

5
Effective Data Structures beyond STL

The C++ Standard Library provides a rich set of **generic containers** that can be employed for a wide variety of common programming tasks. These include sequence containers like `std::vector`, `std::deque`, `std::list`, `std::forward_list`, and ordered and unordered associative containers like `std::map`, `std::set`, `std::unordered_map`, `std::unordered_set`, and so on.

Containers are traversed, and their individual elements accessed, using **iterators**. C++ defines a hierarchy of iterator categories based on the kind of access they provide to the elements of the container (read, write, forward traversal, bidirectional traversal, and random access). The type of iterator available for traversing a container is dependent on the internal structure of a container.

Available alongside the containers is a library of **generic algorithms** that read and manipulate generic containers, using one or more iterators. These libraries heavily rely on **generic programming**, in which program interfaces are abstracted from and are parameterized in terms of data types.

This collection of generic containers, algorithms, and a bunch of accompanying utilities originated in the **Standard Template Library** or **STL**, developed at HP Labs by Alexander Stepanov and Meng Lee, and were accepted as part of the C++ Standard Library in 1994. The name STL has stuck on for those parts of the Standard Library that originated in this work, and we will loosely use it to mean such parts of the library. STL containers and algorithms have been heavily used in C++ software ever since, but have had several limitations. Before C++11, you could only store copyable objects in containers. Certain classes of containers like hash-based associative containers, were absent in the Standard Library while others, like priority queues, were under-represented.

As of C++14, there are no containers yet in the Standard Library suitable for storing pointers to dynamically-allocated objects, though with the availability of `std::unique_ptr`, this is easier to deal with since C++11. You cannot efficiently search the contents of an associative container, like `std::map` by value rather than key, nor can you easily write iterators for your custom container classes that work well with STL algorithms. There is no easy library to read property sets or key-value pairs from various standard formats (XML, JSON, etc.) into in-memory data structures. There are many more such routine uses that require significant effort if you are limited to the Standard Library.

In this chapter and the next, we will look at the leading Boost libraries that fill many of these gaps. The chapter is divided into the following sections:

- The Boost Container library
- Fast lookups using Boost Unordered containers
- Containers for dynamically-allocated objects
- Expressive initialization and assignment using Boost.Assign
- Iteration patterns with Boost.Iterator

This chapter should provide you a solid foundation for using the wide variety of data structure libraries in Boost.

Boost Container library

The Boost Container library implements majority of the STL container templates in addition to providing a few nifty nonstandard containers. So, what is the point of reimplementing STL containers? To understand this, let us look at what kind of objects can be stored in STL containers and what kind cannot be.

To store objects of type T in a `std::vector`, for example, the type T must be a complete type (that is, must be completely defined, not just declared) at the point where the object of type `std::vector<T>` is defined. Moreover, in pre-C++11, objects of type T must be copyable and assignable. These requirements generally hold for other STL containers besides `std::vector`. In general, till before C++11, STL was a copy-intensive framework: you copied objects into STL containers to store them, the containers copied them around while being resized or restructured, and the containers destroyed those copies when they went out of scope. Copying being an expensive operation in terms of time and memory is also more error prone and thus the exception safety of several operations on STL containers was weak.

C++11 introduced move semantics that made it possible to **move-construct** new objects by moving or usurping the state of an existing object, typically by only exchanging integers and pointers and completely avoiding any non-trivial and error-prone copy operations. Likewise, the state or contents of an object could be moved into another existing object in an operation called **move-assignment**. Move semantics are applied by default when constructing or assigning from a temporary object while it can be explicitly enforced when copying from an l-value object (see *Appendix, C++11 Language Features Emulation*). These capabilities allow operations on Standard Library containers in C++11 to be significantly optimized and independent of **copy semantics**. The objects stored in C++11 STL containers need not be **copyable** if they are **move constructible**. C++11 also allows objects to be constructed in-place in the container's layout instead of requiring them to be constructed first and then copied.

The Boost Container library provides move-aware implementations of Standard Library containers that work not only with C++11 compilers, but also with Boost move emulation for C++03 compilers (see *Appendix, C++11 Language Features Emulation emulation*). In addition, they also support in-place construction of objects. This is a significant functionality if you are on a C++03 compiler. In addition, the containers in Boost Container library can hold objects of incomplete types, making it possible to define interesting recursive structures that are simply not possible with the standard containers.

In addition to the standard containers, the Boost Container library also implements several useful nonstandard containers that are useful for various specific uses.

Move-awareness and in-place construction

Consider the following class for encapsulating `char` strings, which is movable but not copyable. We use the Boost move emulation macros to define its move semantics. In a C++11 environment, this code translates to C++11 move syntax, while on C++03, it emulates the move semantics:

Listing 5.1: Movable but not copyable String

```
 1 #include <boost/move/move.hpp>
 2 #include <boost/swap.hpp>
 3 #include <cstring>
 4
 5 class String
 6 {
 7 private:
 8   BOOST_MOVABLE_BUT_NOT_COPYABLE(String)
 9
10 public:
```

```
11    String(const char *s = nullptr) : str(nullptr), sz(0) {
12      str = heapcpy(s, sz);
13    }
14
15    ~String() {
16      delete[] str;
17      sz = 0;
18    }
19
20    String(BOOST_RV_REF(String) that) : str(nullptr), sz(0) {
21      swap(that);
22    }
23
24    String& operator = (BOOST_RV_REF(String) rhs) {
25      String tmp(boost::move(rhs));
28
29     return *this;
30    }
31
32    void swap(String& rhs) {
33      boost::swap(this->sz, rhs.sz);
34      boost::swap(this->str, rhs.str);
35    }
36
37    const char *get() const {
38      return str;
39    }
40
41 private:
42    char *str;
43    size_t sz;
44
45    static char *heapcpy(const char *str, size_t& sz) {
46      char *ret = nullptr;
47
48      if (str) {
49        sz = std::strlen(str) + 1;
50        ret = new char[sz];
51        std::strncpy(ret, str, sz);
52      }
53
54      return ret;
55    }
56 };
```

On a pre-C++11 compiler, trying to store instances of String in a standard container will result in compiler errors because String is not copyable. Here is some code that moves String instances into a boost::container::vector, which is the Boost counterpart of std::vector:

Listing 5.2: Pushing String objects onto Boost vectors

```
 1 #include <boost/container/vector.hpp>
 2 #include "String.h"  // for class String
 3 #include <cassert>
 4
 5 int main() {
 6   boost::container::vector<String> strVec;
 7   String world("world");
 8   // Move temporary (rvalue)
 9   strVec.push_back(String("Hello"));
10   // Error, copy semantics needed
11   //strVec.push_back(world);
12   // Explicit move
13   strVec.push_back(boost::move(world));
14   // world nulled after move
15   assert(world.get() == nullptr);
16   // in-place construction
17   strVec.emplace_back("Hujambo Dunia!"); // Swahili
18
19   BOOST_FOREACH(String& str, strVec) {
20     std::cout <<str.get() << '\n';
21   }
22 }
```

In the preceding code, we create a Boost vector (line 6) and append a temporary String "Hello" to it (line 9). This automatically invokes move semantics, as the expression String("Hello") is an **rvalue**. We construct a String variable called world (line 7), but if we tried to append it to strVec, it would fail because it would try to copy world, but it is not copyable (line 11).

In order to put world into strVec, we need to explicitly move it, using boost::move (line 13). Once world is moved into strVec, its contents are moved out into a String object stored in strVec, and hence, its contents become null (line 15).Finally, we construct a String object in-place by calling the emplace_back member of the vector and passing it the constructor arguments of String (line 17). The code in listings 5.1 and 5.2 will compile and work correctly on pre-C++11 compilers as well as C++11. Moreover, on C++11, the Boost macros for move emulation simply translate to the C++ rvalue reference syntax. Note that we use the BOOST_FOREACH macro instead of a C++11 range-based for-loop to iterate through the vector (see *Appendix, C++11 Language Features Emulation*).

The code prints the following lines:

```
Hello
world
Hujambo Dunia!
```

Notice that in the range-based for-loop, the loop variable `str` is introduced using `auto&`. If we did not use the trailing ampersand after `auto`, the compiler would try to generate code to copy each element of `strVec` into `str`, which would fail because `String` is not copyable. Using the trailing ampersand ensures that `str` is a reference to successive elements.

In addition to `vector`, the Boost Container library implements other standard containers, like `deque`, `list`, `set`, `multiset`, `map` and `multimap`, and also `basic_string`. These are move-aware containers that are very similar to their C++11 counterparts and can be used in pre-C++11 environments using move emulation (via Boost.Move).

Nonstandard containers

In addition to the standard containers, the Boost Container library provides several useful nonstandard containers. This section is a quick overview of these containers and their applicability.

Flat associative containers

There are two flavors of the standard associative containers: **ordered** and **unordered**. Ordered containers like `std:set`, `std::multiset`, `std::map`, and `std::multimap` are typically implemented using a balanced search tree (an optimized Red-Black Tree implementation is **de facto**). Thus, they store their elements in sorted order. The unordered containers `std::unordered_set`, `std::unordered_multiset`, `std::unordered_map`, and `std::unordered_multimap`, are based on hash tables. They originated in the Boost Container library before becoming part of the C++TR1 release and C++11 Standard Library. These containers store objects in an array of buckets called a **hash table**, based on hash value computed for the object. There is no inherent ordering in how the objects are stored in the hash tables, hence the name unordered containers.

Associative containers support fast lookup. Ordered containers use balanced search trees which support logarithmic time searches, and unordered containers use hash tables which support amortized constant-time searches. These are not the only data structures that support fast lookups. Binary search on a sorted sequence that allows random positional access to its elements also performs in logarithmic time. The four flat associative containers: flat_set, flat_multiset, flat_map, and flat_multimap use a sorted vector to store data and use binary search on the vector to perform lookups. They are drop-in replacements for their ordered and unordered counterparts from the Standard Library but have different performance characteristics for insertions and lookups:

Listing 5.3: Using flat maps

```
 1 #include <iostream>
 2 #include <string>
 3 #include <boost/container/flat_map.hpp>
 4
 5 int main()
 6 {
 7   boost::container::flat_map<std::string, std::string>
 8       newCapitals;
 9
10   newCapitals["Sri Lanka"] = "Sri Jayawardenepura Kotte";
11   newCapitals["Burma"] = "Naypyidaw";
12   newCapitals["Tanzania"] = "Dodoma";
13   newCapitals["Cote d'Ivoire"] = "Yamoussoukro";
14   newCapitals["Nigeria"] = "Abuja";
15   newCapitals["Kazakhstan"] = "Astana";
16   newCapitals["Palau"] = "Ngerulmud";
17   newCapitals["Federated States of Micronesia"] = "Palikir";
18
19   for (const auto& entries : newCapitals) {
20     std::cout<< entries.first << ": " << entries.second
21               << '\n';
22   }
23 }
```

This first example lists a set of countries, whose capitals were moved in the last few decades. If you thought Lagos is still Nigeria's capital, you're in for a surprise. Geography apart, there isn't a whole lot surprising going on in the preceding code. We create a `typedef` for `boost::container::flat_map<std::string, std::string>`, and instantiate a map `newCapitals` of this type, inserting string pairs of countries and their new capitals. If we replace `boost::container::flat_map` with `std::map`, the code will work without any changes.

The flat associative containers can store objects that are either copyable or movable. Objects are stored in a contiguous layout without using pointers for indirection. Thus, in order to store a given number of objects of a certain type, the flat containers will less memory than the tree-based and hash-based containers too. Insertions maintain sorted order and are thus costlier than in the other associative containers; in particular, for value types that are copyable but not movable. Also, unlike with the standard associative containers, all the iterators are invalidated by insertion of any new element or deletion of existing elements.

Iterations and lookups tend to be faster, and cache performance better than that of the standard containers due to the contiguous layout and faster performance of binary search. Insertions into flat containers can cause reallocations and elements to get moved or copied if the initial capacity of flat containers is exceeded. This can be prevented by reserving sufficient space using the `reserve` member function before performing insertions. The following example illustrates this aspect:

Listing 5.4: Using flat sets

```
1 #include <boost/container/flat_set.hpp>
2 #include <iostream>
3 #include <string>
4
5 template<typename C>
6 void printContainerInternals(const C& container) {
7   std::cout << "Container layout" << '\n'
8             << "-------------\n";
9
10  for (const auto& elem : container) {
11    std::cout << "[Addr=" << &elem
12              << "] : [value=" << elem << "]\n";
13  }
14 }
15
16 int main()
17 {
18   boost::container::flat_set<std::string> someStrings;
19   someStrings.reserve(8);
```

```
20
21    someStrings.insert("Guitar");
22    printContainerInternals(someStrings);
23
24    someStrings.insert("Mandolin");
25    printContainerInternals(someStrings);
26
27    someStrings.insert("Cello");
28    printContainerInternals(someStrings);
29
30    someStrings.insert("Sitar");
31    printContainerInternals(someStrings);
32 }
```

This example shows one way to figure out how the internal layout of the flat associative containers changes with successive insertions. We define a `flat_set` container called `someStrings` (line 18) and insert names of eight string instruments. The `printContainer` template is called on the container after each insertion to print out the successive address in the internal vector, where each string is present. We reserve capacity for eight elements before the insertion (line 19), and insert eight elements thereafter. As there is sufficient capacity at the outset, none of the insertions should trigger reallocations and you should see a fairly stable set of addresses with only the order of strings changing to maintain sorted order. If we commented out the call to reserve (line 19) and ran the code, we might see reallocations and changing addresses.

slist

The `boost::container::slist` container is a singly-linked list abstraction similar to a container template of the same name that was available in the SGI STL implementation but never made it to the standard. The `std::list` container is a doubly linked list. C++ finally got its own singly linked list with `std::forward_list` introduced in C++11. The `slist` is move-aware.

Singly-linked lists have a lesser memory overhead than doubly linked lists, although the time complexity of certain operations goes from constant to linear. If you need a sequence container that should support relatively frequent insertions and you do not need backward traversals, singly linked lists are a good choice:

Listing 5.5: Using slist

```
1 #include <boost/container/slist.hpp>
2 #include <iostream>
3 #include <string>
4
```

```
 5  int main()
 6  {
 7    boost::container::slist<std::string> geologic_eras;
 8
 9    geologic_eras.push_front("Neogene");
10    geologic_eras.push_front("Paleogene");
11    geologic_eras.push_front("Cretaceous");
12    geologic_eras.push_front("Jurassic");
13    geologic_eras.push_front("Triassic");
14    geologic_eras.push_front("Permian");
15    geologic_eras.push_front("Carboniferous");
16    geologic_eras.push_front("Devonian");
17    geologic_eras.push_front("Silurian");
18    geologic_eras.push_front("Ordovician");
19    geologic_eras.push_front("Cambrian");
20
21    for (const auto& str : geologic_eras) {
22      std::cout << str << '\n';
23    }
24  }
```

In this simple example, we use an `slist` to store successive geologic eras. Unlike the standard sequence container `std::list`, `slist` does not have a `push_back` method to append an element to the end of the list. This is because computing the end of the list for each append would make it a linear operation instead of a constant one. Instead, we use the `push_front` member to add each new element at the head of the list. The final order of the strings in the list is the reverse of the order of insertion (and in the chronological order of the periods, oldest first).

Certain operations on singly-linked lists have higher time-complexity than their equivalents on doubly linked lists. The `insert` method which inserts an element before another is constant time in `std::list` but is linear time in `slist`. This is because the element preceding the position of insertion can be located using the link to the previous element in a doubly linked list like `std::list` but would require traversal from the beginning of the list in `slist`. For the same reason, the `erase` member function for erasing an element at a given position and the `emplace` member function for the in-place construction of an element *before* another also have linear complexity compared to their `std::list` counterparts. For this reason, `slist` provides member functions `insert_after`, `erase_after`, and `emplace_after` that provide similar functionality with slightly altered semantics of inserting, erasing, and emplacing objects in constant time after a given position. In order to allow these functions to add an element to the beginning of an `slist`, you can use the `before_begin` member function to get an iterator to a `head` pointer — a non-dereferenceable iterator which when incremented, points to the first element in the `slist`.

We can now rewrite listing 5.5 to insert the geologic periods into the `slist` in chronological order:

Listing 5.6: Adding elements to the end of slist

```
1  #include <boost/container/slist.hpp>
2  #include <iostream>
3  #include <string>
4  #include <cassert>
5
6  int main()
7  {
8      boost::container::slist<std::string> eras;
9      boost::container::slist<std::string>::iterator last =
10                                         eras.before_begin();
11
12     const char *era_names [] = {"Cambrian", "Ordovician",
13                         "Silurian", "Devonian", "Carboniferous",
14                         "Permian", "Triassic", "Jurassic",
15                         "Cretaceous", "Paleogene", "Neogene"};
16
17     for (const char *period :era_names) {
18         eras.emplace_after(last, period);
19         ++last;
20     }
21
22     int i = 0;
23     for (const auto& str : eras) {
24         assert(str == era_names[i++]);
25     }
26 }
```

Splicing

Besides `insert` and `emplace`, you can also add elements at any given position in an `slist` using an operation called `splice`. Splicing is a useful operation on linked lists in which one or more successive elements from one given list are moved to a particular position in another linked list or to a different position in the same list. The `std::list` container provides a `splice` member function that allows you to do this in constant time. In an `slist`, the time complexity of the `splice` member function is linear in the number of elements spliced, due to the need for linear traversal to locate the element before the position of insertion. The `splice_after` member function, like `insert_after` and `emplace_after`, moves elements into a list after a specified position:

Listing 5.7: Splicing slists

```
1  #include <boost/container/slist.hpp>
2  #include <string>
3  #include <iostream>
4
5  typedef boost::container::slist<std::string> list_type;
6  typedef list_type::iterator iter_type;
7
8  int main()
9  {
10   list_type dinos;
11   iter_type last = dinos.before_begin();
12
13   const char *dinoarray[] = {"Elasmosaurus", "Fabrosaurus",
14                       "Galimimus", "Hadrosaurus", "Iguanodon",
15                       "Appatosaurus", "Brachiosaurus",
16                       "Corythosaurus", "Dilophosaurus"};
17
18   // fill the slist
19   for (const char *dino : dinoarray) {
20     dinos.insert_after(last, dino);
21     ++last;
22   }
23
24   // find the pivot
25   last = dinos.begin();
26   iter_type iter = last;
27
28   while (++iter != dinos.end()) {
29     if (*last > *iter) {
30       break;
31     }
32     ++last;
33   }
34
35   // find the end of the tail
36   auto itend = last;
37   while (iter != dinos.end()) {
38     ++itend;
39     ++iter;
40   }
41
```

```
42    // splice after
43    dinos.splice_after(dinos.before_begin(), dinos,
44                      last, itend);
45    for (const auto& str: dinos) {
46     std::cout <<str<< '\n';
47    }
48 }
```

In this code example, we have an array of eight dinosaur names, starting with the first eight letters of the English alphabet (lines 13-16). It is a sorted list, which is rotated by four positions, so it starts with Elasmosaurus and has Appatosaurus somewhere in the middle. We make an slist out of these, using insert_after (line 20), and then locate the pivot at which the lexically smallest string lies (lines 29-30). At the end of the loop, iter points to the lexically smallest string in the dinos list and last points to the element immediately before iter. Here is the prototype of the splice_after overload we want to use to move the tail of the list to the beginning:

```
void splice_after(const_iterator add_after, slist& source,
        const_iterator start_after, const_iterator end);
```

The sequence of elements that are to be moved from the source container to the target starts at the element following start_after and ends at end, both ends inclusive, that is, the half-open interval (start_after, end). These elements are inserted into the target slist after the position is identified by add_after. We can use the iterator last for the third argument. For the fourth argument, we compute the position of the last element in the list (lines 36-40). The iterator itend now points to the last element in the list. Using the chosen splice_after overload, we move all elements, following last and till the end of the list, to the beginning of the list (lines 43-44).

The std::forward_list container does not provide a size member function to return the number of elements in a list. This helps ensure that its splice_after implementation is constant time. Otherwise, during each splice_after operation, the number of elements transferred to the list would need to be counted, and the total count of elements need to be incremented by that much. Solely to support this, splice_after would have to be linear in the number of elements transferred instead of constant time. The slist container provides a size member and several overloads of splice_after. The overload of splice_after that we used is linear in the number of elements transferred, as it computes this number using a linear traversal. However, if we computed this number in our code without extra loops and passed it to the splice_after function, then it could avoid iterating again and use the passed number. There are two overloads of splice_after that take the count of the elements from the user and avoid the linear computation, thus providing constant-time splice.

Here is a slightly altered snippet to do this:

```
35    // find the end of the tail
36    size_t count = 0;
37    auto itend = last;
38
39    while (iter != dinos.end()) {
40      ++itend;
41      ++iter;
42      ++count;
43    }
44
45    // splice after
46    dinos.splice_after(dinos.before_begin(), dinos,
47                       last, itend, count);
```

We compute `count` while determining the iterator range to move, and pass that to `splice_after`. We must make sure that our computation of `count` is correct, or the behavior will be undefined. This overload is useful because we had a way to determine the count without increasing the complexity of our calling code.

For `std::forward_list`, the `splice_after` signature differs slightly in semantics from that of `boost::container::slist`. Here is the prototype of one overload of the `splice_after` member of `std::forward_list`:

```
void splice_after(const_iterator pos, std::forward_list& list,
        const_iterator before_first, const_iterator after_last);
```

The iterators `before_first` and `after_last` identify an open interval, and the actual elements transferred would be the sequence starting at the element following `before_first` and ending at the element before `after_last`, that is, the open interval (`before_first`, `after_last`). Using this function, we would not need to write the loop to determine the last element in this case because we could simply use `dinos.end()` as the marker for one-past-the-end position. If `dinos` were an instance of `std::forward_list`, we would have edited listing 5.7, thus saving six lines of code:

```
37    dinos.splice_after(dinos.before_begin(), dinos,
38                       last, dinos.end());
```

All `splice_after` overloads in `std::forward_list` that transfer a range of elements are linear in the number of elements transferred. While we saw a constant-time overload in `boost::container::slist`, we had to write linear complexity logic to pass the correct count of elements to it. So, in many cases, code using `std::forward_list` might be more maintainable and no less efficient if you can make do without the constant-time `size` member function.

stable_vector

The `std::vector` container stores objects in contiguous memory. The `vector` reallocates internal storage and copies or moves objects to new storage as needed, so as to accommodate additional new objects. It allows fast random access to the stored objects using an index. Inserting elements at arbitrary positions in the vector is expensive compared to appending elements at the end, because insertion requires elements after the point of insertion to be moved in order to make room for the new element. There is one more implication of this behavior. Consider the following code:

Listing 5.8: Iterator invalidation in std::vector

```
 1 #include <vector>
 2 #include <cassert>
 3
 4 int main() {
 5   std::vector<int>v{1, 2, 3, 5};
 6   auto first = v.begin();
 7   auto last = first + v.size() - 1;
 8   assert(*last == 5);
 9   v.insert(last, 4);
10   // *last = 10;  // undefined behavior, invalid iterator
11   for (int i = 0; i < 1000; ++i) {
12     v.push_back(i);
13   }
14
15   // *first = 0; // likely invalidated
16 }
```

In the preceding code, we create a `vector` of integers v and initialize it with four integers (line 5). The brace-enclosed list of comma-separated values used to initialize the vector is a very handy C++11 construct called **initializer list**. In pre-C++11, you had to manually append values or, as we will see later in this chapter, use the `Boost.Assign` library. We then compute the iterator to the last element of the object as an offset from the first iterator (line 7). We assert that the last element is 5 (line 8). Next, we insert an element before the last element (line 9). Past this point, the iterator `last` will be invalidated and any access of the iterator `last` will be undefined behavior. In fact, in the two random access containers, vectors and deques, iterator invalidations happen all too often. Any write operation on the vector can invalidate iterators. For example, if you erase an element at a particular iterator position, all existing iterators to later positions are invalidated. Even appending an element to the end of the vector could trigger a resize of the vector's internal storage, requiring elements to be moved. Such an event will invalidate all existing iterators. The Standard Library `vector` is an **unstable container**. The `boost::container::stable_vector` is a sequence container that provides random access coupled with stable iterators, which are not invalidated unless the element they point to is erased. Have a look at the following image from the Boost documentation pages on stable_vector (`http://www.boost.org/doc/libs/1_58_0/doc/html/container/non_standard_containers.html#container.non_standard_containers.stable_vector`):

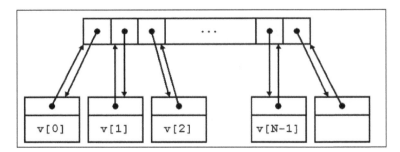

As illustrated here, `stable_vector` does not store the objects in a contiguous memory layout. Instead, each object is stored in a separate node, and a contiguous array stores pointers to these nodes in the order of insertion. Each node contains the actual object and also a pointer to its position in the array. The iterators point to these nodes rather than to positions in the array. Thus, nodes with existing objects do not change after insertion of new objects or deletion of some existing objects and their iterators also remain valid. Their back pointers are updated however when they change positions due to insertions/removals. The contiguous array of node pointers still allows random access to elements. Because of the extra pointers and indirections, `stable_vector` tends to be slower than `std::vector`, but that is the trade-off for stable iterators. Here is some code to boot:

Listing 5.9: Stable vector example

```
1 #include <boost/container/stable_vector.hpp>
2 #include <cassert>
3 #include <string>
4
5 int main()
6 {
7   const char *cloud_names[] = {"cumulus", "cirrus", "stratus",
8                  "cumulonimbus", "cirrostratus", "cirrocumulus",
9                  "altocumulus", "altostratus"};
10
11  boost::container::stable_vector<std::string> clouds;
12  clouds.reserve(4);
13  clouds.resize(4);    // To circumvent a bug in Boost 1.54
14
15  size_t name_count = sizeof(cloud_names)/sizeof(const char*);
16  size_t capacity = clouds.capacity();
17
18  size_t i = 0;
19  for (i = 0; i < name_count && i < capacity; ++i) {
20    clouds[i] = cloud_names[i];
21  }
22
23  auto first = clouds.begin();
24
25  for (; i < name_count; ++i) {
26    clouds.push_back(cloud_names[i]);
27  }
28
29  auto sixth = clouds.begin() + 5;
30
31  // 1 erase @4
32  clouds.erase(clouds.begin() + 4);
33  // 2 inserts @3
34  clouds.insert(clouds.begin() + 3, "stratocumulus");
35  clouds.insert(clouds.begin() + 3, "nimbostratus");
36
37  assert(*first == cloud_names[0]);
38  assert(sixth == clouds.begin() + 6); // not +5
39  assert(*sixth == cloud_names[5]);
40 }
```

Using `stable_vector` is no different from using `vector`, and it is move-aware too. In the preceding example, we want to store the names of different types of clouds in a `stable_vector` of `std::string`. There are eight cloud names present in an array called `cloud_names` (lines 7-9). We create a `stable_vector` called `clouds` to store these names, and reserve a capacity for only four elements (lines 12-13). What we want to show is that once we add elements beyond the capacity of the `stable_vector`, requiring an expansion of the underlying array and movement of the existing data, iterators computed before the change in capacity still remain valid. It is entirely possible for `reserve` to allocate more capacity than that requested, and if this is more than the total number of cloud names we have, our example is moot.

We first store names of clouds (lines 18-21) without overshooting the capacity, and compute the iterator to the first element (line 23). We then append remaining cloud names, if any (lines 25-27). If there were any remaining cloud names, then they would have caused a resize when the first of them got stored.

We compute the iterator to the sixth element (line 29), erase the fifth element (line 32), and insert two more cloud names before the fourth element (lines 34-35). After all this, the iterator `first` still points to the first element (line 37). At the time we computed the iterator `sixth`, it pointed to the sixth element and its value was `"cirrocumulus"`, the sixth string in the `cloud_names` array. Now with one deletion and two insertions before it, it should be the seventh element (line 38), but its value should remain unchanged (line 39) — as stable as iterators get!

Since Boost 1.54, the `capacity` member function of `stable_vector` returns an incorrect value for the capacity after a call to `reserve`. By calling the `resize` member function with an argument as large as what was passed to `reserve` (line 13) before calling `capacity`, we can circumvent the bug and ensure that a subsequent call to `capacity` returns the correct value. Once the bug is fixed in a later release, the call to `resize` following the call to `reserve` should not be needed.

static_vector

The `boost::container::static_vector` template is a vector-like container with an upper limit on the size defined at compile time. It allocates a fixed size, uninitialized storage in its layout, rather than dynamically in a separate buffer. It does not try to value-initialize all the elements upon instantiation, unlike `vector` or `stable_vector`, both of which try to value-initialize elements when an initial size is specified as a constructor argument. The absence of heap allocation and value-initialization makes `static_vector` instantiation almost zero overhead.

A `static_vector` is used just as a regular vector with one important caveat. Trying to insert one element too many into a `static_vector` would result in a runtime error, so you should always make sure that there is enough room in the `static_vector` before trying to insert an additional element:

Listing 5.10: Using a static_vector

```
 1 #include <boost/current_function.hpp>
 2 #include <boost/container/static_vector.hpp>
 3 #include <iostream>
 4
 5 class ChattyInit
 6 {
 7 public:
 8   ChattyInit() {
 9     std::cout << BOOST_CURRENT_FUNCTION << '\n';
10   }
11 };
12
13 int main()
14 {
15   boost::container::static_vector<ChattyInit, 10> myvector;
16   std::cout << "boost::container::static_vector initialized"
17             <<'\n';
18   while (myvector.size() < myvector.capacity()) {
19     myvector.push_back(ChattyInit());
20   }
21
22   // cisv.push_back(ChattyInit()); // runtime error
23 }
```

We construct a `static_vector` of `ChattyInit` objects, `ChattyInit` being a simple class whose constructor prints its own name. The fixed size of the `static_vector` is specified as a numeric template argument (line 15). Running the preceding code prints the following on my GNU Linux box with a g++ 4.9 compiler:

```
boost::container::static_vector initialized
ChattyInit::ChattyInit()
ChattyInit::ChattyInit()
… 8 more lines …
```

We can see that no objects are created as part of `static_vector` initialization, and individual objects are instantiated as they are appended. We make sure that the total number of elements inserted does not exceed the capacity of the container (line 18). Because the elements of `static_vector` are not value-initialized by default, the `size` member function returns zero when no elements are explicitly added. Compare this with `std::vector`:

```
std::vector<ChattyInit> myvector(10); // 10 elems value-inited
assert(myvector.size() == 10);
```

If we actually tried appending one element too many (line 22), the program would crash. `boost::container::static_vector` is a useful container if you are looking for a fast, size-bounded `vector` replacement.

Fast lookups using Boost Unordered containers

The four standard associative containers in C++03: `std::set`, `std::map`, `std::multiset`, and `std::multimap` are ordered containers and store their keys in some sorted order using balanced binary search trees. They require an ordering relationship to be defined for their keys and provide logarithmic complexity insertions and lookups. Given the ordering relationship and two keys, A and B, we can determine whether A precedes B or B precedes A in the relationship. If neither precedes the other, the keys A and B are said to be equivalent; this does not mean A and B are equal. In fact, the ordered containers are agnostic to equality and there need not be a notion of equality defined at all. This is the reason, such a relation is called a **strict weak ordering**.

Consider the following example:

```
1 #include <string>
2 #include <tuple>
3
4 struct Person {
5   std::string name;
6   int age;
7   std::string profession;
8   std::string nationality;
9 };
10
11 bool operator < (const Person& p1, const Person& p2)
12 {
13   return std::tie(p1.nationality, p1.name, p1.age)
```

```
14              < std::tie(p2.nationality, p2.name, p2.age);
15  }
```

We define a type `Person` that represents a human individual, using the fields `name`, `age`, `profession`, and `nationality` (lines 3-9), and then define an ordering relation using the `operator<` that does not take the `profession` field into account (lines 11-15). This allows `Person` objects to be ordered, but not compared for equality. Two `Person` objects `p1` and `p2` would be deemed equivalent if `!(p1 < p2)` and `!(p2 < p1)` both hold. This would be true of any two `Person` objects with the same `name`, `age`, and `nationality`, irrespective of their `profession`. The ordered container `std::set` does not allow multiple keys that are equivalent to each other while `std::multiset` does. Likewise, `std::map` does not allow multiple key-value pairs, whose keys are equivalent, while `std::multimap` does. Thus, adding a key-value pair to a `std::map` that already contains an equivalent key overwrites the older value.

The ordered containers are implemented using a kind of balanced binary search tree known as Red-Black Trees, with several optimizations. They offer one key capability besides the ability to lookup and insert keys in logarithmic time — an ordered traversal of the keys in the container. However, if you do not need ordered traversal, then there are more efficient alternatives available — hash tables being the most obvious one. Appropriate implementations of hash tables support constant-time lookups on average, and amortized constant-time inserts that outperform the ordered containers with better cache performance, while having a somewhat higher space overhead.

The Boost Unordered library introduced four hash table-based counterparts of the ordered containers: `boost::unordered_set`, `boost::unordered_map`, `boost::unordered_multiset`, and `boost::unordered_multimap`, which became part of the C++ TR1 release in 2007 and were included in the Standard Library in C++11. Of course, you can use Boost Unordered even with a C++03 compiler.

Unordered containers require the notion of equality to be defined for the objects they store, but not the notion of ordering. Thus, for unordered containers, equivalence is defined in terms of equality rather than ordering. In addition, unordered containers need a way to compute a hash value of each key to determine the position in the table, where the key is stored. In the following code examples, we will see how to use unordered containers and compute hash values for objects, reusing the `Person` type we introduced earlier:

Listing 5.11: Using unordered_sets

```
1 #include <boost/unordered_set.hpp>
2 #include <boost/functional/hash.hpp>
3 #include <iostream>
4 #include <cassert>
```

```
 5 #include "Person.h" // struct Person definition
 6
 7 bool operator==(const Person& left, const Person& right){
 8   return (left.name == right.name
 9           && left.age == right.age
10           && left.profession == right.profession
11           && left.nationality == right.nationality);
12 }
13
14 namespace boost
15 {
16   template <>
17   struct hash<Person>
18   {
19     size_t operator()(const Person& person) const{
20       size_t hash = 0;
21       boost::hash_combine(hash,
22                           boost::hash_value(person.name));
23       boost::hash_combine(hash,
24                           boost::hash_value(person.nationality));
25       return hash;
26     }
27   };
28 }
29
30 int main() {
31   boost::unordered_set<Person> persons;
32
33   Person p{"Ned Land", 40, "Harpooner","Canada"};
34   persons.insert(p); // succeeds
35
36   Person p1{"Ned Land", 32, "C++ Programmer","Canada"};
37   persons.insert(p1);  // succeeds
38
39   assert(persons.find(p) != persons.end());
40   assert(persons.find(p1) != persons.end());
41
42   Person p2 = p;
43   persons.insert(p2);   // fails
44   assert(persons.size() == 2);
45 }
```

The preceding example shows how an `unordered_set` is used to store objects of the user-defined type `Person` that we defined in the earlier listing. We define an `unordered_set` of `Person` objects (line 31), create two `Person` objects p and p1, and insert them into the `unordered_set` called `Persons` (lines 34, 37). We define a third `Person` object p2, which is a copy of p, and try to insert this element but fail (line 43). The container being a set (`unordered_set`) contains unique elements. Since p2 is a copy of p and is equal to it, its insertion fails.

There are a couple of ways for the `unordered_set` to compute the hash value of each object it stores. We demonstrate one such way: open the `boost` namespace (line 14) to define a specialization for the function template `boost::hash` for the type `Person` in question (line 21-24). To compute the hash of a `Person` object, we consider only two of its fields: `name` and `nationality`. We use the utility functions `boost::hash_value` and `boost::hash_combine` (to generate the hash values for individual fields and combine them). Since we only consider the name and nationality of a person while determining the hash value for that `Person` object, the objects p and p1, both of which represent individuals with the same name and nationality, end up having the same hash value. However, they are not equal, as their other fields are different, and therefore, both objects are successfully added to the set. On the other hand, the object p2 is a copy of p, and when we try inserting p2 into the `persons` set, the insertion fails because sets do not contain duplicates and p2 is a duplicate of p. The `boost::unordered_multiset` and `boost::unordered_multimap` containers are hash-based containers that can store duplicate objects.

Computing good hash values is important in ensuring that objects are well distributed in the hash table. While the `boost::hash_value` and `boost::hash_combine` utility function templates help compute hash values for more complex objects, their indiscriminate application can result in inefficient hashing algorithms. For user-defined types, it may be better in many cases to roll out a mathematically validated hashing algorithm that exploits the semantics of the user-defined type. If you use primitives or standard types like `std::string` as keys in your `unordered_set` or `unordered_map`, then you need not roll out your own hash function, as `boost::hash` does an adequate job.

Looking up values is typically done using the `find` and `count` member functions of the unordered associative containers. While `find` returns an iterator to the actual object stored in the container, corresponding to the key passed, `count` returns just the count of occurrences of the key. The `equal_range` member function of `unordered_multiset` and `unordered_multimap` return the range of matching objects. For `unordered_set` and `unordered_map`, the count member function can never return a value greater than 1.

Containers for dynamically-allocated objects

Object-oriented programming relies heavily on using polymorphic base class references to manipulate objects of an entire class hierarchy. More often than not, these objects are dynamically allocated. When dealing with a whole collection of such objects, STL containers come a cropper; they store concrete objects of a single type and require copy or move semantics. It is impossible to define a single container that can store objects of different classes across a hierarchy. While you may store polymorphic base class pointers in containers, pointers are treated as POD-types and with little support for deep-copy semantics. The life cycle of dynamically-allocated objects is none of STL's business. But it is unwieldy to define a container of pointers whose lifetimes have to be managed separately without any help from the container.

The Boost Pointer Container library addresses these gaps by storing pointers to dynamically-allocated objects and deallocating them at the end of the container's life. The pointer containers provide an interface through which you can operate on the underlying objects without the need for pointer indirection. As they store pointers to objects, these containers naturally support polymorphic containers without any extra machinery.

The following table shows pointer containers and their Standard Library counterparts:

Pointer container from Boost	Standard Library container
boost::ptr_array	std::array
boost::ptr_vector	std::vector
boost::ptr_deque	std::deque
boost::ptr_list	std::list
boost::ptr_set / boost::ptr_multiset	std::set / std::multiset
boost::ptr_unordered_set / boost::ptr_unordered_multiset	std::unordered_set / std::unordered_multiset
boost::ptr_map / boost::ptr_multimap	std::map / std::multimap
boost::ptr_unordered_map / boost::ptr_unordered_multimap	std::unordered_map / std::unordered_multimap

Boost defines the pointer container equivalents for all the standard containers. These containers can be used to store polymorphic pointers, and the underlying objects pointed to by the stored pointers need not be copyable or movable. Here is a basic example to get started with:

Listing 5.12: Using Boost pointer containers

```
 1 #include <boost/ptr_container/ptr_vector.hpp>
 2 #include <boost/noncopyable.hpp>
 3 #include <iostream>
 4 #include <boost/current_function.hpp>
 5
 6 class AbstractJob {
 7 public:
 8   virtual ~AbstractJob() {}
 9
10   void doJob() {
11     doStep1();
12     doStep2();
13   }
14
15 private:
16   virtual void doStep1() = 0;
17   virtual void doStep2() = 0;
18 };
19
20 class JobA : public AbstractJob
21 {
22   void doStep1() override {
23     std::cout << BOOST_CURRENT_FUNCTION << '\n';
24   }
25
26   void doStep2() override {
27     std::cout << BOOST_CURRENT_FUNCTION << '\n';
28   }
29 };
30
31 class JobB : public AbstractJob
```

```
32 {
33   void doStep1() override {
34     std::cout << BOOST_CURRENT_FUNCTION << '\n';
35   }
36
37   void doStep2() override {
38     std::cout << BOOST_CURRENT_FUNCTION << '\n';
39   }
40 };
41
42 int main()
43 {
44   boost::ptr_vector<AbstractJob> basePtrVec;
45
46   basePtrVec.push_back(new JobA);
47   basePtrVec.push_back(new JobB);
48
49   AbstractJob& firstJob = basePtrVec.front();
50   AbstractJob& lastJob = basePtrVec.back();
51
52   for (auto& job : basePtrVec) {
53     job.doJob();
54   }
55 }
```

In the preceding example, AbstractJob is an abstract base class (line 5) which defines two private pure virtual functions doStep1 and doStep2 (lines 16, 17), and a non-virtual public function doJob which calls these two functions (line 10). JobA and JobB are two concrete implementations of AbstractJob, which implement the virtual functions doStep1 and doStep2. The override keyword trailing the function signature (lines 22, 26, 33, and 37) is a C++11 feature that clarifies that a particular function overrides a virtual function in the base class. In the main function, we create a ptr_vector of AbstractJobs. Note that the template argument is not the pointer type (line 44). We then append two concrete instances of JobA and JobB to the vector (lines 46 and 47). We access the first and last elements in the vector using the front (line 49) and back (line 50) member functions, both of which return references to the underlying objects rather than their pointers. Finally, we read off the stored objects in a range-based for-loop (line 52). The loop variable job is declared as a reference (auto&), not a pointer. Member functions of the pointer containers as well as iterators return references not to the stored pointers but to the underlying objects they point to, providing for syntactic ease.

While range-based for-loops and `BOOST_FOREACH` make it easy to iterate through collections, you can also use the iterator interface directly if you need to:

```
49    typedef boost::ptr_vector<AbstractJob>::iterator iter_t;
50
51    for (iter_t it = basePtrVec.begin();
52          it != basePtrVec.end(); ++it) {
53      AbstractJob& job = *it;
54      job.do();
55    }
```

Once again, notice that the iterator returns a reference to the underlying object, not to the pointer (line 53), even though the container stores pointers. The variable `job` is a reference because `AbstractJob` is abstract and cannot be instantiated. But what if the base class was not abstract? Consider the following example of a non-abstract polymorphic base class:

Listing 5.13: Pitfalls of copyable concrete base classes

```
 1 struct ConcreteBase
 2 {
 3   virtual void doWork() {}
 4 };
 5
 6 struct Derived1 : public ConcreteBase
 7 {
 8   Derived1(int n) : data(n) {}
 9   void doWork() override { std::cout <<data <<"\n"; }
10   int data;
11 };
12
13 struct Derived2 : public ConcreteBase
14 {
15   Derived2(int n) : data(n) {}
16   void doWork() override { std::cout <<data << "\n"; }
17   int data;
18 };
19
20 int main()
21 {
22   boost::ptr_vector<ConcreteBase> vec;
23   typedef boost::ptr_vector<ConcreteBase>::iterator iter_t;
24
```

```
25   vec.push_back(new Derived1(1));
26   vec.push_back(new Derived2(2));
27
28   for (iter_t it = vec.begin(); it != vec.end(); ++it) {
29     ConcreteBase obj = *it;
30     obj.doWork();
31   }
32 }
```

The preceding code compiles cleanly but may not do what you expect it to do. In the body of the for-loop, we assign each object of a derived class to a base class instance (line 29). The copy constructor of `ConcreteBase` takes effect, and what we get is a sliced object and incorrect behavior.

Thus, it is a good idea to prevent copying at the outset by deriving the base class itself from `boost::noncopyable`, as follows:

```
1 #include <boost/noncopyable.hpp>
2
3 class ConcreteBase : public boost::noncopyable
```

This would prevent slicing due to an inadvertent copy by causing such code to be flagged as compilation error. Note that this would make all classes in the hierarchy noncopyable. We will look at ways of adding copy semantics to such a hierarchy in the next section. But before that, a look at using associative pointer containers.

We can store dynamically-allocated objects, including polymorphic objects in `boost::ptr_set` or `boost::ptr_multiset`. Since these are ordered containers, we must define a strict weak ordering relation for the value-type stored in the container. This is typically done by defining the `bool operator<` for the type. If you store polymorphic pointers to objects of a class hierarchy, you must define an ordering relationship for all objects of the hierarchy, not just among objects of a particular concrete type:

Listing 5.14: Using associative pointer containers – ptr_set

```
1 #include <boost/ptr_container/ptr_set.hpp>
2 #include <boost/noncopyable.hpp>
3 #include <string>
4 #include <iostream>
5
6 class Animal : boost::noncopyable
7 {
8 public:
9   virtual ~Animal()
10  {};
```

```
11
12   virtual std::string name() const = 0;
13 };
14
15 class SnowLeopard : public Animal
16 {
17 public:
18   SnowLeopard(const std::string& name) : name_(name) {}
19
20   virtual ~SnowLeopard() { std::cout << "~SnowLeopard\n"; }
21
22   std::string name() const override
23   {
24     return name_ + ", the snow leopard";
25   }
26
27 private:
28   std::string name_;
29 };
30
31 class Puma : public Animal
32 {
33 public:
34   Puma(const std::string& name) : name_(name) {}
35   virtual ~Puma() { std::cout << "~Puma\n"; }
36
37   virtual std::string name() const
38   {
39     return name_ + ", the puma";
40   }
41
42 private:
43   std::string name_;
44 };
45
46 bool operator<(const Animal& left, const Animal& right)
47 {
48   return left.name() < right.name();
49 }
50
51 int main()
52 {
53   boost::ptr_set<Animal>animals;
54   animals.insert(new Puma("Kaju"));
```

```
55    animals.insert(new SnowLeopard("Rongi"));
56    animals.insert(new Puma("Juki"));
57
58    for (auto&animal :animals) {
59      std::cout <<animal.name() << '\n';
60    }
61 }
```

This shows the use of `std::ptr_set` to store polymorphic pointers to dynamically-allocated objects. The `Animal` abstract base declares a pure virtual function `name`. Two two derived classes, `SnowLeopard` and `Puma`, (representing two real mammal species) override them. We define a `ptr_set` of `Animal` pointers called `animals` (line 53). We create two pumas named `Kaju` and `Juki` and a snow leopard named `Rongi`, inserting them into the set `animals` (lines 54-56). When we iterate through the list, we get references to the dynamically-allocated objects, not pointers (lines 58, 59). The `operator<` (line 46) compares any two animals and orders them lexically by name. Without this operator, we would not be able to define the `ptr_set`. Here is the output of the preceding code:

```
Juki, the puma
Kaju, the puma
Rongi, the snow leopard
~Puma
~Puma
~SnowLeopard
```

The three animals are listed in the first three lines, and then the destructor of each object is invoked and prints its identity as the `ptr_set` container instance goes out of scope.

Another common use of associative pointer containers is to store polymorphic objects in a map or a multimap:

Listing 5.15: Using associative pointer containers

```
1 #include <boost/ptr_container/ptr_map.hpp>
2 #include <iostream>
3 // include definitions of Animal, SnowLeopard, Puma
4
5 int main() {
6   boost::ptr_multimap<std::string, Animal> animals;
7   std::string kj = "Puma";
8   std::string br = "Snow Leopard";
9
10  animals.insert(kj, new Puma("Kaju"));
11  animals.insert(br, new SnowLeopard("Rongi"));
```

```
12    animals.insert(kj, new Puma("Juki"));
13
14    for (const auto&entry : animals) {
15      std::cout << "[" << entry.first << "]->"
16                 << entry.second->name() << '\n';
17    }
18 }
```

We create a multimap called `animals` (line 6) that keeps the species name as a key of type `std::string`, and stores one or more polymorphic pointers to animals of that species for each key (lines 10-12). We use the same `Animal` hierarchy we used in listing 5.14. We loop through all the entries in the multimap, printing the name of the species followed by the given name of the specific animal. Here is the output:

```
[SnowLeopard]->Rongi, the snow leopard
[Puma]->Kaju, the puma
[Puma]->Juki, the puma
```

Each `Animal` entry is of type `std::pair<std::string, Animal*>`, and thus the key and value are accessed using the members `first` and `second`. Note that `entry.second` returns the stored pointer, not a reference to the underlying object (line 16).

Ownership semantics of pointer containers

We have already seen that pointer containers "own" the dynamically-allocated objects we store in them, in the sense that the container takes care of deallocating them at the end of its own life. The objects themselves need to support neither copy nor move semantics, so it is natural to wonder what it would mean to copy a pointer container. Actually, the pointer containers are copyable and support simple copy semantics — upon copy-construction or copy assignment of a pointer-container, it dynamically allocates a copy of each object in the source container and stores the pointer to that object. This works fine for any non-polymorphic type that is either a POD-type or has a copy constructor. For polymorphic types, this behavior leads to slicing or failure to compile when the base classes are abstract or noncopyable. In order to create deep copies of containers with polymorphic objects, the objects must support the clone interface.

To support creating copies of objects of a polymorphic type `T`, in a namespace `X`, you must define a free function in the namespace `X` with the following signature:

```
1 namespace X {
2   // definition of T
3   ...
4
5   T* new_clone(const T& obj);
6 }
```

The function `new_clone` is found via **Argument Dependent Lookup (ADL)** and is expected to return a copy of the object `obj` passed to it, whose runtime type should be the same as that of `obj`. We can extend the animal example; we can do this by defining a `clone` virtual function that is overridden in each subclass of `Animal` to return a copy of the object. The `new_clone` free function then simply has to call the clone function on the passed object and return the cloned pointer:

Listing 5.16: Making objects and pointer containers cloneable

```
 1 #include <boost/ptr_container/ptr_vector.hpp>
 2 #include <boost/noncopyable.hpp>
 3 #include <string>
 4 #include <iostream>
 5
 6 namespace nature
 7 {
 8
 9 class Animal : boost::noncopyable
10 {
11 public:
12   // ...
13   virtual Animal *clone() const = 0;
14 };
15
16 class SnowLeopard : public Animal
17 {
18 public:
19   // ...
20   SnowLeopard *clone() const override
21   {
22     return new SnowLeopard(name_);
23   }
24
25 private:
26   std::string name_;
27 };
28
29 class Puma : public Animal
30 {
31 public:
32   // ...
33   Puma *clone() const override
34   {
35     return new Puma(name_);
```

```
36    }
37
38 private:
39    std::string name_;
40 };
41
42 Animal *new_clone(const Animal& animal)
43 {
44    return animal.clone();
45 }
46
47 } // end of namespace nature
48
49 int main()
50 {
51    boost::ptr_vector<nature::Animal> animals, animals2;
52
53    animals.push_back(new nature::Puma("Kaju"));
54    animals.push_back(new nature::SnowLeopard("Rongi"));
55    animals.push_back(new nature::Puma("Juki"));
56
57    animals2 = animals.clone();
58
59    for (auto&animal : animals2) {
60      std::cout <<animal.name() << '\n';
61    }
62 }
```

For full generality, we put the `Animal` and its derived classes into a namespace called nature (line 6), and add a pure virtual function called `clone` in `Animal` (line 13). We override the clone method in each of the two derived classes (line 33, 42), and implement the `new_clone` free function in terms of the `clone` method. We declare two `ptr_vector` containers of `nature::Animal` pointers: `animals` and `animals2` (line 51), initialize `animals` with three furry mammals (lines 53-55), and finally, assign the clone of `animals` to `animals2` (line 57). What if instead of the call to `clone`, we write the following:

```
57    animals2 = animals;
```

In this case, the line would fail to compile because `Animal` is abstract and noncopyable, and the preceding line would try to slice each stored object in `animals` and copy it to `animals2`. If `Animal` was copyable and nonabstract, such a line would have compiled, but `animals2` would contain some hapless, sliced `Animals`.

The pointer containers support moving ownership of objects from one container to another, even when the containers are of different types. You can move a single element, a range of elements, or the entire contents of one container to another, in operations reminiscent of `slice` in Standard Library `std::list`. The following example illustrates some of these techniques:

Listing 5.17: Moving pointers between containers

```
1  #include <boost/ptr_container/ptr_vector.hpp>
2  #include <boost/ptr_container/ptr_list.hpp>
3  #include <cassert>
4  #include <iostream>
5  // definitions of Animal, SnowLeopard, Puma in namespace nature
6
7  int main()
8  {
9    boost::ptr_vector<nature::Animal> mountA;
10   boost::ptr_vector<nature::Animal> mountB;
11   boost::ptr_list<nature::Animal> mountC;
12
13   mountA.push_back(new nature::Puma("Kaju"));
14   mountA.push_back(new nature::SnowLeopard("Rongi"));
15   mountA.push_back(new nature::Puma("Juki"));
16   mountA.push_back(new nature::SnowLeopard("Turo"));
17
18   size_t num_animals = mountA.size();
19
20   for (auto&animal : mountA) {
21     std::cout << "MountA: " <<animal.name() << '\n';
22   }
23
24   // Move all contents
25   mountB = mountA.release();
26   assert(mountA.size() == 0);
27   assert(mountB.size() == num_animals);
28
29   // move one element
30   mountC.transfer(mountC.begin(), mountB.begin() + 1, mountB);
31   assert(mountB.size() == num_animals - 1);
32   assert(mountC.size() == 1);
33
34   // move one element, second way
35   auto popped = mountB.pop_back();
36   mountC.push_back(popped.release());
```

```
37
38    assert(mountB.size() + mountC.size() == num_animals);
39    assert(mountC.size() == 2);
40
41    // move a range of elements
42    mountC.transfer(mountC.end(), mountB.begin(),
43                    mountB.end(), mountB);
44    assert(mountB.size() + mountC.size() == num_animals);
45    assert(mountC.size() == num_animals);
46
47    for (auto&animal : mountC) {
48      std::cout << "MountC: " <<animal.name() << '\n';
49    }
50 }
```

The preceding example illustrates all the different techniques of moving elements from one container to another. Two Pumas (Kaju and Juki) and two SnowLeopards (Rongi and Turo) are on mountain A, so the vector mountA stores the animals on mountain A. The four animals decide to move to mountain B; the vector mountB is empty to start with. Then, the four Animals move to mountain B, so we move the contents of mountA to mountB, using the release method of mountA (line 25). Following this, there are no more Animals in mountA (line 26) while mountB contains all four (line 27). Now the animals want to cross over to mountain C, and it is a different kind of mountain that is difficult to climb. The animals on mountain C are tracked in a ptr_list called mountC (rather than a ptr_vector). To start with, Rongi, the snow leopard (the second element in mountB) shows the way and is the first to climb mountain C. So we move the second element of mountB to the beginning of mountC, using the transfer member function of mountC (line 30). Next, Turo, the other snow leopard ventures to cross over to C. We move the last element of mountB to the end of mountC by first popping it off the end of mountB (line 35), then calling release on the popped object, and appending the returned pointer to mountC (line 36). At this point, there are two more Animals on mountB (line 39). The remaining elements (two pumas) are moved from mountB to the end of mountC by a call to the transfer member function of mountC (lines 42, 43), thus completing the exodus of the animals (line 45).

The first argument to transfer is the iterator identifying the position in the destination container, where the moved elements are inserted. In the three-parameter overload (line 30), the second argument identifies the iterator to the element in the source container, which needs to be moved, and the third argument is a reference to the source container. In the four-parameter overload, the second and third arguments identify the range of elements from the source container that need to be moved, and the fourth argument is the reference to the source container.

If you are on pre-C++11, you cannot use the `auto` keyword to do away with type names you do not care about (line 35). In that case, you will need to store the result of `pop_back()` (or other methods that remove and return an element from the container) in a variable of type `container::auto_type`. For example:

```
33   boost::ptr_vector<nature::Animal>::auto_type popped =
34                                    mountB.pop_back();
```

Null pointers in pointer containers

Given the fact that pointer containers store pointers and give out references to the underlying objects, what happens if you store a null pointer? By default, pointer containers do not allow null pointers and trying to store a null pointer would duly cause an exception to be thrown at runtime. You can override this behavior and tell the compiler to allow storing nulls. To do this, you have to modify your container definition slightly, to use:

```
boost::ptr_container<boost::nullable<Animal>> animals;
```

Instead of:

```
boost::ptr_container< Animal> animals;
```

The advantages are limited, and you have to additionally make sure you do not dereference a potential null pointer. Your code becomes complex, and it becomes difficult to use range-based for-loops. Here is an example:

```
1 std::ptr_vector< boost::nullable<Animal>> animalsAndNulls;
2 ... // assign animals
3
4 for (auto it = animalsAndNulls.begin();
5 it != animalsAndNulls.end(); ++it)
6 {
7   if (!boost::is_null(it)) {
8     Animal& a = *it;
9     // do stuff ...
10   }
11 }
```

It is best to avoid storing null pointers, and instead, use the Null Object Pattern that the library author recommends. You can see the Boost online documentation for more details on the Null Object Pattern (http://www.boost.org/doc/libs/1_57_0/libs/ptr_container/doc/guidelines.html#avoid-null-pointers-in-containers-if-possible).

In summary, the Boost Pointer Containers are a full-featured set of containers for pointers to dynamically-allocated objects and are well suited for handling polymorphic objects. In C++11, one alternative way of achieving similar semantics is via containers of `std::unique_ptr<T>`. With sufficient optimization, the overhead of the `unique_ptr` wrapper is likely to be minimal, and the performance comparable to that of Boost's pointer container. While using containers of `boost::shared_ptr<T>` (T being the type of the dynamically-allocated objects) serves the use cases described here, they have higher memory and runtime overhead and are not optimal unless shared ownership semantics are needed.

Expressive initialization and assignment using Boost.Assign

Initializing an object or assigning some literal value to it using a single statement is a succinct way of generating the contents of the object. It is easy to do this for simple variables like numeric variables or strings, because there are readily available literals. On the other hand, there are no simple syntactic means of initializing containers with arbitrary sets of values. This is because expressing more complex objects with nontrivial internal data structures as literals is difficult. Using some ingenious patterns and overloaded operators, the Boost.Assign library makes it possible to initialize and assign values to a whole host of STL and Boost containers, using a very expressive syntax.

With the availability of the new **initializer list** and **uniform initialization** syntax in C++11, these tasks can be accomplished without Boost.Assign. Still Boost.Assign is the only means of getting the job done on pre-C++11, and also provides some nifty additional capabilities not easily available via initializer lists and uniform initialization.

Assigning lists of values to containers

Boost.Assign is one of those nifty little libraries in Boost, which you get into the habit of using at the smallest opportunity. Here is an example:

Listing 5.18: Assigning a list of values to a vector

```
1 #include <string>
2 #include <vector>
3 #include <boost/assign.hpp>
4 #include <cassert>
5
```

```
 6 using namespace boost::assign;
 7
 8 int main()
 9 {
10   std::vector<std::string>greetings;
11   greetings += "Good morning", "Buenos dias", "Bongiorno";
12   greetings += "Boker tov", "Guten Morgen", "Bonjour";
13
14   assert(greetings.size() == 6);
15 }
```

Assigning a list of values to a vector was never as much fun as with Boost.Assign. By overloading the comma operator (`operator,`) and `operator+=`, the Boost Assign library provides an easy way to append a list of values to a vector. In order to use the operators, we include `boost/assign.hpp` (line 3). The `using namespace` directive makes the operators defined in Boost Assign available in the global scope (line 6). Without this, we would not be able to freely use the operators and the expressiveness would be gone. We append three "good morning" greetings in English, French, and Italian to the vector `greetings` (line 11), and then three more in Hebrew, German, and French (line 12). The net effect is a vector with six strings (line 14). We could have replaced the vector with a deque and this would have still worked. If you wanted an alternate mode of insertion like inserting at the head of a list or deque or inserting into a map, Boost Assign can still work for you. Here is one more example:

Listing 5.19: Assigning elements to other containers

```
 1 #include <string>
 2 #include <map>
 3 #include <list>
 4 #include <deque>
 5 #include <boost/assign.hpp>
 6 #include <iostream>
 7 #include <boost/tuple/tuple.hpp>
 8
 9 using namespace boost::assign;
10
11 int main(){
12   std::deque<std::string>greets;
13   push_front(greets) = "Good night", "Buenas noches",
14        "Bounanotte", "Lyla tov", "Gute nacht", "Bonne nuit";
15
16   std::map<std::string, std::string> rockCharacters;
17   insert(rockCharacters)
18        ("John Barleycorn", "must die")       // Traffic
19        ("Eleanor Rigby", "lives in a dream") // Beatles
20        ("Arnold Layne", "had a strange hobby")   // Floyd
```

```
21              ("Angie", "can't say we never tried")     // Stones
22              ("Harry", "play the honkytonk"); // Dire Straits
23
24      std::list<boost::tuple<std::string, std::string,
25                          std::string>> trios;
25      push_back(trios)("Athos", "Porthos", "Aramis")
26                      ("Potter", "Weasley", "Granger")
27                      ("Tintin", "Snowy", "Haddock")
28                      ("Geller", "Bing", "Tribbiani")
29                      ("Jones", "Crenshaw", "Andrews");
30
31      std::cout << "Night greets:\n";
32      for (const auto& greet: greets) {
33        std::cout << greet << '\n';
34      }
35
36      std::cout << "\nPeople:\n";
37      for (const auto&character: rockCharacters) {
38        std::cout << character.first << ": "
39                  << character.second << '\n';
40      }
41
42      std::cout << "Trios:\n";
43      for (auto& trio: trios) {
44        std::cout << boost::get<0>(trio) << ", "
45                  << boost::get<1>(trio) << ", "
46                  << boost::get<2>(trio) << '\n';
47      }
48 }
```

Here, we see examples of assigning values to three different kinds of containers. We first push six "good night" greets in different languages into the head of a std::deque (lines 13-14). We do this using the push_front adaptor from Boost Assign which invokes the method of the same name push_front on the deque greets. It should be clear that after this operation, the last string in the list ("Bonne nuit") sits at the front of the queue.

If you have had a thing for rock 'n' roll and are as old as I am, you would perhaps identify the characters in the next example: an std::map of characters from rock 'n' roll songs and albums, and what they did (according to those songs). Using the insert adaptor, which calls the method of the same name, on the map rockCharacters, we insert five pairs of strings—each mapping a character to an act (lines 17-22). The insert adaptor and other adaptors like it return an object with an overloaded operator() which can be chained. By chaining calls to this operator, the list of values is created.

The last container we use is a `std::list`, and for fun, we keep a list of famous trios from fiction. The `boost::tuple` template can be used to define tuples of an arbitrary number of elements of different types. Here, we use a `boost::tuple` of three strings to represent a trio, and keep a list of such trios in the variable `trios` (line 24). The `push_back` adaptor from Boost Assign is used to append the trios to the end of the list. The operator `+=` used in listing 5.17 with `std::vector` calls `push_back` on the underlying container. However, in this case, the `push_back` adaptor needs to be used to allow tuples of values to be pushed into the list.

Next, we print the content of the data structures. To access each element of each tuple in the list `trios`, we use the `boost::get` template that accesses the elements in tuples by a 0-based index (lines 44-45). Running this code prints the following output:

```
Night greets:
Bonne nuit
Gute nacht
Lyla tov
Bounanotte
Buenas noches
Good night
People:
Angie: can't say we never tried
Arnold Layne: had a strange hobby
Eleanor Rigby: lives in a dream
John Barleycorn: must die
Harry: play the honkytonk
People:
Athos,Porthos, Aramis
Potter,Weasley, Granger
Tintin,Snowy, Haddock
Jones,Crenshaw, Andrews
```

Initializing containers with lists of values

In the previous examples, we saw various ways of appending or inserting values into a container, but Boost.Assign also lets you initialize containers with values at the time of construction. The syntax is slightly different from what is used for assignments:

Listing 5.20: Aggregate initialization with Boost Assign

```
1 #include <boost/assign.hpp>
2 #include <boost/rational.hpp>
3 #include <iterator>
4
```

```
 5 using namespace boost::assign;
 6
 7 int main()
 8 {
 9   std::cout << "Catalan numbers:\n";
10   const std::vector<int> catalan = list_of(1)(1)(2)(5)
11                         (14)(42)(132)(429)(1430)(4862);
12
13   std::ostream_iterator<int>os(std::cout, " ");
14   std::copy(catalan.begin(), catalan.end(), os);
15
16   std::cout << "\nBernoulli numbers:\n";
17   const std::map<int, boost::rational<int>>bernoulli =
18                         map_list_of(0, boost::rational<int>(1))
19                             (1, boost::rational<int>(1, 2))
20                             (2, boost::rational<int>(1, 6))
21                             (3, boost::rational<int>(0))
22                             (4, boost::rational<int>(-1, 30))
23                             (5, boost::rational<int>(0))
24                             (6, boost::rational<int>(1, 42))
25                             (7, boost::rational<int>(0));
26
27   for (auto&b : bernoulli) {
28     std::cout << 'B' << b.first << ": " << b.second << ", ";
29   }
30   std::cout << '\n';
31 }
```

The preceding example constructs a vector of the first ten Catalan Numbers.
The nth Catalan number (n being a nonnegative integer) equals the number of
permutations of a string containing n left parentheses and n right parentheses in
which all parentheses are correctly matched. We use the `list_of` adaptor from the
`boost::assign` namespace to construct the list of first ten Catalan numbers with
which the vector `catalan` is initialized (lines 10-11). We use an `ostream_iterator`
to print this list (lines 13-14).

Next, we create a `std::map` containing the first eight Bernoulli numbers: the keys are
the ordinal positions and the values are the numbers themselves. Bernoulli numbers
are a sequence of rational numbers (expressible as a ratio of two integers) that arise
in number theory and combinatorics. For initializing such a map, we use the `map_`
`list_of` adaptor passing keys and values as shown (lines 17-25). For representing
a rational number, we use the `boost::rational` template defined in the header
`boost/rational.hpp`.

This code prints the following output:

```
Catalan numbers:
1 1 2 5 14 42 132 429 1430 4862
Bernoulli numbers:
B0: 1/1, B1: 1/2, B2: 1/6, B3: 0/1, B4: -1/30, B5: 0/1, B6: 1/42, B7:
0/1,
```

Interestingly, you can also create anonymous sequences using Boost Assign. These sequences can be constructed either as a sequence of non-constant l-value references or as a sequence of const l-value references that can admit literals. They are more efficient to construct than `list_of` and can be used in its place for initializing sequence containers like vectors. These sequences comply with the Boost Range concept and can be used anywhere a range can be used. Here is an example:

Listing 5.21: Creating anonymous sequences

```
 1 #include <boost/assign.hpp>
 2 #include <iostream>
 3
 4 using namespace boost::assign;
 5
 6 template<typename RangeType>
 7 int inspect_range(RangeType&& rng)
 8 {
 9   size_t sz = boost::size(rng);
10
11   if (sz > 0) {
12     std::cout << "First elem: " << *boost::begin(rng) << '\n';
13     std::cout <<"Last elem: " << *(boost::end(rng) - 1) << '\n';
14   }
15
16   return sz;
17 }
18
19 int main()
20 {
21   std::cout << inspect_range(
22             cref_list_of<10>(1)(2)(3)(4)(5)(6)(7)(8));
23
24   typedef std::map<std::string, std::string> strmap_t;
25   strmap_t helloWorlds =
26           cref_list_of<3, strmap_t::value_type>
```

```
27                    (strmap_t::value_type("hello", "world"))
28                    (strmap_t::value_type("hola", "el mundo"))
29                    (strmap_t::value_type("hallo", "Welt"));
30 }
```

We create an anonymous sequence of size ten using the `cref_list_of` adaptor, but actually put only eight values in it (line 22). If we had variables to put in the sequence instead of character literals, we could have used the `ref_list_of` adaptor, and this would have created a mutable sequence. We use `boost::size`, `boost::begin` and `boost::end` functions for operating on ranges to determine the length of the sequence (line 9) and its first and last elements (lines 12-13). Next, we use an anonymous list of string pairs to initialize a `std::map` (lines 26-29). Note that `value_type` nested typedef in a map represents the type of each key-value pair in the map.

C++11 introduces the very handy aggregate initialization syntax using which arbitrary containers can be initialized. It is syntactically simpler to perform initialization using the aggregate initializer syntax than Boost Assign and is likely more efficient. In pre-C++11 environments, Boost Assign's initialization syntax remains the only choice. Here are a few examples of C++11 aggregate initialization:

```
1 std::vector<std::string>scholars{"Ibn Sina", "Ibn Rushd",
2                                   "Al Khwarizmi", "Al Kindi"};
3std::map<std::string, std::string> scholarsFrom
4={{scholars[0], "Bukhara"},
5     {scholars[1], "Cordoba"},
6{scholars[2], "Khwarezm"},
7                                 {scholars[3], "Basra"}};
```

This snippet shows the way to use a comma-separated list of values enclosed in curly braces to initialize collections. The `scholars` vector is initialized with names of four Muslim scholars from the Middle Ages, and then the `scholarsFrom` map is initialized with the names of those scholars as keys and their places of origin as the values. Note how each key-value pair is enclosed in braces in a comma-separated list of such pairs. Also, note that we freely use l-values (like `scholars[0]`) as well as literals in the initializer.

Initializing pointer containers and assigning values

The Boost Assign library provides special support for assigning values to pointer containers and initializing pointer containers in an exception-safe way.

The following short example summarizes the usage:

Listing 5.22: Boost Assign with pointer containers

```cpp
 1 #include <boost/ptr_container/ptr_vector.hpp>
 2 #include <boost/ptr_container/ptr_map.hpp>
 3 #include <boost/assign/ptr_list_inserter.hpp>
 4 #include <boost/assign/ptr_map_inserter.hpp>
 5 #include <boost/assign/ptr_list_of.hpp>
 6 #include <string>
 7 #include <iostream>
 8
 9 using namespace boost::assign;
10
11 struct WorkShift
12 {
13   WorkShift(double start = 9.30, double end = 17.30)
14     : start_(start), end_(end)
15   {}
16
17   double start_, end_;
18 };
19
20 std::ostream& operator<<(std::ostream& os, const WorkShift& ws)
21 {
22   return os << "[" << ws.start_ <<" till " << ws.end_ << "]";
23 }
24
25 int main()
26 {
27   boost::ptr_vector<WorkShift> shifts = ptr_list_of<WorkShift>
28                             (6.00, 14.00)();
29   ptr_push_back(shifts)(14.00, 22.00)(22.00, 6.00);
30
31   boost::ptr_map<std::string, WorkShift> shiftMap;
32   ptr_map_insert(shiftMap)("morning", 6.00, 14.00)("day")
33           ("afternoon", 14.00, 22.00)("night", 22.00, 6.00);
34
35   for (const auto& entry: shiftMap) {
36     std::cout << entry.first <<" " <<shiftMap.at(entry.first)
37               << '\n';
38   }
39 }
```

In this example, we define a type `WorkShift` that represents a shift at a workplace and encapsulates information about work hours for a particular shift. Its constructor takes two arguments, the start and end time of the shift, and defaults them to 9.30 and 17.30 (line 12). We create a `ptr_vector` of `WorkShift` objects and initialize them, using the `ptr_list_of` adaptor. Instead of passing constructed objects, we pass constructor arguments for two objects: a shift between 6.00 and 14.00 and another shift with a default start and end time (line 28).

The template argument to `ptr_list_of` denotes which type to instantiate. We add two more shifts to the `ptr_vector` called `shifts`, using the `ptr_push_back` adaptor. Next, we make a `ptr_map` called `shiftMap` with string keys, identifying the type of shifts and pointers to shift objects for values (line 31). We then use the `ptr_map_insert` adaptor to insert the elements into the map. We create each entry by invoking `operator()`, passing the string key as the first argument and the constructor arguments for the `WorkShift` object as the remaining arguments (lines 32-33). We print the contents of the `ptr_map` (line 35-38), using the overloaded streaming operator for `WorkShift` (line 19). The following is the output of this program:

```
afternoon [14 till 22]
general [9.3 till 17.3]
morning [6 till 14]
night [22 till 6]
```

It is important to understand why a separate class of adaptors is used for initializing pointer containers. The following, for example, is a perfectly a valid code:

```
1 boost::ptr_vector<WorkShift> shifts;
2 boost::assign:push_back(shifts)(new WorkShift())
3                         (new WorkShift(6.00, 14.00));
```

However, in this example, the user of the library (that is us) manually allocates two new `WorkShift` objects. The order in which these get allocated is not guaranteed by the compiler. Only the order in which they are appended to `shifts` is guaranteed (via calls to the overloaded `operator()` in the adaptor returned by `boost::assign::push_back`). So, for the preceding sample, the compiler could generate code roughly equivalent to the following:

```
1 boost::ptr_vector<WorkShift> shifts;
2 WorkShift *w1 = new WorkShift(6.00, 14.00);
3 WorkShift *w2 = new WorkShift();
4 boost::assign::push_back(shifts)(w2)(w1);
```

If the constructor of `WorkShift` threw while `w2` was constructed (line 3), then `w1` would be leaked. In order to ensure exception-safety, we should use `ptr_push_back`:

```
1 boost::ptr_vector<WorkShift> shifts;
2 boost::assign::ptr_push_back(shifts)()(6.00, 14.00);
```

Instead, the overloaded `operator()` in the `boost::assign::ptr_push_back` adaptor takes the constructor arguments for each `WorkShift` object that needs to be in the `shifts` container and constructs each `WorkShift` object, forwarding those arguments to the `WorkShift` constructor. The call returns only after the constructed object is in the container. This ensures that at the time of construction of a `WorkShift` object, all previously constructed `WorkShift` objects are already part of the container. So if the constructor throws, the container along with the previously-constructed objects are released.

Iteration patterns using Boost.Iterator

Iteration is a fundamental task in most programming problems, whether it is iterating through the elements of a container, a series of natural numbers, or the files in a directory. By abstracting how a collection of values is iterated through, we can write generic code to process such a collection without depending on methods of iteration specific to each collection.

The Standard Library containers expose iterators for this purpose, and the generic algorithms in the Standard Library can operate on any conforming container through its iterators, without depending on the specific type of the container or its internal structure.

The Boost.Iterator library provides a framework for writing iterators for custom classes that conform to the standards and are compatible with algorithms in the Standard Library. It also helps generalize iteration concepts to more abstract object collections, not limited to containers.

Smart iteration using Boost.Iterator

The Boost Iterator library provides a number of iterator adaptors that make iterating over containers and sequences of values more expressive and efficient. An iterator adaptor wraps an iterator to produce another iterator. The adapted iterator may or may not iterate over the entire range of elements addressed by the underlying iterator. Also, they can be designed to return a different value, potentially of a different type than the underlying iterator. In this section, we look at a few examples of such iterator adaptors from Boost.

Filter Iterator

The filter iterators iterate over a subsequence of an underlying sequence of elements. They wrap an underlying iterator sequence and take a unary Boolean predicate, which is used to determine which elements to include from the underlying range, and which ones to skip. The predicate takes an element of the underlying sequence as a single argument and returns true or false. The ones for which true is returned are included in the iteration, the rest are filtered out; hence the name.

You can create filter iterators by using the `boost::make_filter_iterator` function template. You pass it a unary function object (functor, lambda, or function pointer) that returns `bool`. You also pass it not one, but two iterators: the one it wraps and another one marking the end of sequence. In the following example, we have a list of `Person` objects, and we need to write code to make a payout of 100 dollars to the bank account of each person who is seventy years of age or older:

Listing 5.23: Using filter iterators

```
 1 #include <boost/iterator/filter_iterator.hpp>
 2 #include <boost/assign.hpp>
 3 #include <vector>
 4 #include <string>
 5 #include <iostream>
 6
 7 struct Person
 8 {
 9   std::string name;
10   int age;
11   std::string bank_ac_no;
12
13   Person(const std::string& name, int years,
14         const std::string& ac_no) :
15         name(name), age(years), bank_ac_no(ac_no) {}
16 };
17
17 void payout(double sum, const std::string& ac_no) {
19   std::cout << "Credited a sum of "<< sum
20           <<" to bank account number " << ac_no << '\n';
21 }
22
23 template<typename Itertype>
24 void creditSum(Itertype first, Itertype last, double sum)
```

```
25 {
26   while (first != last) {
27     payout(sum, first->bank_ac_no);
28     first++;
29   }
30 }
31
32 bool seventyOrOlder(const Person& person)
33 {
34   return person.age >= 70;
35 }
36
37 int main()
38 {
39   std::vector<Person> people{{"A Smith", 71, "5702750"},
40                   {"S Bates", 56, "3920774"},
41                   {"L Townshend", 73, "9513914"},
42                   {"L Milford", 68, "1108419"},
43                   {"F Cornthorpe", 81, "8143919"}};
44
45   auto first = boost::make_filter_iterator(seventyOrOlder,
46                              people.begin(), people.end());
47
48   auto last = boost::make_filter_iterator(seventyOrOlder,
49                              people.end(), people.end());
50
51   creditSum(first, last, 100);
52 }
```

In this example, the function payout takes an account number and an amount and initiates a payment to the account (line 17). The function creditSum takes a pair of iterators defining a sequence of Person objects and an amount, and initiates a payment of that amount to each Person in the sequence, calling payout for each (line 23-24). We have a vector of Person objects (line 39), which we initialize with the details of five people, using the uniform initialization syntax from C++11. We cannot directly call creditSum on the entire range of elements in the vector because we only want to credit it to people who are seventy or older. To do this, we first define the predicate function seventyOrOlder (line 32) that helps us select the candidate entries, and then define the filter iterators first and last (lines 45-49). Finally, we call creditSum with the pair of filter iterators and the sum to credit (line 51).

Transform Iterator

Transform iterators allow you to traverse a sequence, and when dereferenced, return the result of applying a unary function to the underlying element of the sequence. You can construct transform iterators using `boost::make_tranform_iterator`, passing it the unary function object and the underlying iterator.

Consider `std::map` objects containing subject names as keys and subjects scores as values. We use transform iterators to compute the sum of the scores in all the subjects, as shown in the following example:

Listing 5.24: Using transform iterators

```
 1 #include <iostream>
 2 #include <string>
 3 #include <vector>
 4 #include <map>
 5 #include <algorithm>
 6 #include <functional>
 7 #include <boost/assign.hpp>
 8 #include <boost/iterator/transform_iterator.hpp>
 9 #include <numeric> // for std::accumulate
10 using namespace boost::assign;
11
12 typedef std::map<std::string, int> scoremap;
13
14 struct GetScore : std::unary_function<
15                         const scoremap::value_type&, int>
16 {
17   result_type operator()(argument_type entry) const
18   {
19     return entry.second;
20   }
21 };
22
23 int main()
24 {
25   scoremap subjectScores{{"Physics", 80}, {"Chemistry", 78},
26                       {"Statistics", 88}, {"Mathematics", 92}};
27
28   boost::transform_iterator<GetScore,
```

```
29                              scoremap::iterator>
30                          first(subjectScores.begin(), GetScore()),
31                          last(subjectScores.end(), GetScore());
32
33    std::cout << std::accumulate(first, last, 0) << '\n';
34 }
```

The map `subjectScores` contains the scores in individual subjects stored against each subject name. We use the C++11 uniform initialization syntax to initialize the map (lines 25-26). We want to iterate through the values in this map and compute their sum. Iterating through `subjectScores` will give us key-value pairs of subject names and scores. To extract the score from a pair, we define a functor `GetScore` (lines 14-15). We then define a pair of transform iterators `first` and `last`, each constructed using an instance of the `GetScore` functor and the underlying iterator, and pointing to the beginning and end of the `subjectScores` map (lines 28-31). By calling `std::accumulate` from `first` to `last`, we sum over the scores in the map (line 33) and print the result.

Notice that `GetScore` derives from `std::unary_function<ArgType, RetType>`, where `ArgType` is the type of the functor's single argument and `RetType` is return type of the functor. This is not required for C++11, and you do not need to derive `GetScore` from any specific class in C++11.

Like `boost::transform_iterator`, the `std::transform` algorithm allows applying a transform to each element in a sequence, but you must also store the results in a sequence. The transform iterator allows you to create a lazy sequence whose elements are evaluated, as they are accessed without the binding need to store them anywhere.

Function Output Iterator

The function output iterators apply a unary function to each element that is assigned to them. You can create a function output iterator using the `boost::make_function_output_iterator` function template, passing it a unary function object. You can then use `std::copy` or a similar algorithm to assign elements from a sequence to the function output iterator. The function output iterator simply calls the function on each element assigned to it. You can encapsulate any logic in the function object you provide, print them enclosed in quotes, add them to another container, keep a count of elements processed, and so on.

In the following example, we have a list of directory names, and using the `boost::function_output_iterator`, we concatenate them together separated by spaces, making sure to quote any strings with embedded spaces:

Listing 5.25: Using function output iterators

```
 1 #include <iostream>
 2 #include <string>
 3 #include <vector>
 4 #include <algorithm>
 5 #include <boost/assign.hpp>
 6 #include <boost/function_output_iterator.hpp>
 7
 8 struct StringCat
 9 {
10   StringCat(std::string& str) : result_(str) {}
11
12   void operator()(const std::string& arg) {
13     if (arg.find_first_of(" \t") != std::string::npos) {
14       result_ += " \"" + arg + "\"";
15     } else {
16       result_ += " " + arg;
17     }
18   }
19
20   std::string& result_;
21 };
22
23 int main()
24 {
25   std::vector<std::string> dirs{"photos", "videos",
26                                 "books", "personal docs"};
27
28   std::string dirString = "";
29   std::copy(dirs.begin(), dirs.end(),
30           boost::make_function_output_iterator(
31   StringCat(dirString)));
32   std::cout << dirString << '\n';
33 }
```

We define a functor `StringCat` that stores a non-const reference to a `std::string` passed to its constructor (line 12) in a member called `result_`. It defines a unary `operator()`, which takes a single string parameter and appends it to `result_`. If the passed string has embedded spaces or tabs, it is quoted and appended with a leading space (line 14). Otherwise it is appended with a leading space without quoting (line 16).

We have a list of directory names called `dirs` (line 25-27), and we want to append them following this scheme to a string called `dirString` (line 28). To do this, we create an instance of `StringCat`, passing it a reference to `dirString` (line 31), and pass this to `boost::make_function_output_iterator`, which returns an output iterator (line 30). We use `std::copy` to copy the elements from `dirs` into the output iterator returned, which has the effect of concatenating the strings by making repeated calls to the `StringCat` functor. When `std::copy` returns, `dirString` has the following content:

```
photos videos books "personal docs"
```

You can see that `personal docs`, which is the name of a single directory, is appropriately quoted.

There are other iterator adaptors besides the ones listed above that we did not cover here, including `boost::indirect_iterator`, `boost::function_input_iterator`, `boost::zip_iterator`, `boost::counting_iterator`, and `boost::permutation_iterator`. Use the documentation on the Boost website to familiarize yourself with the patterns of their uses, and explore how you can use them in your own code.

Iterator adaptors provide a set of common idioms from functional programming languages and libraries like Python's **itertools**. Iterator adaptors are particularly useful when you have APIs that take a pair of iterators but have no option to filter or adapt the elements via functors or predicates. Much of what iterator adaptors enable can also be achieved by using the more modern Boost Range Adaptors, perhaps with less verbose syntax. However, if your APIs expect iterators instead of ranges, then these iterator adaptors will be handy.

Creating conforming iterators for custom classes

In addition to providing iterator adaptor templates, the Boost.Iterator library provides a framework for creating conforming iterators. In this section, we will use the Boost. Iterator library to create conforming iterators for a threaded binary search tree. A binary search tree is an abstract data type that stores elements in a tree structure. Loosely speaking, each node in the tree has zero, one, or two children. All elements in the left sub-tree of a node are smaller than the node, and all elements in the right sub-tree of a node are larger than the node. Nodes with zero children are called leaves. A threaded binary search tree is optimized for traversing its elements in a sorted order, the so-called **inorder traversal**.

We implement a naïve version of a threaded binary search tree, in which we will maintain pointers to the predecessor and successor of a node in each node. We will then provide a bidirectional iterator interface that will allow forward and reverse traversal of the tree in the order of its elements.

Listing 5.26: A naïve threaded binary search tree

```
 1 #include <iostream>
 2 #include <algorithm>
 3 #include <vector>
 4 #include <boost/assign.hpp>
 5 #include <boost/iterator.hpp>
 6 #include <boost/iterator/iterator_facade.hpp>
 7
 8 template<typename T>
 9 struct TreeNode
10 {
11   T data;
12   TreeNode<T> *left, *right;
13   TreeNode<T> *prev, *next;
14
15   TreeNode(const T& elem) : data(elem),
16           left(nullptr), right(nullptr),
17           prev(nullptr), next(nullptr)
18   {}
19
20   ~TreeNode()
21   {
22     delete left;
23     delete right;
24   }
25 };
26
27 template<typename T>
28 class BSTIterator :
29   public boost::iterator_facade <BSTIterator<T>, T,
30                     boost::bidirectional_traversal_tag>
31 {
32 public:
33   BSTIterator() : node_ptr(nullptr) {}
34   explicit BSTIterator(TreeNode<T> *node) :
35       node_ptr(node) {}
36   BSTIterator(const BSTIterator<T>& that) :
37       node_ptr(that.node_ptr) {}
38
```

```
39 private:
40    TreeNode<T> *node_ptr;
41
42    friend class boost::iterator_core_access;
43
44    void increment() { node_ptr = node_ptr->next; }
45    void decrement() { node_ptr = node_ptr->prev; }
46
47    bool equal(const BSTIterator<T>& that) const {
48      return node_ptr == that.node_ptr;
49    }
50
51    T& dereference() const { return node_ptr->data; }
52 };
53
54 template<typename T>
55 class BinarySearchTree
56 {
57 public:
58    BinarySearchTree() : root(nullptr), first(nullptr),
59                          last(nullptr) {}
60    ~BinarySearchTree() {
61      delete root;
62      delete last;
63    }
64
65    void insert(const T& elem) {
66      if (!root) {
67        root = new TreeNode<T>(elem);
68        first = root;
69        last = new TreeNode<T>(T());
70        first->next = last;
71        last->prev = first;
72      } else {
73        insert(elem, root);
74      }
75    }
76
```

```
 77    BSTIterator<T>begin() { return BSTIterator<T>(first); }
 78    BSTIterator<T>end() { return BSTIterator<T>(last); }
 79
 80    BSTIterator<T>begin() const {
 81      return BSTIterator<const T>(first);
 82    }
 83    BSTIterator<T>end() const {
 84      return BSTIterator<const T>(last);
 85    }
 86
 87 private:
 88    TreeNode<T> *root;
 89    TreeNode<T> *first;
 90    TreeNode<T> *last;
 91
 92    void insert(const T& elem, TreeNode<T> *node) {
 93      if (elem < node->data) {
 94        if (node->left) {
 95          insert(elem, node->left);
 96        } else {
 97          node->left = new TreeNode<T>(elem);
 98          node->left->prev = node->prev;
 99          node->prev = node->left;
100          node->left->next = node;
101
102          if (!node->left->prev) {
103            first = node->left;
104          } else {
105            node->left->prev->next = node->left;
106          }
107        }
108      } else if (node->data < elem) {
109        if (node->right) {
110          insert(elem, node->right);
111        } else {
112          node->right = new TreeNode<T>(elem);
113          node->right->next = node->next;
114          node->next = node->right;
115          node->right->prev = node;
116
```

```
117              if (node->right->next) {
118                node->right->next->prev = node->right;
119              }
120            }
121          }
122        }
123    };
```

We can use the `BinarySearchTree` template in the following code:

```
125  int main()
126  {
127    BinarySearchTree<std::string> bst;
128    bst.insert("abc");
129    bst.insert("def");
130    bst.insert("xyz");
131
132    for(auto& x: bst) {
133      std::cout << x << '\n';
134    }
135  }
```

This example helps us illustrate the techniques for creating custom iterators for a not too trivial data structure, using the Boost Iterator framework. The threaded tree implementation is made deliberately simple to aid understanding. `TreeNode<T>` represents each node in a tree containing values of a parameterized type `T`. `BinarySearchTree<T>` represents a binary search tree that supports inorder traversal. It stores three pointers of type `TreeNode<T>`: the root of the tree, the pointer `first` to the smallest element, and a sentinal pointer `last`, representing the end of the traversal (lines 68-70). Finally, `BSTIterator<T>` represents the type of a bidirectional iterator to `BinarySearchTree<T>`, one that allows inorder traversal through the elements of the tree in both directions.

`TreeNode<T>` stores two pointers to its `left` and `right` children and two more to its nodes that precede (`prev`) and follow (`next`) it in order of the values they store (lines 12-13). A new node is always inserted as a leaf node, and the `prev` and `next` pointers of the new node and the ones that precede and follow it in a traversal order are readjusted appropriately. New elements are inserted into the tree using the `insert` public method, and the actual logic for insertion is in the private overload of the `insert` method (lines 72-102).The `begin` and `end` methods of `BinarySearchTree` return iterators to the first element in the tree and another node, marking the end of traversal.

The BSTIterator template, which is the iterator implementation that we are most interested in, derives from a specialization of boost::iterator_facade (lines 29-30). The specialization takes three arguments: BSTIterator<T> itself, the type parameter T, and a tag boost::bidirectional_traversal_tag to identify the type of traversal the iterator supports (bidirectional in this case). The base template taking the derived class as an argument is a well-known C++ idiom called **Curiously Recurring Template Parameter** and is used to achieve the effect of virtual method calls without the runtime cost of it. We now define a set of members to finish the implementation.

The BSTIterator template keeps a TreeNode<T> pointer to a node in the tree (line 40). This is initialized using a default constructor and the one that takes a node pointer (lines 33-35). Also, importantly, we must make BSTIterator copyable (lines 36-37). We define a set of private member functions, which are accessed by the Boost Iterator framework. The framework code accesses these functions via a class called boost::iterator_core_access, which is therefore defined as a friend class (line 42). The functions increment (line 44) and decrement (line 45) are called when we increment or decrement the iterator using operator++ or operator--. They change the internal node pointer to point to the next or previous node in the traversal order (inorder). The function dereference is called when we dereference the iterator using operator*. It returns a reference to the data element stored in each node (line 51). The equal method is used to check whether two iterators are equal to each other. This is invoked when, for example, you check if an iterator has reached the end of the sequence of values in a container with code like:

```
if (it == container.end())
```

This is all we need to do to define a fully functional iterator. There is one additional bit of work that has to be done inside the container. We define the begin and end methods that return the start and end of the sequence of values in the container (lines 77-78). These pointers, first (line 89) and last (line 90), are maintained as additional members and suitably updated by the BinarySearchTree template. The pointer first is updated each time a new smallest element is inserted into the container. The pointer last, which represents a sentinel beyond which the forward traversal can never proceed, is created initially and never updated (line 69). Each time a new largest element is added to the tree, its next pointer points to last. The const versions of begin and end member functions (lines 80-85) are provided to ensure that calling them on a constant container give immutable iterators. Following essentially the same pattern, you can roll out your own iterators for your containers that are compliant with the Standard Library's iterator concepts. A number of Standard Library algorithms may be used on your custom container via such an iterator interface. The concise implementation of the iterator (lines 27-51) is made possible by the abstractions provided by the Boost Iterator framework.

Self-test questions

For multiple choice questions, choose all the options that apply:

1. Which of the following are true for flat associative containers compared to ordered/unordered associative containers?

    a. Require less memory

    b. Insertion is faster

    c. Traversal is slower

    d. Lookups are faster

2. The `std::forward_list` does not provide a `size()` member function because:

    a. Linear time size members cannot be supported for singly-linked lists

    b. Both splice and size members cannot be constant time

    c. It would be thread-unsafe

    d. All of the above

3. Where is the internal memory of a `static_vector` allocated:

    a. Stack

    b. Depends on where the static vector is created

    c. Free store

    d. Depends on the allocator used

4. In order to store objects of type X in an unordered container, which of the following must be defined/available for objects of type X?

    a. Ordering relation

    b. Hash function

    c. Equality comparison

    d. Copy constructor

5. Which data structure allows random access to its elements and supports iterators that are not invalidated upon insertion and erase of other elements?

    a. `static_vector`

    b. `unordered_map`

    c. `stable_vector`

    d. `circular_buffer`

Summary

This chapter laid out a wide array of Boost libraries that provide different kinds of containers or make it easier to work with them. We looked at several useful nonstandard containers that extend the Standard Library containers, looked at containers designed to store dynamically-allocated object pointers, saw some expressive ways of assigning elements to containers, learned about hash-based unordered containers, and learned different patterns of iterating over collections and enabling iteration for custom collections.

In the next chapter, we will continue our study of container libraries from Boost and focus on specialized containers that support efficient lookup of objects based on multiple criteria.

References

Avoid null-pointers in containers (if possible): `http://www.boost.org/doc/libs/1_57_0/libs/ptr_container/doc/guidelines.html#avoid-null-pointers-in-containers-if-possible`

6
Bimap and Multi-index Containers

The Standard Library has ordered and unordered associative containers for storing objects and looking them up efficiently using some **key**. The key could be a text type, numeric type, or first-class objects. For ordered containers such as `std::set` and `std::map`, the keys must have a well-defined ordering relation that allows any set of keys to be sorted. For unordered containers, it must be possible to compute an integer hash value for each key, and additionally, determine whether any two keys are equivalent for some definition of equivalence. The key represents an index or criterion for lookup, and all the Standard Library associative containers support lookup using only a single criterion. In other words, you cannot efficiently look up objects using multiple, independent criteria.

Let us suppose you have a type called `PersonEntry` to describe a person. The `PersonEntry` type has attributes like name, age, phone number, and so on. You would end up storing several objects of type `PersonEntry` in containers and at different times, you may need to look up `PersonEntry` objects using different attributes like name, age, phone number, and so on. While the Standard Library containers do an admirable job for a lot of common tasks involving collections, they cut a sorry figure when you want a data structure that stores data and searches them efficiently based on multiple criteria. Boost provides a small number of generic containers geared for this need, two of which we study in this chapter. The chapter is divided into the following sections:

- Containers for multi-criteria lookups
- Boost Multi-index containers
- Boost Bimap

Containers for multi-criteria lookups

Consider a collection of objects of type `PersonEntry`, as defined in the following code:

```
1 struct PersonEntry
2 {
3   std::string name;
4   std::string phoneNumber;
5   std::string city;
6 };
```

An object of this type represents an entry in a telephone directory perhaps. How would you design a data structure that allows you to look up a person by name? We can use a `std::set` of `PersonEntry` objects for it, with an appropriate ordering relation defined for `PersonEntry`. Since we want to search by name, we should define the ordering relationship by name:

```
1 bool operator<(const PersonEntry& left,
2                const PersonEntry& right) {
3   return left.name< right.name;
4 }
```

Now `std::set` stores only unique elements and any two `PersonEntry` objects with the same name would be considered duplicates. Since namesakes are common in real life, we should choose a container that allows duplicates, that is, `std::multiset`. We can then insert elements and look them up by name using the following code:

Listing 6.1: Lookups using multimaps

```
1 #include <set>
2 #include <iostream>
3 #include <string>
4
5 struct PersonEntry {
6   std::string name;
7   std::string phoneNumber;
8   std::string city;
9 };
10
11 int main() {
```

```
12    std::multiset<PersonEntry> directory;
13    PersonEntry p1{"Arindam Mukherjee", "550 888 9999", "Pune"};
14    PersonEntry p2{"Arindam Mukherjee", "990 770 2458",
15                    "Calcutta"};
16    directory.insert(p1);
17    directory.insert(p2);
18    auto it1 = directory.lower_bound(
19                    PersonEntry{ "Arindam Mukherjee", "", "" });
20    auto it2 = directory.upper_bound(
21                    PersonEntry{ "Arindam Mukherjee", "", "" });
22
23    while (it1 != it2) {
24      std::cout << "Found: [" <<it1->name << ", "
25                  <<it1->phoneNumber << ", " <<it1->city << "]\n";
26      ++it1;
27    }
28  }
```

We create two `PersonEntry` objects of two people with the same name (lines 13-15) and insert them into a `multiset` (lines 16-17). The objects are initialized using C++11's nifty uniform initializer syntax. We then look up the name `"Arindam Mukherjee"`. The correct way to do this in a `multiset` is to determine the range of matching elements. The `lower_bound` member function returns the iterator to the first matching element (lines 18-19). The `upper_bound` member function returns the iterator to the first element to follow the last matching element (lines 20-21). If there are no matching elements, both return the iterator to the first element that would follow a matching element if there was one. We then iterate over the range defined by [low, high) and print all matching elements. If you noticed, we constructed temporary `PersonEntry` objects to perform the lookups. Now, it is perfectly reasonable to want to do a reverse lookup, given a phone number, and find out who it belongs to. How can we do this with the preceding arrangement? We could always perform a linear search through the container, or we could use a separate container of references to the `PersonEntry` objects in a dictionary that stores objects ordered by phone number; neither method is particularly elegant or efficient. This is where the Boost Multi-index library steps in.

Boost Multi-index containers

The Boost Multi-index library actually provides a single generic container called `multi_index_container` to store your objects and options to specify one or more indexes, using which you may look up the objects. Each index will use a different criterion on potentially different fields of the object. The indexes are defined and specified as template parameters to the container and this does make the container declaration a little daunting. But, this ultimately makes the container implementation tighter with a lot of compile-time optimizations. Indeed, the hardest part of using these containers is really getting their declaration right; so let us deconstruct a declaration of such a container of `PersonEntry` objects:

Listing 6.2: Defining multi-index containers

```
1 #include <boost/multi_index_container.hpp>
2 #include <boost/multi_index/indexed_by.hpp>
3 #include <boost/multi_index/ordered_index.hpp>
4 #include <boost/multi_index/identity.hpp>
5
6 using namespace boost::multi_index;
7
8 typedef ordered_non_unique<identity<PersonEntry>> by_person;
9 typedef multi_index_container<PersonEntry,
10                       indexed_by<by_person>> directory_t;
```

In the preceding snippet, we create a typedef for a `multi_index_container` of the `PersonEntry` objects (lines 9-10). We use a single index called `person_index` that we defined earlier (line 8). The `person_index` is the type of index that will be used for looking up objects in the container. It is defined as `ordered_non_unique<identity<PersonEntry>>`. This means that the index keeps the `PersonEntry` objects ordered by their defined ordering relationship and allows for duplicates (non-unique). This index provides the same semantics as `std::multiset<PersonEntry>`. Now, if we want to look up `PersonEntry` objects by telephone number, we would need to define additional indexes:

Listing 6.3: Defining multi-index containers

```
1 #include <boost/multi_index_container.hpp>
2 #include <boost/multi_index/indexed_by.hpp>
3 #include <boost/multi_index/ordered_index.hpp>
4 #include <boost/multi_index/identity.hpp>
5 #include <boost/multi_index/member.hpp>
```

```
 6 #include "PersonEntry.h"  // contains PersonEntry definition
 7 using namespace boost::multi_index;
 8
 9 typedef ordered_non_unique<member<PersonEntry, std::string,
10                        &PersonEntry::name>> by_name;
11 typedef ordered_unique<member<PersonEntry, std::string,
12                        &PersonEntry::phoneNumber>>by_phone;
13
14 typedef multi_index_container<PersonEntry,
15                        indexed_by<by_name,
16                            by_phone>> directory_t;
```

Here we define two index types: an index type `by_name` for looking up objects by the name field and a second index type `phone_index` for looking up by phone numbers (lines 9-12). We use the `member` template to indicate that we want an index based on a data member of `PersonEntry` called `name` or `phoneNumber` of type `std::string`.

We pass a specialization of the `indexed_by` template to the `multi_index_container` template as an argument. All the indexes that we want to enable are listed as arguments of this specialization (lines 15-16). Let us now see these types in action. We assume that all the header files from the listing 6.3 are included and all the types defined in listing 6.3 are available in the following listing:

Listing 6.4: Using Boost Multi-index containers

```
 1 int main()
 2 {
 3   directory_t phonedir;
 4   PersonEntry p1{"Arindam Mukherjee", "550 888 9999", "Pune"};
 5   PersonEntry p2{"Arindam Mukherjee", "990 770 2458",
 6                  "Calcutta"};
 7   PersonEntry p3{"Ace Ventura", "457 330 1288", "Tampa"};
 8
 9   phonedir.insert(p1);
10   phonedir.insert(p2);
11   phonedir.insert(p3);
12
13   auto iter = phonedir.find("Ace Ventura");
14   assert(iter != phonedir.end() && iter->city == "Tampa");
15
16   auto& ph_indx = phonedir.get<1>();
```

```
17    auto iter2 = ph_indx.find("990 770 2458");
18    assert(iter2 != ph_indx.end());
19    assert(iter2->city == "Calcutta");
20
21    for (auto& elem: ph_indx) {
22      std::cout << elem.name <<" lives in " << elem.city
23          << " and can be reached at "<< elem.phoneNumber
24          << '\n';
25    }
26 }
```

In this example, we create a multi-index container of `PersonEntry` objects indexed by `name` and `phoneNumber` fields, as defined in listing 6.3. We insert three `PersonEntry` objects (lines 8-10). We then perform a lookup by name on the container (lines 12-13). The container's behavior defaults to that of the first index, which is `by_name` (listing 6.3, lines 9-10). Thus, the call to the `find` method uses the first index (`by_name`) for the lookup. To look up by phone numbers, we need to get a reference to the second index. To do this, we use the `get` member template of `multi_index_container`, passing it `1`, which is the zero-based position of the `by_phone` index (line 15). We can then call methods on the returned index reference just like on `std::set` (lines 16-18). We can even iterate through the index using a range-based for-loop construct (line 21) or using actual iterators.

In the preceding example both indexes are ordered, which requires that whichever element they are based on (`name` or `phoneNumber` fields) should define an ordering relationship. In this case, both fields are of type `std::string`, so the ordering relationship is well-defined. But if it is not available, we need to roll our own definition of ordering as an overloaded `operator<`. Alternatively, we can define a functor to perform the ordering comparisons between two elements of the type in question and pass its type as a trailing argument to the `member` template. The online documentation for Boost Multi-index has more details.

If specifying numeric positions for index types seems less than ideal, you can use tags instead. This changes the declaration of the `by_phone` index a wee bit but makes for more readable code where it matters. Here is how to do it for the `phone_index`:

```
1 struct phone_tag {};
2 typedef ordered_unique< <tag<phone_tag>, member<PersonEntry,
3         std::string, &PersonEntry::phoneNumber>> by_phone;
4
5 auto& ph_indx = phonedir.get<phone_tag>();
```

In the preceding snippet, we define an empty struct called `phone_tag` just to act as a tag for a particular index (line 1). We then define the index type `by_phone`, as specialization of the `ordered_unique` template. The first parameter of the `ordered_unique` template specifies the tag to use for retrieving this index (`phone_tag`). The second template parameter to `ordered_unique` is `member<PersonEntry, std::string, &PersonEntry::phoneNumber>`; it specifies that the `phoneNumber` member of each `PersonEntry` object is to be used as the key for this index, and that it is of type `std::string` (lines 2-3). Finally, we access the index by calling the `get` member template of `phonedir`, but pass it the tag `phone_tag` rather than a numeric index (line 5).

Index types

The `ordered_unique` and `ordered_non_unique` indexes correspond to the semantics of `std::set` and `std::multiset` respectively. Using these indexes, you not only get logarithmic lookup and insertions, but can also perform an ordered traversal of the container's elements. If you do not care about ordered traversal, you can also use `hashed_unique` and `hashed_non_unique` indexes, which provide excellent insertion and lookup performance (constant expected time). Naturally, the hashed indexes do not require any ordering relationship to be defined on the elements but require a way to generate their hash values. This can be enabled using the techniques shown for unordered containers in listing 5.11.

Sometimes, it is important to get objects in the order of insertion and also perform lookups based on different criteria. To get objects in the order in which they were inserted, we need to use the `sequenced` index. Sequenced indexes do not take any arguments other than an optional tag. We can add the `sequenced<>` index to the `directory_t` type we defined in listing 6.3, as shown in the following code:

```
1 #include <boost/multi_index/sequenced_index.hpp>
2 typedef multi_index_container<PersonEntry,
3                       indexed_by<by_name,
4                                  by_phone,
5                       sequenced<>>> directory_t;
```

We could have passed a tag as a template argument to `sequenced` if we wanted to. If we also want a random access iterator to this sequence in insertion order, we may use the `random_access<>` index instead:

```
1 #include <boost/multi_index/random_access_index.hpp>
2 typedef multi_index_container<PersonEntry,
3                   indexed_by<by_name,
4                        by_phone,
5                   random_access<>>> directory_t;
```

Now let us suppose that you look up a `PersonEntry` by name using the `by_name` index and want to find out the position of the element in insertion order. Iterators are associated with an index and the iterator we have is associated with the `by_phone` index. Now you want an iterator to the same element on the `random_access` index as well. You can then compute the difference between that iterator and the beginning iterator of the `random_access` index to compute the ordinal position of the element. The general way to do this is to use the `project` member template of the `multi_index_container`, as shown in the following example:

Listing 6.5: Using iterator projections

```
 1  // the necessary includes for Boost Multi-index
 2
 3  typedef multi_index_container<PersonEntry,
 4  indexed_by<by_name,by_phone,
 5                              random_access<>>> directory_t;
 6
 7  int main()
 8  {
 9    directory_t phonedir;  // directory_t defined in listing 6.3
10
11    phonedir.insert(PersonEntry{"Dr. Dolittle", "639 420 7624",
12                        "Atlanta"});
13    phonedir.insert(PersonEntry{"Arindam Mukherjee",
14                        "990 770 2458", "Calcutta"});
15    phonedir.insert(PersonEntry{"Ace Ventura", "457 330 1288",
16                        "Tampa"});
17    phonedir.insert(PersonEntry{"Arindam Mukherjee",
18                        "550 888 9999", "Pune"});
19
20    auto& name_index = phonedir.get<0>();
21    auto it = name_index.find("Ace Ventura");
22    auto& random_index = phonedir.get<2>();
23    if (it != name_index.end()) {
24      auto rit = phonedir.project<2>(it);
25      std::cout << "Element found: " << it->name
26        << ", position = " <<rit - random_index.begin() << '\n';
27    }
28  }
```

We look up an element by name using the find member, which returns an iterator it to the element (line 21). We then get a reference to the random access index at index 2, using the get member template (line 22). Using the project member template of phonedir, we get the iterator corresponding to it in the random_access index (line 24). The returned iterator rit being a random access iterator, we compute the zero-based position of the element as the difference between rit and the begin iterator on random_index. If we had used a sequenced<> index in place of random_access<> (line 5), we would not be able to compute the position by computing the difference of the two iterators (line 26). Instead, we would need to use the std::distance Standard Library function to compute the offset between the beginning of the sequenced container and the looked up iterator. This would be of linear time complexity rather than constant.

Range lookups using lambda

Sometimes we want to find elements whose attributes fall in a certain range of values. Instead of using the lower_bound and upper_bound members of the multi_index_container and its indexes, we can perform range lookups using a more expressive syntax that uses Boost Lambda. Lambda expressions are discussed later in this book (see *Chapter 7, Higher Order and Compile-time Programming*), but you really do not need to understand any of it to follow the example:

Listing 6.6: Expressive range lookup

```
 1 // include required Boost Multi-index headers
 2 #include <boost/lambda/lambda.hpp>
 3
 4 namespace bl = boost::lambda;  // lambda placeholder
 5
 6 int main()
 7 {
 8   directory_t phonedir;  // directory_t defined in listing 6.3
 9
10   phonedir.insert(PersonEntry{"Dr. Dolittle", "639 420 7624",
11                               "Atlanta"});
12   phonedir.insert(PersonEntry{"Arindam Mukherjee",
13                               "990 770 2458", "Calcutta"});
14   phonedir.insert(PersonEntry{"Ace Ventura", "457 330 1288",
15                               "Tampa"});
16   phonedir.insert(PersonEntry{"Arindam Mukherjee",
```

```
17                                   "550 888 9999", "Pune"});
18
19    auto& name_index = phonedir.get<0>();
20    auto range = name_index.range("Ar" <= bl::_1, "D" > bl::_1);
21
22    for (auto start = range.first; start != range.second;
23        ++start) {
24      std::cout << start->name << ", " << start->phoneNumber
25              << ", " << start->city << "\n";
26    }
27 }
```

Using the `multi_index_container` type called `directory_t` defined in listing 6.3, which uses the indexes `by_name` and `by_phone`, we define a multi-index container of `PersonEntry` objects called `phonedir` (line 8) and insert four entries into it (lines 10-17). We then look for all entries with names lexically greater or equal to `"Ar"` and lexically less than `"D"`. To do this, we first get the appropriate index, the `by_name` index, which is the zeroth index or default index. We then call the `range` member function on this index, passing it the two criteria for determining the ends of the range using a lambda placeholder `_1` (`boost::lambda::_1`). Semantically, `std::string("Ar") <= _1` says we are looking for strings, which are lexically not smaller than `"Ar"`, and `std::string("D") > _1` says we are looking for strings that are lexically smaller than `"D"`. These two criteria together determine which elements fall in the range and which ones fall outside. Turns out, my two namesakes are in the range while their more famous friends are out. This program prints:

```
Arindam Mukherjee, 550 888 9999, Pune
Arindam Mukherjee, 990 770 2458, Calcutta
```

Insertions and updates

You can add new elements into the `multi_index_container` and erase them using the container interface or any of its indexes. How you add and erase elements via the index interfaces depends on the type of the index. How you add and erase them via the container's public interface is defined by the type of the first index of the container.

We already used the `insert` member function in previous examples to add a single element to `multi_index_containers`. We used the overload of `insert` that takes a single object and adds it to the container at the appropriate location. We may also use this method on an individual index of type `ordered_unique`, `ordered_non_unique`, `hashed_unique`, or `hashed_non_unique`. But on the `random_access` or `sequenced` indexes, and on containers that use such an index as their first index, a single argument overload of `insert` is not available. You may use `push_back` or `push_front` to add elements to the ends. You may also use an overload of `insert` that takes the iterator to the position to insert at as an additional argument. Likewise for `erase`, with `sequenced<>` and `random_access<>` indexes, you can only use overloads that specify the element to erase with an iterator; while with ordered and hashed indexes, you can actually use an overload that takes a value to look up and erases all matching elements.

You can also update values in a multi-index container using either the `replace` or the `modify` method. The following snippet illustrates these concepts:

Listing 6.7: Inserts, erases and updates on multi-index containers

```
 1 // include required Boost Multi-Index headers
 2 #include <boost/lambda/lambda.hpp>
 3
 4 // by_name, by_phone defined Listing 6.3
 5 using namespace boost::multi_index;
 6
 7 typedef ordered_non_unique<member<PersonEntry, std::string,
 8                             &PersonEntry::name>> by_name;
 9 typedef ordered_unique<member<PersonEntry, std::string,
10                         &PersonEntry::phoneNumber>> by_phone;
11 typedef multi_index_container<PersonEntry,
12                         indexed_by<random_access<>,
13                             by_name, by_phone>> phdir_t;
14
15 int main()
16 {
17   phdir_t phonedir;
18
19   phonedir.push_back(PersonEntry{"Dr. Dolittle",
20           "639 420 7624", "Atlanta"}); // insert won't work
21   auto& phindx = phonedir.get<2>();
```

```
22    phindx.insert(PersonEntry{"Arindam Mukherjee",
23                             "550 888 9999", "Pune"});
24    auto& nameindx = phonedir.get<1>();
25    nameindx.insert(PersonEntry{"Arindam Mukherjee",
26                               "990 770 2458", "Calcutta"});
27    phonedir.push_front(PersonEntry{"Ace Ventura",
28                                   "457 330 1288", "Tampa"});
29
30    nameindx.erase("Arindam Mukherjee");   // erases 2 matching
31    phonedir.erase(phonedir.begin());      // erases Ace Ventura
32    assert(phonedir.size() == 1);
33    std::cout <<"The lonesome "<< phonedir.begin()->name << '\n';
34
35    phonedir.push_back(PersonEntry{"Tarzan", "639 420 7624",
36                                   "Okavango"});
37    assert(phonedir.size() == 1);
38    std::cout <<"Still alone "<< phonedir.begin()->name << '\n';
39
40    phonedir.push_back(PersonEntry{"Tarzan", "9441500252",
41                                   "Okavango"});
42    assert(phonedir.size() == 2);
43
44    PersonEntry tarzan = *(phonedir.begin() + 1);
45    tarzan.phoneNumber = "639 420 7624";
46    assert(!phonedir.replace(phonedir.begin() + 1, tarzan));
47 }
```

In this example, we create a multi-index container of `PersonEntry` objects with three indexes: the default `random_access` index, an ordered non-unique index on the `name` field, and an ordered unique index on the `phoneNumber` field. We first use the public interface of the container to add a `PersonEntry` record using the `push_back` method (lines 19-20). We then access a reference to the phone index (line 21) and name index (line 24). We add a second record using the single argument `insert` overload on the phone index (line 22), and a third record using the same overload on the name index (lines 25-26). Next, we use the `push_front` method on the container to add a fourth record (lines 27-28), which puts this record at the front or beginning of the `random_access` index.

We then call the single argument `erase` overload on the name index passing it the string to match against the `name` field (line 30). This erases the two matching records (inserted on lines 22-23 and 25-26). We then erase the record at the beginning of the container (line 31), which deletes the `"Ace Ventura"` record. The sole remaining record (line 32) is printed to the console (line 33) and this should print:

```
The lonesome Dr. Dolittle
```

Next we use `push_back` to add another record for a person called `Tarzan` (line 35-36). Interestingly, Mr. Tarzan has the same phone number as Dr. Dolittle. But because there is a unique index on the `phoneNumber` field, this insertion does not succeed and the container still retains the record of Dr. Dolittle (lines 37, 38). We fix this by adding a new record for Tarzan with a unique phone number (lines 40-41), which succeeds (line 42).

Next, we access the record for Tarzan, which would be the second record in insertion order, and create a copy of that object (line 44). We then change the `phoneNumber` field of the `tarzan` object to the same number as Dr. Dolittle's. We try to replace the object for Tarzan in the container with this modified object using the `replace` member function, but because the replacement violates the uniqueness constraint on the phone number, the `replace` method fails to update the record returning a Boolean false. We can also use the more efficient `modify` method instead of `replace`. We will not cover `modify` in this book; the online documentation is a good place to look for reference.

Each insertion updates all indexes and like the associative containers and `std::list` from the Standard Library, they do not invalidate any existing iterators, not even those generated from other indexes. Erase operations invalidate only iterators to the erased elements.

Boost Bimap

Storing objects and looking them up using a key is a very common programming chore, and every language has some measure of support for it through native constructs or libraries in the form of dictionaries or lookup tables. In C++, the `std::map` and `std::multimap` containers (and their unordered variants) provide the lookup table abstraction. Traditionally, such libraries support lookups in one direction. Given a key you can look up a value and this is adequate for many cases. But sometimes, we also need a way to look up a key given a value, and the standard library associative containers are of little help in such cases; what we need there is the Boost Bimap library.

The Boost Bimap library provides bimaps or bidirectional map data structures that allow lookups using keys as well as values. Let us start with an example to get a feel of how it works. We will use a Boost bimap to store names of countries and territories, with their capitals:

Listing 6.8: Using a bimap

```
 1 #include <boost/bimap.hpp>
 2 #include <boost/assign.hpp>
 3 #include <string>
 4 #include <iostream>
 5 #include <cassert>
 6 using namespace boost::assign;
 7
 8 typedef boost::bimap<std::string, std::string> string_bimap_t;
 9
10 int main()
11 {
12   string_bimap_t countryCapitals;
13
14   insert(countryCapitals)("Slovenia", "Ljubljana")
15                          ("New Zealand", "Wellington")
16                          ("Tajikistan", "Bishkek")
17                          ("Chile", "Santiago")
18                          ("Jamaica", "Kingston");
19
20   string_bimap_t::left_map& countries = countryCapitals.left;
21   string_bimap_t::left_map::const_iterator it
22       = countries.find("Slovenia");
23   if (it != countries.end()) {
24     std::cout << "Capital of "<< it->first << " is "
25               << it->second << "\n";
26   }
27
28   string_bimap_t::right_map& cities = countryCapitals.right;
29   string_bimap_t::right_map::const_iterator it2
30       = cities.find("Santiago");
31   if (it2 != cities.end()) {
32     std::cout << it2->first <<" is the capital of "
33               << it2->second << "\n";
34   }
```

```
35
36    size_t size = countryCapitals.size();
37    countryCapitals.insert(
38        string_bimap_t::value_type("Chile", "Valparaiso"));
39    assert(countries.at("Chile") == "Santiago");
40    assert(size == countryCapitals.size());
41
42    countryCapitals.insert(
43      string_bimap_t::value_type("Norfolk Island", "Kingston"));
44    assert(cities.at("Kingston") == "Jamaica");
45    assert(size == countryCapitals.size());
46 }
```

The type `bimap<string, string>` that will hold names of the countries and map them to the capitals is named `string_bimap_t` (line 8). We define a bimap of this type called `countryCapitals` (line 12), and add the names of five countries and their capitals using the `insert` adaptor from Boost Assign (lines 14-18).

A bimap defines a relation or mapping between values in two containers: a *left container* consisting of country names and a *right container* consisting of names of capital cities. We can get a *left view* of the bimap that maps the keys (country names) to values (capitals) and a *right view* that maps the values (capitals) to the keys (country names). These represent two alternative views of the bimap. We can access these two alternate views using the members `left` and `right` of the bimap (lines 20, 28). These two views have a very similar public interface as `std::map` or, to borrow a succinct description from the online documentation, they are *signature-compatible* with `std::map`.

So far, there is a one-to-one mapping between the set of countries and the set of capitals. We now try to insert an entry for Chile's second capital, Valparaiso (lines 37-38). It fails (lines 39-40) because, just like `std::map` and unlike `std::multimap`, the keys must be unique.

Now consider what happens if we try to insert a new entry into the bimap (lines 42-43) for a new country `Norfolk Island` (a territory under Australia), whose capital `Kingston` shares its name with that of another country on the map (`Jamaica`). Unlike what would have happened in a `std::map`, the insertion fails and there is no change in the number of entries in the bimap (lines 44-45). In this case, the values too must be unique, which is not a constraint for `std::map`. But what if we actually want to represent a one-to-many or many-to-many kind of a relation using Boost Bimap? We will see the options we have in the next section.

Collection types

The default behavior of Boost Bimap is one-to-one mapping, that is, unique keys and unique values. But, we can support one-to-many and many-to-many mappings by varying a couple of template parameters. To illustrate such use with an example, we use a map of given names to nicknames (listing 6.9). A given name can sometimes be associated with multiple nicknames and a nickname too can occasionally apply to multiple given names. So we would like to model a many-to-many relationship. To define a bimap that allows many-to-many relations, we have to choose a collection type for the left and right containers different from the default (which has set semantics). Since both names and nicknames can be non-unique, both the left and right containers should have the semantics of multisets instead. Boost Bimap provides collection type specifiers (refer to the following table), which can be used as template arguments to the `boost::bimap` template. Depending on the collection type, the semantics of the left or right view of the bimap also change. Here is a short table summarizing the available collection types, their semantics, and the corresponding views (based on the online documentation at `www.boost.org`):

Collection type	Semantics	View type
`set_of`	Ordered, unique.	map
`multiset_of`	Ordered, non-unique.	multimap
`unordered_set_of`	Hashed, unique.	unordered_map
`unordered_multiset_ of`	Hashed, non-unique.	unordered_multimap
`unconstrained_set_of`	Unconstrained.	No view available
`list_of`	Non-ordered, non-unique.	Linked list of key-value pairs
`vector_of`	Non-ordered, non-unique, random access sequence.	Vector of key-value pairs

Note that the collection types are defined in the `boost::bimaps` namespace and each collection type comes in its own header, which must be included separately. The following example shows you how to use collection types in conjunction with the `boost::bimap` template to define many-to-many relations:

Listing 6.9: Bimaps for many-to-many relations

```
1 #include <boost/bimap.hpp>
2 #include <boost/bimap/multiset_of.hpp>
3 #include <boost/assign.hpp>
4 #include <string>
5 #include <iostream>
```

```
 6  #include <cassert>
 7  using namespace boost::assign;
 8  namespace boostbi = boost::bimaps;
 9
10  typedef boost::bimap<boostbi::multiset_of<std::string>,
11              boostbi::multiset_of<std::string>> string_bimap_t;
12
13  int main()
14  {
15    string_bimap_t namesShortNames;
16
17    insert(namesShortNames)("Robert", "Bob")
18                           ("Robert", "Rob")
19                           ("William", "Will")
20                           ("Christopher", "Chris")
21                           ("Theodore", "Ted")
22                           ("Edward", "Ted");
23
24    size_t size = namesShortNames.size();
25    namesShortNames.insert(
26            string_bimap_t::value_type("William", "Bill"));
27    assert(size + 1 == namesShortNames.size());
28
29    namesShortNames.insert(
30            string_bimap_t::value_type("Christian", "Chris"));
31    assert(size + 2 == namesShortNames.size());
32
33    string_bimap_t::left_map& names = namesShortNames.left;
34    string_bimap_t::left_map::const_iterator it1
35        = names.lower_bound("William");
36    string_bimap_t::left_map::const_iterator it2
37        = names.upper_bound("William");
38
39    while (it1 != it2) {
40      std::cout << it1->second <<" is a nickname for "
41                << it1->first << '\n';
42      ++it1;
43    }
44
45    string_bimap_t::right_map& shortNames =
```

```
46                                    namesShortNames.right;
46
47    auto iter_pair = shortNames.equal_range("Chris");
48    for (auto it3 = iter_pair.first; it3 != iter_pair.second;
49        ++it3) {
50      std::cout << it3->first <<" is a nickname for "
51                << it3->second << '\n';
52    }
53 }
```

The specific bimap container type we need to use is bimap<multiset_of<string>, multiset_of<string>> (lines 10-11). Using bimap<string, string> would have given us a one-to-one mapping. If we wanted a one-to-many relation, we could have used bimap<set_of<string>, multiset_of<string>>, or simply bimap<string, multiset_of<string>> since set_of is the default collection type used when we do not specify one. Note that in the code, we use boostbi as an alias for the boost::bimaps namespace (line 8).

We define the namesShortNames bimap to hold the name and nickname entries (line 15).We add some entries, including a duplicate name Robert and a duplicate nickname Ted (lines 17-22). Using the insert member function of bimap, add one more duplicate name William (lines 25-26) and one more duplicate nickname Chris (lines 29-30); both insertions succeed.

We access the left view with names as keys and the right view with nicknames as keys, using the left and right members of bimap (lines 33, 45). Both the left and right views are signature compatible with std::multimap, and we perform lookups on them just as we would on std::multimaps. Thus, given a name, to find the first matching entry for it, we use the lower_bound member function (line 35). To find the first entry lexically greater than the name, we use the upper_bound member function (line 37).We can iterate over the range of matching entries using the iterators returned by these two functions (line 39). In general, lower_bound returns the first element with name lexically equal or greater than the passed key; so if there are no matching elements, lower_bound and upper_bound return the same iterator. We can also use the equal_range function, which returns both the lower bound and upper bound iterators as an iterator pair (line 47).

If we did not care about ordered traversal of the maps, we could have used unordered_set_of or unordered_multiset_of collection types. Like with all unordered containers, the notion of equality of elements and a mechanism to compute the hash values of the elements must be available.

A container such as `std::map<T, U>`, has the same semantics as `bimap<T, unconstrained_set_of<U>>`. The `unconstrained_set_of` collection type does not provide a way to iterate through elements in it or look them up, and does not require the elements to be unique. While `bimap<T, multiset_of<U>>` allows non-unique values, it also supports looking up by values, something that `std::map` does not.

The `list_of` and `vector_of` collection types, like the `unconstrained_set_of` collection type, do not enforce either uniqueness or any structure that allows look up. However, they can be iterated through element by element, unlike `unconstrained_set_of` and thus, you can use a Standard Library algorithm like `std::find` to perform linear searches. `vector_of` provides random access. One can sort the entities it contains using its `sort` member function following which one could perform binary searches using `std::binary_search`.

More ways to use bimaps

There are several ways to make the use of bimaps more expressive. In this section, we explore a few of these.

Tagged access

Instead of using `left` and `right` to access each of the two opposing views in the container, you may like to use a more descriptive name to access them. You can do this using tags or empty structures that are used as markers. This is very similar to how indexes in Boost's multi-index containers are accessed by a tag instead of a numeric position. The following code snippet illustrates this technique:

```
 1 struct name {};
 2 struct nickname {};
 3
 4 typedef boost::bimap<
 5         boostbi::multiset_of<
 6            boostbi::tagged<std::string, name>>,
 7         boostbi::multiset_of<
 8            boostbi::tagged<std::string, nickname>>>
 9      string_bimap_t;
10
11 string_bimap_t namesShortNames;
12
13 auto& names = namesShortNames.by<name>();
14 auto& nicknames = namesShortNames.by<nickname>();
```

We define an empty struct for a tag for each view we want to access by name (lines 1-2). We then define the bimap container type, tagging the individual collections with our tags using the `tagged` template (lines 6, 8). We finally use the `by` member template to access the individual views. While the syntax for using tags is not the most straightforward, the expressiveness of accessing views using `by<tag>` can certainly make your code clearer and less error-prone.

Searches on views can be written more succinctly using the `range` member function and Boost Lambda placeholders, just like we did with Boost Multi-index. Here is an example:

```
 1 #include <boost/bimap/support/lambda.hpp>
 2
 3 ...
 4 string_bimap_t namesShortNames;
 5 ...
 6 using boost::bimaps::_key;
 7 const auto& range = namesShortNames.right.range("Ch" <= _key,
 8                                                 _key < "W");
 9
10 for (auto i1 = range.first; i1 != range.second; ++i1) {
11   std::cout << i1->first << ":" << i1->second << '\n';
12 }
```

The call to the `range` member function of the `right` view returns a Boost.Range object called `range`, which is really a pair of iterators (lines 7-8). We extract the two individual iterators (line 10) and then run through the returned range, printing the nicknames and the full names (lines 10-11). With range-aware algorithms, we can simply pass the range object without bothering to extract iterators from them. If you want to constrain only one end of the range, you can use `boost::bimaps::unbounded` for the other end.

Projections

From an iterator on one view, you can get to an iterator on another view using the `project` member template or the `project_left`/`project_right` member functions. Let us suppose that given a name, you want to find out all other names that share the same nickname. Here is one way to do this:

```
1 auto i1 = names.find("Edward");
2 auto i2 = namesShortNames.project<nickname>(i1);
3
4 const auto& range = shortNames.range(_key == i2->first,
```

```
5                                            _key == i2->first);
6
7 for (auto i3 = range.first; i3 != range.second; ++i3) {
8   std::cout << i3->first << ":" << i3->second << '\n';
9 }
```

We first obtain an iterator to a matching name by using the `find` member function on the `names` view (line 1).We then project this iterator to the nicknames view using the `project` member template. If we do not use tagged keys and values, we should use `project_left` and `project_right` member functions instead, depending on which view we want to project to. This returns an iterator to the same element on the nicknames view (line 2). Next, using the `range` member function, we find all entries whose nickname equals `i2->first` (lines 4-5). We then print the pairs of nicknames by looping through the iterator range returned by `range` (lines 7-9).

There are several other useful features of Boost Bimap, including a view of the container as a collection of relations between pairs of elements and the ability to modify keys and values in a bimap, in-place. The online Bimap documentation on `www.boost.org` is comprehensive and you should refer to it for more details on these features.

Self-test questions

For multiple choice questions, choose all options that apply:

1. The `ordered_non_unique` index on Boost `multi_index_container` has the semantics of:

   a. `std::set`

   b. `std::multiset`

   c. `std::unordered_set`

   d. `std::unordered_multiset`

2. Deleting an element in a `multi_index_container` will only invalidate the iterator to the deleted element, irrespective of the index.

   a. True

   b. False

   c. Depends on the type of index

3. Which of the following bimap types has semantics equivalent to a `multimap<T, U>`?

   a. `bimap<T, multiset_of<U>>`

   b. `bimap<multiset_of<T>, U>`

   c. `bimap<multiset_of<T>, unconstrained_set_of<U>>`

   d. `bimap<multiset_of<T>, multiset_if<U>>`

Summary

In this chapter, we focused on containers specialized for looking up objects based on multiple criteria. Specifically, we looked at Boost Bimap which is a bidirectional map object, whose keys and values can both be looked up efficiently. We also looked at Boost Multi-index containers, which are generic associative containers with multiple associated indexes, each assisting the efficient look up of an object on one criterion.

In the next chapter, we change gears to look at functional composition and metaprogramming techniques that enable us to write powerful and expressive applications with excellent runtime performance.

References

Multi-index modify method: `http://www.boost.org/doc/libs/release/libs/multi_index/doc/reference/ord_indices.html#modif`

7
Higher Order and Compile-time Programming

A number of Standard Library algorithms take callable entities called **function objects** (function pointers, functors, and so on) as parameters. They call these function objects on individual elements of containers to compute some value or perform some action. Thus, a part of the runtime logic of the algorithm is encapsulated in a function or functor and supplied as an argument to the algorithm. A function may also return function objects instead of data values. The returned function object can be applied on a set of parameters and may in turn return either a value or another function object. This gives rise to higher order transforms. This style of programming involving passing and returning functions is called **higher order programming**.

C++ templates enable us to write type generic code. Using templates, it is possible to execute branching and recursive logic at compile time and conditionally include, exclude, and generate code from simpler building blocks. This style of programming is called **compile-time programming** or **template metaprogramming**.

In the first part of this chapter, we will learn the applications of higher order programming in C++ using the Boost Phoenix Library and C++11 facilities like bind and lambda. In the next part of this chapter, we will learn C++ template metaprogramming techniques that execute at compile time to help generate more efficient and expressive code. In the last part of this chapter we look at domain-specific languages created within C++ by applying higher order programming techniques in combination with metaprogramming. The topics of this chapter are divided into the following sections:

- Higher order programming using Boost
- Compile-time programming using Boost
- Domain Specific Embedded Languages

In this chapter, we will explore an alternate paradigm of programming, which is different from object-oriented and procedural programming and draws heavily from functional programming. We will also develop generic programming techniques that ultimately help us implement more efficient template libraries.

Higher order programming with Boost

Consider a type `Book` with three string fields: the ISBN, title, and author (for our purposes, assume that there is only one author). Here is how we can choose to define this type:

```
1 struct Book
2 {
3   Book(const std::string& id,
4         const std::string& name,
5         const std::string& auth)
6         : isbn(id), title(name), author(auth)
7   {}
8
9   std::string isbn;
10   std::string title;
11   std::string author;
12 };
13
14 bool operator< (const Book& lhs, const Book& rhs)
12 {  return lhs.isbn < rhs.isbn;  }
```

It is a `struct` with three fields and a constructor that initializes these three fields. The `isbn` field uniquely identifies the book and therefore is used to define an ordering of `Book` objects, using the overloaded `operator<` (line 14).

Now imagine that we have a list of these `Book` objects in a `std::vector`, and we want to sort these books. Thanks to the overloaded `operator<`, we can easily sort them using the Standard Library `sort` algorithm:

```
1 #include <vector>
2 #include <string>
3 #include <algorithm>
4 #include <iostream>
5
6 // include the definition of struct Book
7
8 int main()
9 {
```

```
10    std::vector<Book> books;
11    books.emplace_back("908..511..123", "Little Prince",
12                      "Antoine St. Exupery");
13    books.emplace_back("392..301..109", "Nineteen Eighty Four",
14                      "George Orwell");
15    books.emplace_back("872..610..176", "To Kill a Mocking Bird",
16                      "Harper Lee");
17    books.emplace_back("392..301..109", "Animal Farm",
18                      "George Orwell");
19
20    std::sort(books.begin(), books.end());
21 }
```

In the preceding code, we put four `Book` objects in the vector `books`. We do this by calling the `emplace_back` method (lines 11-18) rather than `push_back`. The `emplace_back` method (introduced in C++11) takes the constructor arguments for the stored type (`Book`) and constructs an object in the vector's layout rather than copying or moving in a pre-constructed object. We then sort the vector using `std::sort`, which ultimately uses the `operator<` for `Book` objects. Without this overloaded operator, `std::sort` would have failed to compile.

This is all great, but what if you wanted to sort the books in descending order of the ISBN? Or you could want to sort the books by their authors instead. Also, for two books with the same author, you might want to sort them further by their title. We will see a method to sort them this way in the next section.

Function objects

There is a three-argument overload of `std::sort` algorithm that takes a function object for comparing two elements as the third argument. This function object should return true if the first argument appears before the second argument in the final ordering and false otherwise. So, even without an overloaded `operator<`, you can tell `std::sort` how to compare two elements and sort the vector. Here is how we do the sorting using an ordering function:

Listing 7.1: Passing functions to algorithms

```
1 bool byDescendingISBN(const Book& lhs, const Book& rhs)
2 {  return lhs.isbn > rhs.isbn; }
3
4 ...
5 std::vector<Book> books;
6 ...
7 std::sort(books.begin(), books.end(), byDescendingISBN);
```

The function byDescendingISBN takes const references to two books and returns true if the ISBN of the first book (lhs) is lexically greater than that of the second (rhs) and false otherwise. The signature of the function compatible with the function object that std::sort algorithm expects as its third argument. To sort the books vector in descending order, we pass to std::sort, a pointer to this function (line 7).

Function pointers are by no means the only callable entities you can pass around. A *functor* is a type that overloads the function call operator member (operator()). By applying or calling an instance of a functor on a set of arguments, you invoke the overloaded operator() member. In the following example, we define a functor to order books by author names, and in case of a tie with author names, by titles:

Listing 7.2: Defining and passing functors to algorithms

```
1  ...
2  struct CompareBooks
3  {
4    bool operator()(const Book& b1, const Book& b2) const {
5      return (b1.author < b2.author)
6             || (b1.author == b2.author
7                 && b1.title < b2.title);
8    }
9  };
10
11 ...
12 std::vector<Book> books;
13 ...
14 std::sort(books.begin(), books.end(), CompareBooks());
```

We define a functor called CompareBooks with an overloaded operator() that takes two Book objects to compare (line 4). It returns true if the name of the first book's author is lexicographically smaller than the name of second book's author. In case the authors of the two books are same, it returns true if the title of the first book is lexicographically smaller than that of the second. To use this functor as the sorting criterion, we pass a temporary instance of CompareBooks as the third argument of the std::sort algorithm (line 14). Functors like CompareBooks, that map one or more arguments to a Boolean truth value are called **predicates**.

A note on terminology

We use the term **function object** to refer to all callable entities that can be passed around and stored for later use by the application. These include function pointers and functors as well as other kinds of callable entities like unnamed functions or **lambdas**, which we will explore in this chapter.

A **functor** is simply a class or struct that defines an overloaded function call operator.

A function object that takes one or more arguments and maps them to a Boolean truth value is usually called a **predicate**.

The **arity** of a function object is the number of arguments it takes. A function with no arguments has 0-arity or is **nullary**, a function with one argument has 1-arity or is **unary**, a function with two arguments has 2-arity or is **binary**, and so on.

A **pure function** is a function whose return value depends solely on the values of the arguments passed to it and which has no side effects. Modifying states of objects not local to the function, performing I/O, or otherwise modifying the execution environment — all qualify as side effects.

Functors are especially useful when you want them to retain some state between calls. For example, imagine you have an unsorted list of names, and you just want to make a comma-separated list of all names, starting with a particular letter. Here is a way to do this:

Listing 7.3: Functors with states

```
1  #include <vector>
2  #include <string>
3  #include <iostream>
4  #include <algorithm>
5
6  struct ConcatIfStartsWith {
7    ConcatIfStartsWith(char c) : startCh(c) {}
8
9    void operator()(const std::string& name) {
10     if (name.size() > 0 && name.at(0) == startCh) {
11       csNames += name + ", ";
12     }
```

```
13   }
14
15   std::string getConcat() const {
16     return csNames;
17   }
18
19   void reset() { csNames = ""; }
20
21 private:
22   char startCh;
23   std::string csNames;
24 };
25
26 int main() {
27   std::vector<std::string> names{"Meredith", "Guinnevere",
28       "Mabel", "Myrtle", "Germaine", "Gwynneth", "Mirabelle"};
29
30   const auto& fe = std::for_each(names.begin(), names.end(),
31                       ConcatIfStartsWith('G'));
32   std::cout << fe.getConcat() << '\n';
33 }
```

We define a functor called ConcatIfStartsWith (line 6), which stores some
state, namely the starting character to match (startCh) and a string to contain
the comma-separated list of names (csNames). When the functor is invoked on a
name, it checks whether it starts with the specified character, and if so, concatenates
it to csNames (lines 10-11). We use the std::for_each algorithm to apply the
ConcatIfStartsWith functor to each name in a vector of names (lines 30-31),
looking for names starting with the letter G. The functor we pass is a temporary
one (line 31), but we need a reference to it in order to access the concatenated
string stored in it. The std::for_each algorithm actually returns a reference to
the passed functor, which we then use to get the concatenated string. Here is the
output, listing the names starting with G:

```
Guinnevere, Germaine, Gwynneth,
```

This illustrates an important point about functors; they are particularly useful
when you want to maintain state that persists between successive calls to the
function. They are also great if you need to use them at multiple places in your code.
By naming them intuitively, their purpose can be made evident at the point of use:

```
const auto& fe = std::for_each(names.begin(), names.end(),
                    ConcatIfStartsWith('G'));
```

But sometimes, what a functor needs to do is trivial (for example, to check whether a number is even or odd). Often, we don't need it to maintain any state between calls. We may not even need to use it at multiple places. Sometimes, the functionality we are looking for may already be there in some form, maybe as a member function of the objects. In such cases, writing a new functor seems like overkill. C++11 introduced lambdas or unnamed functions to address precisely such cases.

Lambdas – unnamed function literals

The character string "hello" is a valid C++ expression. It has a well-defined type (const char[6]), can be assigned to variables of type const char*, and passed to functions that take arguments of type const char*. Likewise, there are numeric literals like 3.1415 or 64000U, Boolean literals like true and false, and so on. C++11 introduces **lambda expressions** for generating anonymous functions defined at the site, where they are invoked. Often, simply called **lambdas** (from Alonzo Church's λ-calculus), they consist of a function body not bound to a function name and are used to generate a function definition at any point in the lexical scope of a program, where you would expect to pass a function object. Let us first understand how this is done with the help of an example.

We have a list of integers, and we want to find the first odd number in the list using the std::find_if algorithm. The predicate passed to std::find_if is defined using a lambda.

Listing 7.4: Using lambdas

```
 1 #include <vector>
 2 #include <algorithm>
 3 #include <cassert>
 4
 5 int main() {
 6   std::vector<int> vec{2, 4, 6, 8, 9, 1};
 7
 8   auto it = std::find_if(vec.begin(), vec.end(),
 9                     [](const int& num) -> bool
10                     {  return num % 2 != 0; }
11                     );
12
13   assert(it != vec.end() && *it == 9);
14 }
```

The lambda to compute whether a number is odd or even is a block of code passed as the third argument to `std::find_if` (lines 9-10). Let us look at the lambda in isolation to understand the syntax. First, consider what this function does; given an integer, it returns true if it is odd and false otherwise. So, we have an unnamed function that maps an `int` to a `bool`. The way to write this in lambda-land is as follows:

```
[](const int& num) -> bool
```

We introduce the unnamed function with an empty pair of square brackets, and we describe the mapping by writing a parameter list like that of a conventional function, followed by an arrow and the return type. Following this, we write the body of the function just like you would for a normal function:

```
{ return num % 2 != 0; }
```

The pair of square brackets, often called **lambda introducers**, need not be empty, as we will see shortly. There are several other variations possible with this syntax, but you can define a lambda using just this bit of syntax. The return type specification for lambdas is optional in simple cases, where the compiler can easily deduce the return type from the function body. Thus, we could have rewritten the lambda from the preceding example without the return type because the function body is really simple:

```
[](const int& num) { return num % 2 != 0; }
```

Lambda captures

The lambda we defined in the previous example was a pure function without any state. In fact, how could a lambda conceivably store the state that persists between calls? Actually, lambdas can access local variables from the surrounding scope (in addition to global variables). To enable such an access, we can specify **capture clauses** in the lambda introducer to list which variables from the surrounding scope are accessible to the lambda and *how*. Consider the following example in which we filter out names longer than a user-specified length from a vector of names and return a vector containing only the shorter names:

Listing 7.5: Lambdas with captures

```
1 #include <vector>
2 #include <string>
3 #include <algorithm>
4 #include <iterator>
5 typedef std::vector<std::string> NameVec;
6
7 NameVec getNamesShorterThan(const NameVec& names,
```

```
 8                                    size_t maxSize) {
 9     NameVec shortNames;
10     std::copy_if(names.begin(), names.end(),
11                    std::back_inserter(shortNames),
12                    [maxSize](const std::string& name) {
13                        return name.size() <= maxSize;
14                    }
15                    );
16     return shortNames;
17 }
```

The `getNamesShorterThan` function takes two parameters: a vector called `names` and a variable `maxSize` that caps the size of strings to be filtered. It copies names shorter than `maxSize` from the `names` vector into a second vector called `shortNames`, using the `std::copy_if` algorithm from the standard library. We use a lambda expression (lines 12-14) to generate the predicate for `std::copy_if`. You can see that we name the `maxSize` variable from the surrounding lexical scope inside the square brackets (line 12), and access it inside the body of the lambda to compare the size of the passed string (line 13). This enables read-only access to the `maxSize` variable inside the lambda. If we wanted to potentially access any variable from the surrounding scope instead of a specific one, we could instead write the lambda with an equals sign in the square brackets; this would *implicitly capture* any variable used from the surrounding scope:

```
[=](const std::string& name) {
    return name.size() <= maxSize;
}
```

You may want to modify a local copy of a variable from the surrounding scope, without affecting its value in the surrounding scope. To enable your lambda to do this, it must be declared as mutable:

```
[=](const std::string& name) mutable -> bool {
    maxSize *= 2;
    return name.size() <= maxSize;
}
```

The `mutable` keyword trails the parameter list but appears before the return type if you specify one. This does not affect the value of `maxSize` in the surrounding scope.

You can also modify a variable from the surrounding scope inside a lambda. To do this, you must capture the variable by reference, by prefixing an ampersand to its name in the square brackets.

Here is listing 6.3 rewritten using a lambda:

Listing 7.6: Reference captures in lambda

```
1  #include <vector>
2  #include <string>
3  #include <algorithm>
4  #include <iostream>
5
6  int main() {
7    std::string concat;
8    char startCh = 'M';
9    std::vector<std::string> names{"Meredith", "Guinnevere", "Mabel"
10                  , "Myrtle", "Germaine", "Gwynneth", "Mirabelle"};
11
12   std::for_each(names.begin(), names.end(),
13               [&concat, startCh](const std::string& name) {
14                 if (name.size() > 0 && name[0] == startCh) {
15                   concat += name + ", ";
16                 }
17               });
18   std::cout << concat << '\n';
19 }
```

In the preceding example, we concatenate all names from the vector `names` that start with a specific character. The starting character is picked up from the variable `startCh`. The concatenated string is stored in the variable `concat`. We call `std::for_each` on the elements of the vector and pass a lambda, which explicitly captures `concat` as a reference (with a leading ampersand) and `startCh` as a read-only value from the surrounding scope (line 13). Thus, it is able to append to `concat` (line 15). This code prints the following output:

```
Meredith, Mabel, Myrtle, Mirabelle
```

In the latest revision of the C++ Standard, dubbed C++14, lambdas get a little niftier. You can write a *generic lambda* whose parameter types are deduced based on the context. For example, in C++14, you can write the call to `std::for_each` in the previous example, as follows:

```
std::for_each(names.begin(), names.end(),
            [&concat, startCh](const auto& name) {
              if (name.size() > 0 && name[0] == startCh) {
                concat += name + ", ";
              }
            });
```

The type of the argument to lambda is written as `const auto&`, and the compiler deduces it as `const std::string&` based on the type of elements in the iterated sequence.

Delegates and closures

Let us suppose you are writing a high-level C++ API for reading incoming messages on a message queue. The client of your API must register for the types of messages it is interested in and pass a callback—a function object that will be invoked when messages of your interest arrive. Your API could be a member of a `Queue` class. Here is one possible API signature:

```
class Queue
{
public:
    . . .
    template <typename CallbackType>
    int listen(MsgType msgtype, CallbackType cb);
    . . .
};
```

The `listen` member template takes two parameters: the message type `msgtype`, which identifies the messages of interest, and a callback function object `cb` that will be called when a new message arrives. Since we want the client to be able to pass function pointers, pointer to member functions, functors, as well as lambdas for the callback, we make `listen` a member template parameterized on the type of the callback. Of course, the callback should have a specific signature. Let us suppose it should be compatible with the signature of the following function:

```
void msgRead(Message msg);
```

Here, `Message` is the type of messages read from the queue. The `listen` member template is a little too permissive because it can be instantiated with function objects that do not conform to the preceding signature. For a signature-incompatible callback, a compilation error occurs at the point where the callback is invoked inside `listen` rather than the point where the nonconforming callback is passed. This can make debugging the compiler errors more difficult.

The Boost.Function library and its C++11 incarnate `std::function` offer function object wrappers that are tailor-made to fix such problems. We can write the type of the function `msgRead` as `void (Message)`. The general syntax for the type of a function of arity N is as follows:

```
return-type(param1-type, param2-type, ..., paramN-type)
```

The more familiar **function pointer type** corresponding to the preceding **function type** would be:

```
return-type (*)(param1-type, param2-type, ..., paramN-type)
```

Thus, the type of a function `int foo(double, const char*)` would be:

```
int(double, const char*);
```

A pointer to will be of type:

```
int (*)(double, const char*);
```

Using `std::function` with the appropriate function type, we can declare `listen` so that it accepts only function objects that conform to the correct signature:

```
#include <boost/function.hpp>

class Queue
{
public:
    ...
    int listen(MsgType msgtype, boost::function<void(Message)> cb);
    ...
};
```

The callback is now declared to be of type `boost::function<void(Message)>`. You can now call `listen` with a pointer to a global function, a functor, or even a lambda, and it will only compile if the function object has a conforming signature. We could have used `std::function` in place of `boost::function` if we were using a C++11 compiler. On pre-C++11 compilers, `boost::function` supports signatures with up to ten arguments, while `std::function` does not have any such limitation as it uses C++11 *variadic templates*. For more features of `boost::function` and its differences from `std::function` (which are minor), you can refer to the online documentation.

Passing a nonstatic member function as a callback requires a little bit more work, because a non-static member must be called on an instance of its class. Consider the following class `MessageHandler` with a member `handleMessage`:

```
class MessageHandler
{
public:
    ...
    void handleMessage(Message msg);
};
```

The `handleMessage` member function is implicitly passed a pointer to the `MessageHandler` object on which it is invoked as its first parameter; so its effective signature is:

```
void(MessageHandler*, Message);
```

When we want to pass this as a callback to `Queue::listen`, we probably already know which object we want `handleMessage` to be called on, and it would be great if we could somehow attach that object instance too in the call to listen. There are a couple of ways in which this can be done.

The first method involves wrapping the call to `handleMessage` in a lambda and passing it to `listen`. The following snippet illustrates this:

Listing 7.7: Member function callbacks using closures

```
1 MessageHandler *handler = new MessageHandler(...);
2 Queue q(...);
3 ...
4 q.listen(msgType, [handler](Message msg)
5                    {  handler->handleMessage(msg);  }
6                    );
```

Here, the second argument to `listen` is generated using a lambda expression, which also captures a pointer to the `handler` object from the surrounding scope. In this example, `handler` is a local variable in the calling scope, but the lambda captures it and binds it into the function object it generates. This function object is not invoked immediately on it but delayed until a message of interest is received on the queue, when it forwards the call to the `handleMessage` method on the `handler` object pointer.

The `handler` pointer is created in the calling scope but becomes indirectly accessible in another scope via the lambda capture. This is referred to as **dynamic scoping**, and functions of this kind that bind to variables in the lexical scope, in which they are created, are called **closures**. Of course, the handler pointer must still point to a valid `MessageHandler` object at the time when `handleMessage` is called on it, not just when the lambda is created.

More often than not, such lambdas would be generated from inside a member function, like a member function of the `MessageHandler` class and would capture the `this` pointer with some consequent syntactic simplifications:

Listing 7.8: Capturing this-pointer in lambdas

```
1 class MessageHandler
2 {
3 public:
```

```
 4    ...
 5    void listenOnQueue(Queue& q, MessageType msgType) {
 6      q.listen(msgType, [this](Message msg)
 7                        { handleMsg(msg); } );
 8    }
 9
10    void handleMsg(Message msg) { ... }
11  };
```

In the preceding example, we create a closure using a lambda expression that captures the `this` pointer (line 6). The call to `handleMsg` inside the lambda automatically binds to the `this` pointer, just as it would in a member function. Callbacks, especially when bound to specific objects, as mentioned earlier, are sometimes called **delegates**.

The `boost::function` / `std::function` wrapper provides an effective and type-checked way of passing and returning function objects as callbacks or delegates. They are sometimes called polymorphic function wrappers because they completely abstract the type of the underlying callable entity (function pointer, functor, and so on) from the caller. Most implementations allocate memory dynamically though, so you should pay due diligence to assess their impact on runtime performance.

Partial function application

Given the Standard Library function `pow`:

```
double pow(double base, double power);
```

Consider the effect of the line of code `x = pow(2, 3)`. When this line is encountered, the function `pow` is immediately called with two arguments, the values 2 and 3. The function `pow` computes 2 raised to 3 and returns the value 8.0, which is then assigned to `x`.

Now, say you have a list of numbers, and you want to put their cubes into another list. The Standard Library algorithm `std::transform` is a perfect fit for this. We just need to find the right functor to raise the numbers to their cubic power. The following functor takes a single numeric argument and raises it to a specific power, using the `pow` function:

```
#include <cmath>

struct RaiseTo {
  RaiseTo(double power) : power_(power) {}

  double operator()(double base) const {
```

```
    return pow(base, power_);
  }

  double power_;
};
```

We could also have used a lambda expression to generate the function object, as shown in listing 7.7 and 7.8 in the last section. Using `RaiseTo` with the `std::transform` algorithm, the following code does the job:

```
std::vector<double> nums, raisedToThree;
...
std::transform(nums.begin(), nums.end(),
               std::back_inserter(raisedToThree),
               RaiseTo(3));
```

The core computation in `RaiseTo` is done by the `pow` function. The `RaiseTo` functor provides a way to fix the power through the constructor argument and a call signature compatible with what `std::transform` expects.

Imagine if you could do this in C++ without functors or lambdas. What if using the following *imaginary* syntax, you could do the same thing?

```
std::transform(nums.begin(), nums.end(),
               std::back_inserter(raisedToThree),
               pow(_, 3));
```

It is as if you are passing the `pow` function with one of its two arguments fixed at 3 and asking the `transform` algorithm to fill in the blank; supply the number to raise to. The expression `pow(_, 3)` would have evaluated to a function object, taking one argument instead of 2. We essentially achieved this using the `RaiseTo` functor, but the Boost Bind library and its C++11 incarnate `std::bind` help us do this with less syntax. Formally, what we have just done is referred to as **partial function application**.

To create a partially applied function object for `pow` using `bind`, you would need to write:

```
boost::bind(pow, _1, 3)
```

The preceding expression generates an unnamed functor which takes a single argument and returns its value raised to the power of 3, using the standard library function `pow`. The similarity with our imaginary syntax should be evident. The value to be cubed is passed as the sole argument of the generated functor and is mapped to the special placeholder `_1`.

Listing 7.9: Using Boost Bind

```
1 #include <boost/bind.hpp>
2
3 std::vector<double> nums, raisedToThree;
4 std::transform(nums.begin(), nums.end(),
5                std::back_inserter(raisedToThree),
6                boost::bind(pow, _1, 3));
```

If the generated functor takes more arguments, then they could be mapped to the placeholders _2, _3, and so on, based on their positions in the argument list. In general, the nth argument maps to the placeholder _n. Boost Bind by default supports maximum nine positional placeholders (_1 through _9); std::bind might support more (varies from one compiler to the next), but you will need to access them from the std::placeholders namespace, using one of the following directives:

```
using std::placeholders::_1;
using std::placeholders::_2;
// etc. OR
using namespace std::placeholders;
```

You may adapt functions by reordering their arguments without changing function arity to achieve a new functionality. For example, given the functor std::less that returns true if its first argument is less than its second argument, we can generate a functor, which returns true if its first argument is greater than its second argument by swapping the arguments. The following expression generates this:

```
boost::bind(std::less<int>(), _2, _1)
```

Here, std::less<int> takes two arguments, and we generate a wrapper function object, which also takes two arguments but swaps their positions before passing them to std::less. We can directly call the generated functor in-place, like this:

```
boost::bind(std::less<int>(), _2, _1)(1, 10)
```

We can safely assert that 1 is not greater than 10 but is, in fact, less:

```
assert( std::less<int>()(1, 10) );
assert( !boost::bind(std::less<int>(), _2, _1)(1, 10) );
```

Boost Bind is also useful for generating delegates, and other methods of generating delegates were illustrated in listing 7.7 and 7.8. Here is Listing 7.8 rewritten using boost::bind:

Listing 7.10: Generating delegates with Boost Bind

```
1 class MessageHandler
2 {
3 public:
```

```
 4   ...
 5   void listenOnQueue(Queue& q, MessageType msgType) {
 6     q.listen(msgType, boost::bind(&MessageHandler::handleMsg,
 7                                     this, _1));
 8   }
 9
10   void handleMsg(Message msg) { ... }
11 };
```

We must bind a member function to an object instance. We do this by binding `this` to the first argument of `MessageHandler::handleMsg` (lines 6-7). This technique is generally useful for invoking member functions on each object in a collection. Moreover, `boost::bind` / `std::bind` intelligently deal with objects, pointers, smart pointers, and so on, so you do not need to write different binders, depending on whether it is a copy of an object, a pointer, or a smart pointer. In the following example, we take a vector of `std::strings`, compute their lengths using the `size` member function, and put them in a vector of lengths:

Listing 7.11: Generating delegates with Boost Bind

```
1 #include <functional>
2 ...
3 std::vector<std::string> names{"Groucho", "Chico", "Harpo"};
4 std::vector<std::string::size_type> lengths;
5 using namespace std::placeholders;
6
7 std::transform(names.begin(), names.end(),
8                std::back_inserter(lengths),
9                std::bind(&std::string::size, _1));
```

The lengths are computed by calling the `size` member function on each `std::string` object. The expression `std::bind(&std::string::size, _1)` generates an unnamed functor, which calls the `size` member on the `string` object passed to it.

Even if `names` was a vector of pointers to `std::string` objects, or smart pointers, the bind expression (line 9) would not need to change. The `bind` function takes its parameters by value. Thus, in the preceding example, each string is copied into the generated functor—a source of potential performance issue.

Another function template called `boost::mem_fn` and its Standard Library counterpart `std::mem_fn` make it a tad easier to call member functions on objects and generate delegates. The `mem_fn` function template creates a wrapper around pointers to class members. For a member function `f` of arity `N` in class `X`, `mem_fn(&X::f)` generates a functor of arity `N+1`, whose first argument must be a reference, pointer, or smart pointer to the object on which the member function is invoked.

We can write listing 7.11 to use `mem_fn` instead:

```
1 #include <boost/mem_fn.hpp> // <functional> for std
2
...
7 std::transform(names.begin(), names.end(),
8                std::back_inserter(lengths),
9                boost::mem_fn(&std::string::size));
```

Because `std::string::size` is nullary, the functor generated by `boost::mem_fn` is unary and can be readily used with `transform`, without additional binding. The savings are in not having to write the `_1` placeholder, and thus have less syntactic noise.

When we generate a function object using `bind`, it does not immediately check whether the type and number of arguments match the signature of the function being bound to. Only when the generated function object is invoked, does the compiler detect parameter type and arity mismatch:

```
1 std::string str;
2 auto f = boost::bind(&std::string::size, 5); // binds to literal 5
3 auto g = boost::bind(&std::string::size, _1, 20); // binds two args
```

For example, the preceding code would compile even though you cannot call the `size` member function of `std::string` on a numeric literal 5 (line 2). Nor does the `size` member function take an additional numeric argument (line 3). But as soon as you try to call these generated function objects, you will get errors due to type and arity mismatch:

```
4 f(); // error: operand has type int, expected std::string
5 g(str); // error: std::string::size does not take two arguments
```

Binding member functions that are overloaded requires more syntactic effort. Generating functions of even moderate complexity with `bind` is an exercise in nesting binds, which more often than not produces unmaintainable code. In general, with the availability of C++11 lambda and its further refinement in C++14, lambdas rather than bind should be the preferred mechanism of generating unnamed functors. Use `bind` only when it makes your code more expressive than a lambda can.

Compile-time programming with Boost

Templates allow us to write C++ code that is independent of specific types of operands and can thus work unchanged with a large family of types. We can create both **function templates** and **class templates** (or struct templates), which take type parameters, nontype parameters (like constant integers), as well as template parameters. When a *specialization* of a class template is instantiated, member functions that are not directly or indirectly called are never instantiated.

The power of C++ templates goes beyond the ability to write generic code though. C++ templates are a powerful computation subsystem using which we can introspect C++ types, glean their properties, and write sophisticated recursive and branching logic that executes at compile time. Using these capabilities, it is possible to define generic interfaces to implementations that are highly optimized for each type they operate upon.

Basic compile-time control flow using templates

In this section, we briefly look at branching and recursive logic generated using templates.

Branching

Consider the function template `boost::lexical_cast`, introduced in *Chapter 2*, *The First Brush with Boost's Utilities*. To convert a `string` to a `double`, we would write code like the following:

```
std::string strPi = "3.141595259";
double pi = boost::lexical_cast<double>(strPi);
```

The primary template of `lexical_cast` is declared this way:

```
template <typename Target, typename Source>
Target lexical_cast(const Source&);
```

The default implementation of `lexical_cast` (called the **primary template**) writes the source object to a memory buffer via an interface like `ostringstream` and reads back from it via another interface like `istringstream`. This conversion may incur some performance overhead but has an expressive syntax. Now let us suppose that for a particularly performance-intensive application, you want to improve the performance of these string-to-double conversions, but do not want to replace `lexical_cast` with some other function calls. How would you do it? We can create an **explicit specialization** of the `lexical_cast` function template to perform a branching at compile time based on the types involved in the conversion. Since we want to override the default implementation for `string` to `double` conversions, this is how we would write the specialization:

Listing 7.12: Explicit specialization of function templates

```
 1 namespace boost {
 2 template <>
 3 double lexical_cast<double, std::string>(
 4                         const std::string& str)
 5 {
 6   const char *numstr = str.c_str();
 7   char *end = nullptr;
 8   double ret = strtod(numstr, &end);
 9
10   if (end && *end != '\0') {
11     throw boost::bad_lexical_cast();
12   }
13
14   return ret;
15 }
16 } // boost
```

The `template` keyword with an empty argument list (`template<>`) indicates that this is a specialization for specific type arguments (line 2). The **template identifier** `lexical_cast <double, std::string>` lists the specific types for which the specialization takes effect (line 3). With this specialization available, the compiler invokes it whenever it sees code like this:

```
std::string strPi = "3.14159259";
double pi = boost::lexical_cast<double>(strPi);
```

Note that it is possible to *overload function templates* (not just functions). For example:

```
template<typename T> void foo(T);      // 1
template<typename T> void foo(T*);     // 2
template<typename T> T foo(T, T);      // 3
```

```
void foo(int);                      // 4
template<> void foo<double>(double); // 5

int x;
foo(&x);    // calls 2
foo(4, 5);  // calls 3
foo(10);    // calls 4
foo(10.0);  // calls 5
```

In the preceding example, `foo` is a function template (1) that is overloaded (2 and 3). The function `foo` itself is overloaded (4). The function template `foo` (1) is also specialized (5). When the compiler encounters a call to `foo`, it first looks for a matching non-template overload, failing which it looks for the most specialized template overload. In the absence of a matching specialized overload, this would simply resolve to the primary template. Thus, the call to `foo(&x)` resolves to `template<typename T> void foo(T*)`. If such an overload was not present, it would resolve to `template<typename T> void foo(T)`.

It is possible to create specializations for class templates too. In addition to explicit specializations, which specialize a class template for a fixed set of type and non-type arguments, we can also create **partial specializations** of class templates that specialize a class template for a family or category of types:

```
template <typename T, typename U>
class Bar { /* default implementation */ };

template <typename T>
class Bar<T*, T> { /* implementation for pointers */ };
```

In the preceding example, the primary template `Bar` takes two type arguments. We create a partial specialization for `Bar` for those cases, where the first of these two arguments is a pointer-type and the second argument is the pointer-type for the first. Thus, instantiating `Bar<int, float>` or `Bar<double, double*>` will instantiate the primary template, but `Bar<float*, float>`, `Bar<Foo*, Foo>`, etc. will instantiate the partially specialized template. Note that functions cannot be partially specified.

Recursion

Recursion using templates is best illustrated using an example of calculating factorials at compile time. Class templates (as well as function templates) can take integer arguments as long as the values are known at compile time.

Listing 7.13: Compile-time recursion using templates

```
 1  #include <iostream>
 2
 3  template <unsigned int N>
 4  struct Factorial
 5  {
 6    enum {value = N * Factorial<N-1>::value};
 7  };
 8
 9  template <>
10  struct Factorial<0>
11  {
12    enum {value = 1};  // 0! == 1
13  };
14
15  int main()
16  {
17    std::cout << Factorial<8>::value << '\n';  // prints 40320
18  }
```

The primary template for calculating factorials defines a compile-time constant enum `value`. The `value` enum in `Factorial<N>` contains the value of the factorial of N. This is calculated recursively by instantiating the `Factorial` template for N-1 and multiplying its nested `value` enum with N. The stopping condition is provided by the specialization of `Factorial` for 0. These calculations happen at compile time, as the `Factorial` template gets instantiated with successively smaller arguments until `Factorial<0>` stops further instantiation. Thus, the value 40320 is computed completely at compile time and baked into the binary that is built. For example, we could have written the following and it would have compiled and generated an array of 40320 integers on the stack:

```
int arr[Factorial<8>::value];  // an array of 40320 ints
```

Boost Type Traits

The Boost Type Traits library provides a set of templates used to query types for properties and generate derivative types at compile time. They are useful in generic code, that is, code which uses parameterized types, for purposes such as choosing an optimal implementation based on the properties of a type parameter.

Consider the following template:

```
1 #include <iostream>
2
3 template <typename T>
4 struct IsPointer {
5   enum { value = 0 };
6 };
7
8 template <typename T>
9 struct IsPointer <T*> {
10   enum { value = 1 };
11 };
12
13 int main() {
14   std::cout << IsPointer<int>::value << '\n';
15   std::cout << IsPointer<int*>::value << '\n';
16 }
```

The `IsPointer` template has a nested enum called `value`. This is set to 0 in the primary template. We also define a partial specialization of `IsPointer` for pointer-type arguments and set the nested `value` to 1. How is this class template useful? For any type `T`, `IsPointer<T>::value` is 1 if and only if `T` is a pointer-type and 0 otherwise. The `IsPointer` template maps its type argument to a compile-time constant value 0 or 1, which can be used for further branching decisions at compile time.

The Boost Type Traits library is chock full of such templates (including `boost::is_pointer`) that can glean information about types and also generate new types at compile time. They can be used for selecting or generating the optimal code for the types at hand. Boost Type Traits was accepted for the C++ TR1 release in 2007 and as of C++11, there is a Type Traits library in the Standard Library.

Each type trait is defined in its own header so that you can include only those type traits that you need. For example, `boost::is_pointer` would be defined in `boost/type_traits/is_pointer.hpp`. The corresponding `std::is_pointer` (introduced in C++11) is defined in the standard header `type_traits`, there being no separate standard header for it. Each type trait has an embedded type called `type`, and in addition, it may have a member `value` of type bool. Here is an example of using a few type traits.

Listing 7.14: Using type traits

```
1 #include <boost/type_traits/is_pointer.hpp>
2 #include <boost/type_traits/is_array.hpp>
```

```
 3 #include <boost/type_traits/rank.hpp>
 4 #include <boost/type_traits/extent.hpp>
 5 #include <boost/type_traits/is_pod.hpp>
 6 #include <string>
 7 #include <iostream>
 8 #include <cassert>
 8
 9 struct MyStruct {
10   int n;
11   float f;
12   const char *s;
13 };
14
15 int main()
16 {
17 // check pointers
18   typedef int* intptr;
19   std::cout << "intptr is "
20             << (boost::is_pointer<intptr>::value ?"" :"not ")
21             << "pointer type\n";
22 // introspect arrays
23   int arr[10], arr2[10][15];
24   if (boost::is_array<decltype(arr)>::value) {
25     assert(boost::rank<decltype(arr)>::value == 1);
26     assert(boost::rank<decltype(arr2)>::value == 2);
27     assert(boost::extent<decltype(arr)>::value == 10);
28     assert(boost::extent<decltype(arr2)>::value == 10);
29     assert((boost::extent<decltype(arr2), 1>::value) == 15);
30     std::cout << "arr is an array\n";
31   }
32
33 // POD vs non-POD types
34   std::cout << "MyStruct is "
35             << (boost::is_pod<MyStruct>::value ?"" : "not ")
36             << "pod type." << '\n';
37   std::cout << "std::string is "
38             << (boost::is_pod<std::string>::value ?"" : "not ")
40             << "pod type." << '\n';
41 }
```

In this example, we use a number of type traits to query information about types. We define a type `intptr` as an integer pointer (line 18). Applying `boost::is_pointer` to `intptr` yields true (line 20).

The `decltype` specifier used here was introduced in C++ 11. It generates the type of the expression or entity it is applied to. Thus, `decltype(arr)` (line 24) yields the declared type of arr, including any `const` or `volatile` qualifiers. It is a useful means of computing the type of an expression. We apply the `boost::is_array` trait to an array type, which obviously yields true (line 24). To find the number of dimensions or the rank of an array, we use the trait `boost::rank` (lines 25 and 26). The rank of `arr[10]` is 1 (line 25), but the rank of `arr2[10][15]` is 2 (line 26). The `boost::extent` trait is used to find the extent of an array's rank. It must be passed the array's type and rank. If the rank is not passed, it defaults to 0 and returns the extent for one-dimensional arrays (line 27) or the zeroth dimension of multi-dimensional arrays (line 28). Otherwise, the rank should be explicitly specified (line 29).

The `boost::is_pod` trait returns whether a type is a Plain Old Data type or not. It returns true for a simple struct without any constructors or destructors like `MyStruct` (line 34) and false for `std::string`, which is obviously not a POD type (line 38).

As mentioned before, there is also an embedded type in these traits called `type`. This is defined as `boost::true_type` or `boost::false_type`, depending on whether the trait returned true or false. Now consider that we are writing a generic algorithm to copy arrays of arbitrary objects into an array on the heap. For POD-types, a shallow copy or `memcpy` of the whole array is good enough, while for non-POD types, we need to perform element by element copies.

Listing 7.15: Leveraging type traits

```
 1 #include <boost/type_traits/is_pod.hpp>
 2 #include <cstring>
 3 #include <iostream>
 4 #include <string>
 5
 6 struct MyStruct {
 7   int n; float f;
 8   const char *s;
 9 };
10
11 template <typename T, size_t N>
12 T* fastCopy(T(&arr)[N], boost::true_type podType)
13 {
14   std::cerr << "fastCopy for POD\n";
15   T *cpyarr = new T[N];
16   memcpy(cpyarr, arr, N*sizeof(T));
17
18   return cpyarr;
19 }
```

```
20
21 template <typename T, size_t N>
22 T* fastCopy(T(&arr)[N], boost::false_type nonPodType)
23 {
24   std::cerr << "fastCopy for non-POD\n";
25   T *cpyarr = new T[N];
26   std::copy(&arr[0], &arr[N], &cpyarr[0]);
27
28   return cpyarr;
29 }
30
31 template <typename T, size_t N>
32 T* fastCopy(T(&arr)[N])
33 {
34   return fastCopy(arr, typename boost::is_pod<T>::type());
35 }
36
37 int main()
38 {
39   MyStruct podarr[10] = {};
40   std::string strarr[10];
41
42   auto* cpyarr = fastCopy(podarr);
43   auto* cpyarr2 = fastCopy(strarr);
44   delete []cpyarr;
45   delete []cpyarr2;
46 }
```

The fastCopy function template creates a copy of the array on the heap (lines 31-35). We create two overloads of it: one for copying POD-types (lines 11-12) and the other for copying non-POD types (lines 21-22), by adding a second parameter of type boost::true_type in the first case and boost::false_type in the second case. We create two arrays: one of the POD-type MyStruct and the other of the non-POD type std::string (lines 42-43). We call fastCopy on both, which are resolved to the one argument overload (line 32). This forwards the call to the two argument overloads of fastCopy, passing an instance of boost::is_pod<T>::type as the second argument (line 34). This automatically routes the call to the correct overload, depending on whether the stored type T is POD-type or not.

There are many, many more type traits than we can cover in the scope of this book. You have type traits to check whether one type is a base class of another (boost::is_base), whether a type is copy constructible (boost::is_copy_constructible), has specific operators (for example, boost::has_pre_increment), is same as another type (boost::is_same), and so on. The online documentation is a good place to go dig traits and see which ones fit a job at hand.

SFINAE and enable_if / disable_if

Each time a compiler encounters a call to a function with the same name as a function template, it creates an overload resolution set of matching template and non-template overloads. The compiler deduces template arguments as needed to determine which function template overloads (and specializations thereof) qualify, and the qualifying template overloads are instantiated in the process. If substitution of the deduced type arguments in the template's argument list or the function parameter list causes an error, this does not cause the compilation to abort. Instead, the compiler removes the candidate from its overload resolution set. This is referred to as **Substitution Failure Is Not An Error** or **SFINAE**. The compiler only flags an error if, at the end of the process, the overload resolution set is empty (no candidates) or has multiple equally good candidates (ambiguity).

Using a few clever tricks involving compile-time type computation, it is possible to leverage SFINAE to conditionally include templates or exclude them from the overload resolution set. The most succinct syntax to do this is provided by the `boost::enable_if` / `boost::disable_if` templates that are part of the Boost. Utility library.

Let us write a function template to copy an array of elements into another array. The signature of the primary template is as follows:

```
template <typename T, size_t N>
void copy(T (&lhs)[N], T (&rhs)[N]);
```

Thus, you pass two arrays of same size storing the same type of elements, and the elements of the second arguments are copied into the first array in the correct order. We also assume that the arrays never overlap; this keeps the implementation simple. Needless to say this is not the most general setting in which such an assignment can take place, but we will relax some of these restrictions a little later. Here is a generic implementation for this template:

```
1 template <typename T, size_t N>
2 void copy(T (&lhs)[N], T (&rhs)[N])
3 {
4   for (size_t i = 0; i < N; ++i) {
5     lhs[i] = rhs[i];
6   }
7 }
```

The first opportunity for optimization here is when T is a POD-type and a bitwise copy is good enough and possibly faster. We will create a special implementation for POD-types and use SFINAE to choose this implementation only when we are dealing with arrays of POD-types. Our technique should exclude this overload from the overload set when dealing with non-POD type arrays. Here is the special implementation for POD-types:

```
1  // optimized for POD-type
2  template <typename T, size_t N>
3  void copy(T (&lhs)[N], T (&rhs)[N])
4  {
5    memcpy(lhs, rhs, N*sizeof(T));
6  }
```

If you noticed, the two implementations have identical signature and obviously cannot coexist. This is where the boost::enable_if template comes in. The boost::enable_if template takes two parameters: a type T and a second type E, which defaults to void. enable_if defines an embedded type called type, which is typedef'd to E only when T has an embedded type called type and T::type is boost::true_type. Otherwise, no embedded type is defined. Using enable_if, we modify the optimized implementation:

Listing 7.16: Using enable_if

```
#include <boost/utility/enable_if.hpp>
#include <boost/type_traits/is_pod.hpp>

// optimized for POD-type
template <typename T, size_t N>
typename boost::enable_if<boost::is_pod<T>>::type
copy(T (&lhs)[N], T (&rhs)[N])
{
  memcpy(lhs, rhs, N*sizeof(T));
}
```

The typename keyword is required because otherwise the compiler has no way of knowing whether the expression boost::enable_if<boost::is_pod<T>>::type names a type or a member.

If we now instantiate an array of a non-POD type, it will resolve to the default implementation:

```
std::string s[10], s1[10];
copy(s1, s);  // invokes the generic template
```

The call to `copy` causes the compiler to instantiate both templates but `boost::is_pod<std::string>::type` is `boost::false_type`. Now `enable_if<false_type>` does not have a nested type as required by the return type specification of the version of `copy` optimized for POD-arrays. Therefore, there is a substitution failure, and this overload is removed from the overload resolution set, and the first or generic implementation is invoked. Now consider what happens in the following case, where we try to copy an array of POD-types (`double`):

```
double d[10], d1[10];
copy(d1, d);
```

In the current state of affairs, the POD-optimized version will no longer encounter a substitution failure, but the default implementation would also be signature-compatible with this call. Thus, there would be ambiguity and this would result in a compiler error. To fix this, we would have to make sure that the generic implementation excuses itself from the overload set this time. This is done using `boost::disable_if` (which is really `boost::enable_if` negated) in the return type of the generic implementation.

Listing 7.17: Using disable_if

```
1 template <typename T, size_t N>
2 typename boost::disable_if<boost::is_pod<T>>::type
3 copy(T (&lhs)[N], T (&rhs)[N])
4 {
5   for (size_t i = 0; i < N; ++i) {
6     lhs[i] = rhs[i];
7   }
8 }
```

When `T` is a POD-type, `is_pod<T>::type` is `boost::true_type`. `boost::disable_if<true_type>` does not have a nested `type` and thus a substitution failure occurs with the generic implementation. This way, we build two mutually exclusive implementations that are correctly resolved at compile time.

We can also use the `boost::enable_if_c<>` template which takes a Boolean parameter instead of a type. `boost::enable_if_c<true>` has an embedded `type`, while `boost::enable_if_c<false>` does not. With these, the return type in listing 7.17 would look like this:

```
typename boost::disable_if_c<boost::is_pod<T>::value>::type
```

The Standard Library, as of C++11, has `std::enable_if` only, and it behaves like `boost::enable_if_c`, taking a Boolean argument rather than a type. It is available from the standard header `type_traits`.

The Boost Metaprogramming Library (MPL)

The **Boost Metaprogramming Library**, **MPL** for short, is a general purpose library for template metaprogramming. It is ubiquitous in the Boost codebase, and most libraries use some metaprogramming facility from MPL. Some libraries like Phoenix, BiMap, MultiIndex, and Variant use it very heavily. It is used heavily for type manipulation and optimization through conditional selection of specific template implementations. This section is a short overview of some of the concepts and techniques involving MPL.

Metafunctions

The heart of the MPL library is a **metafunction**. Formally, a metafunction is either a class template with only type parameters or a class, which exposes a single embedded type called `type`. In effect, type parameters if any are analogous to parameters to a function and the embedded `type`, which is computed at compile time based on the parameters, is analogous to the return value of a function.

Type traits provided by Boost Type Traits library are first-class metafunctions. Consider the `boost::add_pointer` type trait:

```
template <typename T>
struct add_pointer;
```

The type `add_pointer<int>::type` is `int*`. The `add_pointer` template is a unary metafunction with a single type parameter and an embedded type called `type`.

Sometimes, the effective result of a type computation is numeric – case in point `boost::is_pointer<T>` (Boolean truth value) or `boost::rank<T>` (a positive integer). In such cases, the embedded `type` will have a static member called `value` containing this result, and it will also be directly accessible from the metafunction as a non-type member called `value`. Thus, `boost::is_pointer<T>::type::value` and `boost::is_pointer<T>::value` are both valid, the latter being more concise.

Using MPL metafunctions

The MPL working in conjunction with Boost Type Traits makes a lot of metaprogramming jobs easy. For this, the MPL provides a number of metafunctions to compose existing metafunctions together.

Like type traits, MPL facilities are partitioned into independent, highly granular header files. All metafunctions are in the `boost::mpl` namespace. We can compose unnamed metafunctions together into composite metafunctions using the MPL library. This is not unlike lambdas and bind at runtime. The following snippet uses `boost::mpl::or_` metafunction to check whether a type is either an array or a pointer:

Listing 7.18: Using MPL metafunctions

```
 1 #include <boost/mpl/or.hpp>
 2 #include <boost/type_traits.hpp>
 3
 4 if (boost::mpl::or_<
 5                     boost::is_pointer<int*>,
 6                     boost::is_array<int*>
 7                   >::value) {
 8   std::cout << "int* is a pointer or array type\n";
 9 }
10
11 if (boost::mpl::or_<
12                     boost::is_pointer<int[]>,
13                     boost::is_array<int[]>
14                   >::value) {
15   std::cout << "int* is a pointer or array type\n";
16 }
```

The `boost::mpl::or_` metafunction checks whether any of its argument metafunctions evaluates to true. We can create our own reusable metafunction that packages the preceding logic by using a technique called **metafunction forwarding**:

Listing 7.19: Creating your own metafunction

```
 1 #include <boost/mpl/or.hpp>
 2 #include <boost/type_traits.hpp>
 3
 4 template <typename T>
 5 struct is_pointer_or_array
 6      : boost::mpl::or_<boost::is_pointer<T>,
 7                        boost::is_array<T>>
 8 {};
```

We combine the existing type trait metafunctions using `boost::mpl::or_` and inherit from the composed entity, as shown in the preceding listing (line 6). We can now use `is_pointer_or_array` like any type trait.

Sometimes, we need to pass numeric arguments, which are clearly non-type, to metafunctions. For example, to compare whether the size of a type T is smaller than that of another type U, we ultimately need to compare two numeric sizes. Let us write the following trait to compare the size of two types:

```
template <typename T, typename U> struct is_smaller;
```

is_smaller<T, U>::value will be true if and only if sizeof(T) is less than sizeof(U), and will be false otherwise.

Listing 7.20: Using integral wrappers and other metafunctions

```
 1 #include <boost/mpl/and.hpp>
 2 #include <boost/mpl/int.hpp>
 3 #include <boost/mpl/integral_c.hpp>
 4 #include <boost/mpl/less.hpp>
 5 #include <iostream>
 6 namespace mpl = boost::mpl;
 7
 8 template <typename L, typename R>
 9 struct is_smaller : mpl::less<
10                         mpl::integral_c<size_t, sizeof(L)>
11                         , mpl::integral_c<size_t, sizeof(R)>>
12 {};
13
14 int main()
15 {
16   if (is_smaller<short, int>::value) {
17     std::cout << "short is smaller than int\n";
18   } else { ... }
19 }
```

MPL provides a metafunction boost::mpl::integral_c to wrap integral values of a specified type (size_t, short, etc.). We use it to wrap the sizes of the two types. The boost::mpl::less metafunction compares the two sizes and its nested value is set to true only if the first argument is numerically less than the second. We can use it like any other trait.

We will now try to write something slightly less trivial. We want to write a function to assign arrays. Here is the function template signature:

```
template <typename T, size_t M,
          typename S, size_t N>
void arrayAssign(T(&lhs)[M], S(&rhs)[N]);
```

The type T(&)[M] is a reference to an array of M elements of type T; likewise for S (&)[N]. We want to assign the second argument rhs to the first argument lhs.

You can assign an array of type S[] to an array of type T[] as long as S and T are the same types, or the conversion from S to T is allowed and does not cause loss of information. Also, M must not be smaller than N. We will define a trait is_array_assignable which captures these constraints. Thus, is_array_assignable<T(&)[M], S(&)[N]>::value will be true only if the preceding constraints are met.

First, we need to define three helper metafunctions: is_floating_assignable, is_integer_assignable, and is_non_pod_assignable. The is_floating_assignable<T, S> metafunction checks whether it is possible to assign a numeric value of type S to a floating point type T. The is_integer_assignable<T, S> metafunction checks whether both T and S are integers, and an assignment for T and S does not cause any potential loss or narrowing. Thus, signed integers cannot be assigned to unsigned integers, unsigned integers can only be assigned to larger signed integer types, and so on. The is_non_pod_assignable<T, S> trait checks whether at least one of S and T is non-POD type and whether an assignment operator from S to T exists.

We will then define is_array_assignable using these and other metafunctions.

Listing 7.21: Defining useful type traits using MPL

```
 1 #include <boost/type_traits.hpp>
 2 #include <type_traits>
 3 #include <boost/mpl/and.hpp>
 4 #include <boost/mpl/or.hpp>
 5 #include <boost/mpl/not.hpp>
 6 #include <boost/mpl/greater.hpp>
 7 #include <boost/mpl/greater_equal.hpp>
 8 #include <boost/mpl/equal.hpp>
 9 #include <boost/mpl/if.hpp>
10 #include <boost/mpl/integral_c.hpp>
11 #include <boost/utility/enable_if.hpp>
12 #include <iostream>
13
14 namespace mpl = boost::mpl;
15
16 template <typename T, typename S>
17 struct is_larger
18     : mpl::greater<mpl::integral_c<size_t, sizeof(T)>
19                 , mpl::integral_c<size_t, sizeof(S)>>
20 {};
```

```
21 template <typename T, typename S>
22 struct is_smaller_equal
23   : mpl::not_<is_larger<T, S>>
24 {};
25
26 template <typename T, typename S>
27 struct is_floating_assignable
28   : mpl::and_<
29       boost::is_floating_point<T>
30     , boost::is_arithmetic<S>
31     , is_smaller_equal<S, T>
32     >
33 {};
34
35 template <typename T, typename S>
36 struct is_integer_assignable
37   : mpl::and_<
38       boost::is_integral<T>
39     , boost::is_integral<S>
40     , is_smaller_equal<S, T>
41     , mpl::if_<boost::is_signed<S>
42             , boost::is_signed<T>
43             , mpl::or_<boost::is_unsigned<T>
44                     , mpl::and_<boost::is_signed<T>
45                             , is_larger<T, S>>
46                 >
47           >
48     >
49 {};
50
51 template <typename T, typename S>
52 struct is_non_pod_assignable
53   : mpl::and_<
54           mpl::not_<mpl::and_<boost::is_pod<T>
55                           , boost::is_pod<S>>
56             >
57         , std::is_assignable<T, S>
58         >
59 {};
60
61 template <typename T, typename U>
62 struct is_array_assignable
```

```
63      : boost::false_type
64 {};
65
66 template <typename T, size_t M, typename S, size_t N>
67 struct is_array_assignable<T (&)[M], S (&)[N]>
68      : mpl::and_<
69            mpl::or_<
70                  boost::is_same<T, S>
71                , is_floating_assignable<T, S>
72                , is_integer_assignable<T, S>
73                , is_non_pod_assignable<T, S>
74              >
75          , mpl::greater_equal<mpl::integral_c<size_t, M>
76                              , mpl::integral_c<size_t, N>>
77          >
78 {};
79
80
81 template <typename T, size_t M, typename S, size_t N>
82 typename boost::enable_if<is_array_assignable<T(&)[M],
83                                               S(&)[N]>>::type
84 assignArray(T (&target)[M], S (&source)[N])
85 { /* actual copying implementation */ }
```

The primary template of the is_array_assignable metafunction always returns
false (lines 61-64). The partial specialization of is_array_assignable (line 66-78)
is the heart of the implementation. It uses the mpl::or_ metafunction to check
whether any one of the following conditions is met:

- The source and target types are the same (line 70)

- The target type is a floating point, the source type is numeric, and an
  assignment is possible without narrowing (line 71)

- The target type is integral (signed or unsigned), the source type is integral,
  and an assignment is possible without narrowing (line 72)

- At least one of the source and target types is a non-POD type and a
  conversion from the source to the target type is possible (line 73)

The mpl::or_ metafunction is analogous to the logic or operator of C++, and its
static member value is set to true if any one of the passed conditions is true. Along
with this composite condition being true, the following condition must also hold:

The number of elements in the target array should be at least as much as the
elements in the source array.

We use the `mpl::greater_equal` metafunction to compare these two values `M` and `N`. Since the metafunction needs to take type parameters, we generate type parameters corresponding to `M` and `N` using `boost::mpl::integral_c` wrapper (lines 75-76). We compute the logical-OR of conditions 1-4 and its logical-AND with condition 5 using the `mpl::and_` metafunction (line 61).

We use `boost::enable_if` that leverages SFINAE to disable `assignArray` when `is_array_assignable` returns false.

Let us now look at the implementation of the `is_integer_assignable`. It checks if the target and source types are both integral, (lines 38-39) and the source type is not bigger than the target type (line 40). In addition, we use `boost::mpl::if_` metafunction, which takes three metafunctions; if the first metafunction evaluates to `true`, the second metafunction is returned, otherwise the third metafunction is returned. Using `mpl::if_`, we express the constraints on the source and target types (lines 41-47). If the source type is a signed integer (line 41), then the target type must also be a signed integer (line 42). But if the source type be an unsigned integer, then the target type must either be an unsigned integer (line 43) or a signed integer larger than the source type (lines 44-45). The rest of the traits are similarly defined using Boost MPL library facilities.

Metaprogramming is not just a tool for choosing optimal implementations or catching violations at compile time. It actually helps create expressive libraries like `boost::tuple` or `boost::variant`, involving significant type manipulation. We introduced only a few basic abstractions from the Boost MPL library to help you ease into template metaprogramming. If you have worked through the examples in this chapter, you should have no problems exploring MPL further on your own.

Domain Specific Embedded Languages

In the last third of this chapter, we look at the applications of higher order and compile-time programming mainly in the area Domain Specific Embedded Languages.

Lazy evaluation

In C++, when we see the following code:

```
z = x + y();
```

We know that the value of z is immediately computed when the control reaches past the statement z = x + y(). In fact, the act of computing the sum involves evaluating the expressions x and y() themselves. Here, y is presumably a function or a functor instance, so the call to y() will in turn trigger more evaluations. Irrespective of whether z is ever used for anything later, its value would still be computed. This is the model of **eager evaluation** that a lot of programming languages follow. The actual story is slightly more complex because compilers can reorder and optimize away computations but there is little control the programmer has on the process.

What if we could defer the evaluation of such expressions and any of their sub-expressions until we have to make use of the result? This is the **lazy evaluation** model seen in a lot of functional programming languages, like Haskell. If we could construct arbitrary language expressions that are lazily evaluated, then such expressions could be passed around just like functors and evaluated where necessary. Imagine a function called integrate that evaluates definite integrals of arbitrary functions, given boundary values:

```
double integrate(std::function<double(double)> func,
                 double low, double high);
```

Imagine being able to evaluate the integral $\int_{1}^{10}(x+1/x)\,dx$ by calling the following code:

```
double result = integrate(x + 1/x, 1, 10);
```

The key would be to not evaluate the expression x + 1/x eagerly but pass it to the integrate function as a lazy expression. Now C++ does not have any built-in mechanism to create lazy expressions like these using regular variables. But we can quite easily write a lambda to get our job done:

```
result = integrate([](double) { return x + 1/x; }, 1, 10);
```

This works albeit with some syntactic noise, but in many applications, lambda and bind just do not scale with complexity. In this section, we briefly study **expression templates** and more generally, **Domain Specific Embedded Languages (DSELs)**, which are the means of constructing lazily evaluated function objects within C++ that get your job done without sacrificing on expressive syntax.

Expression templates

So, how do we express a function $f(x)=x+1/x$ in the language of the domain rather than through a syntactic compromise within the confines of C++? To create a generic solution, we must be able to support a variety of algebraic expressions. Let us start with the most basic function—a constant function, such as $f(x)=5$. Irrespective of the value of x, this function should always return 5.

The following functor can be used for this purpose:

Listing 7.22a: An expression template mini-library – lazy literals

```
 1 #include <iostream>
 2
 3 struct Constant {
 4   Constant(double val = 0.0) : val_(val) {}
 5   double operator()(double) const { return val_; }
 6
 7   const double val_;
 8 };
 9
10 Constant c5(5);
11 std::cout << c5(1.0) << '\n';  // prints 5
```

The `operator()` returns the stored `val_` and ignores its argument, which is unnamed. Now let us see how we can represent a function like *f(x)=x*, using a similar functor:

Listing 7.22b: An expression template mini-library – lazy variables

```
1 struct Variable {
2   double operator()(double x) { return x; }
3 };
4
5 Variable x;
6 std::cout << x(8) << '\n';   // prints 8
7 std::cout << x(10) << '\n';  // prints 10
```

We now have a functor that yields whatever value is passed to it; exactly what *f(x)=x* does. But how do we express an expression like *x + 1/x*? The general form of a functor that represents an arbitrary function of a single variable should be as follows:

```
struct Expr {
  ...
  double operator()(double x) {
    return (value computed using x);
  }
};
```

Both `Constant` and `Variable` conform to this form. But consider a more complex expression like *f(x)=x+1/x*. We can break it down to two sub-expressions *x* and *1/x* acted upon by the binary operation +. The expression *1/x* can be further broken down to two sub-expressions *1* and *x* acted upon by the binary operation /.

This can be represented by an **Abstract Syntax Tree (AST)**, as shown here:

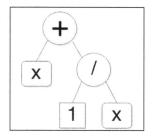

The non-leaf nodes in the tree represent operations. Binary operation nodes have two children: the left operand is the left child and the right operand is the right child. The AST has an operation (+) at the root and two sub-expressions as two children. The left sub-expression is *x*, while the right sub-expression is *1/x*. This *1/x* is further deconstructed in a sub-tree with operation (/) at the root, *1* as the left child, and *x* as the right child. Notice that values like *1* and *x* only appear at the leaf level and correspond to the `Constant` and `Variable` classes we defined. All non-leaf nodes represent operators.

We can model a complex expression as one that is composed of two sub-expressions with an operator:

Listing 7.22c: An expression template mini-library – complex expressions

```
1 template <typename E1, typename E2, typename OpType>
2 struct ComplexExpression {
3   ComplexExpression(E1 left, E2 right) : left_(left),
4                right_(right)
5   {}
6
7   double operator()(double x) {
8     return OpType()(left_(x), right_(x));
9   }
10
11   E1 left_; E2 right_;
12 };
```

When the `ComplexExpression` functor is invoked, that is, when it evaluates its left and right sub-expressions and then applies the operator on them (line 7), this in turn triggers the evaluation of the left and right sub-expressions. If they are `ComplexExpression`s themselves, then they trigger further evaluations that traverse down the tree, depth-first. This is definitive **lazy evaluation**.

Now, in order to easily generate complex expression functors, we need to overload the arithmetic operators to combine sub-expressions of type `Constant`, `Variable`, `ComplexExpression<>`, or primitive arithmetic types. To do this better, we create an abstraction for all kinds of expressions called `Expr`. We also modify our definition of `ComplexExpression` to use `Expr`.

Listing 7.22d: An expression template mini-library – generic expressions

```
 1 template <typename E, typename Enable = void>
 2 struct Expr {
 3   Expr(E e) : expr_(e) {}
 4
 5   double operator()(double x) { return expr_(x); }
 6
 7 private:
 8   E expr_;
 9 };
10
11 template <typename E1, typename E2, typename Op>
12 struct ComplexExpression
13 {
14   ComplexExpression(Expr<E1> left, Expr<E2> right) :
15                     left_(left), right_(right) {}
16
17   double operator()(double d) {
18     return Op()(left_(d), right_(d));
19   }
20
21 private:
22   Expr<E1> left_;
23   Expr<E2> right_;
24 };
```

We will pass around all kinds of expressions wrapped in `Expr`, for example, `Expr<Constant>`, `Expr<ComplexExpression>`, and so on. If you are unsure why we need the second template parameter `Enable`, then hang on for the answer in a bit. Before that, we will define the arithmetic operators between any two `Expr`s, starting with `operator+`:

Listing 7.22e: An expression template mini-library – overloaded operators

```
 1 #include <functional>
 2
```

```
 3 template <typename E1, typename E2>
 4 Expr<ComplexExpression<E1, E2, std::plus<double>>>
 5          operator+ (E1 left, E2 right)
 6 {
 7   typedef ComplexExpression <E1, E2,
 8                                  std::plus<double>> ExprType;
 9   return ExprType(Expr<E1>(left), Expr<E2>(right));
10 }
```

Any binary operation will produce a `ComplexExpression`. Since we will pass everything abstracted as `Expr`, we return `Expr<ComplexExpression<...>>` from the arithmetic operators. It is easy to write an `operator-`, `operator*`, or `operator/` on the same lines. We can replace `std::plus` with `std::minus`, `std::multiples`, or `std::divides` in the preceding implementation.

There is only one more detail to take care of. With the preceding code, we can write expressions of the following form:

```
Variable x;
Constant c1(1);
integrate(x + c1/x, 1, 10);
```

But we cannot write $x + 1/x$ using numeric literals. To do this, we must automatically convert numeric literals to `Constant`. For this, we will create a partial specialization of `Expr` and use `boost::enable_if` to enable it for numeric types. This is where the `Enable` argument of the `Expr` template comes in handy. It defaults to `void` for the primary template, but it helps us write the partial specialization for wrapping arithmetic-type literals.

Listing 7.22f: An expression template mini-library – a small trick

```
 1 #include <boost/utility/enable_if.hpp>
 2 #include <boost/type_traits/is_arithmetic.hpp>
 3
 4 template <typename E>
 5 struct Expr<E, typename boost::enable_if<
 6                         boost::is_arithmetic<E>>::type>
 7 {
 8   Expr(E& e) : expr_(Constant(e)) {}
 9
10   double operator()(double x) { return expr_(x); }
11
12   Constant expr_;
13 };
```

This partial specialization is invoked only when E is an arithmetic type (int, double, long, etc.). This stores the arithmetic value as a Constant. With this change, we can use numeric literals in our expressions, and as long as there is a single Variable in the expression, the literals would get wrapped in a Constant via the partial specialization in listing 7.22f. We can now generate a functor using just natural algebraic expressions:

Listing 7.22g: An expression template mini-library – using the expressions

```
Variable x;
std::cout << (x + 1/x)(10) << '\n';
std::cout << ((x*x - x + 4)/(2*x))(10) << '\n';
```

We can add many more refinements to this very basic *expression template* library of not even a hundred lines of code. But it already allows us to generate arbitrary algebraic functions of a single variable using very simple syntax. This is an example of a *Domain Specific Language*. Also, specifically, because we use valid C++ syntax to do all this instead of defining a new syntax, it is specifically called **Domain Specific Embedded Language (DSEL)** or sometimes **Embedded Domain Specific Language (EDSL)**. We will now look at Boost Phoenix, an elaborate library of lazy expressions.

Boost Phoenix

Boost Phoenix 3 is a library for enabling functional programming constructs in C++. It defines an elaborate and very readable DSEL with scores of functors and operators, which can be used to generate fairly involved lambdas. It provides a comprehensive library for constructing lazy expressions and an excellent example of what expression templates can achieve. This section features a very short introduction to using Phoenix expressions as lambdas, and we will see some examples of using Phoenix with Boost Spirit Parser Framework. It is too extensive a library to cover in a single chapter, let alone a subsection of it, but this introduction should still provide enough tail wind to master Phoenix, with the benefit of the excellent online documentation.

Phoenix expressions are composed of **actors**, which are abstractions for lazy functions. Actors are used to generate unnamed functions or lambdas. They support partial function application by binding some arguments to values and keeping others unspecified. They can be composed to generate more complex functors. In that sense, Phoenix is a lambda language library.

Actors are categorized based on functionality and exposed through a set of header files. The most basic actor is `val` which represents a lazy immutable value (not unlike the `Constant` functor in our expression template example). The `ref` actor is used to create a lazy mutable variable reference, and the `cref` actor generates a lazy immutable reference. There is a whole set of actors that define lazy operators, including arithmetic (`+`, `-`), comparison (`<`, `==`, `>`), logical (`&&`, `||`), bitwise operators (`|`, `^`, `&`), and other kinds of operators. Using just these, we can construct algebraic expressions, as we do in the following example:

Listing 7.23: Lazy algebraic expressions with Phoenix

```
1  #include <boost/phoenix/core.hpp>
2  #include <boost/phoenix/operator.hpp>
3  #include <iostream>
4
5  int main() {
6    namespace phx = boost::phoenix;
7    double eX;
8    auto x = phx::ref(eX);
9
10   eX = 10.0;
11   std::cout << (x + 1/x)() << '\n';                // prints 10.1
12   std::cout << ((x*x -x + 4) / (2*x))() << '\n'; // prints 4.7
13 }
```

Using `boost::phoenix::ref`, we generate an actor for lazily evaluating the variable eX (**e** for **eager**) and cache it in a variable x. The expressions x + 1/x and x*x - x + 4 generate anonymous functors just like the expression templates from listing 7.22, except that x is already bound to the variable eX. The actor x is said to **infect** the numeric literals in the expressions by its presence; the literals get wrapped in `boost::phoenix::val`. The operators +, -, *, and / used in the expression are lazy operators from Phoenix (just like the operators we defined for our expression template in listing 7.22e) and generate anonymous functors.

Writing simple lambdas can sometimes be extremely succinct using Phoenix. Look at how we can print each element in a vector using `std::for_each` and Phoenix's lazy `operator<<`:

Listing 7.24: Simpler lambdas with Phoenix

```
1  #include <boost/phoenix/core.hpp>
2  #include <boost/phoenix/operator.hpp>
3  #include <vector>
```

```
 4 #include <string>
 5 #include <iostream>
 6 #include <algorithm>
 7
 8 int main() {
 9   using boost::phoenix::arg_names::arg1;
10   std::vector<std::string> vec{"Lambda", "Iota",
11                               "Sigma", "Alpha"};
12   std::for_each(vec.begin(), vec.end(),
13                 std::cout << arg1 << '\n');
14 }
```

The expression `std::cout << arg1` is actually a lambda that generates a functor. The actor `arg1` (`boost::phoenix::arg_names::arg1`) represents the first argument to the functor and is lazily evaluated. The presence of `arg1` in the expression `std::cout << arg1` invokes the lazy `operator<<` and infects the entire expression to generate an unnamed function that prints its argument to the standard output. In general, you can use `arg1` through `argN` to refer to the lazy arguments of an N-ary functor generated with Phoenix. By default, up to ten argument actors (`arg1` through `arg10`) are supported. These are akin to `_1`, `_2`, etc. for `boost::bind`. You can also use `boost::phoenix::placeholders::_1`, `_2`, etc.

Phoenix actors are not limited to expressions involving operators. We can generate actors that lazily evaluate entire blocks of code with branching and looping constructs. Let us say we have a vector of the names of personnel in a band's lineup, and we want to print whether a person is a vocalist or instrumentalist:

Listing 7.25: Lazy control structures with Phoenix

```
 1 #include <boost/phoenix/core.hpp>
 2 #include <boost/phoenix/statement/if.hpp>
 3 #include <boost/phoenix/operator.hpp>
 4 #include <algorithm>
 5 #include <vector>
 6 #include <iostream>
 7
 8 int main() {
 9   namespace phx = boost::phoenix;
10   using namespace phx;
11   using phx::arg_names::arg1;
12
13   std::vector<std::string> names{"Daltrey", "Townshend",
14                                  "Entwistle", "Moon"};
15   std::for_each(names.begin(), names.end(),
16                 if_(arg1 == "Daltrey") [
```

```
17              std::cout << arg1 << ", vocalist" << '\n'
18            ].else_[
19              std::cout << arg1 << ", instrumentalist" << '\n'
20            ]
21          );
22 }
```

We want to run through the vector of last names of the four legendary members of *The Who* and list them with their roles. For (Roger) Daltrey, the role would be of a vocalist and for the others, instrumentalist. We use `std::for_each` to iterate the list of names. We pass a unary functor to it generated using Phoenix's statement actors, specifically `boost::phoenix::if_`.

The syntax is intuitive enough to look at and understand what is going on. The actual statements in the `if_` and `else_` blocks are put in square brackets instead of braces (which cannot be overloaded) and are lazily evaluated. If there were multiple statements, they would need to be separated by commas. Notice how the `else_` is a member call invoked with a dot on the preceding expression (line 18). The presence of `arg1` is said to *infect* the statements, that is, it invokes the lazy `operator<<` and causes the literal character strings to be automatically wrapped in `boost::phoenix::val` (lines 16, 17, 19). Running this code prints the following:

```
Daltrey, vocalist
Townshend, instrumentalist
Entwistle, instrumentalist
Moon, instrumentalist
```

The power of Phoenix should be evident already. It defines an expressive sub-language using, standard C++ operator overloading and functors that easily generates unnamed functions or lambdas as needed, and starts to mimic the host language itself. There is more to the Phoenix library. It is chock-full of actors for lazy evaluation of STL container member functions and STL algorithms. Let us look at an example to understand this better:

Listing 7.26: Actors for STL algorithms and container member functions

```
1 #include <vector>
2 #include <string>
3 #include <iostream>
4 #include <boost/phoenix/core.hpp>
5 #include <boost/phoenix/stl/algorithm.hpp>
6 #include <boost/phoenix/stl/container.hpp>
7 #include <cassert>
8
9 int main() {
```

```
10    namespace phx = boost::phoenix;
11    using phx::arg_names::arg1;
12    std::vector<std::string> greets{ "Hello", "Hola", "Hujambo",
13                                     "Hallo" };
14    auto finder = phx::find(greets, arg1);
15    auto it = finder("Hujambo");
16
17    assert (phx::end(greets)() != it);
18    std::cout << *it << '\n';
19    assert (++it != greets.end());
20    std::cout << *it << '\n';
21 }
```

We have a vector greets of hello greetings in different languages (English, Spanish, Swahili, and German), and we want to search for a specific greet. We want to do so lazily using Phoenix. Phoenix provides actors for generating lazy versions of most STL algorithms. We use the lazy form of the std::find algorithm available via the header boost/phoenix/stl/algorithm.hpp (line 5), and call the boost::phoenix::find actor to generate a unary functor named finder (line 14). The finder functor takes as its only argument, the string to look for in greets. The call boost::phoenix::find(greets, arg1) takes two arguments and generates a unary functor. The first argument is a reference to the vector greets, which is automatically wrapped in a cref actor and stored for lazy evaluation later. The second argument to find is the Phoenix placeholder arg1.

When finder is called with the string to lookup as its sole argument, it evaluates the arg1 actor to get this string argument. It also evaluates the cref actor it stored earlier to get a reference to greets. It then calls std::find on the greets vector, looking for the string passed, which returns an iterator. We look for the string Hujambo which is the present in the vector(line 15).

To check whether the iterator returned is valid, we need to compare it against greets.end(). Just to show that it can be done, we generate the lazy version of the end member function call using the boost::phoenix::end actor available from the header boost/phoenix/stl/algorithm.hpp. The call boost::phoenix::end(greets) generates a functor, and we call it in-place by suffixing parentheses. We compare the result with the iterator returned by finder (line 17). We print the greeting pointed by the iterator returned by find and the element after that (lines 18-20):

```
Hujambo
Hallo
```

Actors from Phoenix are polymorphic. You can apply `boost::phoenix::find` on any kind of container that supports searching via `std::find`, and you can look up an object of any type that the underlying container can store.

In the final example on Phoenix, we look at how we can define our own actors, which can fit in with the rest of Phoenix. We have a vector of names from which we print the first name in each entry, using `std::for_each` and functors generated using Phoenix. We extract first names from a name string by looking up the first space character in the string and extracting the prefix up to that point. We can use the `find` actor to locate the space but to extract the prefix, we need a lazy way to call the `substr` member of `std::string`. There is no `substr` actor currently available in Phoenix, so we need to roll out our own:

Listing 7.27: User defined actors and STL actors

```
 1 #include <vector>
 2 #include <string>
 3 #include <iostream>
 4 #include <algorithm>
 5 #include <boost/phoenix/core.hpp>
 6 #include <boost/phoenix/function.hpp>
 7 #include <boost/phoenix/operator.hpp>
 8 #include <boost/phoenix/stl/container.hpp>
 9 #include <boost/phoenix/stl/algorithm.hpp>
10
11 struct substr_impl {
12   template<typename C, typename F1, typename F2>
13   struct result  {
14     typedef C type;
15   };
16
17   template<typename C, typename F1, typename F2>
18   C operator()(const C& c, const F1& offset,
19               const F2& length) const
20   {  return c.substr(offset, length); }
21 };
22
23 int main() {
24   namespace phx = boost::phoenix;
25   using phx::arg_names::arg1;
26
27   std::vector<std::string> names{"Pete Townshend",
28             "Roger Daltrey", "Keith Moon", "John Entwistle"};
29   phx::function<substr_impl> const substr = substr_impl();
30
```

```
31    std::for_each(names.begin(), names.end(), std::cout <<
32                  substr(arg1, 0, phx::find(arg1, ' ')
33                                 - phx::begin(arg1))
34                  << '\n');
35  }
```

We write the `substr_impl` functor, which has a member template `operator()` (line 17) and a metafunction called `result` (line 12). The `operator()` is a template used to make `substr_impl` polymorphic. Any type `C` with a member function called `substr`, which takes two parameters of type `F1` and `F2` (which may or may not be of different types) can be covered by this single implementation (lines 17-20). The embedded `type` in the `result` metafunction is the return type of the wrapped function (`substr`). The actual `substr` actor is an instance of type `boost::phoenix::function<substr_impl>` (line 29). We use the `substr` actor, we just defined, to generate a unary functor, which we pass to the `std::for_each` algorithm (lines 32-33). Since we want to extract the first name from each string in the `names` vector, the first argument is `arg1` (the name passed to the functor), the second offset argument is 0, while the third length argument is the offset of the first space character in the string. The third argument is calculated lazily as the expression `boost::phoenix::find(arg1, ' ')` – `boost::phoenix::begin(arg1)`. The `find(arg1, ' ')` is an actor that looks up the first space in the string passed to it using the generic find actor from Phoenix that we also used in listing 7.26. The `begin(arg1)` is an actor that returns the begin iterator of its argument (in this case the string). The difference between them returns the length of the first name.

Boost Spirit Parser Framework

Boost Spirit is a very popular DSEL used for generating lexers and parsers, which uses Boost Phoenix. Writing custom lexers and parsers used to be heavily reliant on specialized tools like lex/flex, yacc/bison, and ANTLR that generated C or C++ code from a language neutral specification in the **Extended Backus-Naur Form** (EBNF). Spirit eliminates the need for creating such a specification outside the language, and for tools to translate from such specifications. It defines a declarative DSEL with intuitive syntax in C++ and uses only the C++ compiler to generate parsers. Spirit makes heavy use of template metaprogramming, resulting in slower compile times but generates parsers that are efficient at runtime.

Spirit is a rich framework that includes Spirit Lex – a lexer, Spirit Qi – a parser, and Spirit Karma – a generat. You can use these separately, or use them all in collaboration to build powerful data translation engines.

In this book we only look at Spirit Qi. It is used primarily to parse *text data* according to some specified *grammar* that the data is supposed to obey, with the following objectives:

- Verifying that the input conforms to the grammar
- Decomposing a conforming input into meaningful semantic components

For example, we can parse some input text to verify whether it is a valid timestamp, and if it is, extract the components of the timestamp, such as year, month, day, hours, minutes, and so on. For this, we need to define a grammar for the timestamp, and we need to define the actions to be taken, as we parse the data in terms of its semantic constituents. Let us see a concrete example.

Using Spirit Qi

Spirit provides **predefined parsers**, which can be combined using **parser operators** defined by Spirit, to define a parser for our needs. Once defined, we can store the parser or its components as **rules** that can be combined with other rules. Or we can directly pass it to a Qi **parsing API**, such as `parse` or `phrase_parse`, along with the input to parse.

Predefined parsers

Qi provides a number of predefined parsers that can be used to parse basic pieces of data. The parsers are available or aliased under the namespace `boost::spirit::qi`. Here is a listing of these parsers with their purpose:

Input class	Parsers	Purpose
Integers	`int_`, `uint_`, `short_`, `ushort_`, `long_`, `ulong_`, `long_long`, `ulong_long`	Parse signed and unsigned integers
Real numbers	`float_`, `double_`, `long_double`	Parse real numbers with decimal points
Boolean	`bool_`, `true_`, `false_`	Parse either or both the strings, `true` and `false`
Characters	`char_`, `alpha`, `lower`, `upper`, `digit`, `xdigit`, `alnum`, `space`, `blank`, `punct`, `cntrl`, `graph`, `print`	Parse characters of different classes, like letters, digits, hexadecimal digits, punctuation, etc.
Strings	`String`	Parse specific strings

The parsers listed in the preceding table are predefined objects rather than types. There are generic parser templates corresponding to each of these parsers. For example, the template `boost::spirit::qi::int_parser` can be used to define custom parsers for signed integers. There are many other templates, including `boost::spirit::qi::uint_parser`, `boost::spirit::qi::bool_parser`, and so on.

The parsing API

Qi provides two function templates, `parse` and `phrase_parse`, that are used to parse text input. Each takes a pair of iterators that define the input range and a parser expression. In addition, `phrase_parse` takes a second parser expression that is used to match and skip whitespace. The following short example shows you the essence of using Spirit:

Listing 7.28: A simple Spirit example

```
 1 #include <boost/spirit/include/qi.hpp>
 2 #include <cassert>
 3 namespace qi = boost::spirit::qi;
 4
 5 int main()
 6 {
 7   std::string str = "Hello, world!";
 8
 9   auto iter = str.begin();
10   bool success = qi::parse(iter, str.end(), qi::alpha);
11
12   assert(!success);
13   assert(iter - str.begin() == 1);
14 }
```

We include the header file `boost/spirit/include/qi.hpp` in order to access Spirit Qi functions, types, and objects. Our input is the string `Hello, world!`, and using the predefined parser `alpha`, we want to enforce that the first character is a letter from the Latin alphabet, as opposed to a digit or a punctuation symbol. For this, we use the `parse` function, passing it a pair of iterators defining the input and the `alpha` parser (line 10). The `parse` function returns `true` if the parser successfully parses the input and false otherwise. The iterator to the start of the range is incremented to point to the first unparsed character in the input. Since the first character of `Hello, world!` is H, the `alpha` parser parses it successfully, incrementing the `iter` by 1 (line 13) and `parse` returns `true` (line 12). Note that the first iterator is passed as a non-const reference to `parse` and is incremented by parse; the reason we pass a copy of `str.begin()`.

Parser operators and expressions

Spirit defines a number of overloaded operators called **parser operators** which can be used to compose a complex parser expression out of simpler parsers, including the predefined ones. The following table summarizes some of these operators:

Operator	Type	Purpose	Example
>> (Sequence operator)	Binary, infix	Two parsers serially parse two tokens	`string("Hello") >> string("world")` Matches `Helloworld`.
| (Disjunction operator)	Binary, infix	Any one of the two parsers is able to parse the token, but not both	`string("Hello") | string("world")` Matches either `Hello` or `world` but not `Helloworld`.
* (Kleene operator)	Unary, prefix	Parses the empty string or one or more matching tokens	`*string("Hello")` Matches the empty string, `Hello`, `HelloHello`, and so on.
+ (Plus operator)	Unary, prefix	Parses one or more matching tokens	`+string("Hello")` Matches `Hello`, `HelloHello`, and so on, but not the empty string.
~ (Negation operator)	Unary, prefix	Parses a token that does not match the parser	`~xdigit` Will parse any character that is not a hexadecimal digit.
- (Optional operator)	Unary, prefix	Parses the empty string or a single matching token	`-string("Hello")` Matches `Hello` or the empty string.
- (Difference operator)	Binary, infix	*P1* - *P2* parses any token that P1 can parse and P2 cannot	`uint_ - ushort_` Matches any `unsigned int` that is not also an `unsigned short`. Matches 65540 but not 65530 on a system with 2-byte `short`.
% (List operator)	Binary, infix	*P1* % *D* splits the input into tokens that match P1 at delimiters that match D	`+alnum % +(space|punct)` Splits input text strings into alphanumeric strings, using spaces and punctuations as delimiters.
|| (Sequential OR operator)	Binary, infix	*P1* || *P2* is equivalent to *P1* | *(P1 >> P2)*	`string("Hello") || string("world")` Matches either `Hello` or `Helloworld` but not `world`.

Note that there is a unary `operator-`, which is the optional operator, and binary `operator-`, which is the difference operator.

The `boost::spirit::qi::parse` function template does not skip any characters whitespaces while parsing. Sometimes, it is convenient to ignore intervening spaces between tokens while parsing, and the `boost::spirit::qi::phrase_parse` does this. For example, the parser `string("Hello") >> string("world")` would parse `Helloworld` when we use `boost::spirit::qi::parse`, but not `Hello, world!`. But if we used `phrase_parse` and ignored spaces and punctuation, then it would parse `Hello, world!` too.

Listing 7.29: Using phrase_parse

```
1 #include <boost/spirit/include/qi.hpp>
2 #include <cassert>
3 namespace qi = boost::spirit::qi;
4
5 int main()
6 {
7   std::string str = "Hello, world!";
8
9   auto iter = str.begin();
10  bool success = qi::parse(iter, str.end(),
11                  qi::string("Hello") >> qi::string("world"));
12
13  assert(!success);
14
15  iter = str.begin();
16  success = qi::phrase_parse(iter, str.end(),
17                  qi::string("Hello") >> qi::string("world"),
18                  +(qi::space|qi::punct));
19
20  assert(success);
21  assert(iter - str.begin() == str.size());
22 }
```

Note that we pass `+(space|punct)` as the fourth argument to `phrase_parse`, which tells it which characters to ignore; spaces and punctuation.

Parsing directives

Parsing directives are modifiers that can be used to alter the behavior of parsers in some way. For example, we can perform case-insensitive parses using the `no_case` directive, as shown in the following snippet:

```
1    std::string str = "Hello, WORLD!";
2    iter = str.begin();
3    success = qi::phrase_parse(iter, str.end(),
4                    qi::string("Hello") >>
5                      qi::no_case[qi::string("world")],
6                    +(qi::space|qi::punct));
7    assert(success);
```

The `skip` directive can be used to skip whitespace over a section of the input:

```
1    std::string str = "Hello world";
2    auto iter = str.begin();
3    bool success = qi::parse(iter, str.end(),
4                    qi::skip(qi::space)[qi::string("Hello") >>
5                                        qi::string("world")]);
6    assert( success);
```

The directive `qi::skip(qi::space)[parser]` ignores spaces even though we called `parse` and not `phrase_parse`. It can be selectively applied to parser sub-expressions.

Semantic actions

More often than not, while using Spirit, we are not just looking to verify that a piece of text conforms to a certain grammar; we want to extract the tokens and perhaps use them in some kind of calculation or store them away. We can associate some action to a parser instance to be run when it successfully parses text, and this action can perform the necessary computation using the result of the parse. Such actions are defined using a function object enclosed in square brackets, trailing the parser it is associated with.

Listing 7.30: Defining actions associated with parsers

```
1 #include <boost/spirit/include/qi.hpp>
2 #include <iostream>
3 namespace qi = boost::spirit::qi;
4
5 void print(unsigned int n) {
```

```
 6    std::cout << n << '\n';
 7  }
 8
 9  int main() {
10    std::string str = "10 20 30 40 50 60";
11
12    auto iter = str.begin();
13    bool success = qi::phrase_parse(iter, str.end(),
14                                    +qi::uint_[print],
15                                    qi::space);
16    assert(success);
17    assert(iter == str.end());
18  }
```

In the preceding example, we parse a list of unsigned integers separated by spaces (line 10) using the uint_ parser (line 14). We define a function print (line 5) to print unsigned integers and associate it as an action with the uint_ parser (line 14). For each unsigned integer parsed, the preceding code prints it on a new line by invoking the specified action. Actions can also be specified using functors, including those generated by Boost Bind and Boost Phoenix.

Each parser, from the primitive to the most complex, has an associated *attribute*, which is set to the result of a successful parse, that is, the text it matches when it is applied to some input converted to the appropriate type. For a simple parser like uint_, this attribute would be of type unsigned int. For complex parsers, this could be an ordered tuple of attributes of its constituent parsers. When an action associated with a parser is invoked, it is passed the value of the parser's attribute.

The expression +qi::uint_[print] associates the print function with the uint_ parser. If instead we wanted to associate an action with the composite parser +qi::uint_, then we would need to use a function with a different signature—one with a parameter of type std::vector<unsigned int> that would contain all the parsed numbers:

```
1  #include <vector>
2
3  void printv(std::vector<unsigned int> vn)
4  {
5    for (const int& n: vn) {
6      std::cout << n << '\n';
```

```
 7   }
 8 }
 9
10 int main() {
11   std::string str = "10 20 30 40 50 60";
12
13   auto iter = str.begin();
14   bool success = qi::phrase_parse(iter, str.end(),
15                            (+qi::uint_) [printv],
16                            qi::space);
17 }
```

We can use Boost Bind expressions and Phoenix actors too for generating the action.
Thus, we could have written +qi::uint_[boost::bind(print, ::_1)] to call
print on each parsed number. The placeholders ::_1 through ::_9 are defined
by the Boost Bind library in the global namespace. Spirit provides Phoenix actors
that can be used for a variety of actions. The following snippet shows a way to add
parsed numbers into a vector:

```
 1 #include <boost/spirit/include/qi.hpp>
 2 #include <boost/spirit/include/phoenix_core.hpp>
 3 #include <boost/spirit/include/phoenix_operator.hpp>
 4 #include <boost/spirit/include/phoenix_stl.hpp>
 5
 6 int main() {
 7   using boost::phoenix::push_back;
 8
 9   std::string str = "10 20 30 40 50 60";
10   std::vector<unsigned int> vec;
11   auto iter = str.begin();
12   bool status = qi::phrase_parse(iter, str.end(),
13               +qi::uint_[push_back(boost::phoenix::ref(vec),
14                                    qi::_1)],
15               qi::space);
16 }
```

The action expression push_back(boost::phoenix::ref(vec), qi::_1) uses the
boost::phoenix::push_back actor to append each parsed number (represented by
the placeholder qi::_1) to the vector vec.

There are overloads of the `parse` and `phrase_parse` function templates that take an attribute argument in which you can directly store the data parsed by the parser. Thus, we can pass a `vector` of `unsigned ints` as the attribute argument, while parsing the list of unsigned integers:

```
std::vector<unsigned int> result;
bool success = qi::phrase_parse(iter, str.end(),
                                +qi::uint_, result,
                                qi::space);
for (int n: result) {
  std::cout << n << '\n';
}
```

Rules

So far, we have generated parsers using inline expressions. When dealing with more complex parsers, it is useful to cache the components and reuse them. For this purpose, we use the `boost::spirit::qi::rule` template. The rule template takes up to four arguments of which the first, that is, the iterator type for the input, is mandatory. Thus, we can cache a parser that parses spaces in `std::string` objects, as shown here:

```
qi::rule<std::string::iterator> space_rule = qi::space;
```

Notice that `space_rule`, defined as above, is a parser that follows the same grammar as `qi::space`.

More often than not, we are interested in consuming the value parsed by the parser. To define a rule containing such a parser, we need to specify the signature of a method that would be used to obtain the parsed value. For example, the `boost::spirit::qi::double_` parser's attribute is of type `double`. So, we consider a function taking no arguments and returning a `double` as the appropriate signature `double()` to use. This signature is passed as the second template argument to the rule:

```
qi::rule<std::string::iterator, double()> double_rule =
                                          qi::double_;
```

If the rule is meant to skip spaces, we specify the type of parser that is used to identify the characters to skip as the third template argument to `rule`. Thus, to define a parser for a list of `doubles` separated by spaces, we can use the following rule with `qi::space_type`, specifying the type of the space parser:

```
qi::rule<std::string::iterator, std::vector<double>(),
         qi::space_type> doubles_p = +qi::double_;
```

When a rule is defined in terms of a combination of parsers, the value parsed by the rule is synthesized from the values parsed by the individual component parsers. This is called the **synthesized attribute** of the rule. The signature argument to the rule template should be compatible with the type of the synthesized attribute. For example, the parser +qi::double_ returns a sequence of doubles, and therefore, the type of the synthesized attribute is std::vector<std::double>:

```
qi::rule<std::string::iterator, std::vector<double>(),
                           qi::space_type> doubles_p;
doubles_p %= +qi::double_;
```

Notice that we assign the parser to the rule on a separate line, using operator %=. If we did not use the %= operator and used the plain assignment operator instead, then the result of a successful parse using +qi::double_ would not be propagated to the synthesized attribute of doubles_p. Thanks to the %= operator, we can associate a semantic action with doubles_p to access its synthesized value as a std::vector<double>, as shown in the following example:

```
std::string nums = "0.207879576 0.577215 2.7182818 3.14159259";
std::vector<double> result;
qi::phrase_parse(iter1, iter2,
            doubles_p[boost::phoenix::ref(result) == qi::_1],
            qi::space);
```

Parsing timestamps

Consider timestamps of the form YYYY-mm-DD HH:MM:SS.ff, in which the date part is mandatory and the time part is optional. Moreover, the seconds and fractional seconds part of the time are also optional. We need to define a suitable parser expression.

The first thing we require is a way to define parsers for fixed-length unsigned integers. The boost::spirit::qi::int_parser template comes in handy for this purpose. Using template parameters of int_parser, we specify the base integral type to use, the radix or base of the number system, and the minimum and maximum number of digits to allow. Thus, for 4-digit years, we can use a parser type int_parser<unsigned short, 10, 4, 4>, both the minimum and maximum width being 4, as we need fixed-length integers. The following are the rules constructed using int_parser:

```
#include <boost/spirit/include/qi.hpp>

namespace qi = boost::spirit::qi;

qi::int_parser<unsigned short, 10, 4, 4> year_p;
```

```
qi::int_parser<unsigned short, 10, 2, 2> month_p, day_p, hour_p,
                                         min_p, sec_p;
qi::rule<std::string::iterator> date_p =
  year_p >> qi::char_('-') >> month_p >> qi::char_('-') >> day_p;

qi::rule<std::string::iterator> seconds_p =
          sec_p >> -(qi::char_('.') >> qi::ushort_);

qi::rule<std::string::iterator> time_p =
  hour_p >> qi::char_(':') >> min_p
          >> -(qi::char_(':') >> seconds_p);

qi::rule<std::string::iterator> timestamp_p = date_p >> -
                                         (qi::space >> time_p);
```

Of course, we need to define actions to capture the components of the timestamp. For simplicity, we will associate actions with the component parsers. We will define a type to represent timestamps and associate actions with parsers to set attributes of an instance of this type.

Listing 7.31: Simple date and time parser

```
 1 #include <boost/spirit/include/qi.hpp>
 2 #include <boost/bind.hpp>
 3 #include <cassert>
 4 namespace qi = boost::spirit::qi;
 5
 6 struct timestamp_t
 7 {
 8   void setYear(short val) { year = val; }
 9   unsigned short getYear() { return year; }
10   // Other getters / setters
11
12 private:
13   unsigned short year, month, day,
14             hours, minutes, seconds, fractions;
15 };
16
17 timestamp_t parseTimeStamp(std::string input)
18 {
```

```
19    timestamp_t ts;
20
21    qi::int_parser<unsigned short, 10, 4, 4> year_p;
22    qi::int_parser<unsigned short, 10, 2, 2> month_p, day_p,
23                                      hour_p, min_p, sec_p;
24    qi::rule<std::string::iterator> date_p =
25     year_p [boost::bind(&timestamp_t::setYear, &ts, ::_1)]
26     >> qi::char_('-')
27     >> month_p [boost::bind(&timestamp_t::setMonth, &ts, ::_1)]
28     >> qi::char_('-')
29     >> day_p [boost::bind(&timestamp_t::setDay, &ts, ::_1)];
30
31    qi::rule<std::string::iterator> seconds_p =
32        sec_p [boost::bind(&timestamp_t::setSeconds, &ts, ::_1)]
33          >> -(qi::char_('.')
34          >> qi::ushort_
35          [boost::bind(&timestamp_t::setFractions, &ts, ::_1)]);
36
37    qi::rule<std::string::iterator> time_p =
38     hour_p  [boost::bind(&timestamp_t::setHours, &ts, ::_1)]
39     >> qi::char_(':')
40     >> min_p [boost::bind(&timestamp_t::setMinutes, &ts, ::_1)]
41      >> -(qi::char_(':') >> seconds_p);
42
43    qi::rule<std::string::iterator> timestamp_p = date_p >> -
44                                      (qi::space >> time_p);
45    auto iterator = input.begin();
46    bool success = qi::phrase_parse(iterator, input.end(),
47                                      timestamp_p, qi::space);
48    assert(success);
49
50    return ts;
51 }
```

The timestamp_t type (line 6) represents a timestamp, with getters and setters for each of its fields. We have omitted most of the getters and setters for conciseness. We define actions associated with parsers for individual fields of the timestamp, setting appropriate attributes of a timestamp_t instance using boost::bind (lines 25, 27, 29, 32, 35, 38, 40).

Self-test questions

For multiple choice questions, choose all the options that apply:

1. Which of the following overloads/specializations does the call `foo(1.0, std::string("Hello"))` resolve to?

    a. `template <typename T, typename U> foo(T, U);`

    b. `foo(double, std::string&);`

    c. `template <> foo<double, std::string>`

    d. There is ambiguity

2. What is the interface that a metafunction must satisfy?

    a. It must have a static `value` field

    b. It must have an embedded type called `type`

    c. It must have a static `type` field

    d. It must have an embedded type called `result`

3. What does the following statement do: `boost::mpl::or_<boost::is_floating_point<T>, boost::is_signed<T>>`?

    a. Checks whether type T is signed and a floating point type

    b. Generates a metafunction that checks (a)

    c. Checks whether type T is signed or a floating point type

    d. Generates a metafunction that checks (b)

4. We have a template declared as: `template <typename T, typename Enable = void> class Bar` and does not use the `Enable` parameter in any way. How do you declare a partial specialization of Bar that would be instantiated only when T is a non-POD type?

    a. `template <T> class Bar<T, boost::is_non_pod<T>>`

    b. `template <T> class Bar<T, boost::enable_if<is_non_pod<T>>::type>`

    c. `template <T> class Bar<T, boost::mpl::not<boost::is_pod<T>>>`

    d. `template <T> class Bar<T, boost::disable_if<is_pod<T>>::type>`

5. Which of the following is true of C++ lambda expressions and Boost Phoenix actors?

   a. Lambda expressions are unnamed, Phoenix actors are not

   b. Phoenix actors are polymorphic, while polymorphic lambda expressions are only available from C++14

   c. Phoenix actors can be partially applied, while lambda expressions cannot

   d. Lambda expressions can be used as closures but Phoenix actors cannot

Summary

This chapter was an interlude in our exploration of the Boost libraries. There were two key underlying themes: more expressive code and faster code. We saw how higher order programming helps us achieve more expressive syntaxes using functors and operator overloading. We saw how template metaprogramming techniques allow us to write code that executes at compile time and chooses the most optimal implementations for the task at hand.

We covered a diverse amount of material in a single chapter and introduced a paradigm of programming that may be new to some of you. We solved a few problems with different functional patterns and saw the power of C++ functors, templates, and operator overloading put together. Understanding the subject of this chapter will be of immediate help if you are reading the implementation of most Boost libraries or trying to write a fast general purpose library that is efficient, expressive, and extensible.

There is a lot that we did not cover in this chapter and do not cover in this book, including many, but the most basic details of Boost Spirit, a DSEL construction kit, Boost Proto; an expression template-based fast regular expression library, Boost Xpressive; and a more advanced tuple library, Boost Fusion. Hopefully, this chapter gives you enough of a head start to explore them further. Starting with the next chapter, where we cover Boost libraries for date and time calculations, we switch gears to focus on systems programming libraries in Boost.

References

- *C++ Common Knowledge, Stephen C. Dewhurst, Addison Wesley Professional*

- *Modern C++ Design, Andrei Alexandrescu, Addison Wesley Professional*

- *C++ Template Metaprogramming, David Abrahams and Aleksey Gurtovoy, Addison Wesley Professional*

- **Proto:** http://web.archive.org/web/20120906070131/http://cpp-next.com/archive/2011/01/expressive-c-expression-optimization/

- **Boost Xpressive FTW:** http://ericniebler.com/2010/09/27/boost-xpressive-ftw/

- **Fusion:** www.boost.org/libs/fusion

8
Date and Time Libraries

This is a short chapter that shows you how to use different Boost libraries for performing basic date and time calculations. Most practical software use date and time measurements in some form. Applications compute current date and time to produce chronological logs of application activity. Specialized programs compute schedules for jobs based on complex scheduling policies, and wait for specific points in time, or time intervals to elapse. Sometimes, applications even monitor their own performance and speed of execution, taking remedial steps as needed or raising notifications.

In this chapter, we look at Boost libraries for performing date and time calculations, and measuring code performance. These topics are divided into the following sections:

- Date and time calculations with Boost `Date Time`
- Using Boost Chrono to measure time
- Measuring program performance using Boost Timer

Date and time calculations with Boost Date Time

Date and time calculations are important in many software applications, yet C++03 had limited support for manipulating dates and performing calculations with them. The Boost `Date Time` library provides a set of intuitive interfaces for representing dates, timestamps, durations, and time intervals. By allowing simple arithmetic operations involving dates, timestamps, durations, and supplementing them with a set of useful date/time algorithms, it enables fairly sophisticated time and calendar calculations using little code.

Dates from the Gregorian calendar

The Gregorian calendar, also known as the Christian calendar, was introduced by Pope Gregory XIII in February 1582 and over the next few centuries, replaced the Julian calendar in the vast majority of the western world. The Date_Time library provides a set of types for representing dates and related quantities:

- boost::gregorian::date: We use this type to represent a date in the Gregorian calendar.

- boost::gregorian::date_duration: In addition to dates, we also need to represent durations — the length of time between two given dates in the calendar — in the unit of days. For this, we use the type boost::gregorian::date_duration. It refers to the same type as boost::gregorian::days.

- boost::date_period: A fixed date period of the calendar starting at a given date and extending for a specific duration is represented using the type boost::date_period.

Creating date objects

We can create objects of type boost::gregorian::date using constituent parts of a date, namely the year, month, and day of the month. In addition, there are a number of factory functions that parse date strings in different formats to create objects of date. In the following example, we illustrate the different ways of creating date objects:

Listing 8.1: Using boost::gregorian::date

```
1  #include <boost/date_time.hpp>
2  #include <iostream>
3  #include <cassert>
4  namespace greg = boost::gregorian;
5
6  int main() {
7    greg::date d0;  // default constructed, is not a date
8    assert(d0.is_not_a_date());
9    // Construct dates from parts
10   greg::date d1(1948, greg::Jan, 30);
11   greg::date d2(1968, greg::Apr, 4);
12
13   // Construct dates from string representations
14   greg::date dw1 = greg::from_uk_string("15/10/1948");
15   greg::date dw2 = greg::from_simple_string("1956-10-29");
16   greg::date dw3 = greg::from_undelimited_string("19670605");
```

```
17    greg::date dw4 = greg::from_us_string("10-06-1973");
18
19    // Current date
20    greg::date today = greg::day_clock::local_day();
21    greg::date londonToday = greg::day_clock::universal_day();
22
23    // Take dates apart
24    std::cout << today.day_of_week() << " " << today.day() << ", "
25            << today.month() << ", " << today.year() << '\n';
26 }
```

A default-constructed date represents an invalid date (line 7); the is_not_a_date member predicate returns true for such dates (line 8). We can construct dates from its constituent parts: year, month, and day. Months can be indicated using enum values named Jan, Feb, Mar, Apr, May, Jun, Jul, Aug, Sep, Oct, Nov, and Dec, which are abbreviated English names of the months of the year. Using special factory functions, dates can be constructed from other standard representations. We use the boost::gregorian::from_uk_string function to construct a date object from a string in the DD/MM/YYYY format, which is standard in UK (line 14). The boost::gregorian::from_us_string function is used to construct a date from a string in the MM/DD/YYYY format used in the US (line 17). The function boost::gregorian::from_simple_string is used to construct a date from a string in the ISO 8601 YYYY-MM-DD format (line 15), and its undelimited form YYYYMMDD can be converted into a date object, using the boost::gregorian::from_undelimited_string function (line 16).

Clocks provide a way to retrieve the current date and time on a system. Boost provides a couple of clocks for this purpose. The day_clock type provides the local_day (line 20) and universal_day (line 21) functions, which return the current date in the local and UTC time zones, which could be same or differ by a day, depending on the time zone and time of the day.

Using convenient accessor member functions like day, month, year, and day_of_week, we can get at parts of a date (lines 24-25).

> The Date_Time library is not a header-only library, and in order to run examples in this section, they must be linked to the libboost_date_time library. On Unix, with g++, you can use the following command line to compile and link examples involving Boost Date Time:
>
> `$ g++ example.cpp -o example -lboost_date_time`
>
> See *Chapter 1, Introducing Boost*, for more details.

Handling date durations

The duration of time between two dates is represented by boost::gregorian::date_duration. In the following example, we compute time durations between dates, and add durations to dates or subtract durations from dates to derive new dates:

Listing 8.2: Basic date arithmetic

```
 1 #include <boost/date_time.hpp>
 2 #include <iostream>
 3 namespace greg = boost::gregorian;
 4
 5 int main() {
 6   greg::date d1(1948, greg::Jan, 30);
 7   greg::date d2(1968, greg::Apr, 4);
 8
 9   greg::date_duration day_diff = d2 - d1;
10   std::cout << day_diff.days()
11           << " days between the two dates\n";
12
13   greg::date six_weeks_post_d1 = d1 + greg::weeks(6);
14   std::cout << six_weeks_post_d1 << '\n';
15
16   greg::date day_before_d2 = d2 - greg::days(1);
17   std::cout << day_before_d2 << '\n';
18 }
```

We compute durations (which can be negative) as the difference of two dates (line 9), and print it in the unit of days (line 10). The date_duration object internally represents durations in unit of days. We can also use the types boost::gregorian::weeks, boost::gregorian::months, and boost::gregorian::years to construct date_duration objects in units of weeks, months, or years. Note that boost::gregorian::days and boost::gregorian::date_duration refer to the same types. We get new dates by adding durations to or subtracting them from dates (lines 13, 16).

Date periods

A period starting at a fixed date is represented by the type boost::gregorian::date_period. In the following example, we construct two date periods, a calendar year, and a US fiscal year. We calculate their overlap period, and then determine the date of the last Friday of each month in the overlapping period.

Listing 8.3: Date periods and calendar calculations

```
1 #include <boost/date_time.hpp>
2 #include <iostream>
3 namespace greg = boost::gregorian;
4 namespace dt = boost::date_time;
5
6 int main() {
7   greg::date startCal(2015, greg::Jan, 1);
8   greg::date endCal(2015, greg::Dec, 31);
9
10  greg::date startFiscal(2014, greg::Oct, 1);
11  greg::date endFiscal(2015, greg::Sep, 30);
12
13  greg::date_period cal(startCal, endCal);
14  greg::date_period fisc(startFiscal, endFiscal);
15
16  std::cout << "Fiscal year begins " << fisc.begin()
17    << " and ends " << fisc.end() << '\n';
18
19  if (cal.intersects(fisc)) {
20    auto overlap = cal.intersection(fisc);
21    greg::month_iterator miter(overlap.begin());
22
23    while (*miter < overlap.end()) {
24      greg::last_day_of_the_week_in_month
25                   last_weekday(greg::Friday, miter->month());
26      std::cout << last_weekday.get_date(miter->year())
27                   << '\n';
28      ++miter;
29    }
30  }
31 }
```

We define date periods in terms of a start and an end date (lines 13, 14). We can check whether two periods overlap using the `intersects` member function of `date_period` (line 19), and obtain the overlap period using the `intersection` member function (line 20). We iterate over a period by creating a `month_iterator` at the start date (line 21) and iterating till the end date (line 23) using the preincrement operator (line 28). There are different kinds of iterators with different periods of iteration. We use `boost::gregorian::month_iterator` to iterate over successive months in the period. The `month_iterator` advances the date by a month, each time it is incremented. You can also use other iterators like `year_iterator`, `week_iterator`, and `day_iterator`, which increment the iterator by a year, a week, or a day at a time.

For each month in the period, we want to find the date of the last Friday in that month. The Date Time library has some interesting algorithm classes for calendar calculations of this sort. We use the `boost::gregorian::last_day_of_the_week_in_month` algorithm for performing such calculations as the date of the last Friday of a month. We construct an object of `last_day_of_the_week_in_month`, the constructor arguments being the day of the week (Friday) and the month (lines 24, 25). We then call its `get_date` member function, passing to it the particular year for which we want the date (line 26).

Posix time

The `Date_Time` library also provides a set of types for representing time points, durations, and periods.

- `boost::posix_time::ptime`: A specific point in time, or a **time point**, is represented by the type `boost::posix_time::ptime`.

- `boost::posix_time::time_duration`: Like date durations, the length of time between two time points is called a **time duration** and is represented by the type `boost::posix_time::time_duration`.

- `boost::posix_time::time_period`: A fixed interval starting at a specific time point and ending at another is called a **time period** and is represented by the type `boost::posix_time::time_period`.

These types and the operations on them together define a **time system**. Posix Time uses `boost::gregorian::date` to represent the date part of time points.

Constructing time points and durations

We can create an instance of `boost::posix_time::ptime` from its constituent parts, that is, date, hours, minutes, seconds, and so on or use factory functions that parse timestamp strings. In the following example, we show different ways in which we can create `ptime` objects:

Listing 8.4: Using boost::posix_time

```
1 #include <boost/date_time.hpp>
2 #include <iostream>
3 #include <cassert>
4 #include <ctime>
5 namespace greg = boost::gregorian;
6 namespace pt = boost::posix_time;
7
8 int main() {
9   pt::ptime pt; // default constructed, is not a time
```

```
10      assert(pt.is_not_a_date_time());
11
12      // Get current time
13      pt::ptime now1 = pt::second_clock::universal_time();
14      pt::ptime now2 = pt::from_time_t(std::time(0));
15
16      // Construct from strings
17      // Create time points using durations
18      pt::ptime pt1(greg::day_clock::universal_day(),
19              pt::hours(10) + pt::minutes(42)
20              + pt::seconds(20) + pt::microseconds(30));
21      std::cout << pt1 << '\n';
22
23      // Compute durations
24      pt::time_duration dur = now1 - pt1;
25      std::cout << dur << '\n';
26      std::cout << dur.total_microseconds() << '\n';
27
28      pt::ptime pt2(greg::day_clock::universal_day()),
29          pt3 = pt::time_from_string("2015-01-28 10:00:31.83"),
30          pt4 = pt::from_iso_string("20150128T151200");
31
32      std::cout << pt2 << '\n' << to_iso_string(pt3) << '\n'
33              << to_simple_string(pt4) << '\n';
34  }
```

Just as with date objects, a default-constructed `ptime` object (line 9) is not a valid time point (line 10). There are clocks that can be used to derive the current time of the day, for example, `second_clock` and `microsec_clock`, which give the time with second or microsecond units. Calling the `local_time` and `universal_time` functions (line 13) on these clocks returns the current date and time in the local and UTC time zones respectively.

The `from_time_t` factory function is passed the Unix time, which is the number of seconds elapsed since the Unix epoch (January 1, 1970 00:00:00 UTC), and constructs a `ptime` object representing that point in time (line 14). The C library function `time`, when passed 0, returns the current Unix time in UTC time zone.

The duration between two time points, which can be negative, is computed as the difference between two time points (line 24). It can be streamed to an output stream for printing the duration, by default, in terms of hours, minutes, seconds, and fractional seconds. Using accessor functions `hours`, `minutes`, `seconds`, and `fractional_seconds`, we can get the relevant parts of a duration. Or we can convert the entire duration to a second or subsecond unit using the accessors `total_seconds`, `total_milliseconds`, `total_microseconds`, and `total_nanoseconds` (line 26).

We can create a `ptime` object from a Gregorian date and a duration of type `boost::posix_time::time_duration` (lines 18-20). We can use the shim types `hours`, `minutes`, `seconds`, `microseconds`, and so on in the `boost::posix_time` namespace to generate durations of type `boost::posix_time::time_duration` in appropriate units and combine them using `operator+`.

We can construct a `ptime` object from just a `boost::gregorian::date` object (line 28). This represents the time at midnight on the given date. We can use factory functions to create `ptime` objects from different string representations (lines 29-30). The function `time_from_string` is used to construct an instance of `ptime` from a timestamp string in "YYYY-MM-DD hh:mm:ss.xxx..." format, in which the date and time parts are separated by a whitespace (line 29). The function `from_iso_string` is used to construct a `ptime` instance from a non-delimited string in the "YYYYMMDDThhmmss.xxx..." format, where an uppercase T separates the date and time parts (line 30). In both cases, the minutes, seconds, and fractional seconds are optional and are taken to be zero if not specified. The fractional seconds can follow the seconds, separated by a decimal point. These formats are locale dependent. For example, in several European locales, a comma is used instead of the decimal point.

We can stream `ptime` objects to output streams like `std::cout` (line 32). We can also convert `ptime` instances to `string` using conversion functions like `to_simple_string` and `to_iso_string` (lines 32-33). In English locales, the `to_simple_string` function converts it to the "YYYY-MM-DD hh:mm:ss.xxx..." format. Notice that this is the same format expected by `time_from_string` and is also the format used when `ptime` is streamed. The `to_iso_string` function converts it to the "YYYYMMDDThhmmss.xxx..." format, same as that expected by `from_iso_string`.

Resolution

The smallest duration that can be represented using a time system is called its resolution. The precision with which time can be represented on a particular system, and therefore, the number of digits of the fractional seconds that are significant, depends on the resolution of the time system. The default resolution used by Posix Time is microsecond (10^{-6} seconds), that is, it cannot represent durations shorter than a microsecond and therefore cannot differentiate between two time points less than a microsecond apart. The following example demonstrates how to obtain and interpret the resolution of a time system:

Listing 8.5: Time ticks and resolution

```
1 #include <boost/date_time.hpp>
2 #include <iostream>
3 namespace pt = boost::posix_time;
4 namespace dt = boost::date_time;
```

```
 5
 6 int main() {
 7   switch (pt::time_duration::resolution()) {
 8   case dt::time_resolutions::sec:
 9     std::cout << " second\n";
10     break;
11   case dt::time_resolutions::tenth:
12     std::cout << " tenth\n";
13     break;
14   case dt::time_resolutions::hundredth:
15     std::cout << " hundredth\n";
16     break;
17   case dt::time_resolutions::milli:
18     std::cout << " milli\n";
19     break;
20   case dt::time_resolutions::ten_thousandth:
21     std::cout << " ten_thousandth\n";
22     break;
23   case dt::time_resolutions::micro:
24     std::cout << " micro\n";
25     break;
26   case dt::time_resolutions::nano:
27     std::cout << " nano\n";
28     break;
29   default:
30     std::cout << " unknown\n";
31     break;
32   }
33   std::cout << pt::time_duration::num_fractional_digits()
34             << '\n';
35   std::cout << pt::time_duration::ticks_per_second()
36             << '\n';
37 }
```

The resolution static function of the time_duration class returns the resolution as an enumerated constant (line 7); we interpret this enum and print a string to indicate the resolution (lines 7-32).

The num_fractional_digits static function returns the number of significant digits of the fractional second (line 33); on a system with microsecond resolution, this would be 6, and on a system with nanosecond resolution, this would be 9. The ticks_per_second static function converts 1 second to the smallest representable time unit on the system (line 35); on a system with microsecond resolution, this would be 10^6, and on a system with nanosecond resolution, this would be 10^9.

Time periods

Just as with dates, we can represent fixed time periods using boost::posix_time::time_period. Here is a short example that shows how you can create time periods and compare different time periods:

Listing 8.6: Using time periods

```
 1 #include <boost/date_time.hpp>
 2 #include <iostream>
 3 #include <cassert>
 4 namespace greg = boost::gregorian;
 5 namespace pt = boost::posix_time;
 6
 7 int main()
 8 {
 9   // Get current time
10   pt::ptime now1 = pt::second_clock::local_time();
11   pt::time_period starts_now(now1, pt::hours(2));
12
13   assert(starts_now.length() == pt::hours(2));
14
15   auto later1 = now1 + pt::hours(1);
16   pt::time_period starts_in_1(later1, pt::hours(3));
17
18   assert(starts_in_1.length() == pt::hours(3));
19
20   auto later2 = now1 + pt::hours(3);
21   pt::time_period starts_in_3(later2, pt::hours(1));
22
23   assert(starts_in_3.length() == pt::hours(1));
24
26   std::cout << "starts_in_1 starts at " << starts_in_1.begin()
27            << " and ends at " << starts_in_1.last() << '\n';
28
29   // comparing time periods
30   // non-overlapping
31   assert(starts_now < starts_in_3);
32   assert(!starts_now.intersects(starts_in_3));
33
34   // overlapping
35   assert(starts_now.intersects(starts_in_1));
36
37   assert(starts_in_1.contains(starts_in_3));
38 }
```

We create a time period called `starts_now` that starts at the current instant and extends for 2 hours into the future. For this, we use the two-argument constructor of `time_period`, passing it the current timestamp and a duration of 2 hours (line 11). Using the `length` member function of `time_period`, we verify that the length of the period is indeed 2 hours (line 13).

We create two more time periods: `starts_in_1` that starts 1 hour later and extends for a duration of 3 hours (line 16), and `starts_in_3` that starts 3 hours later and extends for 1 hour (line 20). The member functions `begin` and `last` of `time_period` return the first and last time points in the period (lines 26-27).

We express the relationships between the three time periods, `starts_now`, `starts_in_1`, and `starts_in_3`, using relational operators and two member functions called `intersects` and `contains`. Clearly, the first hour of `starts_in_1` overlaps with the last hour of `starts_now`, so we assert that `starts_now` and `starts_in_1` intersect with each other (line 35). The last hour of `starts_in_1` coincides with the entire period `starts_in_3`, so we assert that `starts_in_1` contains `starts_in_3` (line 37). But `starts_now` and `starts_in_3` do not overlap; therefore, we assert that `starts_now` and `starts_in_3` do not intersect (line 32).

The relational `operator<` is defined such that for two time periods `tp1` and `tp2`, the condition `tp1 < tp2` holds if and only if `tp1.last() < tp2.begin()`. Likewise, `operator>` is defined such that the condition `tp1 > tp2` holds if and only if `tp1.begin() > tp2.last()`. These definitions imply that `tp1` and `tp2` are disjoint. Thus, for the disjoint `time_period`s `starts_now` and `starts_in_3`, the relation `starts_now < starts_in_3` holds (line 31). These relations do not make sense for overlapping time periods.

Time iterator

We can iterate over a time period using `boost::posix_time::time_iterator`, not unlike how we used `boost::gregorian::date_iterator`. The following example shows this:

Listing 8.7: Iterating over a time period

```
1 #include <boost/date_time.hpp>
2 #include <iostream>
3
4 namespace greg = boost::gregorian;
5 namespace pt = boost::posix_time;
6
7 int main()
8 {
9   pt::ptime now = pt::second_clock::local_time();
```

```
10   pt::ptime start_of_day(greg::day_clock::local_day());
11
12   for (pt::time_iterator iter(start_of_day,
13         pt::hours(1)); iter < now; ++iter)
14   {
15     std::cout << *iter << '\n';
16   }
17 }
```

The preceding example prints the timestamp for each completed hour in the current day. We instantiate a `time_iterator` (line 12), passing it the time point from where to begin the iteration (`start_of_day`) and the duration added for each increment of the iterator (1 hour). We iterate till the current time, incrementing printing the timestamp obtained by dereferencing the iterator (line 15) and incrementing the iterator (line 13). Notice that in the expression `iter < now`, we compare the iterator with a time point to decide when to stop iteration – a peculiar property of `posix_time::time_iterator`, which is not shared with other iterators.

Using Chrono to measure time

Boost Chrono is a library for time calculations having some overlapping functionality with the Posix Time part of the `Date Time` library. Like Posix Time, Chrono too uses the notion of time points and durations. Chrono does not deal with dates. It is a newer library than `Date Time`, and implements the facilities proposed in a paper from the C++ Standards Committee working group (WG21). Parts of that proposal made it to the C++11 Standard Library as the `Chrono` library, and much of the discussion on Boost Chrono also applies to Chrono Standard Library (`std::chrono`).

Durations

A duration represents an interval of time. The duration has a numeric magnitude and must be expressed in units of time. The `boost::chrono::duration` template is used to represent any such duration and is declared as follows:

```
template <typename Representation, typename Period>
class duration;
```

The `Representation` type parameter identifies the underlying arithmetic type used for the magnitude of durations. The `Period` type parameter identifies tick period, which is the magnitude of one unit of time used to measure the duration. The period is usually expressed as a ratio or fraction of 1 second, using a template called `boost::ratio`.

Thus, if we want to express a duration in hundredths of seconds (centiseconds), we can use `int64_t` as the underlying type, and the tick period can be represented using the ratio (1/100) because the tick period is a hundredth of a second. Using `boost::ratio`, we can specialize `duration` to express centisecond intervals as follows:

```
typedef boost::chrono::duration<int64_t, boost::ratio<1, 100>>
                                                  centiseconds;
centiseconds cs(1000);  // represents 10 seconds
```

We create a `typedef` called `centiseconds` and pass `1000`, which is the number of centiseconds in the duration, as a constructor argument. `1000` centiseconds amounts to (1/100)*1000 seconds, that is, 10 seconds.

The `boost::ratio` template is used to construct a type representing a rational number, that is, a ratio of two integers. We specialize `ratio` by passing the numerator and denominator of our rational number as its two non-type template arguments, in that order. The second argument defaults to 1; therefore, to express an integer, say 100, we can simply write `boost::ratio<100>` instead of `boost::ratio<100, 1>`. The expression `boost::ratio<100>` does not represent a value 100 but a type encapsulating the rational number 100.

The `Chrono` library already provides a set of predefined specializations of `duration` for constructing durations expressed in commonly used time units. These are:

- `boost::chrono::hours` (tick period = `boost::ratio<3600>`)
- `boost::chrono::minutes` (tick period = `boost::ratio<60>`)
- `boost::chrono::seconds` (tick period = `boost::ratio<1>`)
- `boost::chrono::milliseconds` (tick period = `boost::ratio<1, 1000>`)
- `boost::chrono::microseconds` (tick period = `boost::ratio<1, 1000000>`)
- `boost::chrono::nanoseconds` (tick period = `boost::ratio<1, 1000000000>`)

Duration arithmetic

Durations can be added and subtracted, and durations in different units can be combined to form other durations. Durations in larger units can be implicitly converted to durations in smaller units. Implicit conversion from smaller to larger units is only possible if you are using a floating point representation; with integral representations, such conversions would incur a loss of precision. To handle this, we must use a function akin to a casting operator for explicit conversions from smaller to larger units with integral representations:

Listing 8.8: Using chrono durations

```
 1 #include <boost/chrono/chrono.hpp>
 2 #include <boost/chrono/chrono_io.hpp>
 3 #include <iostream>
 4 #include <cstdint>
 5 namespace chrono = boost::chrono;
 6
 7 int main()
 8 {
 9   chrono::duration<int64_t, boost::ratio<1, 100>> csec(10);
10   std::cout << csec.count() << '\n';
11   std::cout << csec << '\n';
12
13   chrono::seconds sec(10);
14   chrono::milliseconds sum = sec + chrono::milliseconds(20);
15   // chrono::seconds sum1 = sec + chrono::milliseconds(20);
16
17   chrono::milliseconds msec = sec;
18
19   // chrono::seconds sec2 = sum;
20   chrono::seconds sec2 =
21                 chrono::duration_cast<chrono::seconds>(sum);
22 }
```

This example illustrates the different operations you can perform with durations. The `boost/chrono/chrono.hpp` header includes most of the Boost Chrono facilities we need (line 1). We first create a `duration` of 10 centiseconds (line 9). The `count` member function returns the tick count of the duration, that is, the number of time units in the duration in the chosen unit, centiseconds (line 10). We can directly stream a duration to an output stream (line 11) but need to include the additional header `boost/chrono/chrono_io.hpp` for accessing these operators (line 2). Streaming `csec` prints the following:

```
10 centiseconds
```

Boost Ratio provides the appropriate SI unit prefixes based on the time unit used by the duration, and these are used to intelligently print the appropriate SI prefix. This is not available in the C++11 Standard Library Chrono implementation.

We create second and millisecond durations using the appropriate duration specializations, and compute their sum using an overloaded `operator+` (lines 13, 14). The sum of a second and a millisecond duration is a millisecond duration. Implicit conversion of a duration in milliseconds to a duration in a larger unit like seconds would involve loss of precision when the representation of the larger type is an integral type. Hence, such implicit conversions are not supported (line 15). For example, 10 seconds + 20 milliseconds would be computed as 10020 milliseconds. The `boost:::chrono::seconds typedef` uses a signed integral type representation, and to express 10020 milliseconds in seconds, the 20 milliseconds would need to be implicitly rounded off.

We use the `duration_cast` function template, akin to C++ cast operators, to perform this conversion (lines 20-21), making the intent explicit. The `duration_cast` will effect the rounding off. On the other hand, a duration in seconds can always be implicitly converted to a duration in milliseconds, as there is no loss in precision (line 17).

The `Chrono` library is a separately-built library, which also depends on Boost System library. Thus, we must link the examples in this section to `libboost_system`. On Unix with g++, you can use the following command line to compile and link examples involving Boost Chrono:

```
$ g++ example.cpp -o example -lboost_system -lboost_chrono
```

For Boost libraries installed at nonstandard locations, refer to *Chapter 1, Introducing Boost*.

If we specialized the duration to represent seconds using a `double` instead of a signed integer, then things will be different. The following code will compile because the `double` representation would be able to accommodate fractional parts:

```
boost::chrono::milliseconds millies(20);
boost::chrono::duration<double> sec(10);

boost::chrono::duration<double> sec2 = sec + millies;
std::cout << sec2 << '\n';
```

We do not cover Boost Ratio in detail in this book, but this chapter introduces enough details needed for the purposes of dealing with Boost Chrono. Additionally, you can get at the parts of a ratio and print a ratio as a rational number or an SI prefix, where that makes sense. The following code illustrates this:

```
#include <boost/ratio.hpp>
typedef boost::ratio<1000> kilo;
typedef boost::ratio<1, 1000> milli;
typedef boost::ratio<22, 7> not_quite_pi;
std::cout << not_quite_pi::num << "/"
          << not_quite_pi::den << '\n';
std::cout << boost::ratio_string<kilo, char>::prefix()
          << '\n';
std::cout << boost::ratio_string<milli, char>::prefix()
          << '\n';
```

Note how we use the `ratio_string` template and its prefix member function to print SI prefixes. The code prints the following:

```
22/7
kilo
milli
```

The `std::ratio` template in the C++11 Standard Library corresponds to Boost Ratio and is used by `std::chrono`. There is no `ratio_string` in the Standard Library and therefore, SI prefix printing is absent.

Clocks and time points

A time point is a fixed point in time as opposed to a duration. Given a time point, we can add or subtract a duration from it to derive another time point. An epoch is a reference time point in some time system that can be combined with durations to define other time points. The most famous epoch is the Unix or POSIX epoch January 1, 1970 00:00:00 UTC.

Boost Chrono provides several clocks for the purpose of measuring time in different contexts. A clock has the following associated members:

- A typedef called `duration`, which represents the smallest duration that can be expressed using the clock

- A typedef called `time_point`, which is the type used to represent time points for that clock

- A static member function `now`, which returns the current time point

Boost Chrono defines several clocks, some of which may or may not be available on your system:

- The `system_clock` type represents the wall clock or system time.

- The `steady_clock` type represents a monotonic time system, which means that if the `now` function is called twice serially, the second call will always return a time point later than what the first call returned. This is not guaranteed for `system_clock`. The `steady_clock` type is available if and only if the `BOOST_CHRONO_HAS_STEADY_CLOCK` preprocessor macro is defined.

- The `high_resolution_clock` type is defined to be a `steady_clock` if it is available or else it is defined to be a `system_clock`.

The preceding clocks are available as part of `std::chrono` as well. They use an implementation-defined epoch and provide functions to convert between `time_point` and Unix time (`std::time_t`). The following example illustrates how clocks and time points are used:

Listing 8.9: Using chrono system_clock

```
 1 #include <iostream>
 2 #include <boost/chrono.hpp>
 3
 4 namespace chrono = boost::chrono;
 5
 6 int main()
 7 {
 8   typedef chrono::system_clock::period tick_period;
 9   std::cout
10     << boost::ratio_string<tick_period, char>::prefix()
11     << " seconds\n";
12   chrono::system_clock::time_point epoch;
13   chrono::system_clock::time_point now =
14                           chrono::system_clock::now();
15
16   std::cout << epoch << '\n';
17   std::cout << chrono::time_point_cast<chrono::hours>(now)
18           . << '\n';
19 }
```

In this example, we first print the tick period of the duration associated with `system_clock`. The `system_clock::period` is a typedef for `system_clock::duration::period` and is the `boost::ratio` type representing the tick period of the duration associated with `system_clock` (line 8). We pass it to `boost::ratio_string`, and use the `prefix` member function to print the correct SI prefix (lines 9-10).

It constructs two time points: a default-constructed time point for `system_clock` that represents the epoch of the clock (line 12), and the current time returned by the `now` function provided by the `system_clock` (lines 13-14). We then print the epoch (line 16), followed by the current time (line 17). Time points are printed as the number of time units since the epoch. Note that we use the `time_point_cast` function to convert the current time to hours since the epoch. The preceding code prints the following on my system:

```
nanoseconds
0 nanoseconds since Jan 1, 1970
395219 hours since Jan 1, 1970
```

Boost Chrono also provides the following clocks, none of which are available as part of the C++ Standard Library Chrono:

- The `process_real_cpu_clock` type for measuring the total time since a program started.

- The `process_user_cpu_clock` type for measuring the time a program runs for in the user space.

- The `process_system_cpu` type for measuring the time the kernel runs some code on behalf of the program.

- The `thread_clock` type for measuring the total time for which a particular thread is scheduled. This clock is available if and only if the `BOOST_CHRONO_HAS_THREAD_CLOCK` preprocessor macro is defined.

The process clocks are available if and only if the `BOOST_CHRONO_HAS_PROCESS_CLOCKS` preprocessor macro is defined. These clocks can be used akin to the system clocks but their epochs are at program start-up for CPU clocks, or thread start-up for the thread clocks.

Measuring program performance using Boost Timer

As programmers, we often need to measure performance of a section of code. While there are several excellent profiling tools available for this purpose, sometimes, being able to instrument our own code is both simple and more precise. The Boost Timer library provides an easy-to-use, portable interface for measuring the execution times and reporting them by instrumenting your code. It is a separately compiled library, not header-only, and internally uses Boost Chrono.

cpu_timer

The `boost::timer::cpu_timer` class is used to measure the execution time of a section of code. In the following example, we write a function that reads the contents of a file and returns it in a dynamic array wrapped in a `unique_ptr` (see *Chapter 3, Memory Management and Exception Safety*). It also calculates and prints the time taken to read the file using `cpu_timer`.

Listing 8.10: Using cpu_timer

```
 1 #include <fstream>
 2 #include <memory>
 3 #include <boost/timer/timer.hpp>
 4 #include <string>
 5 #include <boost/filesystem.hpp>
 6 using std::ios;
 7
 8 std::unique_ptr<char[]> readFile(const std::string& file_name,
 9                                  std::streampos& size)
10 {
11   std::unique_ptr<char[]> buffer;
12   std::ifstream file(file_name, ios::binary);
13
14   if (file) {
15     size = boost::filesystem::file_size(file_name);
16
17     if (size > 0) {
18       buffer.reset(new char[size]);
19
20       boost::timer::cpu_timer timer;
```

```
21          file.read(buffer.get(), size);
22          timer.stop();
23
24          std::cerr << "file size = " << size
25                    << ": time = " << timer.format();
26      }
27  }
28
29  return buffer;
30 }
```

We create an instance of cpu_timer at the start of the section of code (line 20), which starts the timer. At the end of the section, we call the stop member function on the cpu_timer object (line 22), which stops the timer. We call the format member function to obtain a readable representation of the elapsed time and print it to the standard error (line 25). Calling this function with a file name, prints the following to the standard input:

```
file size = 1697199:  0.111945s wall, 0.000000s user + 0.060000s
system = 0.060000s CPU (53.6%)
```

This indicates that the call to the read member function of fstream (line 21) was blocked for 0.111945 seconds. This is the wall clock time, that is, the total elapsed time measured by the timer. 0.000000 seconds were spent by the CPU in user mode, and 0.060000 seconds were spent by the CPU in the kernel mode (that is, in system calls). Note that the read happened entirely in kernel mode, which is expected, because it involves invoking system calls (like read on Unix) to read the content of the file from the disk. The percentage of elapsed time spent by the CPU executing this code is 53.6. It is computed as the sum of the durations spent in user mode and in kernel mode, divided by the total elapsed time, that is, (0.0 + 0.06)/0.111945, which is around 0.536.

Code using Boost Timer must link with libboost_timer and libboost_system. To build examples involving Boost Timer with g++ on a POSIX system, use the following command line:

```
$ g++ source.cpp -o executable -std=c++11 -lboost_system
-lboost_timer
```

For Boost libraries installed at nonstandard locations, refer to *Chapter 1, Introducing Boost*.

If we want to measure the cumulative time taken to open the file, read from it and close the file, then we can use a single timer to measure the execution times of multiple sections, stopping and resuming the timer as needed.

The following snippet illustrates this:

```
12    boost::timer::cpu_timer timer;
13    file.open(file_name, ios::in|ios::binary|ios::ate);
14
15    if (file) {
16      size = file.tellg();
17
18      if (size > 0) {
19        timer.stop();
20        buffer.reset(new char[size]);
21
22        timer.resume();
23        file.seekg(0, ios::beg);
24        file.read(buffer.get(), size);
25      }
26
27      file.close();
28    }
29
30    timer.stop();
31
```

The resume member function is called on a stopped timer and it restarts the timer, adding to any previous measurements. In the preceding snippet, we stop the timer before allocating heap memory (line 19), and resume it immediately afterwards (line 22).

There is also a start member function, which is called inside the cpu_timer constructor to start measurements. Calling start instead of resume on a stopped timer would wipe out any previous measurements and effectively reset the timer. You can also check whether the timer has stopped using the is_stopped member function, which returns true if the timer has stopped and false otherwise.

We can get at the elapsed time (wall clock time), CPU time spent in user mode, and CPU time spent in kernel mode in nanoseconds by calling the elapsed member function of cpu_timer:

```
20        file.seekg(0, ios::beg);
21        boost::timer::cpu_timer timer;
22        file.read(buffer.get(), size);
23        timer.stop();
24
25        boost::timer::cpu_times times = timer.elapsed();
26        std::cout << std::fixed << std::setprecision(8)
```

```
27                << times.wall / 1.0e9 << "s wall, "
28                << times.user / 1.0e9 << "s user + "
29                << times.system / 1.0e9 << "s system. "
30                << (double)100*(timer.user + timer.system)
31                      / timer.wall << "% CPU\n";
```

The `elapsed` member function returns an object of type `cpu_times` (line 25), which contains three fields called `wall`, `user`, and `system` that carry the appropriate durations in units of nanoseconds (10^{-9} seconds).

auto_cpu_timer

The `boost::timer::auto_cpu_timer` is a subclass of `cpu_timer` that automatically stops the counter at the end of its enclosing scope and writes the measured execution time to the standard output or another output stream provided by the user. You cannot stop and resume it. When you need to measure the execution of a section of code till the end of a scope, you can use just one line of code using `auto_cpu_timer`, as shown in the following snippet adapted from listing 8.10:

```
17      if (size > 0) {
18          buffer.reset(new char[size]);
19
20          file.seekg(0, ios::beg);
21
22          boost::timer::auto_cpu_timer timer;
23          file.read(buffer.get(), size);
24      }
```

This will print the measured execution time in the familiar format to the standard output:

```
0.102563s wall, 0.000000s user + 0.040000s system = 0.040000s CPU
(39.0%)
```

To print it to a different output stream, we would need to pass the stream as a constructor argument to `timer`.

To measure the time taken to read the file, we simply declare the `auto_cpu_timer` instance before the call to `read` (line 22). If the call to read was not the last statement in the scope, and we did not want to measure the execution time of what followed, then this would not have worked. Then, we could either use `cpu_timer` instead of `auto_cpu_timer`, or put only the statements that we are interested in a nested scope with an `auto_cpu_timer` instance created at the start:

```
17      if (size > 0) {
18          buffer.reset(new char[size]);
```

```
19
20        file.seekg(0, ios::beg);
21
22        {
23          boost::timer::auto_cpu_timer timer(std::cerr);
24          file.read(buffer.get(), size);
25        }
26        // remaining statements in scope
27     }
```

In the preceding example, we create a new scope (lines 22-25) to isolate the section of code to measure, using auto_cpu_timer.

Self-test questions

For multiple choice questions, choose all options that apply:

1. Which of the following lines of code is/are not well-formed? Assume that the symbols are from the boost::chrono namespace.

    a. milliseconds ms = milliseconds(5) + microseconds(10);

    b. nanoseconds ns = milliseconds(5) + microseconds(10);

    c. microseconds us = milliseconds(5) + microseconds(10);

    d. seconds s = minutes(5) + microseconds(10);

2. What does the type boost::chrono::duration<std::intmax_t, boost::ratio<1, 1000000>> represent?

    a. A millisecond duration with integral representation

    b. A microsecond duration with integral representation

    c. A millisecond duration with floating point representation

    d. A nanosecond duration with integral representation

3. What are the differences between boost::timer::cpu_timer and boost::timer::auto_cpu_timer?

    a. auto_cpu_timer calls start in the constructor, cpu_timer does not

    b. auto_cpu_timer cannot be stopped and resumed

    c. auto_cpu_timer writes to an output stream at the end of a scope, cpu_timer does not

    d. You can extract the wall, user, and system time from cpu_timer, but not auto_cpu_timer

Summary

This chapter introduced libraries for measuring time and calculating dates. This chapter gets you up and running with the basics of date and time calculations, without covering the intricate details about sophisticated calendar calculations, time zone awareness, and custom and locale-specific formatting. The Boost online documentation is an excellent source for these details.

References

- *The C++ Standard Library: A Tutorial and Reference Guide (2/e)*, *Nicolai M. Josuttis, Addison Wesley Professional*
- *A Foundation to Sleep On*: *Howard E. Hinnant, Walter E. Brown, Jeff Garland, and Marc Paterno* (`http://www.open-std.org/jtc1/sc22/wg21/docs/papers/2008/n2661.htm`)

9
Files, Directories, and IOStreams

Programming for real-world systems requires interacting with various subsystems of the operating system to utilize their services. Starting with this chapter, we look at the various Boost libraries that provide programmatic access to OS subsystems.

In this chapter, we look at the Boost libraries for performing input and output, and interacting with filesystems. We cover these libraries in the following sections of the chapter:

- Managing files and directories with Boost Filesystem
- Extensible I/O with Boost IOStreams

Using the libraries and techniques covered in this chapter, you will be able to write portable C++ programs that interact with filesystems and perform all kinds of I/O using a standard interface. We do not cover network I/O in this chapter, but devote *Chapter 10, Concurrency with Boost*, to this topic.

Managing files and directories with Boost Filesystem

Software written using the Boost libraries runs on multiple operating systems, including Linux, Microsoft Windows, Mac OS, and various other BSD variants. How these operating systems access paths to files and directories may differ in several ways; for example, MS Windows uses backward slashes as the directory separator while all Unix variants, including Linux, BSD, and Mac, use forward slashes. Non-English operating systems may use other characters as directory separators, and sometimes, multiple directory separators may be supported. The Boost Filesystem library hides these platform-specific peculiarities and lets you write code that is much more portable. Using the functions and types in the Boost Filesystem library, you can write OS-agnostic code to perform common operations on the filesystem that an application needs to run, like copying, renaming, and deleting files, traversing directories, creating directories and links, and so on.

Manipulating paths

Filesystem paths are represented using objects of type `boost::filesystem::path`. Given an object of type `boost::filesystem::path`, we can glean useful information from it and derive other `path` objects from it. A `path` object allows us to model a real filesystem path and derive information from it, but it need not represent a path that really exists in the system.

Printing paths

Let us look at our first example of using Boost Filesystem to print the current working directory of a process:

Listing 9.1: The first example of using Boost Filesystem

```
 1 #include <boost/filesystem.hpp>
 2 #include <iostream>
 3
 4 namespace fs = boost::filesystem;
 5
 6 int main() {
 7   // Get the current working directory
 8   fs::path cwd = fs::current_path();
 9
10   // Print the path to stdout
```

```
11    std::cout << "generic: " << cwd.generic_string() << '\n';
12    std::cout << "native: " << cwd.string() << '\n';
13    std::cout << "quoted: " << cwd << '\n';
14
15    std::cout << "Components: \n";
16    for (const auto& dir : cwd) {
17      std::cout <<'[' <<dir.string() << ']'; // each part
18    }
19    std::cout << '\n';
20 }
```

In this example, the program determines its current working directory by calling the current_path (line 8), which is a namespace level function in the boost::filesystem namespace. It returns an object of type boost::filesystem::path representing the path to the current working directory. Most functions in boost::filesystem work on boost::filesystem::path objects rather than strings.

We print the path by calling the generic_string member function of path (line 11), by calling the string member function (line 12), and also by streaming cwd, the path object, to the output stream (line 13). The generic_string member returns the path in a **generic format** supported by Boost Filesytem with forward slashes as separators. The string member function returns the path in the **native format**, which is an implementation-defined format dependent on the operating system. On Windows, the native format uses backslashes as path separator, while on UNIX there is no difference between the generic and native formats. Boost Filesystem recognizes both forward and backward slashes as path separators on Windows.

Streaming the path object too writes the path in the native format but additionally puts double quotes around the path. Putting double quotes around paths with embedded spaces makes it easy to use the result as arguments to commands. If there be embedded double quote characters (") in the path, those are escaped with an ampersand (&).

On Windows, the full paths are stored as wide character (wchar_t) strings, so generic_string or string return the path as a std::string *after* performing conversion. Depending on the specific Unicode characters in the path, there may not be a meaningful conversion of the path to a single-byte character string. On such systems, it is only safe to call the generic_wstring or wstring member functions, which return the path as a std::wstring in generic or native formats.

We print each directory component in the path, iterating through them using a range-based for-loop in C++11 (line 15). If range-based for-loop is not available, we should use the `begin` and `end` member functions in `path` to iterate through path elements. On my Windows box, this program prints the following:

```
generic: E:/DATA/Packt/Boost/Draft/Book/Chapter07/examples
native:E:\DATA\Packt\Boost\Draft\Book\Chapter07\examples
quoted: "E:\DATA\Packt\Boost\Draft\Book\Chapter07\examples"
Components:
[E:] [/] [DATA] [Packt]  [Boost] [Draft] [Book] [Chapter07] [examples]
```

On my Ubuntu box, this is the output I get:

```
generic: /home/amukher1/devel/c++/book/ch07
native: /home/amukher1/devel/c++/book/ch07
quoted: "/home/amukher1/devel/c++/book/ch07"
Components:
[/] [home] [amukher1]  [devel] [c++] [book] [ch07]
```

The program prints its current working directory in the generic and native formats. You can see that there is no difference between the two on Ubuntu (and generally on any Unix).

On Windows, the first component of the path is the drive letter, generally referred to as the **root name**. This is followed by / (the root folder) and each subdirectory in the path. On Unix, there is no root name (as is usually the case), so the listing starts with / (the root directory) followed by each subdirectory in the path.

The `cwd` object of type `path` is streamable (line 19) and printing it to standard output prints it in the native format, enclosed in quotes.

Compiling and linking examples with Boost Filesystem

Boost Filesystem is not a header-only library. The Boost Filesystem shared libraries are installed as part of the Boost operating system packages, or built from source as described in *Chapter 1, Introducing Boost*.

On Linux

If you installed Boost libraries using your native package manager, then you can use the following commands to build your programs. Note that the library names are in system layout.

```
$ g++ <source>.c -o <executable> -lboost_filesystem
-lboost_system
```

If you built Boost from source as shown in *Chapter 1, Introducing Boost*, and installed it under /opt/boost, you can use the following commands to compile and link your sources:

```
$ g++ <source>.cpp -c -I/opt/boost/include
$ g++ <source>.o -o <executable> -L/opt/boost/lib
-lboost_filesystem-mt -lboost_system-mt -Wl,-rpath,/
opt/boost/lib
```

Since we built the libraries with names in tagged layout, we link against appropriately named versions of Boost Filesystem and Boost System. The -Wl,-rpath,/opt/boost/lib part embeds the path to the Boost shared libraries in the generated executable so that the runtime linker knows from where to pick the shared libraries for the executable to run.

On Windows

On Windows, under Visual Studio 2012 or later, you can enable auto-linking and need not explicitly specify the libraries to link. For this, you need to edit the **Configuration Properties** settings in the **Project Properties** dialog box (brought up using *Alt + F7* in the IDE):

1. Under **VC++ Directories**, append <boost-install-path>\ include to the **Include Directories** property.

2. Under **VC++ Directories**, append <boost-install-path>\lib to the **Library Directories** property.

3. Under **Debugging**, set the **Environment** property to PATH=%PATH%;<boost-install-path>\lib.

4. Under **C/C++ > Preprocessor**, define the following preprocessor symbols:

BOOST_ALL_DYN_LINK

BOOST_AUTO_LINK_TAGGED (only if you built using tagged layout)

5. Build by hitting *F7* from the Visual Studio IDE and run your program by hitting *Ctrl + F5* from the IDE.

Constructing paths

You can construct instances of boost::filesystem::path using one of the path constructors or by combining existing paths in some way. Strings and string literals are implicitly convertible to path objects. You can construct relative as well as absolute paths, convert relative paths to absolute paths, append or strip elements from the path and "normalize" paths, as shown in listing 9.2:

Listing 9.2a: Constructing empty path objects

```
1 #define BOOST_FILESYSTEM_NO_DEPRECATED
2 #include <boost/filesystem.hpp>
3 #include <iostream>
4 #include <cassert>
5 namespace fs = boost::filesystem;
6
7 int main() {
8   fs::path p1; // empty path
9   assert(p1.empty());  // does not fire
10  p1 = "/opt/boost";   // assign an absolute path
11  assert(!p1.empty());
12  p1.clear();
13  assert(p1.empty());
14 }
```

A default constructed path object represents an empty path, as illustrated by the preceding example. You can assign a path string to an empty path object (line 10) and it ceases to be empty (line 11). On calling the clear member function on the path (line 12), it once again turns empty (line 13). Over the years, some parts of the Boost Filesystem library have been deprecated and replaced by better alternatives. We define the macro BOOST_FILESYSTEM_NO_DEPRECATED (line 1) to ensure that such deprecated member functions and types are not accessible.

Listing 9.2b: Constructing relative paths

```
15 void make_relative_paths() {
16   fs::path p2(".."); // relative path
17   p2 /= "..";
18   std::cout << "Relative path: " << p2.string() << '\n';
19
20   std::cout << "Absolute path: "
21     << fs::absolute(p2, "E:\\DATA\\photos").string() << '\n';
22   std::cout << "Absolute path wrt CWD: "
23             << fs::absolute(p2).string() << '\n';
24
```

```
25    std::cout << fs::canonical(p2).string() << '\n';
26 }
27
```

We construct a relative path by using .. (double dot), which is a common way to refer to the parent directory relative to any directory on most filesystems (line 16). We then use `operator/=` to append an additional .. path element to the relative path (line 17). We then print the relative path in its native format (line 18) and create absolute paths using this relative path.

The `boost::filesystem::absolute` function constructs an absolute path given a relative path. You may pass it an absolute path to which the relative path must be appended to construct a new absolute path (line 21). Note that we pass a Windows absolute path and make sure to escape the backslashes. If you omit the second parameter to `absolute`, it constructs the absolute path from the relative path by using the current working directory of the process as the base path (line 23).

A file path such as /opt/boost/lib/../include can be *normalized* to the equivalent form, /opt/boost/include. The function `boost::filesystem::canonical` generates a **normalized absolute path** from a given path (line 25), but requires that the path exist. Otherwise, it throws an exception that needs to be handled. It also reads and follows any symbolic links in the path. The preceding code prints the following output on my Windows box:

```
Relative path: ..\..
Absolute path: E:\DATA\photos\..\..
Absolute path wrt CWD: E:\DATA\Packt\Boost\Draft\Book\Chapter07\
examples\..\..
Canonical: E:/DATA\Packt\Boost\Draft\Book
```

Note that the output for the canonical path has the double dots collapsed.

Listing 9.2c: Handling errors

```
28 void handle_canonical_errors() {
29    fs::path p3 = "E:\\DATA"; // absolute path
30    auto p4 = p3 / "boost" / "boost_1_56";  // append elements
31    std::cout << p4.string() << '\n';
32    std::cout.put('\n');
33
34    boost::system::error_code ec;
35    auto p5 = p4 / ".." / "boost_1_100";  // append elements
36    auto p6 = canonical(p5, ec);
37
38    if (ec.value() == 0) {
```

```
39      std::cout << "Normalized: " << p6.string() << '\n';
40    } else {
41      std::cout << "Error (file=" << p5.string()
42            << ") (code=" << ec.value() << "): "
43            << ec.message() << '\n';
44    }
45 }
```

This example illustrates how `canonical` errors out when it is passed a path that does not exist. We create a path object, `p3`, for the absolute path `E:\DATA` on Windows (line 29). We then create a second path object `p4` by appending successive path elements (`boost` and `boost_1_56`) to `p3` using the overloaded `operator/` for `path` objects (line 30). This constructs a path that is equivalent of `E:\DATA\boost\ boost_1_56`.

Next, we append the relative path `../boost_1_100` to `p4` (line 35), which constructs a path that is equivalent of `E:\DATA\boost\boost_1_56\..\boost_1_100`. This path does not exist on my system so when I call `canonical` on this path, it errors out. Notice that we passed an object of type `boost::system::error_code` as a second argument to `canonical`, to capture any error. We check for a non-zero error code returned using the `value` member function of `error_code` (line 38). In case an error occurred, we can also retrieve a system-defined descriptive error message using the message `member` function (line 43). Alternatively, we can invoke another overload of `canonical`, which does not take an `error_code` reference as argument and instead throws an exception if the path passed does not exist. A throwing and a non-throwing overload is a common pattern seen in functions in the Filesystem library and other system programming libraries from Boost.

Breaking paths into components

In the previous section, we saw how we can get the parent directory of a path by calling the `parent_path` member function. In fact, there is a whole slew of member functions in `boost::filesystem::path` to extract the components in a path. Let us first take a look at a path and its components.

We will first understand the Boost Filesystem terminology for path components using the following path from a UNIX system:

`/opt/boost/include/boost/filesystem/path.hpp`

The leading `/` is called the **root directory**. The last component, `path.hpp`, is called the **filename**, even when the path represents a directory rather than a regular file. The path stripped of the filename (`/opt/boost/include/boost/filesystem`) is called the **parent path**. The part following the leading slash (`opt/boost/include/boost/ filesystem/path.hpp`) is called the **relative path**.

In the preceding example, `.hpp` is the **extension** (including the period or dot) and `path` is the **stem** of the filename. In case of a filename with multiple embedded dots (for example, `libboost_filesystem-mt.so.1.56.0`), the extension is considered to start from the last (right-most) dot.

Now consider the following Windows path:

`E:\DATA\boost\include\boost\filesystem\path.hpp`

The component `E:` is called the **root name**. The leading backslash following `E:` is called the **root directory**. The concatenation of the root name with the root directory (`E:\`) is called the **root path**. The following is a short function that prints these different components of a path using member functions of `boost::filesystem::path`:

Listing 9.3: Splitting a path into components

```
 1 #include <boost/filesystem.hpp>
 2 #include <iostream>
 3 #include <cassert>
 4 namespace fs = boost::filesystem;
 5
 6 void printPathParts(const fs::path& p1)
 7 {
 8 std::cout << "For path: " << p1.string() << '\n';
 9
10   if (p1.is_relative()) {
11     std::cout << "\tPath is relative\n";
12   } else {
13     assert(p1.is_absolute());
14     std::cout << "\tPath is absolute\n";
15   }
16
17   if (p1.has_root_name())
18     std::cout << "Root name: "
19             << p1.root_name().string() << '\n';
20
21   if (p1.has_root_directory())
22     std::cout << "Root directory: "
23             << p1.root_directory().string() << '\n';
24
25   if (p1.has_root_path())
26     std::cout << "Root path: "
27             << p1.root_path().string() << '\n';
```

```
28
29   if (p1.has_parent_path())
30     std::cout << "Parent path: "
31               << p1.parent_path().string() << '\n';
32
33   if (p1.has_relative_path())
34     std::cout << "Relative path: "
35               << p1.relative_path().string() << '\n';
36
37   if (p1.has_filename())
38     std::cout << "File name: "
39               << p1.filename().string() << '\n';
40
41   if (p1.has_extension())
42     std::cout << "Extension: "
43               << p1.extension().string() << '\n';
44
45   if (p1.has_stem())
46     std::cout << "Stem: " << p1.stem().string() << '\n';
47
48   std::cout << '\n';
49 }
50
51 int main()
52 {
53   printPathParts ("");                      // no components
54   printPathParts ("E:\\DATA\\books.txt"); // all components
55   printPathParts ("/root/favs.txt");       // no root name
56   printPathParts ("\\DATA\\books.txt");    // Windows, relative
57   printPathParts ("boost");                 // no rootdir, no extn
58   printPathParts (".boost");                // no stem, only extn
59   printPathParts ("..");                    // no extension
60   printPathParts (".");                     // no extension
61   printPathParts ("/opt/boost/");           // file name == .
62 }
```

In the preceding example, the function printPathParts(line 6) prints as many components of a path as are available. To access a path component, it uses a corresponding member function of path. To check whether a component is available, it uses one of the has_ member functions of path. It also checks whether a path is a relative path or an absolute path using the is_relative and is_absolute member functions of path (lines 10, 13).

We call `printPathParts` with different relative and absolute paths. The results may vary across operating systems. For example, on Windows, a call to `has_root_name` (line 17) returns `false` for all the paths except the Windows path `E:\DATA\books.txt` (line 54), which is considered an absolute path. Calling `root_name` on this path returns `E:`. On UNIX however, the backslashes are not recognized as separators and considered part of the path components, so `E:\DATA\books.txt` will be interpreted as a relative path with the filename `E:\DATA\books.txt`, the stem `E:\DATA\books`, and the extension `.txt`. This, coupled with the fact that forward slashes are recognized on Windows as path separators, is a good reason to never use backslashes in path literals like we have done here.

[For maximum portability, always use forward slashes in path literals or generate paths using the overloaded `operator/` and `operator/=`.]

We can also compare two paths to see whether they are **equal** and **equivalent**. Two paths can be compared for equality using the overloaded `operator==`, which returns `true` only if the two paths are decomposable to the same components. Note that this means the paths `/opt` and `/opt/` are not equal; in the former, the filename component is `opt`, while in the latter, it is . (dot). Two paths that are not equal can still be equivalent if they represent the same underlying filesystem entry. For example, `/opt/boost` and `/opt/cmake/../boost/` are equivalent although they are not equal paths. To compute equivalence, we can use the `boost::filesystem::equivalent` function, which returns `true` if the two paths refer to the same entry in the filesystem:

```
boost::filesystem::path p1("/opt/boost"), p2("/opt/cmake");
if (boost::filesystem::equivalent(p1, p2 / ".." / "boost") {
  std::cout << "The two paths are equivalent\n";
}
```

As with `boost::filesystem::canonical`, the `equivalent` function also actually checks for the existence of the paths and throws an exception if either path does not exist. There is also an overload that does not throw but sets a `boost::system::error_code` out-parameter.

The `path` object can be looked upon as a sequence container of path elements and these elements can be iterated through using an iterator interface exposed by `path`. This allows easy application of several standard algorithms to `path` objects. To iterate through each path element, we can use the following snippet:

```
boost::filesystem::path p1("/opt/boost/include/boost/thread.hpp");
for (const auto& pathElem: p1) {
  std::cout <<pathElem.string() <<" ";
}
```

This will print the components separated by a pair of spaces:

```
/ optboost include boost thread.hpp
```

The begin and end member functions of boost::filesystem::path return a random-access iterator of type boost::filesystem::path::iterator, which you can use with Standard Library algorithms in interesting ways. For example, to find the number of components in a path, you can use:

```
size_t count = std::distance(p1.begin(), p1.end());
```

Now, consider two paths: /opt/boost/include/boost/filesystem/path.hpp and /opt/boost/include/boost/thread/detail/thread.hpp. We will now write a function that computes the common subdirectory under which both paths are located:

Listing 9.4: Finding the common prefix path

```
 1 #include <boost/filesystem.hpp>
 2 #include <iostream>
 3 namespace fs = boost::filesystem;
 4
 5 fs::path commonPrefix(const fs::path& first,
 6                       const fs::path& second) {
 7   auto prefix =
 8     [](const fs::path& p1, const fs::path& p2) {
 9       auto result =
10         std::mismatch(p1.begin(), p1.end(), p2.begin());
11       fs::path ret;
12       std::for_each(p2.begin(), result.second,
13               [&ret](const fs::path& p) {
14               ret /= p;
15               });
16       return ret;
17     };
18
19   size_t n1 = std::distance(first.begin(), first.end());
20   size_t n2 = std::distance(second.begin(), second.end());
21
22   return (n1 < n2) ? prefix(first, second)
23                    : prefix(second, first);
24 }
```

Calling the commonPrefix function on the two paths correctly returns /opt/boost/ include/boost. For this function to work correctly, we should pass paths that do not have . or .. components, something that a more complete implementation can take care of. To compute the prefix, we first define a nested function called prefix using a lambda expression (lines 7-17), which performs the actual computation. We compute the element count of the two paths (lines 19, 20) and pass the shorter path as the first argument and the longer one as the second argument to the prefix function (lines 22-23). In the prefix function, we use the std::mismatch algorithm on the two paths to compute the first component where they do not match (line 10). We then construct the common prefix as the path up to this first mismatch and return it (lines 12-15).

Traversing directories

Boost Filesystem provides two iterator classes, directory_iterator and recursive_directory_iterator, that make iterating through directories fairly simple. Both conform to the **input iterator** concept and provide an operator++ for forward traversal. In the first example here, we see directory_iterator in action:

Listing 9.5: Iterating directories

```
1 #include <boost/filesystem.hpp>
2 #include <iostream>
3 #include <algorithm>
4 namespace fs = boost::filesystem;
5
6 void traverse(const fs::path& dirpath) {
7   if (!exists(dirpath) || !is_directory(dirpath)) {
8     return;
9   }
10
11   fs::directory_iterator dirit(dirpath), end;
12
13   std::for_each(dirit, end, [](const fs::directory_entry& entry) {
14        std::cout <<entry.path().string() << '\n';
15      });
16 }
17
18 int main(int argc, char *argv[1]) {
19   if (argc > 1) {
20     traverse(argv[1]);
21   }
22 }
```

The `traverse` function takes a parameter `dirpath` of type `boost::filesystem::path` representing the directory to traverse. Using the namespace level functions, `exists` and `is_directory` (line 7), the function checks to see that `dirpath` actually exists and is a directory before proceeding.

To perform the iteration, we create an instance `dirit` of `boost::filesystem::directory_iterator` for the path and a second default-constructed `directory_iterator` instance called `end` (line 11). The default-constructed `directory_iterator` acts as the end-of-sequence marker. Dereferencing a valid iterator of type `directory_iterator` returns an object of type `boost::filesystem::directory_entry`. The sequence represented by the iterator range [`dirit`, `end`) is the list of entries in the directory. To iterate through them, we use the familiar `std::for_each` standard algorithm. We use a lambda to define the action to perform on each entry, which is to simply print it to the standard output (lines 13-14).

While we can write recursive logic around `boost::directory_iterator` to iterate through a directory tree recursively, `boost::recursive_directory_iterator` provides an easier alternative. We can replace `boost::directory_iterator` with `boost::recursive_directory_iterator` in listing 9.5 and it will still work, performing a depth-first traversal of the directory tree. But the `recursive_directory_iterator` interface provides additional capabilities like skipping descent into specific directories and keeping track of the depth of descent. A hand-written loop serves better to fully leverage these capabilities, as shown in the following example:

Listing 9.6: Recursively iterating directories

```
1  void traverseRecursive(const fs::path& path)
2  {
3    if (!exists(path) || !is_directory(path)) {
4      return;
5    }
6
7    try {
8      fs::recursive_directory_iterator it(path), end;
9
10     while (it != end) {
11       printFileProperties(*it, it.level());
12
13       if (!is_symlink(it->path())
14           && is_directory(it->path())
15           && it->path().filename() == "foo") {
16         it.no_push();
```

```
17        }
18        boost::system::error_code ec;
19        it.increment(ec);
21        if (ec) {
22          std::cerr << "Skipping entry: "
23                       << ec.message() << '\n';
24        }
25      }
26    } catch (std::exception& e) {
27      std::cout << "Exception caught: " << e.what() << '\n';
28    }
29 }
```

We create a `recursive_directory_iterator` and initialize it with a path (line 8) just as we did for a `directory_iterator` in listing 9.5. The `recursive_directory_iterator` constructor may throw an exception if the path does not exist or cannot be read by the program. To catch such exceptions, we put the code in the `try-catch` block.

We use a while-loop to iterate through entries (line 10) and advance the iterator by calling the `increment` member function (line 19). When the `increment` member function encounters a directory, it tries to descend into it in depth-first order. This can sometimes fail due to system issues, like when the program does not have sufficient permissions to look into the directory. In such cases, we want to continue on to the next available entry rather than abort the iteration. For this reason, we do not use `operator++` on the iterator because it throws an exception when it encounters an error and handling this makes the code more convoluted. The `increment` function takes a `boost::system::error_code` argument, and in case of an error, it sets the `error_code` *and* advances the iterator to the next entry. In such a case, we can get the system-defined error message associated with the error using the `message` member function of `error_code`.

Behavior of boost::filesystem::recursive_directory_iterator

Prior to Boost version 1.56, when the `operator++` and `increment` member functions encountered an error, they would only throw an exception or set an `error_code`, without advancing the iterator. This made writing a correct loop that skips on errors more complex. As of Boost 1.56, these functions also advance the iterator to the next entry making the loop code a lot simpler.

We process each entry by a call to a fictitious function `printFileProperties` (line 11), which takes two arguments—the result of dereferencing the `recursive_directory_iterator` instance, and the depth of traversal obtained by a call to the `level` member function of the iterator. The `level` function returns zero for first-level directories and its return value is incremented by 1 for each additional level of descent. The `printFileProperties` function can use this to indent entries in subdirectories, for example. We will implement the `printFileProperties` function in the next section.

To add dimension to the example, we decide not to descend into directories named `foo`. For this, we check for directories named `foo` (lines 13-15) and call the `no_push` member function on the `recursive_directory_iterator` to prevent descending into the directory (line 16). Likewise, we can call the `pop` member function on the iterator at any time to go up a level in the directory tree without necessarily completing iteration at the current level.

On systems that support symbolic links, if the `recursive_directory_iterator` encounters a symbolic link pointing to a directory, it does not follow the link to descend into the directory. If we want to override this behavior, we should pass a second argument of the enum type `boost::filesystem::symlink_option` to the `recursive_directory_iterator` constructor. The `symlink_option` enum provides the values `none` (or `no_recurse`), which is the default, and `recurse`, which indicates that symbolic links should be followed to descend into directories.

Querying filesystem entries

Boost Filesystem provides a set of functions to perform useful operations on files and directories. Most of these are functions in the `boost::filesystem` namespace. Using these functions, we can check whether a file exists, its size in bytes, its last modification time, the file type, whether it is empty, and so on. We use this slew of functions to write the `printFileProperties` function we used in the preceding section:

Listing 9.7: Querying file system entries

```
1 #include <boost/filesystem.hpp>
2 #include <iostream>
3 #include <boost/date_time.hpp>
4 namespace fs = boost::filesystem;
5 namespace pxtm = boost::posix_time;
6
7 void printFileProperties(const fs::directory_entry& entry,
8                          int indent = 0) {
9   const fs::path& path= entry.path();
10    fs::file_status stat = entry.symlink_status();
```

```
11    std::cout << std::string(2*indent, '');
12
13    try {
14      if (is_symlink(path)) {
15        auto origin = read_symlink(path);
16        std::cout <<" L " << " -   - "
17                     << path.filename().string() << " -> "
18                     << origin.string();
19      } else if (is_regular_file(path)) {
20        std::cout << " F " << " "
21           << file_size(path) << " " << " "
22           << pxtm::from_time_t(last_write_time(path))
23              << " " << path.filename().string();
24      } else if (is_directory(path)) {
25          std::cout << " D " << " - " << " "
26 << pxtm::from_time_t(last_write_time(path))
27 << " " << path.filename().string();
28      } else {
29        switch (stat.type()) {
30        case fs::character_file:
31          std::cout << " C ";
32          break;
33        case fs::block_file:
34          std::cout << " B ";
35          break;
36        case fs::fifo_file:
37          std::cout << " P ";
38          break;
39        case fs::socket_file:
40          std::cout << " S ";
41          break;
42        default:
43          std::cout << " - ";
44          break;
45        }
46        std::cout << pxtm::from_time_t(last_write_time(path))
47                  << " ";
48        std::cout << path.filename().string();
49      }
50      std::cout << '\n';
51    } catch (std::exception& e) {
52      std::cerr << "Exception caught: " <<e.what() << '\n';
53    }
54 }
```

The `printFileProperties` is used to print a short summary for a given file, including attributes like type, size, last modification time, name, and for symbolic links, the target file. The first argument to this function is of type `directory_entry`, the result of dereferencing a `directory_iterator` or `recursive_directory_iterator`. The second argument is the depth of traversal. We obtain the path to the file referenced by the `directory_entry` object by calling the `path` member function of `directory_entry` (line 9). We obtain a reference to a `file_status` object by calling the `symlink_status` member function of `directory_entry` (line 10). The `file_status` object contains additional details about a filesystem entry, which we use in our example to print the status of special files. The `symlink_status` function acts on all kinds of files not just symbolic links, but it returns the status of the symbolic link itself without following it to the target. If you need the status of the target each time you query the symbolic link, use the `status` member function instead of `symlink_status`. The `status` and `symlink_status` member functions are faster than the global functions of the same name because they keep the file stats cached instead of querying the filesystem on every call.

We determine the type of each entry before printing information appropriate for the type. To do this, we use the convenience functions `is_symlink`, `is_regular_file` and `is_directory` (lines 14, 19, 24). On POSIX systems like Linux, there are other kinds of files like block and character devices, fifos, and Unix domain sockets. To identify such files, we use the `file_status` object we obtained earlier (line 10). We call the `type` member function on the `file_status` object to determine the exact type of special file (line 29). Note that we first check if the file is a symbolic link and then perform other tests. That is because `is_regular_file` or `is_directory` may also return true for a symbolic link, based on the type of the target file.

This function prints each entry in the following format:

```
file_type  sizetime  name -> target
```

The file type is indicated by a single letter (D: directory, F: regular file, L: symbolic link, C: character device, B: block device, P: fifo, S: Unix domain socket). The size is printed in bytes, the last modification time is printed as a long integer, and the file name is printed without the full path. Only for symbolic links, a trailing arrow followed by the target path is appended after the name. Hyphens (-) appear for missing fields when file size or last write time are not available. For each level of descent, the entry is indented with an extra pair of spaces (line 11).

Here is a sample output from running this function on my Linux system:

```
bash-3.1$ ./listing8_7
D  -   2015-Jan-04 09:26:00  ch07
   F  1855  2014-Dec-28 19:49:34  listing7_5.cpp
   F  2197  2015-Jan-04 08:30:44  listing7_6.cpp
   F  1723  2014-Dec-28 16:30:45  listing7_4.cpp
   D  -   2014-Dec-29 19:13:17  testdir
      D  -   2014-Dec-29 19:14:28  bar
      D  -   2014-Dec-29 19:14:56  baz
         F  0  2014-Dec-29 19:14:56  bz
   L  -  -  bootln -> /opt/boost
   L  -  -  winnie -> pooh
D  -   2014-Dec-27 18:02:23   ch08
   F  6032  2014-Nov-30 21:38:49  threads4.cpp
   F  917   2014-Nov-25 12:53:48  threads2.cpp
   F  2055  2014-Nov-30 17:50:22  threads1.cpp
   F  6117  2014-Nov-30 21:29:39  thread3.cpp

bash-3.1$
```

You can also run this on the /dev directory on Linux to look at how device files are listed.

To get the target file pointed to by a symbolic link, we call the read_symlink function (line 15). To get the size of a file in bytes, we call the file_size function (line 21), and to get the last modification time of a file, we call the last_write_time function (lines 22, 26, and 46). The last_write_time function returns the **Unix time** at which the file was last modified. We print a meaningful representation of this time stamp by calling the boost::posix_time::from_time_t function to convert this numeric timestamp into a printable date time string (see *Chapter 7, Higher Order and Compile-time Programming*).

In order to build this program, you must additionally link against the Boost DateTime library, as shown here:

```
$ g++ listing8_7.cpp -o listing8_7 -std=c++11 -lboost_filesystem -lboost_date_time
```

There are several such functions for querying objects in the filesystem for different kinds of information—for example, finding the number of hard links to a file. We can query the file_status object (line 10) for file permissions. Notice that we do not qualify these namespace level functions with the namespace; they are correctly resolved using Argument Dependent Lookup based on the type of their arguments (boost::filesystem::path).

Performing operations on files

In addition to querying filesystem entries for information, we can also use the Boost Filesystem library to perform operations on files like creating directories and links, copying files and moving them, and so on.

Creating directories

It is easy to create directories using the function `boost::filesystem::create_directory`. You pass it a path and it creates a directory at that path if one does not exist; it does nothing if the directory already exists. If the path exists but is not a directory, `create_directory` throws an exception. There is also a non-throwing version that takes a `boost::system::error_code` reference, which it sets on error. These functions returns `true` if they create the directory and `false` if they do not:

Listing 9.8: Creating directories

```
 1 #include <boost/filesystem.hpp>
 2 #include <iostream>
 3 #include <cassert>
 4 namespace fs = boost::filesystem;
 5
 6 int main() {
 7   fs::path p1 = "notpresent/dirtest";
 8   boost::system::error_code ec;
 9   if (!is_directory(p1.parent_path()) || exists(p1)) {
10     assert( !create_directory(p1, ec) );
11
12     if (is_directory(p1)) assert(!ec.value());
13     else assert(ec.value());
14   }
15
16   try {
17     if (create_directories(p1)) {
18       assert( !create_directory(p1) );
19     }
20   } catch (std::exception& e) {
21     std::cout << "Exception caught: " << e.what() << '\n';
22   }
23 }
```

In this example, calling `create_directory` on the path `notpresent/dirtest` relative to the current directory fails (line 10) either if there is no directory called `notpresent` already in your current directory, or if `notpresent/dirtest` exists. This is because `create_directory` expects the parent directory of the path passed to exist, and it does not create a path that already exists. If we did not pass the error code parameter, this call to `create_directory` would have thrown an exception that would need to be handled. If `notpresent/dirtest` already exists and is a directory, then `create_directory` fails, but does not set the error code (line 12).

The function `boost::filesystem::create_directories` creates all path components needed, akin to `mkdir -p` on Unix systems. The call to it (line 17) succeeds unless there are permission issues or the path already exists. It creates the directory, including any missing directories along the path. Calls to `create_directory` and `create_directories` are idempotent; if the target directory exists, no error is returned or exception thrown, but the functions return `false` because no new directory was created.

Creating symbolic links

Symbolic links, sometimes called soft links, are entries in the filesystem that act like aliases to other files. They can refer to files as well as directories and are often used to provide alternate, simplified names and paths for files and directories. Symbolic links have been around on UNIX systems for quite a while now and have been available in some form on Windows since Windows 2000. We can use the function `boost::filesystem::create_symlink` to create symbolic links. For creating symbolic links to directories, the function `boost::filesystem::create_directory_symlink` is recommended for better portability.

Listing 9.9: Creating symbolic links

```
 1 #include <boost/filesystem.hpp>
 2 namespace fs = boost::filesystem;
 3
 4 void makeSymLink(const fs::path& target, const fs::path& link) {
 5   boost::system::error_code ec;
 6
 7   if (is_directory(target)) {
 8     create_directory_symlink(target, link);
 9   } else {
10     create_symlink(target, link);
11   }
12 }
```

This shows a function `makeSymLink` that creates a symbolic link to a given path. The first parameter to the function is the target path that the link must alias, and the second parameter is the path to the link itself. This order of arguments is reminiscent of the UNIX `ln` command. If the target is a directory, this function calls `create_directory_symlink` (line 8), while for all other cases it calls `create_symlink` (line 10). Note that the target path need not exist at the time of creation of the symbolic link and a dangling symbolic link will be created in such a case. Calling these functions has the same effect as the command `ln -s target link` on POSIX systems. On Windows, you get the same effect by running the command `mklink /D link target` when `target` is a directory, or by running the command `mklink link target` when `target` is not a directory. The function `makeSymLink` will throw if `create_directory_symlink` or `create_symlink` threw an exception.

Copying files

Copying files is another common chore that Boost Filesystem helps in. The `boost::filesystem::copy_file` function copies regular files from source to destination and fails if the file already exists at the destination. Using an appropriate override, it can be made to overwrite the file at the destination instead. The `boost::filesystem::copy_symlink` takes a source symbolic link and creates a second symbolic link at the destination that aliases the same file as the source. You cannot pass a directory as the destination to either function. There is also a `boost::copy_directory` function, which does not seem to do what its name suggests. It creates directories and copies attributes of the source directory to the target directory. So, we will roll out our own recursive directory-copying utility function instead:

Listing 9.10: Recursively copying directories

```
1 void copyDirectory(const fs::path& src, const fs::path& target) {
2   if (!is_directory(src)
3       || (exists(target) && !is_directory(target))
4       || !is_directory(absolute(target).parent_path())
5       || commonPrefix(src, target) == src) {
6     throw std::runtime_error("Preconditions not satisfied");
7   }
8
9   boost::system::error_code ec;
10  fs::path effectiveTarget = target;
11  if (exists(target)) {
12    effectiveTarget /= src.filename();
13  }
14  create_directory(effectiveTarget);
```

```
15
16    fs::directory_iterator iter(src), end;
17    while (iter != end) {
18      auto status = iter->symlink_status();
19      auto currentTarget = effectiveTarget/
20                                    iter->path().filename();
21
22      if (status.type() == fs::regular_file) {
23        copy_file(*iter, currentTarget,
24                       fs::copy_option::overwrite_if_exists);
25      } else if (status.type() == fs::symlink_file) {
26        copy_symlink(*iter, currentTarget);
27      } else if (status.type() == fs::directory_file) {
28        copyDirectory(*iter, effectiveTarget);
29      } // else do nothing
30      ++iter;
31    }
32 }
```

Listing 9.10 defines the copyDirectory function, which recursively copies a source directory to a target directory. It performs basic validations and throws an exception if the requisite initial conditions are not met (line 6). If any of the following conditions hold true, then a necessary precondition is violated:

1. The source path is not a directory (line 2)

2. The target path exists, but is not a directory (line 3)

3. The parent of the target path is not a directory (line 4)

4. The target path is a subdirectory of the source path (line 5)

To detect violation 4, we reuse the commonPrefix function we defined in listing 9.4. If the target path already exists, a subdirectory with the same name as the source directory is created under it to hold the copied contents (lines 11-12, 14). Otherwise, the target directory is created and the content is copied into it.

Beyond this, we iterate recursively through the source directory using directory_ iterator instead of recursive_directory_iterator (line 17). We use copy_file to copy regular files, passing the copy_option::overwrite_if_exists option to make sure a destination file that already exists is overwritten (lines 23-24). We use copy_symlink to copy a symbolic link (line 26). Each time we encounter a subdirectory, we recursively call copyDirectory (line 28). If an exception is thrown from the Boost Filesystem functions called by copyDirectory, it terminates the copy.

Moving and deleting files

You can move or rename files and directories using the
`boost::filesystem::rename` function, which takes the old and new paths as
arguments. The two-argument overload throws an exception if it fails, while the
three-argument overload sets an error code:

```
void rename(const path& old_path, const path& new_path);
void rename(const path& old_path, const path& new_path,
            error_code& ec);
```

If `new_path` does not exist, it is created provided its parent directory exists;
otherwise, the call to rename fails. If `old_path` is not a directory, then `new_path`, if
it exists, cannot be a directory either. If `old_path` is a directory, then `new_path`, if it
exists, must be an empty directory or the function fails. When a directory is moved
to another empty directory, the contents of the source directory are copied inside
the target empty directory, and then the source directory is removed. Renaming
symbolic links acts on the links, not on the files they refer to.

You can delete files and empty directories by calling `boost::filesystem::remove`
passing it the path to the filesystem entry. To recursively remove a directory that is
not empty, you must call `boost::filesystem::remove_all`.

```
bool remove(const path& p);
bool remove(const path& p, error_code& ec);
uintmax_t remove_all(const path& p);
uintmax_t remove_all(const path& p, error_code& ec);
```

The `remove` function returns false if the file named by the path does not exist. This
removes symbolic links without impacting the files they alias. The `remove_all`
function returns the total number of entries it removes. On error, the single-argument
overloads of remove and remove_all throw an exception, while the two-argument
overloads set the error code reference passed to it without throwing an exception.

Path-aware fstreams

In addition, the header file `boost/filesystem/fstream.hpp` provides versions
of Standard file stream classes that work with `boost::filesystem::path` objects.
These are very handy when you are writing code that uses `boost::filesystem` and
also needs to read and write files.

 A C++ Technical Specification based on the Boost Filesystem library
has been recently approved by ISO. This makes way for its inclusion
in a future revision of the C++ Standard Library.

Extensible I/O with Boost IOStreams

The Standard Library IOStreams facility is meant to provide a framework for operations of all kinds on all manner of devices, but it has not proven to be the easiest of frameworks to extend. The Boost IOStreams library supplements this framework with a simpler interface for extending I/O facilities to newer devices, and provides some pretty useful classes that address common needs while reading and writing data.

Architecture of Boost IOStreams

The Standard Library IOStreams framework provides two basic abstractions, **streams** and **stream buffers**. Streams provide a uniform interface to the application for reading or writing a sequence of characters on an underlying device. Stream buffers provide a lower-level abstraction for the actual device, which is leveraged and further abstracted by streams.

The Boost IOStreams framework provides the `boost::iostreams::stream` and `boost::iostreams::stream_buffer` templates, which are generic implementations of the stream and stream buffer abstractions. These two templates implement their functionality in terms of a further set of concepts, which are described as follows:

- A **source** is an abstraction for an object from which a sequence of characters can be read.

- A **sink** is an abstraction for an object to which a sequence of characters can be written.

- A **device** is a source, a sink, or both.

- An **input filter** modifies a sequence of characters read from a source, while an **output filter** modifies a sequence of characters before it is written to a sink.

- A **filter** is an input filter or an output filter. It is possible to write a filter that can be used either as an input filter or as an output filter; this is known as a **dual use filter**.

To perform I/O on a device, we associate a sequence of zero or more filters plus the device with an instance of `boost::iostreams::stream` or an instance of `boost::iostreams::stream_buffer`. A sequence of filters is called a **chain** and a sequence of filters with a device at the end is said to be a **complete chain**.

The following diagram is a unified view of input and output operation, illustrating the I/O path between a stream object and the underlying device:

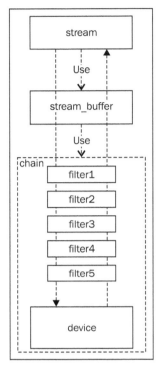

The Boost IOStreams architecture

Input is read from the device and passed through an optional stack of filters to reach the stream buffer from where it is accessible via the stream. Output is written from the stream via the stream buffer and passed through a stack of filters before reaching the device. The filters, if any, act on the data read from the device to present a transformed sequence to the reader of the stream. They also act on the data to be written to the device and transform it before it is written. The preceding diagram is meant for visualizing these interactions but is slightly inaccurate; in code, a filter cannot act both as an input filter and an output filter at the same time.

The Boost IOStreams library comes with several built-in device and filter classes, and it is easy to create our own too. In the following sections, we illustrate the use of different components of the Boost IOStreams library with code examples.

Using devices

A device provides an interface to read and write characters to an underlying medium. It abstracts a real medium like a disk, memory, or network connection. In this book, we will focus on using the number of readily available devices shipped as part of the Boost IOStreams library. Methods of writing our own device classes are beyond the scope of this book, but you should have little difficulty in picking them up from the online documentation once you are familiar with the content we cover in this chapter.

Devices for file I/O

Boost defines a number of devices for performing I/O on files and the one we look at first is a device that abstracts platform-specific file descriptors. Each platform uses some native handle for open files, different from how standard C++ represents open files using `fstreams`. These could be integer file descriptors on POSIX systems and HANDLEs on Windows, for example. The Boost IOStreams library provides the `boost::iostreams::file_descriptor_source`, `boost::iostreams::file_descriptor_sink`, and `boost::iostreams::file_descriptor` devices that adapt POSIX file descriptors and Windows file handles into devices for input and output. In the following example, we use a `file_descriptor_source` object to read successive lines from a file on a POSIX system using the stream interface. This is useful if you want to use a stream interface for I/O on a file that is opened using system calls that deal in file descriptors.

Listing 9.11: Using the file_descriptor device

```
 1 #include <boost/iostreams/stream.hpp>
 2 #include <boost/iostreams/device/file_descriptor.hpp>
 3 #include <iostream>
 4 #include <string>
 5 #include <cassert>
 6 #include <sys/types.h>
 7 #include <fcntl.h>
 8 namespace io = boost::iostreams;
 9
10 int main(int argc, char *argv[]) {
11   if (argc < 2) {
12     return 0;
13   }
14
15   int fdr = open(argv[1], O_RDONLY);
```

```
16    if (fdr >= 0) {
17        io::file_descriptor_source fdDevice(fdr,
18                        io::file_descriptor_flags::close_handle);
19        io::stream<io::file_descriptor_source> in(fdDevice);
20        assert(fdDevice.is_open());
21
22        std::string line;
23        while (std::getline(in, line))
24        std::cout << line << '\n';
25    }
26  }
```

Using this program, we open the first file named on the command line and read successive lines off it. We first open the file using the Unix system call, open (line 15), for which we include the Unix headers sys/types.h and fcntl.h (lines 6-7). If the file is opened successfully (indicated by a positive value of the file descriptor returned by open), then we create an instance of file_descriptor_source passing it the open file descriptor and a flag close_handle to indicate that the descriptor should be appropriately closed when the device is destroyed (lines 17-18).

If we did not want the device to manage the descriptor's lifetime, then we had to pass the flag never_close_handle instead. We then create an instance of boost::iostreams::stream<file_descriptor_source> (line 19) passing it the device object, and read successive lines from it using the std::getline function just as we would use any std::istream instance (line 23). Note that we assert the device is open for reading using the is_open member function (line 19). This code is meant to compile on Unix and Unix-like systems. On Windows, the Visual Studio C Runtime library provides compatible interfaces so that you may be able to compile and run this on Windows as well by including one additional header file io.h.

The types and functions in Boost IOStreams library are split into a set of fairly independent header files, and there is no single header file including which will give you all symbols. Device headers are available under boost/iostreams/device directory and filter headers are under boost/iostreams/filter directory. The rest of the interfaces are available under boost/iostreams.

To build this program, we must link it with the libboost_iostreams library. I use the following command line on my Ubuntu box to build the program using the Boost libraries installed under default paths via the native package manager:

```
$ g++ listing8_11.cpp -o listing8_11 -std=c++11 -lboost_iostreams
```

We may also want to build our program to use the Boost libraries we built from source in *Chapter 1, Introducing Boost*. For this, I use the following command line to build this program on my Ubuntu box, specifying the include path and the library path, as well as the `libboost_iostreams-mt` library to link against:

```
$ g++listing8_11.cpp -o listing8_11-I /opt/boost/include -std=c++11 -L /
opt/boost/lib -lboost_iostreams-mt -Wl,-rpath,/opt/boost/lib
```

To write to a file via a file descriptor, we need to use a `file_descriptor_sink` object. We can also use a `file_descriptor` object to both read and write to the same device. There are other devices that allow writing to files—the `file_source`, `file_sink`, and `file` devices allow you to read and write named files. The `mapped_file_source`, `mapped_file_sink`, and `mapped_file` devices allow you to read and write to files via memory mappings.

Devices for reading and writing to memory

The Standard Library `std::stringstream` family of classes is commonly used for reading and writing formatted data to memory. If you want to read and write from any given contiguous memory area, like an array or byte buffer, the `array` family of devices (`array_source`, `array_sink`, and `array`) from Boost IOStreams library comes in handy:

Listing 9.12: Using array devices

```
 1 #include <boost/iostreams/device/array.hpp>
 2 #include <boost/iostreams/stream.hpp>
 3 #include <boost/iostreams/copy.hpp>
 4 #include <iostream>
 5 #include <vector>
 6 namespace io = boost::iostreams;
 7
 8 int main() {
 9   char out_array[256];
10   io::array_sink sink(out_array, out_array + sizeof(out_array));
11   io::stream<io::array_sink> out(sink);
12   out << "Size of out_array is " << sizeof(out_array)
13       << '\n' << std::ends << std::flush;
14
15   std::vector<char> vchars(out_array,
16                             out_array + strlen(out_array));
17   io::array_source src(vchars.data(),vchars.size());
18   io::stream<io::array_source> in(src);
```

```
19
20    io::copy(in, std::cout);
21 }
```

This example follows the same pattern as Listing 9.11, but we use two devices, a sink and a source, instead of one. In each case, we do the following:

- We create an appropriately initialized device
- We create a stream object and associate the device with it
- We perform input or output on the stream

We first define an `array_sink` device, which is used to write to a contiguous region of memory. The region of memory is passed to the device constructor as a pair of pointers to the first element of an array of `chars` and the one past the last element (line 10). We associate this device with a stream object `out` (line 11) and then write some content to the stream using insertion operators (`<<`). Note that this content can be of any streamable type, not just textual. Using the manipulator `std::ends` (line 13), we make sure that the array has a terminating null character after the text. Using the `std::flush` manipulator, we make sure that this content is not held in the device buffer but finds its way to the backing array `out_array` of the sink device before we call `strlen` on `out_array` (line 16).

Next, we create a `vector` of `chars` called `vchars` initialized with the content of `out_array` (lines 15-16). We then define an `array_source` device backed by this `vector`, passing to the constructor an iterator to the first element of `vchars` and the number of characters in `vchars` (line 17). Finally, we construct an input stream associated with the device (line 18) and then use the `boost::iostreams::copy` function template to copy characters from the input stream to the standard output (line 20). Running the preceding code writes the following line to `out_array` through the `array_sink` device:

```
The size of out_array is 256
```

It then reads each word in this phrase and prints it to the standard output on a new line.

In addition to the `array` devices, the `back_insert_device` device can be used to adapt several standard containers as sinks. The difference between `back_insert_device` and `array_sink` is that `array_sink` requires a fixed memory buffer to operate on, whereas `back_insert_device` can use as its backing store any standard container with an `insert` member function. This allows the underlying memory area for a `back_insert_device` to grow as required by the size of input. We rewrite listing 9.12 using a `back_insert_device` in place of the `array_sink`:

Listing 9.13: Using back_insert_device

```
 1 #include <boost/iostreams/device/array.hpp>
 2 #include <boost/iostreams/device/back_inserter.hpp>
 3 #include <boost/iostreams/stream.hpp>
 4 #include <boost/iostreams/copy.hpp>
 5 #include <iostream>
 6 #include <vector>
 7 namespace io = boost::iostreams;
 8
 9 int main() {
10    typedef std::vector<char> charvec;
11    charvec output;
12    io::back_insert_device<charvec> sink(output);
13    io::stream<io::back_insert_device<charvec>> out(sink);
14    out << "Size of outputis "<< output.size() << std::flush;
15
16    std::vector<char> vchars(output.begin(),
17                             output.begin() + output.size());
18    io::array_source src(vchars.data(),vchars.size());
19    io::stream<io::array_source> in(src);
20
21    io::copy(in, std::cout);
22 }
```

Here, we write to out_vec, which is a vector<char> (line 11), and do so using the
back_insert_device sink (line 12). We write the size of out_vec to the stream, but
this may not print the total number of characters already written to the device at
that point, because the device may buffer some of the output before flushing it to the
vector. Since we intend to copy this data to another vector for reading (lines 16-17),
we ensure that all the data is written to out_vec using the std::flush manipulator
(line 14).

There are other interesting devices, like the tee_device adaptor that allows writing
a character sequence to two different devices, reminiscent of the Unix tee command.
We will now look at how you can write your own device.

Using filters

Filters act on the character stream that is written to a sink or read from a source,
either transforming it before it is written and read, or simply observing some
properties of the stream. The transformation can do a variety of things, like tagging
keywords, translating text, performing regular expression substitution, and
performing compression or decompression. Observer filters can compute line and
word counts or compute a message digest among other things.

Regular streams and stream buffers do not support filters and we need to use **filtering streams** and **filtering stream buffers** instead in order to use filters. Filtering streams and stream buffers maintain a stack of filters with the source or sink at the top and the outermost filter at the bottom in a data structure called a **chain**.

We will now look at several utility filters that are shipped as part of the Boost IOStreams library. Writing our own filters is outside the scope of this book, but the excellent online documentation covers this topic in adequate detail.

Basic filters

In the first example of using filters, we use boost::iostreams::counter filter to keep a count of characters and lines in text read from a file:

Listing 9.14: Using the counter filter

```
 1 #include <boost/iostreams/device/file.hpp>
 2 #include <boost/iostreams/filtering_stream.hpp>
 3 #include <boost/iostreams/filter/counter.hpp>
 4 #include <boost/iostreams/copy.hpp>
 5 #include <iostream>
 6 #include <vector>
 7 namespace io = boost::iostreams;
 8
 9 int main(int argc, char *argv[]) {
10   if (argc <= 1) {
11     return 0;
12   }
13
14   io::file_source infile(argv[1]);
15   io::counter counter;
16   io::filtering_istream fis;
17   fis.push(counter);
18   assert(!fis.is_complete());
19   fis.push(infile);
20   assert(fis.is_complete());
21
22   io::copy(fis, std::cout);
23
24   io::counter *ctr = fis.component<io::counter>(0);
25   std::cout << "Chars: " << ctr->characters() << '\n'
26            << "Lines: " << ctr->lines() << '\n';
27 }
```

We create a `boost::iostream::file_source` device for reading the contents of a file named on the command line (line 14). We create a `counter` filter for counting the number of lines and characters read (line 15). We create an object of `filtering_istream` (line 16) and push the filter (line 17) followed by the device (line 19). Till the device is pushed, we can assert that the filtering stream is incomplete (line 18) and it is complete once the device is pushed (line 20). We copy the contents read from the filtering input stream to the standard output (line 22) and then access the character and line counts.

To access the counts, we need to refer to the `counter` filter object sitting in the chain inside the filtering stream. To get to this, we call the `component` member template function of `filtering_istream` passing in the index of the filter we want and the type of the filter. This returns a pointer to the `counter` filter object (line 24) and we retrieve the number of characters and lines read by calling the appropriate member functions (lines 25-26).

In the next example, we use `boost::iostreams::grep_filter` to filter out blank lines. Unlike the counter filter which did not modify the input stream, this transforms the output stream by removing blank lines.

Listing 9.15: Using the grep_filter

```
 1 #include <boost/iostreams/device/file.hpp>
 2 #include <boost/iostreams/filtering_stream.hpp>
 3 #include <boost/iostreams/filter/grep.hpp>
 4 #include <boost/iostreams/copy.hpp>
 5 #include <boost/regex.hpp>
 6 #include <iostream>
 7 namespace io = boost::iostreams;
 8
 9 int main(int argc, char *argv[]) {
10   if (argc <= 1) {
11     return 0;
12   }
13
14   io::file_source infile(argv[1]);
15   io::filtering_istream fis;
16   io::grep_filter grep(boost::regex("^\\s*$"),
17       boost::regex_constants::match_default, io::grep::invert);
18   fis.push(grep);
19   fis.push(infile);
20
21   io::copy(fis, std::cout);
22 }
```

This example is on the same lines as the listing 9.14 except that we use a different filter, `boost::iostreams::grep_filter`, to filter out blank lines. We create an instance of the `grep_filter` object, passing three arguments to its constructor. The first argument is the regular expression `^\s*$` that matches blank lines — lines that contain zero or more whitespace characters (line 16). Note that the backslash is escaped in code. The second argument is the constant `match_default` to indicate that we use Perl regular expression syntax (line 17). The third argument `boost::iostreams::grep::invert` tells the filter to let only those lines that match the regular expression to be filtered out (line 17). The default behavior is to filter out only those lines that do not match the regular expression.

To build this program on Unix, you must additionally link against the Boost Regex library:

```
$ g++ listing8_15.cpp -o listing8_15 -std=c++11 -lboost_iostreams-lboost_
regex
```

On a system without the Boost native packages and with Boost installed at a custom location, use the following more elaborate command line:

```
$ g++ listing8_15.cpp -o listing8_15-I /opt/boost/include -std=c++11 -L /
opt/boost/lib -lboost_iostreams-mt-lboost_regex-mt -Wl,-rpath,/opt/boost/
lib
```

On Windows, using Visual Studio and enabling auto linking against DLLs, you do not need to explicitly specify the Regex or IOStream DLLs.

Filters for compression and decompression

Boost IOStreams library comes with three different filters for compressing and decompressing data, one each for gzip, zlib, and bzip2 formats. The gzip and zlib formats implement different variants of the **DEFLATE algorithm** for compression, while the bzip2 format uses the more space-efficient **Burrows-Wheeler algorithm**. Since these are external libraries, they must be built and linked to our executables if we use these compression formats. If you have followed the detailed steps outlined in *Chapter 1, Introducing Boost,* to build Boost libraries with support for zlib and bzip2, then the zlib and bzip2 shared libraries should have been built along with the Boost Iostreams shared library.

In the following example, we compress a file named on the command line and write it to the disk. We then read it back, decompress it, and write it to the standard output.

Listing 9.16: Using gzip compressor and decompressor

```
1 #include <boost/iostreams/device/file.hpp>
2 #include <boost/iostreams/filtering_stream.hpp>
```

```
 3  #include <boost/iostreams/stream.hpp>
 4  #include <boost/iostreams/filter/gzip.hpp>
 5  #include <boost/iostreams/copy.hpp>
 6  #include <iostream>
 7  namespace io = boost::iostreams;
 8
 9  int main(int argc, char *argv[]) {
10    if (argc <= 1) {
11      return 0;
12    }
13    // compress
14    io::file_source infile(argv[1]);
15    io::filtering_istream fis;
16    io::gzip_compressor gzip;
17    fis.push(gzip);
18    fis.push(infile);
19
20    io::file_sink outfile(argv[1] + std::string(".gz"));
21    io::stream<io::file_sink> os(outfile);
22    io::copy(fis, os);
23
24    // decompress
25    io::file_source infile2(argv[1] + std::string(".gz"));
26    fis.reset();
27    io::gzip_decompressor gunzip;
28    fis.push(gunzip);
29    fis.push(infile2);
30    io::copy(fis, std::cout);
31  }
```

The preceding code first uses the boost::iostreams::gzip_compressor
filter (line 16) to decompress the file as it is read (line 17). It then writes this
content to a file with the .gz extension appended to the original file name using
boost::iostreams::copy (lines 20-22). The call to boost::iostreams::copy
also flushes and closes the output and input streams passed to it. Thus, it is safe
to read back from the file immediately after the call to copy returns. To read this
compressed file back, we use a boost::iostreams::file_source device with
a boost::iostreams::gzip_decompressor in front (lines 27-28) and write the
decompressed output to the standard output (line 30). We reuse the filtering_
istream object for reading the original file and again for reading the compressed file.
Calling the reset member function on the filtering stream closes and removes the
filter chain and device associated with the stream (line 26), so we can associate a new
filter chain and device (lines 27-28).

It is possible to override several defaults by supplying additional arguments to the constructor of the compressor or decompressor filter, but the essential structure does not change. By changing the header from `gzip.hpp` to `bzip2.hpp` (line 4), and replacing the `gzip_compressor` and `gzip_decompressor` with `bzip2_compressor` and `bzip2_decompressor` in the preceding code, we can test the code for the bzip2 format; likewise for the zlib format. Ideally, the extensions should be changed aptly (.bz2 for bzip2 and .zlib for zlib). On most Unix systems, it will be worthwhile to test the generated compressed files by uncompressing them independently using gzip and bzip2 tools. Command-line tools for zlib archives seem scanty and less standardized. On my Ubuntu system, the `qpdf` program comes with a raw zlib compression/decompression utility called `zlib-flate`, which can compress to and decompress from zlib format.

The steps to build this program are the same as the steps outlined to build listing 9.15. Even if you use the `zlib_compressor` or `bzip2_compressor` filters instead, the necessary shared libraries will be automatically picked up by the linker (and later, the runtime linker during execution) as long as the option `-Wl,-rpath,/opt/boost/lib` is used during linking and the path `/opt/boost/lib` contains the shared libraries for zlib and bzip2.

Composing filters

Filtering streams can apply multiple filters to a character sequence in a pipeline. Using the `push` method on the filtering stream, we form the pipeline starting with the outermost filter, inserting the filters in the desired order, and ending with the device.

This means that for filtering an output stream, you first push the filter that gets applied first and work forward pushing each successive filter, followed at the end by the sink. For example, in order to filter out some lines and compress before writing to a sink, the sequence of pushes would be like the following:

```
filtering_ostream fos;
fos.push(grep);
fos.push(gzip);
fos.push(sink);
```

For filtering input streams, you push the filters, starting with the filter that gets applied last and work backward pushing each preceding filter, followed at the end by the source. For example, in order to read a file, decompress it and then perform a line count, the sequence of pushes will look like this:

```
filtering_istream fis;
fis.push(counter);
fis.push(gunzip);
fis.push(source);
```

Pipelining

It turns out that a little operator overloading can make this much more expressive. We can write the preceding chains using the pipe operator (`operator|`) in the following alternative notation:

```
filtering_ostream fos;
fos.push(grep | gzip | sink);

filtering_istream fis;
fis.push(counter | gunzip | source);
```

The preceding snippet is clearly more expressive with fewer lines of code. From left to right, the filters are strung together in the order you push them into the stream, with the device at the end. Not all filters can be combined in this way, but many readily available ones from the Boost IOStreams library can; more definitively, filters must conform to the **Pipable concept** to be combined this way. Here is a complete example of a program that reads the text in a file, removes blank lines, and then compresses it using bzip2:

Listing 9.17: Piping filters

```
 1 #include <boost/iostreams/device/file.hpp>
 2 #include <boost/iostreams/filtering_stream.hpp>
 3 #include <boost/iostreams/stream.hpp>
 4 #include <boost/iostreams/filter/bzip2.hpp>
 5 #include <boost/iostreams/filter/grep.hpp>
 6 #include <boost/iostreams/copy.hpp>
 7 #include <boost/regex.hpp>
 8 #include <iostream>
 9 namespace io = boost::iostreams;
10
11 int main(int argc, char *argv[]) {
12   if (argc <= 1) { return 0; }
13
14   io::file_source infile(argv[1]);
15   io::bzip2_compressor bzip2;
16   io::grep_filter grep(boost::regex("^\\s*$"),
17         boost::regex_constants::match_default,
18         io::grep::invert);
19   io::filtering_istream fis;
20   fis.push(bzip2 | grep | infile);
21   io::file_sink outfile(argv[1] + std::string(".bz2"));
22   io::stream<io::file_sink> os(outfile);
23
24   io::copy(fis, os);
25 }
```

The preceding example strings together a grep filter for filtering out blank lines (lines 16-18) and a bzip2 compressor (line 15) with a file source device using pipes (line 20). The rest of the code should be familiar from listings 9.15 and 9.16.

Branching data streams with tee

While using filter chains with multiple filters, it is sometimes useful, especially for debugging, to capture the data flowing between two filters. The `boost::iostreams:: tee_filter` is an output filter akin to the Unix `tee` command that sits interposed between two filters and extracts a copy of the data stream flowing between the two filters. Essentially, when you want to capture data at different intermediate stages of processing, you can use a `tee_filter`:

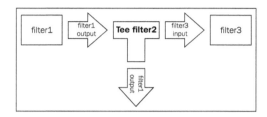

You can also multiplex two sink devices to create a **tee device**, such that writing some content to the tee device writes it to both the underlying devices. The `boost::iostream::tee_device` class template combines two sinks to create such a tee device. By nesting tee devices or pipelining tee filters, we can generate several parallel streams that can be processed differently. The `boost::iostreams::tee` function template can generate tee filters and tee streams. It has two overloads — a single-argument overload that takes a sink and generates a `tee_filter`, and a two-argument overload that takes two sinks and returns a `tee_device`. The following example shows how to compress a file to three different compression formats (gzip, zlib, and bzip2) using very little code:

Listing 9.18: Branching output streams with tees

```
 1 #include <boost/iostreams/device/file.hpp>
 2 #include <boost/iostreams/filtering_stream.hpp>
 3 #include <boost/iostreams/stream.hpp>
 4 #include <boost/iostreams/filter/gzip.hpp>
 5 #include <boost/iostreams/filter/bzip2.hpp>
 6 #include <boost/iostreams/filter/zlib.hpp>
 7 #include <boost/iostreams/copy.hpp>
 8 #include <boost/iostreams/tee.hpp>
 9 namespace io = boost::iostreams;
10
```

```
11 int main(int argc, char *argv[]) {
12   if (argc <= 1) { return 0; }
13
14   io::file_source infile(argv[1]);  // input
15   io::stream<io::file_source> ins(infile);
16
17   io::gzip_compressor gzip;
18   io::file_sink gzfile(argv[1] + std::string(".gz"));
19   io::filtering_ostream gzout;      // gz output
20   gzout.push(gzip | gzfile);
21   auto gztee = tee(gzout);
22
23   io::bzip2_compressor bzip2;
24   io::file_sink bz2file(argv[1] + std::string(".bz2"));
25   io::filtering_ostream bz2out;       // bz2 output
26   bz2out.push(bzip2 | bz2file);
27   auto bz2tee = tee(bz2out);
28
29   io::zlib_compressor zlib;
30   io::file_sink zlibfile(argv[1] + std::string(".zlib"));
31
32   io::filtering_ostream zlibout;
33   zlibout.push(gztee | bz2tee | zlib | zlibfile);
34
35   io::copy(ins, zlibout);
36 }
```

We set up three compression filters for gzip, bzip2, and zlib (lines 17, 23, and 29). We need one `filtering_ostream` for each output file. We create the gzout stream for the gzip-compressed output (line 20) and the bz2out stream for the bzip2-compressed output (line 26). We create tee filters around these two streams (lines 21 and 27). Finally, we string together the filters gztee, bz2tee, and zlib in front of the zlibfile sink and push this chain into the zlibout `filtering_ostream` for the zlib file (line 33). Copying from the input stream ins into the output stream zlibout generates the three compressed output files in a pipeline, as shown in the following diagram:

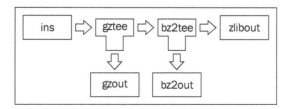

Notice that the calls to tee are not namespace-qualified but get correctly resolved due to Argument Dependent Lookup (see *Chapter 2, The First Brush with Boost's Utilities*).

The Boost IOStreams library provides a very rich framework for writing and using devices and filters. This chapter introduces only the basic uses of this library and there is a whole host of filters, devices, and adaptors that can be combined into useful patterns for I/O.

Self-test questions

For multiple-choice questions, choose all options that apply:

1. What is unique to the `canonical` and `equivalent` functions for manipulating paths?

   a. The arguments cannot name real paths.

   b. Both are namespace-level functions.

   c. The arguments must name real paths.

2. What is the problem with the following code snippet assuming the path is of type `boost::filesystem::path`?

   ```
   if (is_regular_file(path)) { /* … */ }
   else if (is_directory(path)) { /* … */ }
   else if (is_symlink(path)) { /* … */ }
   ```

   a. It must have static `value` field.

   b. It must have an embedded type called `type`.

   c. It must have static `type` field.

   d. It must have an embedded type called `result`.

3. Given this code snippet:

   ```
   boost::filesystem::path p1("/opt/boost/include/boost/thread.hpp");
   size_t n = std::distance(p1.begin(), p1.end());
   ```

   What is the value of n?

   a. 5, the total number of components in the path.

   b. 6, the total number of components in the path.

   c. 10, the sum of the number of slashes and components.

   d. 4, the total number of directory components.

4. You want to read a text file, remove all blank lines using a `grep_filter`, replace specific keywords using the `regex_filter`, and count the characters and lines in the result. Which of the following pipelines will you use?

    a. `file_source | grep_filter| regex_filter | counter`

    b. `grep_filter | regex_filter | counter | file_source`

    c. `counter | regex_filter | grep_filter |file_source`

    d. `file_source | counter | grep_filter | regex_filter`

5. True or false: A tee filter cannot be used with an input stream.

    a. True.

    b. False.

Summary

In this chapter, we covered the Boost Filesystem library for reading file metadata and state of files and directories, and performing operations on them. We also covered the high-level Boost IOStreams framework for performing type-safe I/O with rich semantics.

Working with files and performing I/O are basic system programming tasks that almost any useful piece of software needs to perform and the Boost libraries we covered in this chapter ease those tasks through a set of portable interfaces. In the next chapter, we will turn our attention to another systems programming topic— concurrency and multithreading.

10
Concurrency with Boost

Threads represent concurrent streams of execution within a process. They are a low-level abstraction for **concurrency** and are exposed by the system programming libraries or system call interfaces of operating systems, for example, POSIX threads, Win32 Threads. On multiprocessor or multicore systems, operating systems can schedule two threads from the same process to run in parallel on two different cores, thus achieving true **parallelism**.

Threads are a popular mechanism to abstract concurrent tasks that can potentially run in parallel with other such tasks. Done right, threads can simplify program structure and improve performance. However, concurrency and parallelism introduce complexities and nondeterministic behavior unseen in single-threaded programs, and doing it right can often be the biggest challenge when it comes to threads. A wide variance in the native multithreading libraries or interfaces across operating systems makes the tasks of writing portable concurrent software using threads even more difficult. The Boost Thread library eases this problem by providing a portable interface to create threads and higher level abstractions for concurrent tasks. The **Boost Coroutine** library provides a mechanism to create cooperative *coroutines* or functions which can be exited and resumed, retaining states of automatic objects between such calls. Coroutines can express event-driven logic in a simpler way, and avoid the overhead of threads in some cases.

This chapter is a hands-on introduction to using the Boost Thread library and also features a short account of the Boost Coroutine library. It is divided into the following sections:

- Creating concurrent tasks with Boost Thread
- Concurrency, signaling, and synchronization
- Boost Coroutines

Even if you have never written multithreaded programs or concurrent software, this would be a good starting point. We will also touch upon the thread library in the C++11 Standard Library, which is based on the Boost Thread library and introduces additional refinements.

Creating concurrent tasks with Boost Thread

Consider a program that prints greetings in different languages. There is one list of greetings in Anglo-Saxon languages, such as English, German, Dutch, Danish, and so on. There is a second list of greetings in Romance languages, such as Italian, Spanish, French, Portuguese, and so on. Greetings from both language groups need to be printed, and we do not want to delay printing the greetings from one group because of the other, that is, we want to print greetings from both the groups *concurrently*. Here is one way to print both the groups of greetings:

Listing 10.1: Interleaved tasks

```
 1 #include <iostream>
 2 #include <string>
 3 #include <vector>
 4
 5 int main()
 6 {
 7   typedef std::vector<std::string> strvec;
 8
 9   strvec angloSaxon{"Guten Morgen!", "Godmorgen!",
10                     "Good morning!", "goedemorgen"};
11
12   strvec romance{"Buenos dias!", "Bonjour!",
13                  "Bom dia!", "Buongiorno!"};
14
15   size_t max1 = angloSaxon.size(), max2 = romance.size();
16   size_t i = 0, j = 0;
17
18   while (i < max1 || j < max2) {
19     if (i < max1)
20       std::cout << angloSaxon[i++] << '\n';
```

```
21
22    if (j < max2)
23        std::cout << romance[j++] << '\n';
24    }
25 }
```

In the preceding example, we have two vectors of greetings, and printing the greetings in each is an independent task. We interleave these two tasks by printing one greeting from each array, and thus the two tasks progress concurrently. From the code, we can tell that a Latin and an Anglo-Saxon greeting will be printed alternately in the exact order as shown:

```
Buenos dias!
Guten Morgen!
Bonjour!
Godmorgen!
Bom dia!
Good morning!
Buongiorno!
goedemorgen
```

While the two tasks were run interleaved, and in that sense concurrently, the distinction between them in code was totally muddled to the extent that they were coded in a single function. By separating them into separate functions and running them in separate threads, the tasks can be totally decoupled from each other yet be run concurrently. In addition, threads would allow for their parallel execution.

Using Boost Threads

Every running process has at least one thread of execution. A traditional "hello world" program with a `main` function also has a single thread, often called the **main thread**. Such programs are called **single-threaded**. Using Boost Threads, we can create programs with multiple threads of execution that run concurrent tasks. We can rewrite the listing 10.1 using Boost Threads so that the code for an individual task is cleanly factored out, and the tasks potentially run in parallel when parallel hardware is available. Here is how we can do this:

Listing 10.2: Concurrent tasks as threads

```
1 #include <boost/thread.hpp>
2 #include <string>
3 #include <vector>
```

```
 4 #include <iostream>
 5
 6 typedef std::vector<std::string> strvec;
 7
 8 void printGreets(const strvec& greets)
 9 {
10   for (const auto& greet : greets) {
11     std::cout << greet << '\n';
12   }
13 }
14
15 int main()
16 {
17   strvec angloSaxon{"Guten Morgen!", "Godmorgen!",
18                     "Good morning!", "goedemorgen"};
19
20   strvec romance{"Buenos dias!", "Bonjour!",
21                  "Bom dia!", "Buongiorno!"};
15
16   boost::thread t1(printGreets, romance);
17   printGreets(angloSaxon);
18   t1.join();
19 }
```

We define a function `printGreets` that takes a vector of greetings and prints all the greetings in the vector (lines 8-13). This is the code for the task, simplified and factored out. This function is invoked once each on the two greeting vectors. It is called once from the `main` function, which executes in the main thread (line 17), and once from a second thread of execution that we spawn by instantiating an object of type `boost::thread`, passing it the function to invoke and its arguments (line 16). The header file `boost/thread.hpp` provides types and functions needed for using Boost Threads (line 1).

The object `t1` of type `boost::thread` wraps a native thread, for example, `pthread_t`, Win32 thread HANDLE, and so on. For conciseness, we simply refer to "the thread `t1`" to mean the underlying thread as well as the `boost::thread` object wrapping it, unless it is necessary to distinguish between the two. The object `t1` is constructed by passing a function object (the initial function of the thread) and all the arguments to pass to the function object (line 16). Upon construction, the underlying native thread starts running immediately by calling the passed function with the arguments provided. The thread terminates when this function returns. This happens concurrently with the `printGreets` function called from the `main` function (line 17).

One possible output from this program is:

```
Guten Morgen!
Buenos dias!
Godmorgen!
Bonjour!
Bom dia!
Good morning!
Buongiorno!
goedemorgen
```

The Latin greets are printed in the order they appear in the `romance` vector, and the Anglo-Saxon greets are printed in the order they appear in the `angloSaxon` vector. But there is no predictable order in which they are interleaved. This lack of determinism is a key feature in concurrent programming and a source of some of the difficulty. What is possibly more unnerving is that even the following output is possible:

```
Guten Morgen!
Buenos dGodmorgeias!
n!
Bonjour!
Bom dia! Good morning!
Buongiorno!
goedemorgen
```

Notice that the two greets `Buenos dias!` (Spanish) and `Godmorgen!` (Dutch) are interleaved, and `Good morning!` was printed before the new line following `Bom dia!` could be printed.

We call the `join` member function on `t1` to wait for the underlying thread to terminate (line 18). Since the main thread and the thread `t1` run concurrently, either can terminate before the other. If the `main` function terminated first, it would terminate the program and the `printGreets` function running in the thread `t1` would be terminated before it finished execution. By calling `join`, the main function ensures that it does not exit while `t1` is still running.

Linking against Boost Thread Library

Boost Thread is not a header-only library but has to be built from the sources. *Chapter 1, Introducing Boost*, describes the details of building the Boost libraries from their sources, their **name layout variants**, and naming conventions.

To build a running program from listing 10.2, you need to link your compiled objects with these libraries. To build the preceding example, you must link with Boost Thread and Boost System libraries. On Linux, you must also link against `libpthread`, which contains the Pthreads library implementation.

Assuming the source file is `Listing9_2.cpp`, here is the g++ command line on Linux to compile and link the source to build a binary:
`$ g++ Listing9_2.cpp -o Listing9_2 -lboost_thread -lboost_system -lboost_chrono -pthread`

Linking to `libboost_chrono` is necessary only if we use the Boost Chrono library. The option `-pthread` sets the necessary preprocessor and linker flags to enable compiling a multithreaded application and linking it against `libpthread`. If you did not use your native package manager to install Boost on Linux, or if you are trying to build on another platform, such as Windows, then refer to the detailed build instructions in *Chapter 1, Introducing Boost*.

If you are on C++11, you can use the Standard Library threads instead of Boost Threads. For this, you have to include the Standard Library header `thread`, and use `std::thread` instead of `boost::thread`. Boost Thread and `std::thread` are not drop-in replacements of each other, and therefore some changes would be necessary.

Moving threads and waiting on threads

An object of `std::thread` is associated with and manages exactly one thread in a process. Consider the following code snippet:

```
1 void threadFunc() { ... }
2
3 boost::thread makeThread(void (*thrFunc)()) {
4   assert(thrFunc);
5   boost::thread thr(thrFunc);
6   // do some work
7   return thr;
8 }
9
10 int main() {
11   auto thr1 = makeThread(threadFunc);
```

```
12   // ...
13   thr1.join();
14 }
```

When the `boost::thread` object `thr` is created (line 4), it gets associated with a new native thread (`pthread_t`, handle to a Windows thread, and so on), which executes the function pointed to by `thrFunc`. Now `boost::thread` is a movable but not a copyable type. When the `makeThread` function returns `thr` by value (line 7), the ownership of the underlying native thread handle is moved from the object `thr` in `makeThread` to `thr1` in the `main` function (line 11). Thus you can create a thread in one function and return it to the calling function, *transferring ownership* in the process.

Ultimately though, we wait for the thread to finish execution inside the `main` function by calling `join` (line 13). This ensures that the `main` function does not exit until the thread `thr1` terminates. Now it is entirely possible that by the time `makeThread` returned `thr`, the underlying thread had already completed execution. In this case, `thr1.join()` (line 13) returns immediately. On the other hand, the underlying thread could well continue to execute while the control on the main thread is transferred to the `main` function, and even as `join` was called on `thr1` (line 13). In this case, `thr1.join()` would block, waiting for the thread to exit.

Sometimes, we may want a thread to run its course and exit, and we would never bother to check on it again. Moreover, it may not matter whether the thread terminated or not. Imagine a personal finance desktop application that features a nifty stock ticker thread that keeps displaying stock prices of a configurable set of companies in one corner of the window. It is started by the main application and keeps doing its job of fetching the latest prices of stocks and showing them until the application exits. There is little point for the main thread to wait on this thread before exiting. When the application terminates, the stock ticker thread is also terminated and cleaned up in its wake. We can explicitly request this behavior for a thread by calling `detach` on the `boost::thread` object, as shown in the following snippet:

```
1 int main() {
2   boost::thread thr(thrFunc, arg1, ...);
3   thr.detach();
4   // ...
5 }
```

When we call `detach` on a `boost::thread` object, the ownership of the underlying native thread is passed to the C++ runtime, which continues to execute the thread until either the thread terminates or the program terminates, killing the thread. After the call to `detach`, the `boost::thread` object no longer refers to a valid thread, and the program can no longer check the status of the thread or interact with it in any way.

A thread is said to be joinable if and only if neither `detach` nor `join` has been called on the `boost::thread` object. The `joinable` method on the `boost::thread` returns `true` if and only if the thread is joinable. If you call `detach` or `join` on a `boost::thread` object that is not joinable, the calls return immediately with no other effect. If we do not call `join` on a `boost::thread` object, then `detach` is called in its destructor, when the thread goes out of scope.

Differences between `boost::thread` and `std::thread`

You must call either `join` or `detach` on a `std::thread` object; otherwise, the destructor of `std::thread` calls `std::terminate` and aborts the program. Moreover, calling `join` or `detach` on a `std::thread` that is not joinable will result in a `std::system_error` exception being thrown. Thus you call any one of `join` and `detach` on `std::thread`, and you do so once and only once. This is in contrast to the behavior of `boost::thread` we just described.

We can get `boost::thread` to emulate this behavior of `std::thread` by defining the following preprocessor macros, and it is a good idea to emulate the behavior of `std::thread` in any new code that you write:
```
BOOST_THREAD_TRHOW_IF_PRECONDITION_NOT_SATISFIED
BOOST_THREAD_PROVIDES_THREAD_DESTRUCTOR_CALLS_
TERMINATE_IF_JOINABLE
```

Thread IDs

At any time, each running thread in a process has a unique identifier. This identifier is represented by the type `boost::thread::id` and can be obtained from a `boost::thread` object by calling the `get_id` method. To get the ID of the current thread, we must use `boost::this_thread::get_id()`. A string representation of the ID can be printed to an `ostream` object, using an overloaded insertion operator (`operator<<`).

Thread IDs can be ordered using an `operator<` so they can easily be stored in ordered associative containers (`std::set` / `std::map`). Thread IDs can be compared using an `operator==` and can be stored in unordered associative containers too (`std::unordered_set` / `std::unordered_map`). Storing threads in associative containers indexed by their IDs is an effective means of supporting lookups on threads:

Listing 10.3: Using thread IDs

```
1 #include <boost/thread.hpp>
2 #include <boost/chrono/duration.hpp>
3 #include <vector>
4 #include <map>
```

```
 5 #include <iostream>
 6 #include <sstream>
 7 #include <boost/move/move.hpp>
 8
 9 void doStuff(const std::string& name) {
10   std::stringstream sout;
11   sout << "[name=" << name << "]"
12     << "[id=" << boost::this_thread::get_id() << "]"
13     << " doing work\n";
14   std::cout << sout.str();
15   boost::this_thread::sleep_for(boost::chrono::seconds(2));
16 }
17
18 int main() {
19   typedef std::map<boost::thread::id, boost::thread> threadmap;
20   threadmap tmap;
21
22   std::vector<std::string> tnames{ "thread1", "thread2",
23                                    "thread3", "thread4", "thread5" };
24   for (auto name : tnames) {
25     boost::thread thr(doStuff, name);
26     tmap[thr.get_id()] = boost::move(thr);
27   }
28
29   for (auto& thrdEntry : tmap) {
30     thrdEntry.second.join();
31     std::cout << thrdEntry.first << " returned\n";
32   }
33 }
```

In the preceding example, we create five threads and each runs the function doStuff. The function doStuff is passed an assigned name of the thread it runs; we name the threads thread1 through thread5, and put them in a std::map indexed by their IDs (lines 26). Because boost::thread is movable but not copyable, we move the thread objects into the map. The doStuff function simply prints the ID of the current thread using the method boost::this_thread::get_id (line 12), as part of some diagnostic message, and then sleeps for 2 seconds using boost::this_thread::sleep_for, which is passed a duration of type boost::chrono::duration (see *Chapter 8, Date and Time Libraries*). We can also use duration types provided by Boost Date Time, that is, boost::posix_time::time_duration and its subtypes, instead of boost::chrono, but for that we would need to use the boost::this_thread::sleep function rather than sleep_for.

Cores and threads

Many modern computers have multiple CPU cores on a single die and there might be multiple dice in a processor package. To get the number of physical cores on the computer, you can use the static function `boost::thread::physical_concurrency`.

Modern Intel CPUs support Intel's HyperThreading technology, which maximizes utilization of a single core by using two sets of registers allowing two threads to be multiplexed on the core at any given point and reducing the costs of context switching. On an Intel system with eight cores and supporting HyperThreading, the maximum number of threads that can be scheduled to run in parallel at any given time is then 8x2 = 16. The static function `boost::thread::hardware_concurrency` returns this number for the local machine.

These numbers are useful in deciding the optimal number of threads in your program. However, it is possible for these functions to return 0 if the numbers are not available from the underlying system. You should test these functions thoroughly on each platform where you plan to use them.

Managing shared data

All threads in a process have access to the same global memory, so the results of computations performed in one thread are relatively easy to share with other threads. Concurrent read-only operations on shared memory do not require any coordination, but any write to shared memory requires synchronization with any read or write. Threads that share *mutable data* and other resources need mechanisms to *arbitrate access* to shared data and signal each other about events and state changes. In this section, we explore the mechanisms for coordination between multiple threads.

Creating and coordinating concurrent tasks

Consider a program that generates the difference between two text files à la the Unix `diff` utility. You need to read two files, and then apply an algorithm to identify the parts that are identical and the parts that have changed. For most text files, reading both the files and then applying a suitable algorithm (based on the Longest Common Subsequence problem) works perfectly well. The algorithm itself is beyond the scope of this book and not germane to the present discussion.

Consider the tasks we need to perform:

- R1: Read complete contents of the first file
- R2: Read complete contents of the second file
- D: Apply the diff algorithm to the contents of the two files

The tasks R1 and R2 conceivably produce two arrays of characters containing the file content. The task D consumes the content produced by R1 and R2 and produces the diff as another array of characters. There is no ordering required between R1 and R2, and we can read the two files concurrently in separate threads. For simplicity, D commences only once both R1 and R2 are complete, that is, both R1 and R2 must happen before D. Let us start by writing the code to read a file:

Listing 10.4a: Reading contents of a file

```
1  #include <vector>
2  #include <string>
3  #include <fstream>
4  #include <boost/filesystem.hpp>
5
6  std::vector<char> readFromFile(const std::string& filepath)
7  {
8    std::ifstream ifs(filepath);
9    size_t length = boost::filesystem::file_size(filepath);
10   std::vector<char> content(length);
11   ifs.read(content.data(), length);
12
13   return content;
14 }
15
16 std::vector<char> diffContent(const std::vector<char>& c1,
17                               const std::vector<char>& c2) {
18   // stub - returns an empty vector
19   return std::vector<char>();
20 }
```

Given a file name, the function `readFromFile` reads the contents of the entire file and returns it in a `vector<char>`. We read the file contents into the underlying array of the `vector`, to get at which we call the `data` member function introduced in C++11 (line 11). We open the file for reading (line 8), and obtain the size of the file using the `boost::filesystem::size` function (line 9). We also define a stub of a method `diffContent` to compute the diff between the contents of two files.

How can we employ the `readFromFile` function to read a file in a separate thread and return the vector containing the contents of the file to the calling thread? The calling thread needs a way to wait for the read to complete in the reader thread, and then get at the content read. In other words, the calling thread needs to wait for the future result of an asynchronous operation. The `boost::future` template provides an easy way to enforce such ordering between tasks.

boost::future and boost::promise

The `boost::future<>` template is used to represent the result of a computation that potentially happens in the future. An object of type `boost::future<T>` represents a proxy for an object of type `T` that will potentially be produced in the future. Loosely speaking, `boost::future` enables a calling code to wait or block for an event to happen—the event of producing a value of a certain type. This mechanism can be used to signal events and pass values from one thread to another.

The producer of the value or the source of the event needs a way to communicate with the future object in the calling thread. For this, an object of type `boost::promise<T>`, associated with the future object in the calling thread, is used to signal events and send values. Thus `boost::future` and `boost::promise` objects work in pairs to signal events and pass values across threads. We will now see how we can guarantee that the two file read operations in two threads precede the diff operation using Boost futures and promises:

Listing 10.4b: Returning values from a thread using futures and promises

```
 1 #define BOOST_THREAD_PROVIDES_FUTURE
 2 #include <boost/thread.hpp>
 3 #include <boost/thread/future.hpp>
 4 // other includes
 5
 6 std::vector<char> diffFiles(const std::string& file1,
 7                             const std::string& file2) {
 8   // set up the promise-future pair
 9   boost::promise<std::vector<char>> promised_value;
10   boost::future<std::vector<char>> future_result
11                               = promised_value.get_future();
12   // spawn a reader thread for file2
13   boost::thread reader(
14                   [&promised_value, &file2]() {
15                     std::cout << "Reading " << file2 << '\n';
16                     auto content = readFromFile(file2);
17                     promised_value.set_value(content);
18                     std::cout << "Read of " << file2
19                               << " completed.\n";
20                   });
21
22   std::cout << "Reading " << file1 << '\n';
23   auto content1 = readFromFile(file1);
24   std::cout << "Read of " << file1 << " completed.\n";
25
26   auto content2 = future_result.get(); // this blocks
```

```
27    auto diff = diffContent(content1, content2);
28    reader.join();
29    return diff;
30  }
```

To be able to use `boost::future` and `boost::promise`, we need to include `boost/thread/future.hpp` (line 3). If we did not define the preprocessor symbol `BOOST_THREAD_PROVIDES_FUTURE` (line 1), then we would need to use `boost::unique_future` instead of `boost::future`. This example would work unchanged if we replaced `boost::future` with `boost::unique_future`, but in general there are differences in the capabilities of the two facilities, and we stick to `boost::future` throughout this book.

The function `diffFiles` (lines 6 and 7) takes two file names and returns their diff. It reads the first file synchronously (line 23) using the `readFromFile` function in listing 10.4a, and creates a thread called `reader` to read the second file concurrently (line 13). In order to be notified, when the `reader` thread is done reading and gets the content read, we need to set up a future-promise pair. Since we want to return a value of type `std::vector<char>` from the `reader` thread, we define a promise called `promised_value` of type `boost::promise<std::vector<char>>` (line 9). The `get_future` member of the promise object returns the associated future object and is used to move-construct `future_result` (lines 10-11). This sets up `promised_value` and `future_result` as the promise-future pair we work with.

To read contents of `file2`, we create the `reader` thread passing a lambda (lines 14-20). The lambda captures `promised_value` and the name of the file to read (line 14). It reads the contents of the file and calls `set_value` on the promise object, passing in the content read (line 17). It then prints a diagnostic message and returns. Concurrently, with this, the calling thread also reads in the other file `file1` into the buffer `content1` and then calls `get` on `future_result` (line 26). This call blocks until the associated promise is set via the call to `set_value` (line 17). It returns the `vector<char>` set in the promise and this is used to move-construct `content2`. If the promise was already set, when `get` is called on the future, it returns the value without blocking the calling thread.

We now have the data needed to compute the diff, and we do so by passing the buffers `content1` and `content2` to the `diffContent` function (line 27). Note that we call `join` on the `reader` thread before returning `diff` (line 28). This would be necessary only if we wanted to ensure that the `reader` thread exited before returning from the function. We could also call `detach` instead of `join` to not wait for the reader thread to exit.

Waiting for future

The get member function of boost::future<> blocks the calling thread until the associated promise is set. It returns the value set in the promise. Sometimes, you might want to block for a short duration and go ahead if the promise is not set. To do this, you have to use the wait_for member function and specify the duration to wait using boost::chrono::duration (see *Chapter 8, Date and Time Libraries*):

Listing 10.5: Waiting and timing out on a future

```
 1 #define BOOST_THREAD_PROVIDES_FUTURE
 2 #include <boost/thread.hpp>
 3 #include <boost/thread/future.hpp>
 4 #include <boost/chrono.hpp>
 5 #include <ctime>
 6 #include <cassert>
 7 #include <cstdlib>
 8 #include <iostream>
 9
10 int main() {
11   boost::promise<void> promise;
12   boost::future<void> future = promise.get_future();
13
14   std::cout << "Main thread id="
15                      << boost::this_thread::get_id() << '\n';
16   boost::thread thr([&promise]() {
17         srand(time(0));
18         int secs = 10 + rand() % 10;
19         std::cout << "Thread " << boost::this_thread::get_id()
20                 << " sleeping for "
21                 << secs << " seconds\n";
22         boost::this_thread::sleep_for(
23             boost::chrono::seconds(secs));
24         promise.set_value();
25       });
26
27   size_t timeout_count = 0;
28   size_t secs = 2;
29
30   while (future.wait_for(boost::chrono::seconds(secs))
31           == boost::future_status::timeout) {
32     std::cout << "Main thread timed out\n";
33     ++timeout_count;
34   }
35   assert(future.is_ready());
```

```
36    assert(future.get_state() == boost::future_state::ready);
37
38    std::cout << "Timed out for " << timeout_count * secs
39              << " seconds \n";
40    thr.join();
41 }
```

This example demonstrates how we can wait for a fixed duration on a future object. We create a promise-future pair (lines 11-12), but the template argument for `boost::future<>` and `boost::promise<>` is void. This means that we can use this pair purely for signaling/waiting, but not for transferring any data across threads.

We create a thread `thr` (line 16) passing it a lambda, which captures the promise object. This thread simply sleeps for a random duration between 10 and 19 seconds by passing a random duration to `boost::this_thread::sleep_for` (line 22) and then exits. The duration is constructed using the `boost::chrono::seconds` function (line 23) and passed a random interval `secs` computed using the `rand` function (line 18). We use `rand` for brevity, although more reliable and robust facilities are available in Boost and C++11. To use `rand`, we need to call `srand` to seed the random number generator. On Windows, we must call `srand` in each thread that calls `rand` as we have shown here (line 17), while on POSIX, we should call `srand` once per process, which could be at the start of `main`.

After sleeping for a specific duration, the thread `thr` calls `set_value` on the promise and returns (line 24). Since the promise is of type `boost::promise<void>`, `set_value` does not take any parameters.

In the main thread, we run a loop calling `wait_for` on the future associated with `promise`, passing a duration of 2 seconds each time (line 30). The function `wait_for` returns a value of the enum type `boost::future_state`. Each time `wait_for` times out, it returns `boost::future_state::timeout`. Once the promise is set (line 24), the `wait_for` call returns `boost::future_state::ready` and the loop breaks. The `is_ready` member function of `boost::future` returns `true` (line 35), and the future's state as returned by the `get_state` member function is `boost::future_state::ready` (line 36).

Throwing exceptions across threads

If the initial function passed to the `boost::thread` constructor allows any exceptions to propagate, then the program is immediately aborted by a call to `std::terminate`. This creates a problem if we need to throw an exception from one thread to indicate a problem to another thread, or propagate an exception we caught in one thread to another. The promise/future mechanism comes in handy for this purpose too. Consider how, in Listing 10.4a and 10.4b, you would handle the case when a file does not exist or is not readable:

Listing 10.6: Transporting exceptions across threads

```
1  #define BOOST_THREAD_PROVIDES_FUTURE
2  #include <boost/thread.hpp>
3  #include <boost/thread/future.hpp>
4  // other includes
5
6  std::vector<char> readFromFile(const std::string& filepath)
7  {
8    std::ifstream ifs(filepath, std::ios::ate);
9    if (!ifs) {
10     throw std::runtime_error(filepath + " unreadable");
11   }
12   ... // rest of the code - check Listing 10.4a
13 }
14
15 std::vector<char> diffFiles(const std::string& file1,
16                             const std::string& file2) {
17   // set up the promise-future pair
18   boost::promise<std::vector<char> > promised_value;
19   boost::future<std::vector<char> > future_result
20                     = promised_value.get_future();
21   // spawn a reader thread for file2
22   boost::thread reader(
23                   [&promised_value, &file2]() {
24                     try {
25                       auto content = readFromFile(file2);
26                       promised_value.set_value(content);
27                     } catch (std::exception& e) {
28                       promised_value.set_exception(
29                         boost::copy_exception(e));
30                     }
31                   });
32   ...
33   std::vector<char> diff;
34   try {
35     auto content2 = future_result.get(); // this blocks
36     diff = diffContent(content1, content2);
37   } catch (std::exception& e) {
38     std::cerr << "Exception caught: " << e.what() << '\n';
39   }
40   reader.join();
41   return diff;
42 }
```

If `file2` is the name of a file that does not exist or is not readable (line 25), then the function `readFromFile` throws an exception (line 10) that is caught by the `reader` thread (line 27). The `reader` thread sets the exception in the promise object by using the `set_exception` member function (lines 28-29). Notice that we create a copy of the exception object using `boost::copy_exception` and set it in the promise object (line 29). Once an exception is set in the promise, the call to `get` on the future object (line 35) throws that exception, which needs to be caught and handled (line 38).

shared_future

The `boost::future` object can only be waited upon by one thread. It is not copyable but is movable; thus, its ownership can be transferred from one thread to another and one function to another, but never shared. If we want multiple threads to wait on the same condition using the future mechanism, we need to use `boost::shared_future`. In the following example, we create a publisher thread that waits for a fixed duration before setting a promise with its thread ID. We also create three subscriber threads, which poll a `boost::shared_future` object associated with the promise object at different periodicities until it is ready, and then retrieves the thread ID of the publisher object from the `shared_future`:

Listing 10.7: Using shared_future

```
 1 #include <string>
 2 #include <vector>
 3 #include <iostream>
 4 #define BOOST_THREAD_PROVIDES_FUTURE
 5 #include <boost/lexical_cast.hpp>
 6 #include <boost/thread.hpp>
 7 #include <boost/thread/future.hpp>
 8 #include <boost/chrono.hpp>
 9
10 int main() {
11   boost::promise<std::string> prom;
12   boost::future<std::string> fut(prom.get_future());
13   boost::shared_future<std::string> shfut(std::move(fut));
14   boost::thread publisher([&prom]() {
15           std::string id =
16             boost::lexical_cast<std::string>(
17                          boost::this_thread::get_id());
18           std::cout << "Publisher thread " << id
19                   << " starting.\n";
20           boost::this_thread::sleep_for(
21                          boost::chrono::seconds(15));
22           prom.set_value(id);
```

```
23                      });
24      auto thrFunc = [](boost::shared_future<std::string> sf,
25                        int waitFor) {
26        while (sf.wait_for(boost::chrono::seconds(waitFor))
27              == boost::future_status::timeout) {
28          std::cout << "Subscriber thread "
29                    << boost::this_thread::get_id()
30                    << " waiting ...\n";
31        }
32
33        std::cout << "\nSubscriber thread "
34                  << boost::this_thread::get_id()
35                  << " got " << sf.get() << ".\n";
36      };
37
38      boost::thread subscriber1(thrFunc, shfut, 2);
39      boost::thread subscriber2(thrFunc, shfut, 4);
40      boost::thread subscriber3(thrFunc, shfut, 6);
41
42      publisher.join();
43      subscriber1.join();
44      subscriber2.join();
45      subscriber3.join();
46  }
```

Following the familiar pattern, we create a promise (line 11) and a boost::future (line 12). Using the future object, we move-initialize a shared_future object shfut (line 13). The publisher thread captures the promise (line 14) and sleeps for 15 seconds (line 21) before setting its ID string into the promise (line 22).

For the subscriber threads, we store the function object generated by the lambda expression in a variable called thrFunc (line 24) so that it can be reused multiple times. The initial function for the subscriber thread takes a shared_future parameter by value, and also the waitFor parameter, which specifies the frequency of polling the shared_future in seconds. The subscriber spins in a loop calling wait_for on the shared future, timing out after waitFor seconds. It comes out of the loop once the promise is set (line 22) and retrieves the value set in the promise (the publisher's thread ID) by calling get on the shared_future (line 35).

Three subscriber threads are spawned (lines 38-40). Note how the arguments to their initial function, the shared_future object, and the wait period in seconds, are passed as additional arguments to boost::thread object's variadic constructor template. Note that shared_future is copyable and the same shared_future object shfut is copied into the three subscriber threads.

std::future and std::promise

The C++11 Standard Library provides `std::future<>`, `std::shared_future<>`, and `std::promise<>` templates that are pretty much identical in behavior to their Boost library counterparts. The Boost version's additional member functions are experimental, but leaving those aside, they mirror their Standard Library counterparts. For example, we can rewrite listing 10.5 and 10.7 by replacing the following symbols in the program text:

- Replace `boost::thread` with `std::thread`
- Replace `boost::future` with `std::future`
- Replace `boost::promise` with `std::promise`
- Replace `boost::shared_promise` with `std::shared_promise`
- Replace `boost::chrono` with `std::chrono`

In addition, we would need to replace the included headers `boost/thread.hpp`, `boost/thread/future.hpp`, and `boost/chrono.hpp` with the Standard Library headers `thread`, `future`, and `chrono` respectively.

In listing 10.6, we used the `set_exception` member function of `boost::promise` to enable passing an exception across thread boundaries. This would require some changes to work with `std::promise`. C++11 introduces `std::exception_ptr`, a special smart pointer type with shared ownership semantics that must wrap exception objects so that they can be passed across functions and threads (see *Appendix, C++11 Language Features Emulation*). The `set_exception` member function of `std::promise` takes a parameter of type `std::exception_ptr` instead of a `std::exception`. The following snippet shows how you would change listing 10.6 to use the Standard Library:

```
 1 // include other headers
 2 #include <exception>
... // other code
22   boost::thread reader(
23                    [&promised_value, &file2]() {
24                       try {
25                          auto content = readFromFile(file2);
26                          promised_value.set_value(content);
27                       } catch (std::exception& e) {
28                          promised_value.set_exception(
29                                 std::current_exception());
30                       }
31                    });
```

Here, we call `std::current_exception` (line 29), which returns a `std::exception_ptr` object that wraps the currently active exception in the catch block. This `exception_ptr` is passed to the `set_exception` member function of `std::promise` (line 28). These type and function declarations are available from the Standard Library header `exception` (line 2).

We can also create a `std::exception_ptr` object from an exception object using `std::make_exception_ptr`, as shown in the following snippet (line 29):

```
22    boost::thread reader(
23                        [&promised_value, &file2]() {
24                          try {
25                            auto content = readFromFile(file2);
26                            promised_value.set_value(content);
27                          } catch (std::exception& e) {
28                            promised_value.set_exception(
29                                std::make_exception_ptr(e));
30                          }
31                        });
```

The exception stored in a `std::exception_ptr` can be thrown using `std::rethrow_exception`, as shown here:

```
01 void throwAgain(std::exception_ptr eptr) {
02   // do stuff
03   std::rethrow_exception(eptr);
04 }
```

std::packaged_task and std::async

While threads are powerful constructs, the full generality and control that they provide comes at the cost of simplicity. In a lot of cases, it works best to operate at a higher level of abstraction than creating explicit threads to run tasks. The Standard Library provides the `std::async` function template and `std::packaged_task` class template that provide different levels of abstractions for creating concurrent tasks, freeing the programmer from having to write a lot of boilerplate code in the process. They have counterparts in the Boost library (`boost::async` and `boost::packaged_task`) that are incompletely implemented and less portable to use as of this writing (Boost version 1.57), especially in pre-C++11 environments.

std::packaged_task

The `std::packaged_task<>` class template is used to create asynchronous tasks. You need to explicitly create a thread that runs the task or calls the task manually using the overloaded `operator()` in `packaged_task`. But you do not need to manually set up promise-future pairs or deal with promises in any way. Here is listing 10.6, rewritten using `std::packaged_task`:

Listing 10.8: Using std::packaged_task

```
1  #include <future>
2  #include <thread>
3  #include <vector>
4  // other includes
5
6  std::vector<char> readFromFile(const std::string& filepath)
7  {
8    std::ifstream ifs(filepath, std::ios::ate);
9    if (!ifs) {
10     throw std::runtime_error(filepath + " unreadable");
11   }
12   ... // rest of the code - check Listing 10.4a
13 }
14
15 std::vector<char> diffFiles(const std::string& file1,
16                            const std::string file2)
17 {
18   typedef std::vector<char> buffer_t;
19   std::packaged_task<buffer_t(const std::string&)>
20              readerTask(readFromFile);
21   auto future = readerTask.get_future();
22
23   try {
24     std::thread thread2(std::move(readerTask), file2);
25     auto content1 = readFromFile(file1);
26     std::cout << "Read from file " << file1 << " completed.\n";
27
28     auto content2 = future.get();
29     thread2.detach();
30     return diffContent(content1, content2);
31   } catch (std::exception& e) {
32     std::cout << "Exception caught: " << e.what() << '\n';
33   }
34
35   return std::vector<char>();
36 }
```

In this example, we read two files and compute their diff. To read the files, we use the function `readFromFile`, which returns the file contents in a `vector<char>` or throws an exception if the file is not readable. We read one of the two files by a blocking call to `readFromFile` (line 25), and read the other file on a separate thread.

To read the second file concurrently with the first one, we wrap the `readFromFile` function in a `std::packaged_task` called `readerTask` (lines 19-20) and run it in a separate thread. The specific type of `readerTask` is `std::packaged_task<buffer_t(const std::string&)>`. The template argument to `packaged_task` is the wrapped function type. Before starting this task on a separate thread, we must first get a reference to the associated future object. We get this reference to the future object by calling the `get_future` member function of `packaged_task` (line 21). Next, we create a thread and move the packaged task to this thread (line 24). This is necessary because `packaged_task` is movable but not copyable, which is why the `get_future` method must be called on the `packaged_task` object before it is moved.

The thread `thread2` reads `file2` by calling the `readFromFile` function passed to it in a `packaged_task`. The `vector<char>` returned by `readFromFile` can be obtained from the future object associated with `readerTask` by a call to the `get` member function of the future (line 28). The `get` call will throw any exception originally thrown by `readFromFile`, such as when the named file does not exist.

std::async

The `std::async` function template creates a task from a function object that can potentially run concurrently in a separate thread. It returns a `std::future` object, which can be used to block on the task or wait for it. It is available through the Standard Library header file `future`. With `std::async`, we no longer need to explicitly create threads. Instead, we pass to `std::async` the function to execute, the arguments to pass, and an optional launch policy. `std::async` runs the function either asynchronously in a different thread or synchronously on the calling thread based on the launch policy specified. Here is a simple rewrite of listing 10.5 using `std::async`:

Listing 10.9: Using std::async to create concurrent tasks

```
1 #include <iostream>
2 #include <thread>
3 #include <future>
4 #include <chrono>
5 #include <ctime>
6 #include <cstdlib>
7
8 int main()
9 {
10   int duration = 10 + rand() % 10;
11   srand(time(0));
12   std::cout << "Main thread id="
13             << std::this_thread::get_id() << '\n';
```

```
14
15    std::future<int> future =
16      std::async(std::launch::async,
17        [](int secs) -> int {
18          std::cout << "Thread " << std::this_thread::get_id()
19                    << " sleeping for "
20                    << secs << " seconds\n";
21          std::this_thread::sleep_for(
22                    std::chrono::seconds(secs));
23          return secs;
24        }, duration);
25
26    size_t timeout_count = 0, secs = 2;
27
28    while (future.wait_for(std::chrono::seconds(secs))
29            == std::future_status::timeout) {
30      std::cout << "Main thread timed out\n";
31      ++timeout_count;
32    }
33    std::cout << "Launched task slept for "
34              << future.get() << '\n';
35    std::cout << "Timed out for " << timeout_count * secs
36              << " seconds \n";
37 }
```

While `packaged_task` abstracts promises, `std::async` abstracts threads themselves, and we no longer deal with objects of `std::thread`. Instead, we call `std::async`, passing it a launch policy `std::launch::async` (line 16), a function object (line 17), and any number of arguments that the function object takes. It returns a future object and runs the function passed to it asynchronously.

Like the constructor of `thread`, `std::async` is a variadic function and is passed all the arguments that need to be forwarded to the function object. The function object is created using a lambda expression and does little, besides sleeping for a duration passed to it as a parameter. The `duration` is a random value between 10 and 19 seconds and is passed to the `async` call as the sole argument for the function object (line 24). The function object returns the duration of sleep (line 23). We call the `wait_for` member function on the future object to wait for short periods till the future is set (line 28). We retrieve the return value of the task from the future object by calling its `get` member function (line 34).

Launch policy

We used the launch policy `std::launch::async` to indicate that we want the task to run on a separate thread. This would launch the task immediately in a separate thread. Using the other standard launch policy `std::launch::deferred`, we can launch the task lazily, when we first call `get` or `wait` (non-timed wait functions) on the associated future object. The task would run synchronously in the thread that calls `get` or `wait`. This also means that the task would never be launched if one used the `deferred` policy and did not call `get` or `wait`.

We could not have used `std::launch::deferred` in the listing 10.10. This is because we wait for the future to be ready (line 28) before calling `get` in the same thread (line 34). The task would never be launched until we called `get`, but the future could never be ready unless the task was launched and returned a value; so we would spin eternally in the `while` loop.

While creating a task using `std::async`, we may also omit the launch policy:

```
auto future = std::async([]() {...}, arg1, arg2);
```

In such cases, the behavior is equivalent to the following call:

```
auto future = std::async(std::launch::async|std::launch::deferred,
                         []() {...}, arg1, arg2);
```

It is up to the implementation to choose the behavior conforming to either `std::launch::async` or `std::launch::deferred`. Moreover, the implementation would only create a new thread if the runtime libraries needed to support multithreading are linked to the program. With the default policy, when multithreading is enabled, `std::async` either launches new tasks in new threads or posts them to an internal thread pool. If there are no free threads in the pool or free cores, the tasks would be launched synchronously.

Lock-based thread synchronization methods

So far, we saw how we can delegate functions to be run on separate threads using `boost::thread` and `std::thread`. We saw the use of `boost::future` and `boost::promise` to communicate results and exceptions between threads and to impose order between tasks through blocking calls. Sometimes, you can break down your program into independent tasks that can be run concurrently, producing a value, a side effect, or both, which is then consumed by another part of the program. Launching such tasks and waiting on them using futures is an effective strategy. Once the tasks have returned, you can start on the next phase of computations that consume the results of the first phase.

Often though, multiple threads need to access and modify the same data structures concurrently and repeatedly. These accesses need to be ordered reliably and isolated from each other to prevent inconsistencies from creeping into the underlying data structure due to uncoordinated, concurrent accesses. In this section, we look at the Boost libraries that help us take care of these concerns.

Data races and atomic operations

Consider the following code snippet. We create two threads, and each thread increments a shared integer variable a fixed number of times in a loop:

```
int main() {
  int x = 0;
  const int max = 1000000;

  auto thrFunc = [&x] () {
                         for (int i = 0; i < max; ++i) {
                            ++x;
                         }
                       };

  boost::thread t1(thrFunc);
  boost::thread t2(thrFunc);
  t1.join();
  t2.join();

  std::cout << "Value of x: " << x << '\n';
}
```

What value of x would be printed at the end of the program? Since each thread increments x a million times and there are two threads, one could expect it to be 2000000. You can verify for yourself that the increment operator is called on x no less and no more than N*max times, where N=2 is the number of threads and max is a million. Yet I saw 2000000 being printed not for once; each time it was a smaller number. This behavior might vary depending on the OS and hardware, but it is common enough. Clearly, some increments are not taking effect.

The reason becomes clear when you realize that the operation ++x involves reading the value of x, adding one to the value, and writing this result back into x. Say the value of x is V and two threads perform the operation ++x on V. Each of the two threads can read V as the value of x, perform the increment, and write back V+1. Therefore, after two threads, each incrementing x once, the value of x could still be as if it was incremented only once. Depending on the machine architecture, for some "primitive" data types, it may require two CPU instructions to update the value of a variable. Two such operations executing concurrently could end up setting the value to what neither intended due to *partial writes*.

Interleaved operations like these represent a **data race** — the threads performing them are said to race against each other in performing the operation steps and their exact sequence, and therefore, the results are unpredictable.

Let us use the notation [r=v1, w=v2] to indicate that a thread *read* the value v1 from the variable x and *wrote* back v2. Note that there can be an arbitrary duration between the time a thread reads the value of x and the time when it writes back a value. So the notation [r=v1, ... is used to indicate that a value v1 was read but the write back is yet to happen, and the notation ... w=v2] indicates that the pending write happened. Now consider two threads each incrementing x a million times, as shown in the following sequence:

Time	Operation in Thread 1	Operation in Thread 2	Final value of x
t_1	[r=0, ...	[r=0, w=1]	1
t_2		[r=1, w=2]	2
t_3		[r=2, w=3]	3
...		...	...
t_{999999}		[r=999998,w=999999]	999999
$t_{1000000}$	... w=1]		1
$t_{1000001}$	[r=1, w=2]	[r=1, ...	2
$t_{1000002}$	[r=2, w=3]		3
...	...		...
$t_{1999999}$	[r=999999,w=1000000]		1000000
$t_{2000000}$		..., w=2]	2

For simplicity, assume that partial writes cannot happen. At time **t1**, both Thread 1 and Thread 2 read the value of x as 0. Thread 2 increments this value and writes back the value 1. Thread 2 continues reading and incrementing the value of x for 999998 more iterations until it writes back the value 999999 at time **t999999**. Following this, Thread 1 increments the value 0 that it had read at t1 and writes back the value 1. Next, both Thread 1 and Thread 2 read the value 1, and Thread 1 writes back 2 but Thread 2 hangs on. Thread 1 goes on for 999998 more iterations, reading and incrementing the value of x. It writes the value 1000000 to x at time **t1999999** and exits. Thread 2 now increments the value 1 that it had read at **t1000001** and writes back. For two million increments, the final value of x could well be 2. You can change the number of iterations to any number greater than or equal to 2, and the number of threads to any number greater than or equal to 2, and this result would still hold—a measure of the nondeterminism and nonintuitive aspects of concurrency. When we see the operation ++x, we intuitively think of it as an indivisible or *atomic operation,* when it really is not.

An **atomic operation** runs without any observable intermediate states. Such operations cannot interleave. Intermediate states created by an atomic operation are not visible to other threads. Machine architectures provide special instructions for performing atomic read-modify-write operations, and operating systems often provide library interfaces for atomic types and operations that use these primitives.

The increment operation ++x is clearly nonatomic. The variable x is a shared resource and between a read, increment, and a subsequent write to x by one thread, any number of read-modify-writes to x can take place from other threads—the operations can be interleaved. For such nonatomic operations, we must find means of making them **thread-safe,** that is, by preventing interleaving of operations, such as ++x, across multiple threads.

Mutual exclusion and critical sections

One way to make the ++x operation thread-safe is to perform it in a **critical section**. A critical section is a section of code that cannot be executed simultaneously by two different threads. Thus, two increments of x from different threads can be interleaved. Threads must adhere to this protocol and can use a **mutex** to do so. A mutex is a primitive used for synchronizing concurrent access to shared resources, such as the variable x. We use the `boost::mutex` class for this purpose, as shown in the following example:

Listing 10.10: Using mutexes

```cpp
1 #include <boost/thread/thread.hpp>
2 #include <boost/thread/mutex.hpp>
3 #include <iostream>
4
5 int main()
6 {
7   int x = 0;
8   static const int max = 1000000;
9   boost::mutex mtx;
10
11   auto thrFunc = [&x, &mtx]() {
12     for (int i = 0; i < max; ++i) {
13       mtx.lock();
14       ++x;
15       mtx.unlock();
16     }
17   };
18
19   boost::thread t1(thrFunc);
20   boost::thread t2(thrFunc);
21
22   t1.join();
23   t2.join();
24
25   std::cout << "Value of x: " << x << '\n';
26 }
```

We declare a mutex object of type `boost::mutex` (line 9), capture it in the lambda that generates the initial function for the threads (line 11), and then protect the increment operation on the variable x by locking the mutex before performing it (line 13) and unlocking it afterwards (line 15). The increment operation on x (line 14) is the critical section. This code prints the following each and every time:

```
2000000
```

How does this work? The mutex object has two states: **locked** and **unlocked**. The first thread to call the `lock` member function on a mutex that is unlocked, locks it and the call to `lock` returns. Other threads that call `lock` on the already-locked mutex simply **block**, which means the OS scheduler does not schedule these threads to run, unless some event (like the unlocking of the mutex in question) takes place. The thread with the lock then increments x and calls the `unlock` member function on the mutex to relinquish the lock it is holding. At this point, one of the threads that is blocked in the `lock` call is woken up, the call to `lock` in that thread returns, and the thread is scheduled to run. Which waiting thread is woken up depends on the underlying native implementation. This goes on until all the threads (in our example, just two) have run to completion. The lock ensures that at any point in time, only one thread exclusively holds the lock and is thus free to increment x.

The section we choose to protect with the mutex is critical. We could have alternatively protected the entire for-loop, as shown in the following snippet:

```
12      mtx.lock();
13      for (int i = 0; i < max; ++i) {
14          ++x;
15      }
16      mtx.unlock();
```

The final value of x would still be the same (2000000) as with listing 10.10, but the critical section would be bigger (lines 13-15). One thread would run its entire loop before the other thread could even increment x once. By limiting the extent of the critical section and the time a thread holds the lock, multiple threads can make more equitable progress.

A thread may choose to probe and see whether it can acquire a lock on a mutex but not block if it cannot. To do so, the thread must call the `try_lock` member function instead of the `lock` member function. A call to `try_lock` returns `true` if the mutex was locked and `false` otherwise, and does not block if the mutex was not locked:

```
boost::mutex mtx;
if (mtx.try_lock()) {
  std::cout << "Acquired lock\n";
} else {
  std::cout << "Failed to acquire lock\n";
}
```

A thread may also choose to block for a specified duration while waiting to acquire a lock, using the `try_lock_for` member function. The call to `try_lock_for` returns `true` if it succeeds in acquiring the lock and as soon as it does. Otherwise, it blocks for the entire length of the specified duration and returns false once it times out without acquiring the lock:

```
boost::mutex mtx;
if (mtx.try_lock_for(boost::chrono::seconds(5))) {
  std::cout << "Acquired lock\n";
} else {
  std::cout << "Failed to acquire lock\n";
}
```

 Mutexes should be held for as short a duration as possible over as small a section of code as necessary. Since mutexes serialize the execution of critical sections, holding a mutex over longer durations delays the progress of other threads waiting to lock the mutex.

boost::lock_guard

Acquiring a lock on a mutex and failing to release it is disastrous, as any other thread waiting on the mutex will never make any progress. The bare `lock` / `try_lock` and `unlock` calls on the mutex are not a good idea, and we need some means of locking and unlocking mutexes in an exception-safe way. The `boost::lock_guard<>` template uses the **Resource Acquisition Is Initialization** (**RAII**) idiom to lock and unlock mutexes in its constructor and destructor:

Listing 10.11: Using boost::lock_guard

```
1  #include <boost/thread/thread.hpp>
2  #include <boost/thread/mutex.hpp>
3  #include <iostream>
4
5  int main()
6  {
7    int x = 0;
8    static const int max = 1000000;
9    boost::mutex mtx;
10
11   auto thrFunc = [&x, &mtx]() {
12     for (int i = 0; i < max; ++i) {
13       boost::lock_guard<boost::mutex> lg(mtx);
14       ++x;
16     }
17   };
18
19   boost::thread t1(thrFunc);
20   boost::thread t2(thrFunc);
21
22   t1.join();
```

```
23  t2.join();
24
25  std::cout << "Value of x: " << x << '\n';
26 }
```

Using a `boost::lock_guard` object (line 13), we lock the section of code following the instantiation of the lock guard till the end of the scope. The `lock_guard` acquires the lock in the constructor and releases it in the destructor. This ensures that even in the face of an exception arising in the critical section, the mutex is always unlocked once the scope is exited. You pass the type of the lock as a template argument to `lock_guard`. `boost::lock_guard` can be used not only with `boost::mutex` but with any type that conforms to the **BasicLockable** concept, that is, has accessible `lock` and `unlock` member functions.

We can also use `boost::lock_guard` to encapsulate a mutex that is already locked. To do so we need to pass a second argument to the `lock_guard` constructor indicating that it should assume ownership of the mutex without trying to lock it:

```
1 boost::mutex mtx;
2 ...
3 mtx.lock();  // mutex locked
4 ...
5 {
6   boost::lock_guard<boost::mutex> lk(mtx, boost::adopt_lock);
7   ...
8 } // end of scope
```

`boost::lock_guard` either locks the underlying mutex in its constructor or adopts an already-locked mutex. The only way to release the mutex is to let the `lock_guard` go out of scope. `lock_guard` is neither copyable nor movable, so you cannot pass them around from one function to the next, nor store them in containers. You cannot use `lock_guard` to wait on a mutex for specific durations.

boost::unique_lock

The `boost::unique_lock<>` template is a more flexible alternative that still uses RAII to manage mutex-like locks but provides an interface to manually lock and unlock as required. For this additional flexibility, `unique_lock` has to maintain an additional data member to keep track of whether the mutex is owned by the thread or not. We can use `unique_lock` to manage any class conforming to the **Lockable** concept. A class conforms to the Lockable concept if it conforms to BasicLockable and additionally, defines an accessible `try_lock` member function—just as `boost::mutex` does.

We can use `boost::unique_lock` as a drop-in replacement for `boost::lock_guard`, but `unique_lock` should not be used if `lock_guard` suffices for a purpose. `unique_lock` is typically useful when we want to mix manual locking with exception-safe lock management. For example, we can rewrite listing 10.11 to use `unique_lock`, as shown in the following snippet:

```
7    int x = 0;
8    static const int max = 1000000;
9    boost::mutex mtx;
10
11   auto thrFunc = [&x, &mtx]() {
12     boost::unique_lock<boost::mutex> ul(mtx, boost::defer_lock);
13     assert(!ul.owns_lock());
14
15     for (int i = 0; i < max; ++i) {
16       ul.lock();
17       ++x;
18       assert(ul.owns_lock());
19       assert(ul.mutex() == &mtx);
20
21       ul.unlock();
22     }
23   };
```

Unlike in listing 10.11, we do not create a new `lock_guard` object in each iteration of the loop. Instead, we create a single `unique_lock` object encapsulating the mutex before the loop begins (line 12). The `boost::defer_lock` argument passed to the `unique_lock` constructor tells the constructor not to lock the mutex immediately. The mutex is locked before incrementing the shared variable by calling the `lock` member function of `unique_lock` (line 16) and unlocked after the operation by calling the `unlock` member function of `unique_lock` (line 21). In the event of an exception, the `unique_lock` destructor unlocks the mutex only if it is locked.

The `owns_lock` member function of `unique_lock` returns `true` if the `unique_lock` owns a lock on the mutex, and `false` otherwise (lines 13 and 18). The `mutex` member function of `unique_lock` returns a pointer to the stored mutex (line 19) or `nullptr` if `unique_lock` does not wrap a valid mutex.

Deadlocks

Mutexes provide for exclusive ownership of shared resources and many real-world problems deal with multiple shared resources. Take the case of a multiplayer first-person shooting game. It maintains and updates two lists in real time. There is a set A of shooters who are players with ammunition of some sort, and a second set U of players that are unarmed. When a player exhausts her ammo, she is moved from A to U. When her ammo is replenished, she is moved back from U to A. Thread 1 handles moving elements from A to U and thread 2 handles moving elements from U to A.

When a new player joins the game, she is added to either U or A, depending on whether she has ammo. When a player is killed in the game, she is removed from whichever set (U or A) she was part of. But when ammo is either exhausted or replenished, the player is moved between U and A; so both U and A need to be edited. Consider the following code in which one thread is responsible for moving players from A to U when ammo is exhausted, and another thread is responsible for the movement back (U to A) when ammo is replenished:

Listing 10.12: Deadlock example

```
 1 #include <iostream>
 2 #include <cstdlib>
 3 #include <ctime>
 4 #include <set>
 5 #include <boost/thread.hpp>
 6
 7 struct player {
 8   int id;
 9   // other fields
10   bool operator < (const player& that) const {
11     return id < that.id;
12   }
13 };
14
15 std::set<player> armed, unarmed; // A, U
16 boost::mutex amtx, umtx;
17
18 auto a2u = [&](int playerId) {
19         boost::lock_guard<boost::mutex> lka(amtx);
20         auto it = armed.find(player{playerId});
21         if (it != armed.end()) {
22            auto plyr = *it;
23            boost::unique_lock<boost::mutex> lku(umtx);
24            unarmed.insert(plyr);
```

```
25              lku.unlock();
26              armed.erase(it);
27          }
28      };
29
30  auto u2a = [&](int playerId) {
31          boost::lock_guard<boost::mutex> lku(umtx);
32          auto it = unarmed.find(player{playerId});
33          if (it != unarmed.end()) {
34              auto plyr = *it;
35              boost::unique_lock<boost::mutex> lka(amtx);
36              armed.insert(plyr);
37              lka.unlock();
38              unarmed.erase(it);
39          }
40      };
41
42  void onAmmoExhausted(int playerId) { // event callback
43    boost::thread exhausted(a2u, playerId);
44    exhausted.detach();
45  }
46
47  void onAmmoReplenished(int playerId) { // event callback
48    boost::thread replenished(a2u, playerId);
49    replenished.detach();
50  }
```

Each time a player's ammo is exhausted, the onAmmoExhausted (line 42) function is called with the ID of the player. This function creates a thread that runs the function a2u (line 18) to move this player from set A (armed) to set U (unarmed). Similarly, when player's ammo is replenished, the onAmmoReplenished (line 47) function is called and this, in turn, runs the function u2a in a separate thread to move the player from the set U (unarmed) to the set A (armed).

The mutexes amtx and umtx control access to the sets armed and unarmed. To move a player from A to U, the function a2u first acquires a lock on amtx (line 19) and looks up the player in armed (line 20). If the player is found, the thread acquires a lock on umtx (line 23), puts the player in unarmed (line 23), releases the lock on umtx (line 24), and removes the player from armed (line 25).

The function u2a has essentially the same logic but acquires the lock on umtx first, followed by amtx, and this leads to a fatal flaw. If one player exhausts ammo and another replenishes ammo at around the same time, two threads could run a2u and u2a concurrently. Perhaps rarely, it could happen that the exhausted thread locks amtx (line 19), but before it can lock umtx (line 23), the replenished thread locks umtx (line 31). Now the exhausted thread waits for umtx, which is held by the replenished thread, and the replenished thread waits for amtx, which is held by the exhausted thread. There is no conceivable way for the two threads to proceed from this state, and they are locked in a deadlock.

A **deadlock** is a state in which two or more threads vying for shared resources are blocked, waiting on some resources while holding others, such that it is *impossible* for any of the threads to progress from that state.

In our example, only two threads were involved, and it is relatively easy to debug and fix the problem. The gold standard for fixing deadlocks is to ensure **fixed lock-acquisition order**—any thread acquires two given locks in the same order. By rewriting u2a, as shown in the following snippet, we can ensure that a deadlock is not possible:

```
30 auto u2a = [&](int playerId) {
31     boost::unique_lock<boost::mutex>
32       lka(amtx, boost::defer_lock),
33       lku(umtx, boost::defer_lock);
34
35     boost::lock(lka, lku);  // ordered locking
36     auto it = unarmed.find(player{playerId});
37     if (it != unarmed.end()) {
38       auto plyr = *it;
39       armed.insert(plyr);
40       lka.unlock();
41       unarmed.erase(it);
42     }
43   };
```

In the preceding code, we make sure that u2a locks amtx first before locking umtx, just like a2u does. We could have manually acquired the locks in this order but instead, we demonstrate the use of boost::lock to do this. We create the unique_lock objects, lka and lku, with the defer_lock flag to indicate we do not want to acquire the locks yet. We then call boost::lock, passing the unique_locks in the order we would like to acquire them, and boost::lock ensures that order is observed.

There are two reasons for using `boost::unique_lock` instead of `boost::lock_guard` in this example. First, we can create `unique_lock`s without immediately locking the mutex. Second, we can call `unlock` to release the `unique_lock` early (line 40) and increase lock granularity, which promotes concurrency.

Besides fixed lock-acquisition order, another way to avoid deadlocks is for threads to probe locks (using `try_lock`) and backtrack if they fail to acquire a particular lock. This typically makes code more complex, but may be necessary sometimes.

There are many real-world examples of code with deadlocks, like the one in our example, which might be working correctly for years but with deadlocks lurking in them. Sometimes, the probability of hitting the deadlock could be very low when run on one system, and you might immediately hit it when you run the same code on another system,
all purely because of variances in thread scheduling on the two systems.

Synchronizing on conditions

Mutexes serialize access to shared data by creating critical sections. A critical section is like a room with a lock and a waiting area outside. One thread acquires the lock and occupies the room while others arrive outside, wait for the occupant to vacate the room, and then take its place in some defined order. Sometimes, threads need to wait on a condition becoming true, such as some shared data changing state. Let us look at the producer-consumer problem to see examples of threads waiting on conditions.

Condition variables and producer-consumer problem

The Unix command-line utility **grep** searches files for text patterns specified using regular expressions. It can search through a whole list of files. To search for a pattern in a file, its complete contents must be read and searched for the pattern. Depending on the number of files to search, one or more threads can be employed to concurrently read contents of files into buffers. The buffers can be stored in some data structure that indexes them by file and offset. Multiple threads can then process these buffers and search them for the pattern.

What we just described is an example of a producer-consumer problem in which a set of threads generates some content and puts them in a data structure, and a second set of threads reads the content off the data structure, and performs computations on it. If the data structure is empty, the consumers must wait until a producer adds some content. If data fills up the data structure, then the producers must wait for consumers to process some data and make room in the data structure before trying to add more content. In other words, consumers wait on certain conditions to fulfill and these are fulfilled as a result of the actions of the producers, and vice versa.

One way to model such conditions, wait on them, and signal them, is by using `boost::condition_variable` objects. A **condition variable** is associated with a testable runtime condition or predicate in the program. A thread tests the condition and if it is not true, the thread waits for that condition to become true using a `condition_variable` object. Another thread that causes the condition to become true signals the condition variable, and this wakes up one or more waiting threads. Condition variables are inherently associated with shared data and represent some condition being fulfilled for the shared data. In order for the waiting thread to first test a condition on the shared data, it must acquire the mutex. In order for the signaling thread to change the state of shared data, it too needs the mutex. In order for the waiting thread to wake up and verify the result of the change, it again needs the mutex. Thus we need to use `boost::mutex` in conjunction with a `boost::condition_variable`.

We will now solve the producer-consumer problem for a fixed-sized queue using condition variables. There is a queue of a fixed size, which means the maximum number of elements in the queue is bounded. One or more threads produce content and **enqueue** them (append them to the queue). One or more threads **dequeue** content (remove content from the head of the queue) and perform computations on the content. We use a circular queue implemented on top of a fixed size `boost::array` rather than any STL data structure, such as `std::list` or `std::deque`:

Listing 10.13: Using condition variables for a thread-safe, fixed-size queue

```
 1 #include <boost/thread/thread.hpp>
 2 #include <boost/thread/mutex.hpp>
 3 #include <boost/thread/condition_variable.hpp>
 4 #include <boost/array.hpp>
 5
 6 template <typename T, size_t maxsize>
 7 struct CircularQueue
 8 {
 9   CircularQueue () : head_(0), tail_(0) {}
10
11   void pop() {
12     boost::unique_lock<boost::mutex> lock(qlock);
13     if (size() == 0) {
14       canRead.wait(lock, [this] { return size() > 0; });
15     }
16     ++head_;
17     lock.unlock();
18     canWrite.notify_one();
19   }
```

```
20
21   T top() {
22     boost::unique_lock<boost::mutex> lock(qlock);
23    if (size() == 0) {
24       canRead.wait(lock, [this] { return size() > 0; });
25     }
26     T ret = data[head_ % maxsize];
27     lock.unlock();
28
29     return ret;
30   }
31
32   void push(T&& obj) {
33     boost::unique_lock<boost::mutex> lock(qlock);
34     if (size() == capacity()) {
35       canWrite.wait(lock, [this]
36                          { return size() < capacity(); });
37     }
38     data[tail_++ % maxsize] = std::move(obj);
39     lock.unlock();
40     canRead.notify_one();
41   }
42
43   size_t head() const { return head_; }
44   size_t tail() const { return tail_; }
45
46   size_t count() const {
47     boost::unique_lock<boost::mutex> lock(qlock);
48     return (tail_ - head_);
49   }
50
51 private:
52   boost::array<T, maxsize> data;
53   size_t head_, tail_;
54
55   size_t capacity() const { return maxsize; }
56   size_t size() const { return (tail_ - head_); };
57
58   mutable boost::mutex qlock;
59   mutable boost::condition_variable canRead;
60   mutable boost::condition_variable canWrite;
61 };
62
63 int main()
```

```
64  {
65      CircularQueue<int, 200> ds;
66
67      boost::thread producer([&ds] {
68              for (int i = 0; i < 10000; ++i) {
69                  ds.push(std::move(i));
70                  std::cout << i << "-->"
71                      << " [" << ds.count() << "]\n";
72              }
73          });
74
75      auto func = [&ds] {
76        for (int i = 0; i < 2500; ++i) {
77          std::cout << "\t\t<--" << ds.top() << "\n";
78          ds.pop();
79        }
80      };
81
82      boost::thread_group consumers;
83      for (int i = 0; i < 4; ++i) {
84        consumers.create_thread(func);
85      }
86
87      producer.join();
88      consumers.join_all();
89  }
```

In this listing, we define the CircularQueue<> template and its member functions, including the pop (line 11) and push (line 32) member functions, which are of particular interest. A call to push blocks until there is space in the queue to add a new element. A call to pop blocks until it is able to read and remove an element from the top of the queue. The utility function top (line 21) blocks until it is able to read an element from the top of the queue, a copy of which it returns.

To implement the necessary synchronization, we define the mutex qlock (line 58) and two condition variables, canRead (line 59) and canWrite (line 60). The canRead condition variable is associated with a predicate that checks whether there are any elements in the queue which could thus be read. The canWrite condition variable is associated with a predicate that checks whether there is any space left in the queue where a new element can be added. The mutex qlock needs to be locked to edit the queue and to check the state of the queue in any way.

The `pop` method first acquires a lock on `qlock` (line 12) and then checks whether the queue is empty (line 13). If the queue is empty, the call must block until there is an item available to read. To do this, `pop` calls the `wait` method on the `canRead` condition variable, passing it the lock `lock` and a lambda predicate to test (line 14). The call to `wait` unlocks the mutex in `lock` and blocks. If a call to the `push` method from another thread succeeds and thus data is available, the `push` method unlocks the mutex (line 39) and signals the `canRead` condition variable by calling the `notify_one` method (line 40). This wakes up exactly one thread blocked in the `wait` call inside a `pop` method call. The `wait` call atomically locks the mutex, checks whether the predicate (`size() > 0`) is true and if so, returns (line 14). If the predicate is not true, it once again unlocks the mutex and goes back to waiting.

The `pop` method is either woken up from its wait, and verifies that there is an element to read after reacquiring the mutex lock, or it never has to wait because there were elements to read already. Thus, `pop` proceeds to remove the element at the head of the list (line 16). After removing the element, it unlocks the mutex (line 17) and calls `notify_one` on the `canWrite` condition (line 18). In case it popped an element from a queue that was full, and there were threads blocked in `push`, waiting for some room in the queue, the call to `notify_one` wakes up exactly one thread blocked in `canWrite.wait(...)` inside `push` (line 35) and gives it the chance to add an item to the queue.

The implementation of `push` is really symmetrical and uses the same concepts we described for `pop`. We pass the mutex to the `wait` method on the condition variable, wrapped in a `unique_lock` and not a `lock_guard` because the wait method needs to access the underlying mutex to unlock it manually. The underlying mutex is retrieved from a `unique_lock` by calling the `mutex` member function of `unique_lock`; `lock_guard` does not provide such a mechanism.

To test our implementation, we create a `CircularQueue` of 200 elements of type `int` (line 65), a producer thread that pushes 10,000 elements into the queue (line 67), and four consumer threads that pop 2,500 elements each (lines 82-85).

The consumer threads are not created individually but as part of a **thread group**. A thread group is an object of type `boost::thread_group`, which provides an easy way to manage multiple threads together. Since we want to create four consumer threads using the same initial function and join them all, it is easy to create a `thread_group` object (line 82), create four threads in a loop using its `create_thread` member function (line 84), and wait on all the threads in the group by calling the `join_all` method (line 88).

Condition variable nuances

We call `notify_one` to signal the `canRead` condition variable and wake up exactly one thread waiting to read (line 39). Instead, we could have called `notify_all` to *broadcast* the event and wake up all waiting threads, and it would still have worked. However, we only put one new element in the queue in each call to `push`, so exactly one of the threads woken up would read the new element off the queue. The other threads would check the number of elements in the queue, find it empty, and go back to waiting, resulting in unnecessary context switches.

But if we added a load of elements to the queue, calling `notify_all` might be a better alternative than `notify_one`. Calling `notify_one` would wake up only one waiting thread, which would process the elements serially in a loop (lines 63-65). Calling `notify_all` would wake up all the threads, and they would process the elements concurrently much quicker.

One common conundrum is whether to call `notify_one`/`notify_all` while holding the mutex, as we have done in our examples earlier, or after releasing it. Both options work equally well, but there might be some difference in the performance. If you signal a condition variable while holding the mutex, the woken up threads would immediately block, waiting for the mutex until you release it. So there are two additional context switches per thread and these can have an impact on the performance. Therefore, if you unlock the mutex first before signaling the condition variable, you could see some performance benefits. Therefore, signaling *after* unlocking is the often preferred approach.

The Readers-Writers problem

Take the case of an online catalog of a library. The library maintains a look-up table of books. For simplicity, let us imagine that the books can only be looked up by titles, and titles are unique. Multiple threads representing various clients perform look-ups on the library concurrently. From time to time, the librarian adds new books to the catalog and rarely, takes a book off the catalog. A new book can be added only if a book with the same title is not already present, or if an older edition of the title is present.

In the following snippet, we define a type representing a book entry and the public interface of the `LibraryCatalog` class that represents the library catalog:

Listing 10.14a: Library catalog types and interfaces

```
 1 struct book_t
 2 {
 3   std::string title;
 4   std::string author;
 5   int edition;
 6 };
 7
 8 class LibraryCatalog
 9 {
10 public:
11   typedef boost::unordered_map<std::string, book_t> map_type;
12   typedef std::vector<book_t> booklist_t;
13
14   boost::optional<book_t> find_book(const std::string& title)
15                                                           const;
16   booklist_t find_books(const std::vector<std::string>&
17                                         titles) const;
18   bool add_book(const book_t& book);
19   bool remove_book(const std::string& title);
20 };
```

The member function `find_book` is used to look up a single title and returns it as `book_t` object wrapped in `boost::optional`. Using `boost::optional`, we can return an empty value if a title is not found (see *Chapter 2, The First Brush with Boost's Utilities*). The member function `find_books` looks up a list of titles passed to it as a `vector` and returns a vector of `book_t` objects. The member function `add_book` adds a title to the catalog and `remove_book` removes a title from the catalog.

We want to implement the class to allow multiple threads to look up titles concurrently. We also want to allow the librarian to add and remove titles concurrently with the reads, without hurting correctness or consistency.

As long as data in the catalog does not change, multiple threads can concurrently look up titles without the need for any synchronization; because read-only operations cannot introduce inconsistencies. But since the catalog does allow the librarian to add and remove titles, we must make sure that these operations do not interleave with read operations. In thus formulating our requirements, we just stated the classic concurrency problem known as the Readers-Writers problem. The Readers-Writers problem lays down the following constraints:

- Any writer thread must have exclusive access to a data structure
- Any reader thread can share access to the data structure with other reader threads, in the absence of a writer thread

In the above statements, *reader thread* refers to threads performing only read-only operations like looking up titles, and *writer thread* refers to threads that modify the contents of the data structure in some way, such as adding and removing titles. This is sometimes referred to as **Multiple Readers Single Writer (MRSW)** model, as it allows either multiple concurrent readers or a single exclusive writer.

While `boost::mutex` allows a single thread to acquire an exclusive lock, it does not allow multiple threads to share a lock. We need to use `boost::shared_mutex` for this purpose. `boost::shared_mutex` conforms to the *SharedLockable* concept, which subsumes the Lockable concept, and additionally, defines `lock_shared` and `unlock_shared` member functions, which should be called by reader threads. Because `shared_mutex` also conforms to Lockable, it can be locked for exclusive access using `boost::lock_guard` or `boost::unique_lock`. Let us now look at the implementation of `LibraryCatalog`:

Listing 10.14b: Library catalog implementation

```
1 #include <vector>
2 #include <string>
3 #include <boost/thread.hpp>
4 #include <boost/optional.hpp>
5 #include <boost/unordered/unordered_map.hpp>
6
7 struct book_t { /* definitions */ };
8
9
10 class LibraryCatalog {
11 public:
12   typedef boost::unordered_map<std::string, book_t> map_type;
13   typedef std::vector<book_t> booklist_t;
14
15   boost::optional<book_t> find_book(const std::string& title)
16                                                         const {
17     boost::shared_lock<boost::shared_mutex> rdlock(mtx);
18     auto it = catalog.find(title);
19
20     if (it != catalog.end()) {
21       return it->second;
22     }
23     rdlock.unlock();
24
25     return boost::none;
26   }
```

```
27
28    booklist_t find_books(const std::vector<std::string>& titles)
29                                                      const {
30      booklist_t result;
31      for (auto title : titles) {
32        auto book = find_book(title);
33
34        if (book) {
35          result.push_back(book.get());
36        }
37      }
38
39      return result;
40    }
41
42    bool add_book(const book_t& book) {
43      boost::unique_lock<boost::shared_mutex> wrlock(mtx);
44      auto it = catalog.find(book.title);
45
46      if (it == catalog.end()) {
47        catalog[book.title] = book;
48        return true;
49      }
50      else if (it->second.edition < book.edition) {
51        it->second = book;
52        return true;
53      }
54
55      return false;
56    }
57
58    bool remove_book(const std::string& title) {
59      boost::unique_lock<boost::shared_mutex> wrlock(mtx);
60      return catalog.erase(title);
61    }
62
63 private:
64    map_type catalog;
65    mutable boost::shared_mutex mtx;
66 };
```

The method `find_book` performs read-only operations on the catalog and therefore acquires a shared lock using the `boost::shared_lock` template (line 17). It releases the lock after retrieving a matching book, if any (line 23). The method `find_books` is implemented in terms of `find_book`, which it calls in a loop for each title in the list passed to it. This allows for better overall concurrency between reader threads at the cost of a slight performance hit, due to repeated locking and unlocking of the `shared_mutex`.

Both `add_book` and `remove_book` are mutating functions that potentially change the number of elements in the catalog. In order to modify the catalog, both methods require exclusive or write locks on the catalog. For this reason, we use `unique_lock` instances to acquire an exclusive lock on the `shared_mutex` (lines 43 and 59).

Upgradable locks

There is one glaring problem in the implementation of `add_book` and `remove_book` methods in listing 10.14b. Both methods modify the catalog conditionally, based on the outcome of a look-up that is run first. Yet an exclusive lock is acquired unconditionally at the start of both operations. One could conceivably call `remove_book` with a nonexistent title or `add_book` with an edition of a book that is already in the catalog, in a loop, and seriously hamper the concurrency of the system doing nothing.

If we acquired a shared lock to perform the look up, we would have to release it before acquiring an exclusive lock for modifying the catalog. In this case, the results of the look up would no longer be reliable, as some other thread could have modified the catalog between the time the shared lock is released and the exclusive lock acquired.

This problem can be addressed by using `boost::upgrade_lock` and a set of associated primitives. This is shown in the following rewrite of `add_book`:

```
 1 bool LibraryCatalog::add_book(const book_t& book) {
 2   boost::upgrade_lock<boost::shared_mutex> upglock(mtx);
 3   auto it = catalog.find(book.title);
 4
 5   if (it == catalog.end()) {
 6     boost::upgrade_to_unique_lock<boost::shared_mutex>
 7                                        ulock(upglock);
 8     catalog[book.title] = book;
 9     return true;
10   } else if (it->second.edition > book.edition) {
11     boost::upgrade_to_unique_lock<boost::shared_mutex>
12                                        ulock(upglock);
```

```
13      it->second = book;
14      return true;
15    }
16
17    return false;
18 }
```

Instead of acquiring an exclusive lock to start with, we acquire an *upgrade lock* before performing the look up (line 2), and then *upgrade* it to a unique lock only if we need to modify the catalog (lines 6-7 and 11-12). To acquire an upgrade lock, we wrap the shared mutex in an `upgrade_lock<boost::shared_mutex>` instance (line 2). This blocks if there is an exclusive lock or another upgrade lock on the mutex in effect, but proceeds otherwise even if there be shared locks. Thus, at any point in time, there can be any number of shared locks and at most one upgrade lock on a mutex. Acquiring an upgrade lock thus does not impact read concurrency. Once the look up is performed, and it is determined that a write operation needs to be performed, the upgrade lock is promoted to a unique lock by wrapping it in an instance of `upgrade_to_unique_lock<boost::shared_mutex>` (lines 6-7 and 11-12). This blocks until there are no remaining shared locks, and then *atomically* releases the upgrade ownership and acquires an exclusive ownership on the `shared_mutex`.

 Acquiring an upgrade lock indicates intent to potentially upgrade it to an exclusive lock and perform writes or modifications.

Performance of shared_mutex

`boost::shared_mutex` is slower than `boost::mutex` but acquiring additional read locks on an already read-locked mutex is much faster. It is ideally suited for frequent concurrent reads with infrequent need for exclusive write access. Any time you deal with frequent writes, just use `boost::mutex` to provide exclusive write access.

Most solutions to the MRSW problem either prefer readers over writers or the other way round. In **read-preferring solutions**, when a shared lock is in effect, new reader threads can acquire a shared lock even with a writer waiting to acquire an exclusive lock. This leads to write-starvation as the writer only ever gets an exclusive lock at a point when no readers are around. In **write-preferring solutions**, if there is a writer thread waiting on an exclusive lock, then new readers are queued even if existing readers hold a shared lock. This impacts the concurrency of reads. Boost 1.57 (current release) provides a shared/exclusive lock implementation that is completely fair and does not have either a reader- or a writer-bias.

Standard Library primitives

The C++11 Standard Library introduces `std::mutex` and a whole host of RAII wrappers for locks, including `std::lock_guard`, `std::unique_lock`, and `std::lock`, available in the header `mutex`. C++11 Standard Library also introduces `std::condition_variable` available in the header `condition_variable`. The C++14 Standard Library introduces `std::shared_timed_mutex`, which corresponds to `boost::shared_mutex` and `std::shared_lock`, both available in the header `mutex`. They correspond to their Boost counterparts of the same names, and have very similar interfaces. There is no upgrade lock facility in the Standard Library as of C++14, nor any equivalent of the convenient `boost::thread_group`.

Boost Coroutine

Coroutines are functions that can *yield* or relinquish control to another coroutine, and then given control back, resuming from the point at which they earlier yielded. The state of automatic variables is maintained between a yield and the resumption. Coroutines can be used for complex control flow patterns with surprisingly simple and clean code. The Boost Coroutine library provides two types of coroutines:

- **Asymmetric coroutines**: Asymmetric coroutines distinguish between a caller and a callee coroutine. With asymmetric coroutines, a callee can only yield back to the caller. They are often used for unidirectional data transfer from either the callee to caller, or the other way.

- **Symmetric coroutines**: Such coroutines can *yield* to other coroutines, irrespective of who the caller was. They can be used to generate complex cooperative chains of coroutines.

When a coroutine yields control, it is said to be suspended — its registers are saved and it relinquishes control to another function. On resumption, the registers are restored and execution continues beyond the point of yield. The Boost Coroutine library utilizes the Boost Context library for this purpose.

A distinction is made between *stackful coroutines* versus *stackless coroutines*. A stackful coroutine can be suspended from within a function called by the coroutine, that is, from a nested stackframe. With stackless coroutines, only the top level routine may suspend itself. In this chapter, we only look at asymmetric stackful coroutines.

Asymmetric coroutines

The core template used to define asymmetric coroutines is called `boost::coroutines::asymmetric_coroutine<>`. It takes a single type parameter that represents the type of value transferred from one coroutine to the other. It can be `void` if no value needs to be transferred.

Coroutines that call other coroutines or yield to them must have a way to refer to other coroutines. The nested type `asymmetric_coroutine<T>::push_type` represents a coroutine that provides data of type `T`, and the nested type `asymmetric_coroutine<T>::pull_type` represents a coroutine that consumes the data of type `T`. Both the types are callable types, with an overloaded `operator()`. Using these types, we shall now write a program that uses coroutines to read data from a vector of elements:

Listing 10.15: Using asymmetric coroutines

```
1 #include <iostream>
2 #include <boost/coroutine/all.hpp>
3 #include <boost/bind.hpp>
4 #include <vector>
5 #include <string>
6
7 template <typename T>
8 using pull_type = typename
9   boost::coroutines::asymmetric_coroutine<T>::pull_type;
10
11 template <typename T>
12 using push_type = typename
13   boost::coroutines::asymmetric_coroutine<T>::push_type;
14
15 template <typename T>
16 void getNextElem(push_type<T>& sink,
17                  const std::vector<T>& vec)
18 {
19   for (const auto& elem: vec) {
20     sink(elem);
21   }
22 }
23
24 int main()
25 {
26   std::vector<std::string> vec{"hello", "hi", "hola",
27                                "servus"};
28   pull_type<std::string> greet_func(
```

```
29          boost::bind(getNextElem<std::string>, ::_1,
30          boost::cref(vec)));
31
32   while (greet_func) {
33     std::cout << greet_func.get() << '\n';
34     greet_func();
35   }
36 }
```

To start with, we define two alias templates called `pull_type` and `push_type` referring to `asymmetric_coroutine<T>::pull_type` and `asymmetric_coroutine<T>::push_type` for a type parameter T (lines 7-9 and 11-13).

The function `getNextElem` (line 16) is meant to be used as a coroutine that passes the next element from a vector to the caller each time it is called. The `main` function populates this vector (lines 26-27) and then calls `getNextElem` repeatedly to get each element. Thus data is transferred from `getNextElem` to `main`, `main` being the caller routine, and `getNextElem`, the callee routine.

Depending on whether the coroutine pushes data to the caller or pulls data from it, it should have one of the following two signatures:

* `void (push_type&)`: Coroutine pushes data to caller
* `void (pull_type&)`: Coroutine pulls data from caller

The `pull_type` or `push_type` reference passed to the coroutine refers to the calling context and represents the conduit through which it pushes data to, or pulls data from the caller.

The caller routine must wrap the function in `pull_type` or `push_type`, depending on whether it intends to pull data from it or push data to it. In our case, the `main` function must wrap `getNextElem` in an instance of `pull_type`. However, the signature of `getNextElem` is:

```
void (push_type&, const std::vector<T>&)
```

Thus we must adapt it to a conforming signature using some mechanism such as lambda or `bind`. We use `boost::bind` to bind the second parameter of `getNextElem` to the vector (lines 29-30) and wrap the resulting unary function object in a `pull_type` instance called `greet_func`. Creating the instance of `pull_type` invokes the `getNextElem` coroutine for the first time.

We can use `greet_func` in a Boolean context to check whether a value is available from the callee, and we use this to spin in a loop (line 32). In each iteration of the loop, we call the `get` member function on the `pull_type` instance to obtain the next value furnished by `getNextElem` (line 33). We then invoke the overloaded `operator()` of `pull_type` to relinquish control to the `getNextElem` coroutine (line 34).

On the other side, the `getNextElem` coroutine does not use a conventional return value to send data back to the caller. It iterates through the vector and uses the overloaded `operator()` on the calling context to return each element (line 20). If the caller had to push data to the callee instead, then the caller would have wrapped the callee in `push_type`, and the callee would be passed the caller's reference wrapped in `pull_type`. In the next chapter, we will see how Boost Asio uses coroutines to simplify asynchronous, event-driven logic.

Self-test questions

For multiple choice questions, choose all options that apply:

1. What happens if you do not call `join` or `detach` on a `boost::thread` object and a `std::thread` object?

   a. `join` is called on underlying thread of `boost::thread`.

   b. `std::terminate` is called for `std::thread`, terminating the program.

   c. `detach` is called on underlying thread of `boost::thread`.

   d. `detach` is called on underlying thread of `std::thread`.

2. What happens if an exception is allowed to propagate past the initial function with which a `boost::thread` object is created?

   a. The program is terminated via `std::terminate`.

   b. It is undefined behavior.

   c. The call to `get` on the `future` object throws an exception in the calling thread.

   d. The thread is terminated but the exception is not propagated.

3. Should you call `notify_one` or `notify_all` on a `condition_variable` object without holding the associated mutex?

   a. No, the call will block.

   b. Yes, but it may result in priority inversion in some cases.

   c. No, some waiting threads may miss the signal.

   d. Yes, it may even be faster.

4. What is the advantage of using `boost::unique_lock` over `boost::lock_guard`?

    a. `boost::unique_lock` is more efficient and lightweight.

    b. `boost::unique_lock` can or adopt an already acquired lock.

    c. `boost::lock_guard` cannot be unlocked and relocked mid-scope.

    d. `boost::unique_lock` can defer acquiring a lock.

5. Which of the following are true of `boost::shared_mutex`?

    a. `shared_mutex` is more lightweight and faster than `boost::mutex`.

    b. Boost implementation of `shared_mutex` does not have reader- or writer-bias.

    c. `shared_mutex` can be used as an upgradable lock.

    d. `shared_mutex` is ideal for systems with high-write contention.

Summary

In this chapter, we looked at how to write concurrent logic in terms of threads and tasks using the Boost Thread library and the C++11 Standard Library. We learned how to use the futures and promises paradigm to define ordering of operations across concurrent tasks, and some abstractions around futures and promises in the Standard Library. We also studied various lock-based thread synchronization primitives and applied them to some common multithreading problems.

Multithreading is a difficult and complex topic, and this chapter merely introduces the portable APIs available in Boost to write concurrent programs. The Boost Thread library and the concurrent programming interfaces in the C++ Standard Library are an evolving set, and we did not cover several features: the C++ memory model and atomics, Boost Lockfree, thread cancellation, experimental continuations with `boost::futures`, and several more topics. Architectural concerns in designing concurrent systems and concurrent data structures are other relevant topics that are outside the scope of this book. Hopefully, the concepts and methods presented in this chapter will help you explore further in these directions.

References

- *C++ Concurrency in Action, Anthony Williams, Manning Publications*
- Lockfree data structures: `http://www.boost.org/libs/lockfree`
- *A proposal to add coroutines to the C++ standard library (Revision 1), Oliver Kowalke* and *Nat Goodspeed*: `http://www.open-std.org/jtc1/sc22/wg21/docs/papers/2014/n3985.pdf`
- Lock-Free Programming, Herb Sutter: `https://youtu.be/c1gO9aB9nbs`
- atomic<> Weapons (video), Herb Sutter:
  - `https://channel9.msdn.com/Shows/Going+Deep/Cpp-and-Beyond-2012-Herb-Sutter-atomic-Weapons-1-of-2`
  - `https://channel9.msdn.com/Shows/Going+Deep/Cpp-and-Beyond-2012-Herb-Sutter-atomic-Weapons-2-of-2`

11
Network Programming Using Boost Asio

In today's networked world, Internet servers handling thousands of requests per second have a tough mandate to fulfill — of maintaining responsiveness and not slowing down even with increasing volumes of requests. Building reliable processes that efficiently handle network I/O and scale with the number of connections is challenging because it often requires the application programmer to understand the underlying protocol stack and exploit it in ingenious ways. What adds to the challenge is the variance in the programming interfaces and models for network programming across platforms, and the inherent difficulties of using low-level APIs.

Boost Asio (pronounced ay-see-oh) is a portable library for performing efficient network I/O using a consistent programming model. The emphasis is on performing asynchronous I/O (hence the name Asio), where the program initiates I/O operations and gets on with its other jobs, without blocking for the OS to return with the results of the operation. When the operation is complete in the underlying OS, the program is notified by the Asio library and takes an appropriate action. The problems Asio helps solve and the consistent, portable interfaces it uses to do so, make Asio compellingly useful. But the asynchronous nature of interactions also makes it more complex and less straightforward to reason about. This is the reason we will study Asio in two parts: to first understand its interaction model and then use it to perform network I/O:

- Task execution with Asio
- Network programming using Asio

Asio provides a toolkit for performing and managing arbitrary tasks, and the focus of the first part of this chapter is to understand this toolkit. We apply this understanding in the second part of this chapter, when we look specifically at how Asio helps write programs that communicate with other programs over the network, using protocols from the Internet Protocol (IP) suite.

Task execution with Asio

At its core, Boost Asio provides a task execution framework that you can use to perform operations of any kind. You create your tasks as function objects and post them to a task queue maintained by Boost Asio. You enlist one or more threads to pick these tasks (function objects) and invoke them. The threads keep picking up tasks, one after the other till the task queues are empty at which point the threads do not block but exit.

IO Service, queues, and handlers

At the heart of Asio is the type `boost::asio::io_service`. A program uses the `io_service` interface to perform network I/O and manage tasks. Any program that wants to use the Asio library creates at least one instance of `io_service` and sometimes more than one. In this section, we will explore the task management capabilities of `io_service`, and defer the discussion of network I/O to the latter half of the chapter.

Here is the IO Service in action using the obligatory "hello world" example:

Listing 11.1: Asio Hello World

```
 1 #include <boost/asio.hpp>
 2 #include <iostream>
 3 namespace asio = boost::asio;
 4
 5 int main() {
 6   asio::io_service service;
 7
 8   service.post(
 9     [] {
10       std::cout << "Hello, world!" << '\n';
11     });
12
13   std::cout << "Greetings: \n";
14   service.run();
15 }
```

We include the convenience header `boost/asio.hpp`, which includes most of the Asio library that we need for the examples in this chapter (line 1). All parts of the Asio library are under the namespace `boost::asio`, so we use a shorter alias for this (line 3). The program itself just prints `Hello, world!` on the console but it does so through a task.

The program first creates an instance of `io_service` (line 6) and *posts* a function object to it, using the `post` member function of `io_service`. The function object, in this case defined using a lambda expression, is referred to as a **handler**. The call to `post` adds the handler to a queue inside `io_service`; some thread (including that which posted the handler) must *dispatch* them, that is, remove them off the queue and call them. The call to the `run` member function of `io_service` (line 14) does precisely this. It loops through the handlers in the queue inside `io_service`, removing and calling each handler. In fact, we can post more handlers to the `io_service` before calling `run`, and it would call all the posted handlers. If we did not call `run`, none of the handlers would be dispatched. The `run` function blocks until all the handlers in the queue have been dispatched and returns only when the queue is empty. By itself, a handler may be thought of as an independent, packaged task, and Boost Asio provides a great mechanism for dispatching arbitrary tasks as handlers. Note that handlers must be nullary function objects, that is, they should take no arguments.

Asio is a header-only library by default, but programs using Asio need to link at least with `boost_system`. On Linux, we can use the following command line to build this example:

```
$ g++ -g listing11_1.cpp -o listing11_1 -lboost_system
-std=c++11
```

Most examples in this chapter would require you to link to additional libraries. You can use the following command line to build all the examples in this chapter:

```
$ g++ -g listing11_25.cpp -o listing11_25 -lboost_system
-lboost_coroutine -lboost_date_time -std=c++11
```

If you did not install Boost from a native package, and for installation on Windows, refer to *Chapter 1, Introducing Boost*.

Running this program prints the following:

```
Greetings: Hello, World!
```

Note that `Greetings:` is printed from the main function (line 13) before the call to `run` (line 14). The call to `run` ends up dispatching the sole handler in the queue, which prints `Hello, World!`. It is also possible for multiple threads to call `run` on the same I/O object and dispatch handlers concurrently. We will see how this can be useful in the next section.

Handler states – run_one, poll, and poll_one

While the `run` function blocks until there are no more handlers in the queue, there are other member functions of `io_service` that let you process handlers with greater flexibility. But before we look at this function, we need to distinguish between pending and ready handlers.

The handlers we posted to the `io_service` were all ready to run immediately and were invoked as soon as their turn came on the queue. In general, handlers are associated with background tasks that run in the underlying OS, for example, network I/O tasks. Such handlers are meant to be invoked only once the associated task is completed, which is why in such contexts, they are called **completion handlers**. These handlers are said to be **pending** until the associated task is awaiting completion, and once the associated task completes, they are said to be **ready**.

The `poll` member function, unlike `run`, dispatches all the ready handlers but does not wait for any pending handler to become ready. Thus, it returns immediately if there are no ready handlers, even if there are pending handlers. The `poll_one` member function dispatches exactly one ready handler if there be one, but does not block waiting for pending handlers to get ready.

The `run_one` member function blocks on a nonempty queue waiting for a handler to become ready. It returns when called on an empty queue, and otherwise, as soon as it finds and dispatches a ready handler.

post versus dispatch

A call to the `post` member function adds a handler to the task queue and returns immediately. A later call to `run` is responsible for dispatching the handler. There is another member function called `dispatch` that can be used to request the `io_service` to invoke a handler immediately if possible. If `dispatch` is invoked in a thread that has already called one of `run`, `poll`, `run_one`, or `poll_one`, then the handler will be invoked immediately. If no such thread is available, `dispatch` adds the handler to the queue and returns just like `post` would. In the following example, we invoke `dispatch` from the `main` function and from within another handler:

Listing 11.2: post versus dispatch

```
1 #include <boost/asio.hpp>
2 #include <iostream>
3 namespace asio = boost::asio;
4
5 int main() {
```

```
 6    asio::io_service service;
 7    // Hello Handler - dispatch behaves like post
 8    service.dispatch([]() { std::cout << "Hello\n"; });
 9
10    service.post(
11      [&service] { // English Handler
12        std::cout << "Hello, world!\n";
13        service.dispatch([] {  // Spanish Handler, immediate
14                             std::cout << "Hola, mundo!\n";
15                           });
16      });
17    // German Handler
18    service.post([&service] {std::cout << "Hallo, Welt!\n"; });
19    service.run();
20  }
```

Running this code produces the following output:

```
Hello
Hello, world!
Hola, mundo!
Hallo, Welt!
```

The first call to dispatch (line 8) adds a handler to the queue without invoking it because run was yet to be called on io_service. We call this the Hello Handler, as it prints Hello. This is followed by the two calls to post (lines 10, 18), which add two more handlers. The first of these two handlers prints Hello, world! (line 12), and in turn, calls dispatch (line 13) to add another handler that prints the Spanish greeting, Hola, mundo! (line 14). The second of these handlers prints the German greeting, Hallo, Welt (line 18). For our convenience, let's just call them the English, Spanish, and German handlers. This creates the following entries in the queue:

```
Hello Handler
English Handler
German Handler
```

Now, when we call run on the io_service (line 19), the Hello Handler is dispatched first and prints Hello. This is followed by the English Handler, which prints Hello, World! and calls dispatch on the io_service, passing the Spanish Handler. Since this executes in the context of a thread that has already called run, the call to dispatch invokes the Spanish Handler, which prints Hola, mundo!. Following this, the German Handler is dispatched printing Hallo, Welt! before run returns.

What if the English Handler called `post` instead of `dispatch` (line 13)? In that case, the Spanish Handler would not be invoked immediately but would queue up after the German Handler. The German greeting `Hallo, Welt!` would precede the Spanish greeting `Hola, mundo!`. The output would look like this:

```
Hello
Hello, world!
Hallo, Welt!
Hola, mundo!
```

Concurrent execution via thread pools

The `io_service` object is thread-safe and multiple threads can call `run` on it concurrently. If there are multiple handlers in the queue, they can be processed concurrently by such threads. In effect, the set of threads that call `run` on a given `io_service` form a **thread pool**. Successive handlers can be processed by different threads in the pool. Which thread dispatches a given handler is indeterminate, so the handler code should not make any such assumptions. In the following example, we post a bunch of handlers to the `io_service` and then start four threads, which all call `run` on it:

Listing 11.3: Simple thread pools

```
 1 #include <boost/asio.hpp>
 2 #include <boost/thread.hpp>
 3 #include <boost/date_time.hpp>
 4 #include <iostream>
 5 namespace asio = boost::asio;
 6
 7 #define PRINT_ARGS(msg) do {\
 8   boost::lock_guard<boost::mutex> lg(mtx); \
 9   std::cout << '[' << boost::this_thread::get_id() \
10             << "] " << msg << std::endl; \
11 } while (0)
12
13 int main() {
14   asio::io_service service;
15   boost::mutex mtx;
16
17   for (int i = 0; i < 20; ++i) {
18     service.post([i, &mtx]() {
19                       PRINT_ARGS("Handler[" << i << "]");
20                       boost::this_thread::sleep(
```

```
21                                        boost::posix_time::seconds(1));
22                            });
23    }
24
25    boost::thread_group pool;
26    for (int i = 0; i < 4; ++i) {
27      pool.create_thread([&service]() { service.run(); });
28    }
29
30    pool.join_all();
31 }
```

We post twenty handlers in a loop (line 18). Each handler prints its identifier (line 19), and then sleeps for a second (lines 19-20). To run the handlers, we create a group of four threads, each of which calls run on the io_service (line 21) and wait for all the threads to finish (line 24). We define the macro PRINT_ARGS which writes output to the console in a thread-safe way, tagged with the current thread ID (line 7-10). We will use this macro in other examples too.

To build this example, you must also link against libboost_thread, libboost_date_time, and in Posix environments, with libpthread too:

```
$ g++ -g listing9_3.cpp -o listing9_3 -lboost_system -lboost_thread
-lboost_date_time -pthread -std=c++11
```

One particular run of this program on my laptop produced the following output (with some lines snipped):

```
[b5c15b40] Handler[0]
[b6416b40] Handler[1]
[b6c17b40] Handler[2]
[b7418b40] Handler[3]
[b5c15b40] Handler[4]
[b6416b40] Handler[5]
...
[b6c17b40] Handler[13]
[b7418b40] Handler[14]
[b6416b40] Handler[15]
[b5c15b40] Handler[16]
[b6c17b40] Handler[17]
[b7418b40] Handler[18]
[b6416b40] Handler[19]
```

You can see that the different handlers are executed by different threads (each thread ID marked differently).

 If any of the handlers threw an exception, it would be propagated across the call to the run function on the thread that was executing the handler.

io_service::work

Sometimes, it is useful to keep the thread pool started, even when there are no handlers to dispatch. Neither run nor run_one blocks on an empty queue. So in order for them to block waiting for a task, we have to indicate, in some way, that there is outstanding work to be performed. We do this by creating an instance of io_service::work, as shown in the following example:

Listing 11.4: Using io_service::work to keep threads engaged

```
 1 #include <boost/asio.hpp>
 2 #include <memory>
 3 #include <boost/thread.hpp>
 4 #include <iostream>
 5 namespace asio = boost::asio;
 6
 7 typedef std::unique_ptr<asio::io_service::work> work_ptr;
 8
 9 #define PRINT_ARGS(msg) do {\ …
...
14
15 int main() {
16   asio::io_service service;
17   // keep the workers occupied
18   work_ptr work(new asio::io_service::work(service));
19   boost::mutex mtx;
20
21   // set up the worker threads in a thread group
22   boost::thread_group workers;
23   for (int i = 0; i < 3; ++i) {
24     workers.create_thread([&service, &mtx]() {
25                         PRINT_ARGS("Starting worker thread ");
26                         service.run();
27                         PRINT_ARGS("Worker thread done");
28                       });
29   }
```

```
30
31    // Post work
32    for (int i = 0; i < 20; ++i) {
33      service.post(
34        [&service, &mtx]() {
35          PRINT_ARGS("Hello, world!");
36          service.post([&mtx]() {
37                         PRINT_ARGS("Hola, mundo!");
38                       });
39        });
40    }
41
42    work.reset(); // destroy work object: signals end of work
43    workers.join_all(); // wait for all worker threads to finish
44 }
```

In this example, we create an object of `io_service::work` wrapped in a `unique_ptr` (line 18). We associate it with an `io_service` object by passing to the `work` constructor a reference to the `io_service` object. Note that, unlike listing 11.3, we create the worker threads first (lines 24-27) and then post the handlers (lines 33-39). However, the worker threads stay put waiting for the handlers because of the calls to `run` block (line 26). This happens because of the `io_service::work` object we created, which indicates that there is outstanding work in the `io_service` queue. As a result, even after all handlers are dispatched, the threads do not exit. By calling `reset` on the `unique_ptr`, wrapping the `work` object, its destructor is called, which notifies the `io_service` that all outstanding work is complete (line 42). The calls to `run` in the threads return and the program exits once all the threads are joined (line 43). We wrapped the `work` object in a `unique_ptr` to destroy it in an exception-safe way at a suitable point in the program.

We omitted the definition of `PRINT_ARGS` here, refer to listing 11.3.

Serialized and ordered execution via strands

Thread pools allow handlers to be run concurrently. This means that handlers that access shared resources need to synchronize access to these resources. We already saw examples of this in listings 11.3 and 11.4, when we synchronized access to `std::cout`, which is a global object. As an alternative to writing synchronization code in handlers, which can make the handler code more complex, we can use **strands**.

> Think of a strand as a subsequence of the task queue with the constraint that no two handlers from the same strand ever run concurrently.

The scheduling of other handlers in the queue, which are not in the strand, is not affected by the strand in any way. Let us look at an example of using strands:

Listing 11.5: Using strands

```
 1 #include <boost/asio.hpp>
 2 #include <boost/thread.hpp>
 3 #include <boost/date_time.hpp>
 4 #include <cstdlib>
 5 #include <iostream>
 6 #include <ctime>
 7 namespace asio = boost::asio;
 8 #define PRINT_ARGS(msg) do {\
...
13
14 int main() {
15   std::srand(std::time(0));
16   asio::io_service service;
17   asio::io_service::strand strand(service);
18   boost::mutex mtx;
19   size_t regular = 0, on_strand = 0;
20
21   auto workFuncStrand = [&mtx, &on_strand] {
22           ++on_strand;
23           PRINT_ARGS(on_strand << ". Hello, from strand!");
24           boost::this_thread::sleep(
25                   boost::posix_time::seconds(2));
26         };
27
28   auto workFunc = [&mtx, &regular] {
29                   PRINT_ARGS(++regular << ". Hello, world!");
30                   boost::this_thread::sleep(
31                         boost::posix_time::seconds(2));
32                 };
33   // Post work
34   for (int i = 0; i < 15; ++i) {
35     if (rand() % 2 == 0) {
36       service.post(strand.wrap(workFuncStrand));
37     } else {
38       service.post(workFunc);
39     }
40   }
```

```
41
42    // set up the worker threads in a thread group
43    boost::thread_group workers;
44    for (int i = 0; i < 3; ++i) {
45      workers.create_thread([&service, &mtx]() {
46                      PRINT_ARGS("Starting worker thread ");
47                      service.run();
48                      PRINT_ARGS("Worker thread done");
49                    });
50    }
51
52    workers.join_all(); // wait for all worker threads to finish
53  }
```

In this example, we create two handler functions: workFuncStrand (line 21) and
workFunc (line 28). The lambda workFuncStrand captures a counter on_strand,
increments it, and prints a message Hello, from strand!, prefixed with the value
of the counter. The function workFunc captures another counter regular, increments
it, and prints Hello, World!, prefixed with the counter. Both pause for 2 seconds
before returning.

To define and use a strand, we first create an object of io_service::strand
associated with the io_service instance (line 17). Thereafter, we post all handlers
that we want to be part of that strand by wrapping them using the wrap member
function of the strand (line 36). Alternatively, we can post the handlers to the strand
directly by using either the post or the dispatch member function of the strand, as
shown in the following snippet:

```
33    for (int i = 0; i < 15; ++i) {
34      if (rand() % 2 == 0) {
35        strand.post(workFuncStrand);
37      } else {
...
```

The wrap member function of strand returns a function object, which in turn calls
dispatch on the strand to invoke the original handler. Initially, it is this function
object rather than our original handler that is added to the queue. When duly
dispatched, this invokes the original handler. There are no constraints on the order
in which these wrapper handlers are dispatched, and therefore, the actual order in
which the original handlers are invoked can be different from the order in which
they were wrapped and posted.

On the other hand, calling `post` or `dispatch` directly on the strand avoids an intermediate handler. Directly posting to a strand also guarantees that the handlers will be dispatched in the same order that they were posted, achieving a deterministic ordering of the handlers in the strand. The `dispatch` member of `strand` blocks until the handler is dispatched. The `post` member simply adds it to the strand and returns.

Note that `workFuncStrand` increments `on_strand` without synchronization (line 22), while `workFunc` increments the counter `regular` within the `PRINT_ARGS` macro (line 29), which ensures that the increment happens in a critical section. The `workFuncStrand` handlers are posted to a strand and therefore are guaranteed to be serialized; hence no need for explicit synchronization. On the flip side, entire functions are serialized via strands and synchronizing smaller blocks of code is not possible. There is no serialization between the handlers running on the strand and other handlers; therefore, the access to global objects, like `std::cout`, must still be synchronized.

The following is a sample output of running the preceding code:

```
[b73b6b40] Starting worker thread
[b73b6b40] 0. Hello, world from strand!
[b6bb5b40] Starting worker thread
[b6bb5b40] 1. Hello, world!
[b63b4b40] Starting worker thread
[b63b4b40] 2. Hello, world!
[b73b6b40] 3. Hello, world from strand!
[b6bb5b40] 5. Hello, world!
[b63b4b40] 6. Hello, world!
...
[b6bb5b40] 14. Hello, world!
[b63b4b40] 4. Hello, world from strand!
[b63b4b40] 8. Hello, world from strand!
[b63b4b40] 10. Hello, world from strand!
[b63b4b40] 13. Hello, world from strand!
[b6bb5b40] Worker thread done
[b73b6b40] Worker thread done
[b63b4b40] Worker thread done
```

There were three distinct threads in the pool and the handlers from the strand were picked up by two of these three threads: initially, by thread ID `b73b6b40`, and later on, by thread ID `b63b4b40`. This also dispels a frequent misunderstanding that all handlers in a strand are dispatched by the same thread, which is clearly not the case.

[Different handlers in the same strand may be dispatched by different threads but will never run concurrently.]

Network I/O using Asio

We want to use Asio to build scalable network services that perform I/O over the network. Such services receive requests from clients running on remote machines and send them information over the network. The data transfer between processes across machine boundaries, happening over the wire, is done using certain protocols of network communication. The most ubiquitous of these protocols is IP or the **Internet Protocol** and a **suite of protocols** layered above it. Boost Asio supports TCP, UDP, and ICMP, the three popular protocols in the IP protocol suite. We do not cover ICMP in this book.

UDP and TCP

User Datagram Protocol or UDP is used to transmit **datagrams** or message units from one host to another over an IP network. UDP is a very basic protocol built over IP and is stateless in the sense that no context is maintained across multiple network I/O operations. The reliability of data transfer using UDP depends on the reliability of the underlying network, and UDP transfers have the following caveats:

- A UDP datagram may not be delivered at all

- A given datagram may be delivered more than once

- Two datagrams may not be delivered to the destination in the order in which they were dispatched from the source

- UDP will detect any data corruption in the datagrams and drop such messages without any means of recovery

For these reasons, UDP is considered to be an unreliable protocol.

If an application requires stronger guarantees from the protocol, we choose **Transmission Control Protocol** or TCP. TCP deals in terms of byte streams rather than messages. It uses a handshake mechanism between two endpoints of the network communication to establish a durable **connection** between the two points and maintains state during the life of the connection. All communications between the two endpoints happen over such a connection. At the cost of a somewhat higher latency than UDP, TCP guarantees the following:

- On a given connection, the receiving application receives the stream of bytes sent by the sender in the order they were sent

- Any data lost or corrupted on the wire can be retransmitted, greatly improving the reliability of deliveries

Real-time applications that can handle unreliability and data loss for themselves often use UDP. In addition, a lot of higher level protocols are run on top of UDP. TCP is more frequently used, where correctness concerns supersede real-time performance, for example, e-mail and file transfer protocols, HTTP, and so on.

IP addresses

IP addresses are numeric identifiers used to uniquely identify interfaces connected to an IP network. The older IPv4 protocol uses 32-bit IP addresses in an address space of 4 billion (2^{32}) addresses. The emergent IPv6 protocol uses 128-bit IP addresses in an address space of 3.4×10^{38} (2^{128}) unique addresses, which is practically inexhaustible. You can represent IP addresses of both types using the class `boost::asio::ip::address`, while version-specific addresses can be represented using `boost::asio::ip::address_v4` and `boost::asio::ip::address_v6`.

IPv4 addresses

The familiar IPv4 addresses, such as 212.54.84.93, are 32-bit unsigned integers expressed in the *dotted-quad notation*; four 8-bit unsigned integers or *octets* representing the four bytes in the address, the most significant on the left to the least significant on the right, separated by dots (period signs). Each octet can range from 0 through 255. IP addresses are normally interpreted in network byte order, that is, Big-endian.

Subnets

Larger computer networks are often divided into logical parts called **subnets**. A subnet consists of a set of nodes that can communicate with each other using broadcast messages. A subnet has an associated pool of IP addresses that have a common prefix, usually, called the *routing prefix* or *network address*. The remaining part of the IP address field is called the *host part*.

Given an IP address *and* the length of the prefix, we can compute the prefix using the **netmask**. The netmask of a subnet is a 4-byte bitmask, whose bitwise-AND with an IP address in the subnet yields the routing prefix. For a subnet with a routing prefix of length N, the netmask has the most significant N bits set and the remaining 32-N bits unset. The netmask is often expressed in a dotted-quad notation. For example, if the address 172.31.198.12 has a routing prefix that is 16 bits long, then its netmask would be 255.255.0.0 and the routing prefix would be 172.31.0.0.

In general, the length of the routing prefix must be explicitly specified. The **Classless Interdomain Routing (CIDR) notation** augments the dotted-quad notation with a trailing slash and a number between 0 and 32 that represents the prefix length. Thus, 10.209.72.221/22 represents an IP address with a prefix length of 22. An older scheme of classification, referred to as the *classful scheme*, divided the IPv4 address space into ranges and assigned a *class* to each range (see the following table). Addresses belonging to each range were said to be of the corresponding class, and the length of the routing prefix was determined based on the class, without being specified as, with the CIDR notation.

Class	Address range	Prefix length	Netmask	Remarks
Class A	0.0.0.0 – 127.255.255.255	8	255.0.0.0	
Class B	128.0.0.0 – 191.255.255.255	16	255.255.0.0	
Class C	192.0.0.0 – 223.255.255.255	24	255.255.255.0	
Class D	224.0.0.0 – 239.255.255.255	Not specified	Not specified	Multicast
Class E	240.0.0.0 – 255.255.255.255	Not specified	Not specified	Reserved

Special addresses

Some IPv4 addresses have special meanings. For example, an IP address with all bits set in the host part is known as the **broadcast address** for the subnet and is used to broadcast messages to all hosts in the subnet. For example, the broadcast address in the network 172.31.0.0/16 is 172.31.255.255.

Applications listening for incoming requests use the **unspecified address** 0.0.0.0 (INADDR_ANY) to listen on all available network interfaces, without the need to know addresses plumbed on the system.

The **loopback address** 127.0.0.1 is commonly associated with a virtual network interface that is not associated with any hardware and does not require the host to be connected to a network. Data sent over the loopback interface immediately shows up as received data on the sender host itself. Often used for testing networked applications within a box, you can configure additional loopback interfaces and associate loopback addresses from the range 127.0.0.0 through 127.255.255.255.

Handling IPv4 addresses with Boost

Let us now look at a code example of constructing IPv4 addresses and glean useful information from them, using the type boost::asio::ip::address_v4:

Listing 11.6: Handling IPv4 addresses

```
1 #include <boost/asio.hpp>
2 #include <iostream>
```

```
 3  #include <cassert>
 4  #include <vector>
 5  namespace asio = boost::asio;
 6  namespace sys = boost::system;
 7  using namespace asio::ip;
 8
 9  void printAddrProperties(const address& addr) {
10    std::cout << "\n\n" << addr << ": ";
11
12    if (addr.is_v4()) {
13      std::cout << "netmask=" << address_v4::netmask(addr.to_v4());
14    } else if (addr.is_v6()) { /* ... */ }
15
16    if (addr.is_unspecified()) { std::cout << "is unspecified, "; }
17    if (addr.is_loopback()) { std::cout << "is loopback, "; }
18    if (addr.is_multicast()) { std::cout << "is multicast, "; }
19  }
20
21  int main() {
22    sys::error_code ec;
23    std::vector<address> addresses;
24    std::vector<const char*> addr_strings{"127.0.0.1",
25            "10.28.25.62", "137.2.33.19", "223.21.201.30",
26            "232.28.25.62", "140.28.25.62/22"};
27
28    addresses.push_back(address_v4());        // default: 0.0.0.0
29    addresses.push_back(address_v4::any());   // INADDR_ANY
30
31    for (const auto& v4str : addr_strings) {
32      address_v4 addr = address_v4::from_string(v4str, ec);
33      if (!ec) {
34        addresses.push_back(addr);
35      }
36    }
37
38    for (const address& addr1: addresses) {
39      printAddrProperties(addr1);
40    }
41  }
```

This example highlights a few basic operations on IPv4 addresses. We create a vector of `boost::asio::ip::address` objects (not just `address_v4`) and push IPv4 addresses constructed from their string representations using the `address_v4::from_string` static function (line 32). We use the two-argument overload of `from_string`, which takes the address string, and a non-const reference to an `error_code` object that is set if it is unable to parse the address string. A one-argument overload exists, which throws if there is an error. Note that you can implicitly convert or assign `address_v4` instances to `address` instances. Default constructed instances of `address_v4` are equivalent to the unspecified address 0.0.0.0 (line 28), which is also returned by `address_v4::any()` (line 29).

To print the properties of the address, we have written the `printAddrProperties` function (line 9). We print IP addresses by streaming them to `std::cout` (line 10). We check whether an address is an IPv4 or IPv6 address using the `is_v4` and `is_v6` member functions (lines 12, 14), print the netmask for an IPv4 address using the `address_v4::netmask` static function (line 13), and also check whether the address is an unspecified address, loopback address, or IPv4 multicast address (class D) using appropriate member predicates (lines 16-18). Note that the `address_v4::from_string` function does not recognize the CIDR format (as of Boost version 1.57), and the netmask is computed based on the classful scheme.

In the next section, following a brief overview of IPv6 addresses, we will augment the `printAddrProperties` (line 14) function to print IPv6 specific properties as well.

IPv6 addresses

In its most general form, an IPv6 address is represented as a sequence of eight 2-byte unsigned hexadecimal integers, separated by colons. Digits `a` through `f` in the hexadecimal integers are written in lowercase by convention and leading zeros in each 16-bit number are omitted. Here is an example of an IPv6 address in this notation:

2001:0c2f:003a:01e0:0000:0000:0000:002a

One sequence of two or more zero terms can be collapsed completely. Thus, the preceding address can be written as 2001:c2f:3a:1e0::2a. All leading zeros have been removed and the contiguous zero terms between bytes 16 and 63 have been collapsed, leaving the colon pair (::). If there be multiple zero-term sequences, the longest one is collapsed, and if there is a tie, the one that is leftmost is collapsed. Thus, we can abbreviate this 2001:0000:0000:01e0:0000:0000:001a:002a to this 2001::1e0:0:0:1a:2a. Note that the leftmost sequence of two zero-terms is collapsed, while the other between bits 32 and 63 are not collapsed.

In environments transitioning from IPv4 to IPv6, software frequently supports both IPv4 and IPv6. *IPv4-mapped IPv6 addresses* are used to enable communication between IPv6 and IPv4 interfaces. IPv4 addresses are mapped to an IPv6 address with the ::ffff:0:0/96 prefix and the last 32-bits same as the IPv4 address. For example, 172.31.201.43 will be represented as ::ffff:172.31.201.43/96.

Address classes, scopes, and subnets

There are three classes of IPv6 addresses:

- **Unicast addresses**: These addresses identify a single network interface
- **Multicast addresses**: These addresses identify a group of network interfaces and are used to send data to all the interfaces in the group
- **Anycast addresses**: These addresses identify a group of network interfaces, but data sent to an **anycast** address is delivered to one or more interfaces that are topologically closest to the sender and not to all the interfaces in the group

In unicast and anycast addresses, the least significant 64-bits of the address represent the host ID. In general, the higher order 64-bits represent the network prefix.

Each IPv6 address also has a **scope**, which identifies the segment of the network in which it is valid:

- **Node-local** addresses, including loopback addresses are used for communication within the node.
- **Global** addresses are routable addresses reachable across networks.
- **Link-local** addresses are automatically assigned to each and every IPv6-enabled interface and are accessible only within a network, that is, routers do not route traffic headed for link-local addresses. Link-local addresses are assigned to interfaces even when they have routable addresses. Link-local addresses have a prefix of fe80::/64.

Special addresses

The IPv6 **loopback address** analogous to 127.0.0.1 in IPv4 is ::1. The **unspecified address** (all zeros) in IPv6 is written as :: (`in6addr_any`). There are no broadcast addresses in IPv6, and multicast addresses are used to define groups of recipient interfaces, a topic that is outside the scope of this book.

Handling IPv6 addresses with Boost

In the following example, we construct IPv6 addresses and query properties of these addresses using the `boost::asio::ip::address_v6` class:

Listing 11.7: Handling IPv6 addresses

```
 1 #include <boost/asio.hpp>
 2 #include <iostream>
 3 #include <vector>
 4 namespace asio = boost::asio;
 5 namespace sys = boost::system;
 6 using namespace asio::ip;
 7
 8 void printAddr6Properties(const address_v6& addr) {
 9   if (addr.is_v4_mapped()) { std::cout << "is v4-mapped, "; }
10   else {
11     if (addr.is_link_local()) { std::cout << "is link local";}
12   }
13 }
14
15 void printAddrProperties(const address& addr) { ... }
16
17 int main() {
18   sys::error_code ec;
19   std::vector<address> addresses;
20   std::vector<const char*> addr_strings{"::1", "::",
21     "fe80::20", "::ffff:223.18.221.9", "2001::1e0:0:0:1a:2a"};
22
23   for (const auto& v6str: addr_strings) {
24     address addr = address_v6::from_string(v6str, ec);
25     if (!ec) { addresses.push_back(addr); }
26   }
27
28   for (const auto& addr : addresses) {
29     printAddrProperties(addr);
30   }
31 }
```

This example augments listing 11.6 with IPv6-specific checks. The function `printAddrProperties` (line 15) is the same as that from listing 11.6, so it is not repeated in full. The `printAddr6Properties` function (line 8) checks whether the address is an IPv4-mapped IPv6 address (line 9) and whether it is a link-local address (line 11). Other relevant checks are already performed through version-agnostic members of `address` in `printAddrProperties` (see listing 11.6).

We create a vector of `boost::asio::ip::address` objects (not just `address_v6`) and push IPv6 addresses constructed from their string representations, using the `address_v6::from_string` static function (line 24), which returns `address_v6` objects, which are implicitly convertible to `address`. Notice that we have the loopback address, the unspecified address, IPv4-mapped address, a regular IPv6 unicast address, and a link-local address (lines 20-21).

Endpoints, sockets, and name resolution

Applications **bind** to IP addresses when providing network services, and multiple applications initiate outbound communication with other applications, starting from an IP address. Multiple applications can bind to the same IP address using different **ports**. A port is an unsigned 16-bit integer which, along with the IP address and protocol (TCP, UDP, etc.), uniquely identifies a communication **endpoint**. Data communication happens between two such endpoints. Boost Asio provides distinct endpoint types for UDP and TCP, namely, `boost::asio::ip::udp::endpoint` and `boost::asio::ip::tcp::endpoint`.

Ports

Many standard and widely used network services use fixed, well-known ports. Ports 0 through 1023 are assigned to well-known system services, including the likes of FTP, SSH, telnet, SMTP, DNS, HTTP, and HTTPS. Widely used applications may register standard ports between 1024 and 49151 with the **Internet Assigned Numbers Authority (IANA)**. Ports above 49151 can be used by any application, without the need for registration. The mapping of well-known ports to services is often maintained on a disk file, such as `/etc/services` on POSIX systems and `%SYSTEMROOT%\system32\drivers\etc\services` on Windows.

Sockets

A **socket** represents an endpoint in use for network communication. It represents one end of a communication channel and provides the interface for performing all data communication. Boost Asio provides distinct socket types for UDP and TCP, namely, `boost::asio::ip::udp::socket` and `boost::asio::ip::tcp::socket`. Sockets are always associated with a corresponding local endpoint object. The native network programming interfaces on all modern operating systems use some derivative of the Berkeley Sockets API, which is a C API for performing network communications. The Boost Asio library provides type-safe abstractions built around this core API.

Sockets are an example of **I/O objects**. In Asio, I/O objects are the class of objects that are used to initiate I/O operations. The operations are dispatched to the underlying operating system by an **I/O service** object, which is an instance of boost::asio::io_service. Earlier in this chapter, we saw the I/O service objects in action as task managers. But their primary role is as an interface for operations on the underlying operating system. Each I/O object is constructed with an associated I/O service instance. In this way, high-level I/O operations are initiated on the I/O object, but the interactions between the I/O object and the I/O service remain encapsulated. In the following sections, we will see examples of using UDP and TCP sockets for network communication.

Hostnames and domain names

Identifying hosts in a network by names rather than numeric addresses is often more convenient. The Domain Name System (DNS) provides a hierarchical naming system in which hosts in a network are each identified by a hostname qualified with a unique name identifying the network, known as the **fully-qualified domain name** or simply **domain name**. For example, the imaginary domain name elan.taliesyn. org could be mapped to the IP address 140.82.168.29. Here, elan would identify the specific host and taliesyn.org would identify the domain that the host is part of. It is quite possible for different groups of machines in a single network to report to different domains and even for a given machine to be part of multiple domains.

Name resolution

A hierarchy of DNS servers across the world, and within private networks, maintain name-to-address mappings. Applications ask a configured DNS server to resolve a fully-qualified domain name to an address. The DNS server either resolves the request to an IP address or forwards it to another DNS server higher up in the hierarchy if there is one. The resolution fails if none of the DNS servers, all the way up to the root of the hierarchy, has an answer. A specialized program or a library that initiates such name resolution requests is called a **resolver**. Boost Asio provides protocol-specific resolvers: boost::asio::ip::tcp::resolver and boost::asio::ip::udp::resolver for performing such name resolutions. We query for services on hostnames and obtain one or more endpoints for that service. The following example shows how to do this, given a hostname, and optionally, a service name or port:

Listing 11.8: Looking up IP addresses of hosts

```
1 #include <boost/asio.hpp>
2 #include <iostream>
3 namespace asio = boost::asio;
```

```
 4
 5 int main(int argc, char *argv[]) {
 6   if (argc < 2) {
 7     std::cout << "Usage: " << argv[0] << " host [service]\n";
 8     exit(1);
 9   }
10   const char *host = argv[1];
11   const char *svc = (argc > 2) ? argv[2] : "";
12
13   try {
14     asio::io_service service;
15     asio::ip::tcp::resolver resolver(service);
16     asio::ip::tcp::resolver::query query(host, svc);
17     asio::ip::tcp::resolver::iterator end,
18                             iter = resolver.resolve(query);
19     while (iter != end) {
20       asio::ip::tcp::endpoint endpoint = iter->endpoint();
21       std::cout << "Address: " << endpoint.address()
22                 << ", Port: " << endpoint.port() << '\n';
23       ++iter;
24     }
25   } catch (std::exception& e) {
26     std::cout << e.what() << '\n';
27   }
28 }
```

You run this program by passing it a hostname and an optional service name on the command line. This program resolves these to an IP address and a port, and prints them to the standard output (lines 21-22). The program creates an instance of io_service (line 14), which would be the conduit for operations on the underlying operating system, and an instance of boost::asio::ip::tcp::resolver (line 15) that provides the interface for requesting name resolution. We create a name lookup request in terms of the hostname and service name, encapsulated in a query object (line 16), and call the resolve member function of the resolver, passing the query object as an argument (line 18). The resolve function returns an **endpoint iterator** to a sequence of endpoint objects resolved by the query. We iterate through this sequence, printing the address and port number for each endpoint. This would print IPv4 as well as IPv6 addresses if any. If we wanted IP addresses, specific to one version of IP, we would need to use the three-argument constructor for query and specify the protocol in the first argument. For example, to look up only IPv6 addresses, we can use this:

```
asio::ip::tcp::resolver::query query(asio::ip::tcp::v6(),
                                     host, svc);
```

On lookup failure, the `resolve` function throws an exception unless we use the two-argument version that takes a non-const reference to `error_code`, as a second argument and sets it on error. In the following example, we perform the reverse lookup. Given an IP address and a port, we look up the associated hostname and service name:

Listing 11.9: Looking up hosts and service names

```
 1 #include <boost/asio.hpp>
 2 #include <iostream>
 3 namespace asio = boost::asio;
 4
 5 int main(int argc, char *argv[]) {
 6   if (argc < 2) {
 7     std::cout << "Usage: " << argv[0] << " ip [port]\n";
 8     exit(1);
 9   }
10
11   const char *addr = argv[1];
12   unsigned short port = (argc > 2) ? atoi(argv[2]) : 0;
13
14   try {
15     asio::io_service service;
16     asio::ip::tcp::endpoint ep(
17                 asio::ip::address::from_string(addr), port);
18     asio::ip::tcp::resolver resolver(service);
19     asio::ip::tcp::resolver::iterator iter =
20                            resolver.resolve(ep), end;
21     while (iter != end) {
22       std::cout << iter->host_name() << " "
23                 << iter->service_name() << '\n';
24       iter++;
25     }
26   } catch (std::exception& ex) {
27     std::cerr << ex.what() << '\n';
28   }
29 }
```

We pass the IP address and the port number to the program from the command line, and using them, we construct the `endpoint` (lines 16-17). We then pass the `endpoint` to the `resolve` member function of the `resolver` (line 19), and iterate through the results. The iterator in this case points to `boost::asio::ip::tcp::query` objects, and we print the host and service name for each, using the appropriate member functions (lines 22-23).

Buffers

Data is sent or received over the network as a byte stream. A contiguous byte stream can be represented using a pair of values: the starting address of the sequence and the number of bytes in the sequence. Boost Asio provides two abstractions for such sequences, `boost::asio::const_buffer` and `boost::asio::mutable_buffer`. The `const_buffer` type represents a read-only sequence that is typically used as a data source when sending data over the network. The `mutable_buffer` represents a read-write sequence that is used when you need to add or update data in your buffer, for example, when you receive data from a remote host:

Listing 11.10: Using const_buffer and mutable_buffer

```
 1 #include <boost/asio.hpp>
 2 #include <iostream>
 3 #include <cassert>
 4 namespace asio = boost::asio;
 5
 6 int main() {
 7   char buf[10];
 8   asio::mutable_buffer mbuf(buf, sizeof(buf));
 9   asio::const_buffer cbuf(buf, 5);
10
11   std::cout << buffer_size(mbuf) << '\n';
12   std::cout << buffer_size(cbuf) << '\n';
13
14   char *mptr = asio::buffer_cast<char*>(mbuf);
15   const char *cptr = asio::buffer_cast<const char*>(cbuf);
16   assert(mptr == cptr && cptr == buf);
17
18   size_t offset = 5;
19   asio::mutable_buffer mbuf2 = mbuf + offset;
20   assert(asio::buffer_cast<char*>(mbuf2)
21        - asio::buffer_cast<char*>(mbuf) == offset);
22   assert(buffer_size(mbuf2) == buffer_size(mbuf) - offset);
23 }
```

In this example, we show how a char array is wrapped in a `mutable_buffer` and a `const_buffer` (lines 8-9). While constructing a buffer, you specify the starting address of the memory region and the length of the region in number of bytes. A `const char` array can only be wrapped in a `const_buffer`, not in a `mutable_buffer`. These buffer wrappers *do not* allocate storage, manage any heap-allocated memory, or perform any data copying.

The function `boost::asio::buffer_size` returns the length of the buffer in bytes (lines 11-12). This is the length you passed while constructing the buffer, and it is not dependent on the data present in the buffer. Default-initialized buffers have zero length.

The function template `boost::asio::buffer_cast<>` is used to obtain a pointer to the underlying byte array of a buffer (lines 14-15). Note that we get a compilation error if we try to use `buffer_cast` to get a mutable array from a `const_buffer`:

```
asio::const_buffer cbuf(addr, length);
char *buf = asio::buffer_cast<char*>(cbuf); // fails to compile
```

Finally, you can create a buffer from an offset into another buffer, using the `operator+` (line 19). The length of the resultant buffer would be less than that of the original buffer by the length of the offset (line 22).

Buffer sequences for vectored I/O

Sometimes, it is convenient to send data from a series of buffers or split the received data across a series of buffers. Calling network I/O functions once per sequence would be inefficient, because these calls ultimately translate to system calls and there is an overhead in making each such call. An alternative is to use network I/O functions that can process a **sequence of buffers** passed to it as an argument. This is often called **vectored I/O** or **gather-scatter I/O**. All of Boost Asio's I/O functions deal in buffer sequences, and so they must be passed buffer sequences rather than single buffers. A valid buffer sequence for use with Asio I/O functions satisfies the following conditions:

- Has a member function `begin` that returns a bidirectional iterator, which points to a `mutable_buffer` or `const_buffer`
- Has a member function `end` that returns an iterator pointing to the end of the sequence
- Is copyable

For a buffer sequence to be useful, it must either be a sequence of `const_buffers` or a sequence of `mutable_buffers`. Formally, these requirements are summarized in the **ConstBufferSequence** and **MutableBufferSequence** concepts. This is a slightly simplified set of conditions, but is good enough for our purposes. We can make such sequences using Standard Library containers, such as `std::vector`, `std::list`, and so on, as well as Boost containers. However, since we frequently deal with only a single buffer, Boost provides the `boost::asio::buffer` function that makes it easy to adapt a single buffer as a buffer sequence of length one. Here is a short example illustrating these ideas:

Listing 11.11: Using buffers

```
1 #include <boost/asio.hpp>
2 #include <vector>
3 #include <string>
4 #include <iostream>
5 #include <cstdlib>
6 #include <ctime>
7 namespace asio = boost::asio;
8
9 int main() {
10   std::srand(std::time(nullptr));
11
12   std::vector<char> v1(10);
13   char a2[10];
14   std::vector<asio::mutable_buffer> bufseq(2);
15
16   bufseq.push_back(asio::mutable_buffer(v1.data(),
17                                         v1.capacity()));
18   bufseq.push_back(asio::mutable_buffer(a2, sizeof(a2)));
19
20   for (auto cur = asio::buffers_begin(bufseq),
21        end = asio::buffers_end(bufseq); cur != end; cur++) {
22     *cur = 'a' + rand() % 26;
23   }
24
25   std::cout << "Size: " << asio::buffer_size(bufseq) << '\n';
26
27   std::string s1(v1.begin(), v1.end());
28   std::string s2(a2, a2 + sizeof(a2));
29
30   std::cout << s1 << '\n' << s2 << '\n';
31 }
```

In this example, we create a mutable buffer sequence as a vector of two mutable_buffers (line 14). The two mutable buffers wrap a vector of chars (lines 16-17) and an array of chars (line 18). Using the buffers_begin (line 20) and buffers_end functions (line 21), we determine the entire range of bytes encapsulated by the buffer sequence bufseq and iterate through it, setting each byte to a random character (line 22). As these get written to the underlying vector or array, we construct strings using the underlying vector or array and print their contents (lines 27-28).

Synchronous and asynchronous communications

In the following sections, we put together our understanding of IP addresses, endpoints, sockets, buffers, and other Asio infrastructure we learned so far to write network client and server programs. Our examples use the **client-server model** of interaction, in which a **server** program services incoming requests, and a **client** program initiates such requests. Such clients are referred to as the **active endpoints**, while such servers are referred to as **passive endpoints**.

Clients and servers may communicate **synchronously**, blocking on each network I/O operation until the request has been handled by the underlying OS, and only then proceeding to the next step. Alternatively, they can use **asynchronous I/O**, initiating network I/O without waiting for them to complete, and being notified later upon their completion. With asynchronous I/O, unlike the synchronous case, programs do not wait idly if there are I/O operations to perform. Thus, asynchronous I/O scales better with larger numbers of peers and higher volumes of data. We will look at both synchronous and asynchronous models of communication. While the programming model for asynchronous interactions is event-driven and more complex, the use of Boost Asio coroutines can keep it very manageable. Before we write UDP and TCP servers, we will take a look at the Asio deadline timer to understand how we write synchronous and asynchronous logic using Asio.

Asio deadline timer

Asio provides the `basic_deadline_timer` template, using which you can wait for a specific duration to elapse or for an absolute time point. The specialization `deadline_timer` is defined as:

```
typedef basic_deadline_timer<boost::posix_time::ptime>
                                          deadline_timer;
```

It uses `boost::posix_time::ptime` and `boost::posix_time::time_duration` as the time point and duration type respectively. The following example illustrates how an application can use `deadline_timer` to wait for a duration to elapse:

Listing 11.12: Waiting synchronously

```
1 #include <boost/asio.hpp>
2 #include <boost/date_time.hpp>
3 #include <iostream>
4
5 int main() {
```

```
 6    boost::asio::io_service service;
 7    boost::asio::deadline_timer timer(service);
 8
 9    long secs = 5;
10    std::cout << "Waiting for " << secs << " seconds ..."
11              << std::flush;
12    timer.expires_from_now(boost::posix_time::seconds(secs));
13
14    timer.wait();
15
16    std::cout << " done\n";
17 }
```

We create an object of `io_service` (line 6), which acts as the conduit for operations on the underlying OS. We create an instance of `deadline_timer` associated with the `io_service` (line 7). We specify a 5 second duration to wait for using the member function `expires_from_now` of `deadline_timer` (line 12). We then call the `wait` member function to block until the duration elapses. Notice that we do not need to call `run` on the `io_service` instance. We can instead use the `expires_at` member function to wait until a specific time point, as shown here:

```
using namespace boost::gregorian;
using namespace boost::posix_time;

timer.expires_at(day_clock::local_day(),
                 hours(16) + minutes(12) + seconds(58));
```

Sometimes, programs do not want to block waiting for the timer to go off, or in general, for any future event it is interested in. In the meantime, it can finish off other valuable work and therefore be more responsive than if it were to block, waiting on the event. Instead of blocking on an event, we just want to tell the timer to notify us when it goes off, and proceed to do other work meanwhile. For this purpose, we call the `async_wait` member function and pass it a *completion handler*. A completion handler is a function object we register using `async_wait` to be called once the timer expires:

Listing 11.13: Waiting asynchronously

```
1 #include <boost/asio.hpp>
2 #include <boost/date_time.hpp>
3 #include <iostream>
4
5 void on_timer_expiry(const boost::system::error_code& ec)
```

```
 6 {
 7   if (ec) {
 8     std::cout << "Error occurred while waiting\n";
 9   } else {
10     std::cout << "Timer expired\n";
11   }
12 }
13
14 int main()
15 {
16   boost::asio::io_service service;
17   boost::asio::deadline_timer timer(service);
18
19
20   long secs = 5;
21   timer.expires_from_now(boost::posix_time::seconds(secs));
22
23   std::cout << "Before calling deadline_timer::async_wait\n";
24   timer.async_wait(on_timer_expiry);
25   std::cout << "After calling deadline_timer::async_wait\n";
26
27   service.run();
28 }
```

There are two essential changes in listing 11.13 compared to listing 11.12. We call the async_wait member function of deadline_timer instead of wait, passing it a pointer to the completion handler function on_timer_expiry. We then call run on the io_service object. When we run this program, it prints the following:

```
Before calling deadline_timer::async_wait
After calling deadline_timer::async_wait
Timer expired
```

The call to async_wait does not block (line 24) and therefore the first two lines are printed in quick succession. Following this, the call to run (line 27) blocks until the timer expires, and the completion handler for the timer is dispatched. Unless some error occurred, the completion handler prints Timer expired. Thus, there is a time lag between the appearance of the first two messages and the third message, which is from the completion handler.

Asynchronous logic using Asio coroutines

The `async_wait` member function of `deadline_timer` initiates an asynchronous operation. Such a function returns before the operation it initiates is completed. It registers a completion handler, and the completion of the asynchronous event is notified to the program through a call to this handler. If we have to run such asynchronous operations in a sequence, the control flow becomes complex. For example, let us suppose we want to wait for 5 seconds, print `Hello`, then wait for 10 more seconds, and finally, print `world`. Using synchronous `wait`, it is as easy as shown in the following snippet:

```
boost::asio::deadline_timer timer;
timer.expires_from_now(boost::posix_time::seconds(5));
timer.wait();
std::cout << "Hello, ";
timer.expires_from_now(boost::posix_time::seconds(10));
timer.wait();
std::cout << "world!\n";
```

In many real-life scenarios, especially with network I/O, blocking on synchronous operations is just not an option. In such cases, the code becomes considerably more complex. Using `async_wait` as a model asynchronous operation, the following example illustrates the complexity of asynchronous code:

Listing 11.14: Asynchronous operations

```
 1 #include <boost/asio.hpp>
 2 #include <boost/bind.hpp>
 3 #include <boost/date_time.hpp>
 4 #include <iostream>
 5
 6 void print_world(const boost::system::error_code& ec) {
 7   std::cout << "world!\n";
 8 }
 9
10 void print_hello(boost::asio::deadline_timer& timer,
11                  const boost::system::error_code& ec) {
12   std::cout << "Hello, " << std::flush;
13
14   timer.expires_from_now(boost::posix_time::seconds(10));
15   timer.async_wait(print_world);
16 }
17
18 int main()
19 {
20   boost::asio::io_service service;
```

```
21    boost::asio::deadline_timer timer(service);
22    timer.expires_from_now(boost::posix_time::seconds(5));
23
24    timer.async_wait(boost::bind(print_hello, boost::ref(timer),
25                                              ::_1));
26
27    service.run();
28 }
```

The move from synchronous to asynchronous logic for the same functionality incurs more than double the lines of code and a complex control flow. We register the function `print_hello` (line 10) as the completion handler for the first 5-second wait (lines 22, 24). `print_hello` in turn starts a 10-second wait using the same timer, and registers the function `print_world` (line 6), as the completion handler for this wait (lines 14-15).

Notice that we use `boost::bind` to generate the completion handler for the first 5-second wait, passing the `timer` from the `main` function to the `print_hello` function. The `print_hello` function thus uses the same timer. Why did we need to do it this way? First of all, `print_hello` needs to use the same `io_service` instance to initiate the 10-second wait operation and the earlier 5-second wait. The `timer` instance refers to this `io_service` instance and is used by both completion handlers. Moreover, creating a local `deadline_timer` instance in `print_hello` would be problematic because `print_hello` would return before the timer would go off, and the local timer object would be destroyed, so it would never go off.

Example 11.14 illustrates the problem of *inversion of control flow*, which is a source of significant complexity in asynchronous programming models. We can no longer string together a sequence of statements, and assume that each initiates an operation only once the operation initiated by the preceding statement is completed — a safe assumption for the synchronous model. Instead, we depend on notifications from `io_service` to determine the right time to run the next operation. The logic is fragmented across functions, and any data that needs to be shared across these functions requires more effort to manage.

Asio simplifies asynchronous programming using a thin wrapper around the Boost Coroutine library. Like with Boost Coroutine, it is possible to use stackful as well as stackless coroutines. In this book, we only look at stackful coroutines.

Using the `boost::asio::spawn` function template, we can launch tasks as coroutines. If a coroutine is dispatched and it calls an asynchronous function, the coroutine is suspended. Meanwhile, the `io_service` dispatches other tasks, including other coroutines. Once an asynchronous operation is completed, the coroutine that initiated it is resumed, and it proceeds to the next step. In the following listing, we rewrite listing 11.14 using coroutines:

Listing 11.15: Asynchronous programming using coroutines

```
 1 #include <boost/asio.hpp>
 2 #include <boost/asio/spawn.hpp>
 3 #include <boost/bind.hpp>
 4 #include <boost/date_time.hpp>
 5 #include <iostream>
 6
 7 void wait_and_print(boost::asio::yield_context yield,
 8                     boost::asio::io_service& service)
 9 {
10   boost::asio::deadline_timer timer(service);
11
12   timer.expires_from_now(boost::posix_time::seconds(5));
13   timer.async_wait(yield);
14   std::cout << "Hello, " << std::flush;
15
16   timer.expires_from_now(boost::posix_time::seconds(10));
17   timer.async_wait(yield);
18   std::cout << "world!\n";
19 }
20
21 int main()
22 {
23   boost::asio::io_service service;
24   boost::asio::spawn(service,
25           boost::bind(wait_and_print, ::_1,
26                                   boost::ref(service)));
27   service.run();
28 }
```

The `wait_and_print` function is the coroutine and takes two arguments: an object of type `boost::asio::yield_context` and a reference to an `io_service` instance (line 7). `yield_context` is a thin wrapper around Boost Coroutine. We must use `boost::asio::spawn` to dispatch a coroutine, and such a coroutine must have the signature `void (boost::asio::yield_context)`. Thus, we adapt the `wait_and_print` function using `boost::bind` to make it compatible with the coroutine signature expected by `spawn`. We bind the second argument to a reference to the `io_service` instance (lines 24-26).

The wait_and_print coroutine creates a deadline_timer instance on the stack, and starts a 5-second asynchronous wait, passing its yield_context to the async_wait function in place of a completion handler. This suspends the wait_and_print coroutine, and it is resumed only once the wait is completed. In the meantime, other tasks if any can be processed from the io_service queue. Once the wait is over and wait_and_print is resumed, it prints Hello and starts a 10-second wait. Once again, the coroutine suspends, and it resumes only after the 10 seconds elapse, thereafter printing world. Coroutines make the asynchronous logic as simple and readable as the synchronous one, with very little overhead. In the following sections, we will use coroutines to write TCP and UDP servers.

UDP

The UDP I/O model is relatively simple and the distinction between client and server is blurred. For network I/O using UDP, we create a UDP socket, and use the send_to and receive_from functions to send datagrams to specific endpoints.

Synchronous UDP client and server

In this section, we write a UDP client (listing 11.16) and a synchronous UDP server (listing 11.17). The UDP client tries to send some data to a UDP server on a given endpoint. The UDP server blocks waiting to receive data from one or more UDP clients. After sending data, the UDP client blocks waiting to receive a response from the server. The server, after receiving the data, sends some response back before proceeding to handle more incoming messages.

Listing 11.16: Synchronous UDP client

```
 1 #include <boost/asio.hpp>
 2 #include <iostream>
 3 #include <exception>
 4 namespace asio = boost::asio;
 5
 6 int main(int argc, char *argv[]) {
 7   if (argc < 3) {
 8     std::cerr << "Usage: " << argv[0] << " host port\n";
 9     return 1;
10   }
11
12   asio::io_service service;
13   try {
14     asio::ip::udp::resolver::query query(asio::ip::udp::v4(),
15                                           argv[1], argv[2]);
```

```
16        asio::ip::udp::resolver resolver(service);
17        auto iter = resolver.resolve(query);
18        asio::ip::udp::endpoint endpoint = iter->endpoint();
19
20        asio::ip::udp::socket socket(service,
21                                     asio::ip::udp::v4());
22        const char *msg = "Hello from client";
23        socket.send_to(asio::buffer(msg, strlen(msg)), endpoint);
24        char buffer[256];
25        size_t recvd = socket.receive_from(asio::buffer(buffer,
26                                     sizeof(buffer)), endpoint);
27        buffer[recvd] = 0;
28        std::cout << "Received " << buffer << " from "
29            << endpoint.address() << ':' << endpoint.port() << '\n';
30      } catch (std::exception& e) {
31        std::cerr << e.what() << '\n';
32      }
33 }
```

We run the client by passing it the server hostname and the service (or port) to connect to on the command line. It resolves them to an endpoint (IP address and port number) for UDP (lines 13-17), creates a UDP socket for IPv4 (line 18), and calls the send_to member function on it. We pass to send_to, a const_buffer containing the data to be sent and the destination endpoint (line 23).

Each and every program that performs network I/O using Asio uses an *I/O service*, which is an instance of the type boost::asio::io_service. We have already seen io_service in action as a task manager. But the primary role of the I/O service is that of an interface for operations on the underlying operating system. Asio programs use *I/O objects* that are responsible for initiating I/O operations. Sockets, for example, are I/O objects.

We call the send_to member function on the UDP socket to send a predefined message string to the server (line 23). Note that we wrap the message array in a buffer sequence of length one constructed using the boost::asio::buffer function, as shown earlier in this chapter, in the section on buffers. Once send_to completes, the client calls recv_from on the same socket, passing a mutable buffer sequence constructed out of a writable character array using boost::asio::buffer (lines 25-26). The second argument to receive_from is a non-const reference to a boost::asio::ip::udp::endpoint object. When receive_from returns, this object contains the address and port number of the remote endpoint, which sent the message (lines 28-29).

The calls to `send_to` and `receive_from` are **blocking calls**. The call to `send_to` does not return until the buffer passed to it has been written to the underlying UDP buffer in the system. Dispatching the UDP buffer over the wire to the server may happen later. The call to `receive_from` does not return until some data has been received.

We can use a single UDP socket to send data to multiple other endpoints, and we can receive data from multiple other endpoints on a single socket. Thus, each call to `send_to` takes the destination endpoint as input. Likewise, each call to `receive_from` takes a non-const reference to an endpoint, and on return, sets it to the sender's endpoint. We will now write the corresponding UDP server using Asio:

Listing 11.17: Synchronous UDP server

```
 1 #include <boost/asio.hpp>
 2 #include <exception>
 4 #include <iostream>
 5 namespace asio = boost::asio;
 6
 8 int main()
 9 {
10   const unsigned short port = 55000;
11   const std::string greet("Hello, world!");
12
13   asio::io_service service;
14   asio::ip::udp::endpoint endpoint(asio::ip::udp::v4(), port);
15   asio::ip::udp::socket socket(service, endpoint);
16   asio::ip::udp::endpoint ep;
17
18   while (true) try {
19     char msg[256];
20     auto recvd = socket.receive_from(asio::buffer(msg,
21                                            sizeof(msg)), ep);
22     msg[recvd] = 0;
23     std::cout << "Received: [" << msg << "] from ["
24               << ep << "]\n";
25
26     socket.send_to(asio::buffer(greet.c_str(), greet.size()),
27                    ep);
27     socket.send_to(asio::buffer(msg, strlen(msg)), ep);
28   } catch (std::exception& e) {
29     std::cout << e.what() << '\n';
30   }
31 }
```

The synchronous UDP server creates a single UDP endpoint of type `boost::asio::ip::udp::endpoint` on the port 55000, keeping the address unspecified (line 14). Notice that we use a two-argument `endpoint` constructor, which takes *the protocol* and port as arguments. The server creates a single UDP socket of type `boost::asio::ip::udp::socket` for this endpoint (line 15), and spins in a loop, calling `receive_from` on the socket per iteration, waiting until a client sends some data. The data is received in a `char` array called `msg`, which is passed to `receive_from` wrapped in a mutable buffer sequence of length one. The call to `receive_from` returns the number of bytes received, which is used to add a terminating null character in `msg` so that it can be used like a C-style string (line 22). In general, UDP presents the incoming data as a message containing a sequence of bytes and its interpretation is left to the application. Each time the server receives data from a client, it echoes back the data sent, preceded by a fixed greeting string. It does so by calling the `send_to` member function on the socket twice, passing the buffer to send, and the endpoint of the recipient (lines 26-27, 28).

The calls to `send_to` and `receive_from` are synchronous and return only once the data is passed completely to the OS (`send_to`) or received completely by the application (`receive_from`). If many instances of the client send messages to the server at the same time, the server can still only process one message at a time, and therefore the clients queue up waiting for a response. Of course, if the clients did not wait for a response, they could all have sent messages and exited but the messages would still be received by the server serially.

Asynchronous UDP server

An asynchronous version of the UDP server can significantly improve the responsiveness of the server. A traditional asynchronous model can entail a more complex programming model, but coroutines can significantly improve the situation.

Asynchronous UDP server using completion handler chains

For asynchronous communication, we use the `async_receive_from` and `async_send_to` member functions of `socket`. These functions do not wait for the I/O request to be handled by the operating system but return immediately. They are passed a function object, which is to be called when the underlying operation is completed. This function object is queued in the task queue of the `io_service` and is dispatched when the actual operation on the operating system returns:

```
template <typename MutableBufSeq, typename ReadHandler>
deduced async_receive_from(
    const MutableBufSeq& buffers,
```

```
         endpoint_type& sender_ep,
         ReadHandler handler);


   template <typename ConstBufSeq, typename WriteHandler>
   deduced async_send_to(
      const ConstBufSeq& buffers,
      endpoint_type& sender_ep,
      WriteHandler handler);
```

The signature for both the read handler passed to `async_receive_from` and the write handler passed to `async_send_to` is as follows:

```
   void(const boost::system::error_code&, size_t)
```

The handlers expect to be passed a non-const reference to an `error_code` object, indicating the status of the completed operation and the number of bytes read or written. The handlers can call other asynchronous I/O operations and register other handlers. Thus, the entire I/O operation is defined in terms of a chain of handlers. We now look at a program for an asynchronous UDP server:

Listing 11.18: Asynchronous UDP server

```
 1 #include <boost/asio.hpp>
 2 #include <iostream>
 3 namespace asio = boost::asio;
 4 namespace sys = boost::system;
 5
 6 const size_t MAXBUF = 256;
 7
 8 class UDPAsyncServer {
 9 public:
10   UDPAsyncServer(asio::io_service& service,
11                  unsigned short port)
12     : socket(service,
13         asio::ip::udp::endpoint(asio::ip::udp::v4(), port))
14   {  waitForReceive();  }
15
16   void waitForReceive() {
17     socket.async_receive_from(asio::buffer(buffer, MAXBUF),
18          remote_peer,
19          [this] (const sys::error_code& ec,
20                  size_t sz) {
21             const char *msg = "hello from server";
22             std::cout << "Received: [" << buffer << "] "
23                   << remote_peer << '\n';
```

```
24                 waitForReceive();
25
26                 socket.async_send_to(
27                     asio::buffer(msg, strlen(msg)),
28                     remote_peer,
29                     [this](const sys::error_code& ec,
30                             size_t sz) {});
31             });
32     }
33
34 private:
35     asio::ip::udp::socket socket;
36     asio::ip::udp::endpoint remote_peer;
37     char buffer[MAXBUF];
38 };
39
40 int main() {
41     asio::io_service service;
42     UDPAsyncServer server(service, 55000);
43     service.run();
44 }
```

The UDP server is encapsulated in the class UDPAsyncServer (line 8). To start the server, we first create the obligatory io_service object (line 42), followed by an instance of UDPAsyncServer (line 43) that is passed the io_service instance and the port number it should use. Finally, a call to the run member function of io_service starts the processing of incoming requests (line 44). So how does UDPAsyncServer work?

The constructor of UDPAsyncServer initializes the member UDP socket with a local endpoint (lines 12-13). It then calls the member function waitForReceive (line 14), which in turn calls async_receive_from on the socket (line 18), to start waiting for any incoming messages. We call async_receive_from, passing a mutable buffer made from the buffer member variable (line 17), a non-const reference to the remote_peer member variable (line 18), and a lambda expression that defines a completion handler for the receive operation (lines 19-31). async_receive_from initiates an I/O operation, adds the handler to the task queue in io_service, and returns. The call to run on the io_service (line 43) blocks as long as there are I/O tasks in the queue. When a UDP message comes along, the data is received by the OS, and it invokes the handler to take further action. To understand how the UDP server keeps handling more and more messages ad infinitum, we need to understand what the handlers do.

The *receive handler* is invoked when the server receives a message. It prints the message received and the details of the remote sender (lines 22-23), and then issues a call to waitForReceive, thus restarting the receive operation. It then sends a message hello from server (line 21) back to the sender identified by the remote_ peer member variable. It does so by calling the async_send_to member function of the UDP socket, passing the message buffer (line 27), the destination endpoint (line 28), and another handler in the form of a lambda (lines 29-32), which does nothing.

Note that we capture the this pointer in the lambdas to be able to access the member variables from the surrounding scope (line 20, 29). Also, neither handler does error checking using the error_code argument, which is a must in real-world software.

Asynchronous UDP server using coroutines

Handler chaining fragments the logic across a set of handlers and sharing state across handlers becomes particularly complex. It is the price for better performance, but it is a price we can avoid, as we saw earlier using Asio coroutines to handle asynchronous waits on boost::asio::deadline_timer in listing 11.15. We will now use Asio coroutines to write an asynchronous UDP server:

Listing 11.19: Asynchronous UDP server using Asio coroutines

```
 1 #include <boost/asio.hpp>
 2 #include <boost/asio/spawn.hpp>
 3 #include <boost/bind.hpp>
 4 #include <boost/shared_ptr.hpp>
 5 #include <boost/make_shared.hpp>
 6 #include <iostream>
 7 namespace asio = boost::asio;
 8 namespace sys = boost::system;
 9
10 const size_t MAXBUF = 256;
11 typedef boost::shared_ptr<asio::ip::udp::socket>
12                                 shared_udp_socket;
13
14 void udp_send_to(boost::asio::yield_context yield,
15                 shared_udp_socket socket,
16                 asio::ip::udp::endpoint peer)
17 {
18     const char *msg = "hello from server";
19     socket->async_send_to(asio::buffer(msg, std::strlen(msg)),
20                             peer, yield);
21 }
22
```

```
23 void udp_server(boost::asio::yield_context yield,
24                 asio::io_service& service,
25                 unsigned short port)
26 {
27   shared_udp_socket socket =
28       boost::make_shared<asio::ip::udp::socket>(service,
29           asio::ip::udp::endpoint(asio::ip::udp::v4(), port));
30
31   char buffer[MAXBUF];
32   asio::ip::udp::endpoint remote_peer;
33   boost::system::error_code ec;
34
35   while (true) {
36     socket->async_receive_from(asio::buffer(buffer, MAXBUF),
37                 remote_peer, yield[ec]);
38
39     if (!ec) {
40       spawn(socket->get_io_service(),
41         boost::bind(udp_send_to, ::_1, socket,
42                                 remote_peer));
43     }
44   }
45 }
46
47 int main() {
48   asio::io_service service;
49   spawn(service, boost::bind(udp_server, ::_1,
50                     boost::ref(service), 55000));
51   service.run();
52 }
```

With the use of coroutines, the structure of the asynchronous UDP server changes considerably from listing 11.18 and is closer to the synchronous model of listing 11.17. The function udp_server contains the core logic for the UDP server (line 23). It is meant to be used as a coroutine; hence, one of its arguments is of type boost::asio::yield_context (line 23). It takes two additional arguments: a reference to an io_service instance (line 24) and the UDP server port (line 25).

In the main function, we create an instance of io_service (line 48), and then add a task to run udp_server as a coroutine, using the boost::asio::spawn function template (lines 49-50). We bind the service and port arguments of udp_server appropriately. We then call run on the io_service instance to start processing I/O operations. The call to run dispatches the udp_server coroutine (line 51).

The udp_server coroutine creates a UDP socket associated with the unspecified IPv4 address (0.0.0.0) and the specific port passed as an argument (lines 27-29). The socket is wrapped in a shared_ptr, the reasons for which will become clear in a bit. There are additional variables on the coroutine stack to hold the data received from clients (line 31) and to identify the client endpoint (line 32). The udp_server function then spins in a loop calling async_receive_from on the socket, passing the yield_context for the receive handler (lines 36-37). This suspends the execution of the udp_server coroutine until async_receive_from completes. In the meantime, the call to run resumes and processes other tasks if any. Once a call to async_receive_from function completes, the udp_server coroutine resumes execution and proceeds to the next iteration of its loop.

For each completed receive operation, udp_server sends a fixed greeting string ("Hello from server") in response to the client. The task to send this greeting is also encapsulated in a coroutine, udp_send_to (line 14), which the udp_server coroutine adds to the task queue using spawn (line 40). We pass the UDP socket and the endpoint identifying the client as arguments to this coroutine. Notice that the local variable called remote_peer is passed by value to the udp_send_to coroutine (line 42). This is used inside udp_send_to, as an argument to async_send_to, to specify the recipient of the response (lines 19-20). We pass a copy rather than a reference to remote_peer because when the call to async_send_to is issued, another call to async_receive_from can be active and can overwrite the remote_peer object, before it is used by async_send_to. We also pass the socket wrapped in a shared_ptr. Sockets are not copyable unlike endpoints. If the socket object was on automatic storage in the udp_server function, and udp_server exited while there were still a pending udp_send_to task, the reference to the socket inside udp_send_to would be invalid and possibly lead to crashes. For this reason, the shared_ptr wrapper is the correct choice.

If you noticed, the handler to async_receive_from is written as yield[ec] (line 37). The yield_context class has an overloaded subscript operator using which we can specify a mutable reference to a variable of type error_code. When the asynchronous operation completes, the variable passed as the argument of the subscript operator is set to the error code if any.

> Prefer using coroutines over handler-chaining, when writing asynchronous servers. Coroutines enable simpler code and a more intuitive control flow.

Performance and concurrency

We claimed that the asynchronous mode of communication improves responsiveness of the server. Let us understand exactly what factors contribute to this improvement. In the synchronous model of listing 11.17, a call to `receive_from` could not be issued unless the `send_to` function returned. In the asynchronous code of listing 11.18, `waitForReceive` is called as soon as a message is received and consumed (lines 23-25), and it does not wait for the `async_send_to` to complete. Likewise, in listing 11.19 which illustrates the use of coroutines in asynchronous models, coroutines help suspend a function waiting for an asynchronous I/O operation to complete, and to continue processing other tasks in the queue meanwhile. This is the principal source of improvement in the responsiveness of the asynchronous servers.

It is worth noting that in listing 11.18, all I/O happens on a single thread. This means that at any given point in time, our program handles only one incoming UDP message. This allows us to reuse the `buffer` and `remote_peer` member variables, without worrying about synchronization. We must still ensure that we print the received buffer (lines 22-23) before calling `waitForReceive` again (line 24). If we inverted that order, the buffer could potentially be overwritten by a new incoming message before it could be printed.

Consider what would have happened if we called `waitForReceive` inside the receive handler rather than the send handler like this:

```
18      socket.async_receive_from(asio::buffer(buffer, MAXBUF),
19          remote_peer,
20          [this] (const sys::error_code& ec,
21              size_t sz) {
...             ...
26            socket.async_send_to(
27                asio::buffer(msg, strlen(msg)),
28                remote_peer,
29                [this](const sys::error_code& ec,
30                    size_t sz) {
31                  waitForReceive();
32                });
33          });
```

In this case, the receive would be started only after the send completed; so even with asynchronous calls it would be no better than the synchronous example in listing 11.17.

In listing 11.18, we do not need the buffer received from the remote peer while sending content back, so we do not need to hold on to that buffer till the send is complete. This allows us to start the asynchronous receive (line 24) without waiting for the send to complete. The receive can complete first and overwrite the buffer, but as long as the send operation does not use the buffer, everything is fine. Too often in the real world, this is not the case, so let us see how to fix this without delaying the receive till after the send. Here is a modified implementation of the handlers:

```
17 void waitForReceive() {
18   boost::shared_array<char> recvbuf(new char[MAXBUF]);
19   auto epPtr(boost::make_shared<asio::ip::udp::endpoint>());
20   socket.async_receive_from(
21       asio::buffer(recvbuf.get(), MAXBUF),
22       *epPtr,
23       [this, recvbuf, epPtr] (const sys::error_code& ec,
24                 size_t sz) {
25         waitForReceive();
26
27         recvbuf[sz] = 0;
28         std::ostringstream sout;
29         sout << '[' << boost::this_thread::get_id()
30             << "] Received: " << recvbuf.get()
31             << " from client: " << *epPtr << '\n';
32         std::cout << sout.str() << '\n';
33         socket.async_send_to(
34             asio::buffer(recvbuf.get(), sz),
35             *epPtr,
36             [this, recvbuf, epPtr] (
37                 const sys::error_code& ec, size_t sz) {
38             });
39       });
40 }
```

Now, instead of relying on a buffer that is a shared member variable, we allocate a buffer for receiving each new message (line 18). This obviates the need for the `buffer` member variable in listing 11.18. We use the `boost::shared_array` wrapper because this buffer needs to be passed from the `waitForReceive` call to the receive handler and further; it should be released only when the last reference to it is gone. Likewise, we remove the `remote_peer` member variable that represented the remote endpoint, and use a `shared_ptr`-wrapped endpoint for each new request.

We pass the underlying array to `async_receive_from` (line 21), and make sure it survives long enough by capturing its `shared_array` wrapper in the completion handler for `async_receive_from` (line 23). For the same reason, we also capture the endpoint wrapper `epPtr`. The receive handler calls `waitForReceive` (line 25), and then prints the message received from the client, prefixed with the thread ID of the current thread (with an eye on the future). It then calls `async_send_to`, passing the buffer received instead of some fixed message (line 34). Once again, we need to ensure that the buffer and remote endpoint survive till the send completes; so we capture the `shared_array` wrapper of the buffer and the `shared_ptr` wrapper of the remote endpoint in the send completion handler (line 36).

The changes for the coroutine-based asynchronous UDP server (listing 11.19) are on the same lines:

```
 1 #include <boost/shared_array.hpp>
...
14 void udp_send_to(boost::asio::yield_context yield,
15                  shared_udp_socket socket,
16                  asio::ip::udp::endpoint peer,
17                  boost::shared_array<char> buffer, size_t size)
18 {
19     const char *msg = "hello from server";
20     socket->async_send_to(asio::buffer(msg, std::strlen(msg)),
21                           peer, yield);
22     socket->async_send_to(asio::buffer(buffer.get(), size),
23                           peer, yield);
24 }
25
26 void udp_server(boost::asio::yield_context yield,
27                 asio::io_service& service,
28                 unsigned short port)
29 {
30   shared_udp_socket socket =
31       boost::make_shared<asio::ip::udp::socket>(service,
32           asio::ip::udp::endpoint(asio::ip::udp::v4(), port));
33
34   asio::ip::udp::endpoint remote_peer;
35   boost::system::error_code ec;
36
38   while (true) {
39     boost::shared_array<char> buffer(new char[MAXBUF]);
40     size_t size = socket->async_receive_from(
```

```
41                            asio::buffer(buffer.get(), MAXBUF),
42                            remote_peer, yield[ec]);
43
44    if (!ec) {
45      spawn(socket->get_io_service(),
46        boost::bind(udp_send_to, ::_1, socket, remote_peer,
47                               buffer, size));
43      }
44    }
45  }
```

As the data received from the client needs to be echoed back, the `udp_send_to` coroutine must have access to it. Thus, it takes the buffer containing the received data and the number of bytes read as arguments (line 17). In order to make sure that this data is not overwritten by a subsequent receive, we must allocate buffers for receiving the data in each iteration of the loop in `udp_server` (line 39). We pass this buffer, and also the number of bytes read as returned by `async_receive_from` (line 40) to `udp_send_to` (line 47). With these changes, our asynchronous UDP servers can now maintain the context of each incoming request until it has responded to that peer, without the need to delay the handling of newer requests.

These changes also make the handlers thread-safe because essentially, we removed any shared data across handlers. While the `io_service` is still shared, it is a thread-safe object. We can easily turn the UDP server into a multithreaded server. Here is how we do this:

```
46 int main() {
47   asio::io_service service;
48   UDPAsyncServer server(service, 55000);
49
50   boost::thread_group pool;
51   pool.create_thread([&service] { service.run(); });
52   pool.create_thread([&service] { service.run(); });
53   pool.create_thread([&service] { service.run(); });
54   pool.create_thread([&service] { service.run(); });
55   pool.join_all();
56 }
```

This would create four worker threads that handle incoming UDP messages concurrently. The same would work with coroutines.

TCP

In terms of network I/O, the programming model for UDP is about as simple as it gets—you either send a message, or receive a message, or do both. TCP is a fairly complex beast in comparison and its interaction model has a few additional details to understand.

In addition to reliability guarantees, TCP implements several nifty algorithms to ensure that an overeager sender does not swamp a relatively slow receiver with lots of data (**flow control**), and all senders get a fair share of the network bandwidth (**congestion control**). There is a fair amount of computation that happens at the TCP layer for all of this, and TCP needs to maintain some state information to perform these computations. For this TCP uses **connections** between endpoints.

Establishing a TCP connection

A **TCP connection** consists of a pair of TCP sockets, potentially on different hosts connected by an IP network and some associated state data. Relevant connection state information is maintained at each end of the connection. A **TCP server** typically starts *listening for incoming connections* and is said to constitute the **passive end** of the connection. A **TCP client** initiates a request to connect to a TCP server and is said to be the *active end* of the connection. A well-defined mechanism known as the **TCP 3-way handshake** is used for establishing TCP connections. Similar mechanisms exist for coordinated connection termination. Connections can also be unilaterally reset or terminated, like in case of applications or hosts going down for various reasons or in case of an irrecoverable error of some sort.

Client- and server-side calls

For a TCP connection to be set up, a server process must be listening on an endpoint, and a client process must actively initiate a connection to that endpoint. The server performs the following steps:

1. Create a TCP listener socket.
2. Create a local endpoint for listening to incoming connections and bind the TCP listener socket to this endpoint.
3. Start listening for incoming connections on the listener.
4. Accept any incoming connections, and open a server-side endpoint (different from the listener endpoint) to serve that connection.
5. Perform communication on that connection.
6. Handle the termination of the connection.
7. Continue to listen for other incoming connections.

The client in turn performs the following steps:

1. Create a TCP socket and, optionally, bind it to a local endpoint.
2. Connect to a remote endpoint serviced by a TCP server.
3. Once connection is established, perform communication on that connection.
4. Handle termination of the connection.

Synchronous TCP client and server

We will now write a TCP client which connects to a TCP server on a specified host and port, sends some text to the server, and then receives some messages back from the server:

Listing 11.20: Synchronous TCP client

```
1 #include <boost/asio.hpp>
2 #include <iostream>
3 namespace asio = boost::asio;
4
5 int main(int argc, char* argv[]) {
6   if (argc < 3) {
7     std::cerr << "Usage: " << argv[0] << " host port\n";
8     exit(1);
9   }
10
11  const char *host = argv[1], *port = argv[2];
12
13  asio::io_service service;
14  asio::ip::tcp::resolver resolver(service);
15  try {
16    asio::ip::tcp::resolver::query query(asio::ip::tcp::v4(),
17                                         host, port);
18    asio::ip::tcp::resolver::iterator end,
19                  iter = resolver.resolve(query);
20
21    asio::ip::tcp::endpoint server(iter->endpoint());
22    std::cout << "Connecting to " << server << '\n';
23    asio::ip::tcp::socket socket(service,
24                                 asio::ip::tcp::v4());
25    socket.connect(server);
26    std::string message = "Hello from client";
27    asio::write(socket, asio::buffer(message.c_str(),
28                                     message.size()));
```

```
29        socket.shutdown(asio::ip::tcp::socket::shutdown_send);
30
31        char msg[BUFSIZ];
32        boost::system::error_code ec;
33        size_t sz = asio::read(socket,
34                               asio::buffer(msg, BUFSIZ), ec);
35        if (!ec || ec == asio::error::eof) {
36          msg[sz] = 0;
37          std::cout << "Received: " << msg << '\n';
38        } else {
39          std::cerr << "Error reading response from server: "
40                    << ec.message() << '\n';
41        }
34    } catch (std::exception& e) {
35        std::cerr << e.what() << '\n';
36    }
37 }
```

The TCP client resolves the host and port (or service name) passed to it on the command line (lines 16-19) and creates an endpoint representing the server to connect to (line 21). It creates an IPv4 socket (line 23) and calls the connect member function on it to initiate a connection to the remote server (line 25). The connect call blocks until a connection is established, or throws an exception if the attempt to connect fails. Once the connection is successful, we use the boost::asio::write function to send the text Hello from client to the server (lines 27-28). We call the shutdown member function of the socket with the argument shutdown_send (line 29) to close the write channel to the server. This shows up as an EOF on the server-side. We then use the read function to receive any message sent by the server (lines 33-34). Both boost::asio::write and boost::asio::read are blocking calls. The call to write would throw an exception on failure, for example, if the connection was reset or the send timed out because of a busy server. We call a non-throwing overload of read, and on failure, it sets the non-const reference to the error code we pass to it.

The function boost::asio::read tries to read as many bytes as it can to fill the buffer passed, and blocks until either all the data has arrived, or an end-of-file is received. Although an end-of-file is flagged as an error condition by read, it could simply indicate that the server was done sending data, and we would be interested in whatever data was received. For this reason, we specifically use a non-throwing overload of read, and in case an error was set in the error_code reference, we distinguish between end-of-file and other errors (line 35). For the same reason, we called shutdown to close the write channel on this connection (line 29) so that the server did not wait for more input.

Unlike UDP, TCP is stream-oriented and does not define message boundaries. An application must define its own mechanism to identify message boundaries. Some strategies include prefixing the length of the message to the message, using character sequences as message end-markers, or using messages of a fixed length. In the examples in this book, we use the shutdown member function of tcp::socket, which causes an end-of-file to be read by the receiver, indicating that we are done sending messages. This keeps the examples simple, but in practice, this is not the most flexible strategy.

Let us now write the TCP server, which will handle requests from this client:

Listing 11.21: Synchronous TCP server

```
 1 #include <boost/asio.hpp>
 2 #include <boost/thread.hpp>
 3 #include <boost/shared_ptr.hpp>
 4 #include <boost/array.hpp>
 5 #include <iostream>
 6 namespace asio = boost::asio;
 7
 8 typedef boost::shared_ptr<asio::ip::tcp::socket> socket_ptr;
 9
10 int main() {
11   const unsigned short port = 56000;
12   asio::io_service service;
13   asio::ip::tcp::endpoint endpoint(asio::ip::tcp::v4(), port);
14   asio::ip::tcp::acceptor acceptor(service, endpoint);
15
16   while (true) {
17     socket_ptr socket(new asio::ip::tcp::socket(service));
18     acceptor.accept(*socket);
19     boost::thread([socket]() {
20       std::cout << "Service request from "
21                 << socket->remote_endpoint() << '\n';
22       boost::array<asio::const_buffer, 2> bufseq;
23       const char *msg = "Hello, world!";
24       const char *msg2 = "What's up?";
25       bufseq[0] = asio::const_buffer(msg, strlen(msg));
26       bufseq[1] = asio::const_buffer(msg2, strlen(msg2));
27
28       try {
29         boost::system::error_code ec;
```

```
30          char recvbuf[BUFSIZ];
31          auto sz = read(*socket, asio::buffer(recvbuf,
32                                            BUFSIZ), ec);
33          if (!ec || ec == asio::error::eof) {
34            recvbuf[sz] = 0;
35            std::cout << "Received: " << recvbuf << " from "
36                      << socket->remote_endpoint() << '\n';
37            write(*socket, bufseq);
38            socket->close();
39          }
40        } catch (std::exception& e) {
41          std::cout << "Error encountered: " << e.what() << '\n';
42        }
43      });
44    }
45 }
```

The first thing that a TCP server does is to create a listener socket and bind it to a local endpoint. With Boost Asio, you do this by creating an instance of `asio::ip::tcp::acceptor` and passing it the endpoint to bind to (line 14). We create an IPv4 endpoint specifying only the port and not the address so that it uses the unspecified address 0.0.0.0 (line 13). We bind the endpoint to the listener by passing it to the constructor of the `acceptor` (line 14). We then spin in a loop waiting for incoming connections (line 16). We create a new socket as we need a distinct socket to serve as the server-side endpoint for each new connection (line 17). We then call the `accept` member function on the acceptor (line 18), passing it the new socket. The call to `accept` blocks until a new connection is established. When `accept` returns, the socket passed to it represents the server-side endpoint of the connection established.

We create a new thread to serve each new connection established (line 19). We generate the initial function for this thread using a lambda (line 19-44), capturing the `shared_ptr`-wrapped server-side `socket` for this connection (line 19). Within the thread, we call the `read` function to read data sent by the client (lines 31-32), and then write data back using `write` (line 37). To show how it is done, we send data from a multi-buffer sequence set up from two character strings (lines 22-26). The network I/O in this thread is done inside a try-block to make sure that no exception escapes the thread. Note that we call `close` on the socket after the call to `write` returns (line 38). This closes the connection from the server-side, and the client reads an end-of-file in the received stream.

Concurrency and performance

The TCP server handles each connection independently. But creating a new thread for each new connection scales badly, and the server's resources could be overrun if a large number of connections hit it over a very short interval. One way to handle this is to limit the number of threads. Earlier, we modified the UDP server example from listing 11.18 to use a thread pool and limit the total number of threads. We can do the same with our TCP server from listing 11.21. Here is an outline for how this can be done:

```
12 asio::io_service service;
13 boost::unique_ptr<asio::io_service::work> workptr(
14                           new dummyWork(service));
15 auto threadFunc = [&service] { service.run(); };
16
17 boost::thread_group workers;
18 for (int i = 0; i < max_threads; ++i) { //max_threads
19   workers.create_thread(threadFunc);
20 }
21
22 asio::ip::tcp::endpoint ep(asio::ip::tcp::v4(), port);
23 asio::ip::tcp::acceptor acceptor(service, ep);
24 while (true) {
25   socket_ptr socket(new asio::ip::tcp::socket(service));
26   acceptor.accept(*socket);
27
28   service.post([socket] { /* do I/O on the connection */ });
29 }
30
31 workers.join_all();
32 workptr.reset(); // we don't reach here
```

First, we create a pool of a fixed number of threads (lines 15-20), and make sure they do not exit by posting a dummy work to the io_service's task queue (lines 13-14). Instead of creating a thread for each new connection, we post a handler for the connection to the task queue of the io_service (line 28). This handler can be exactly the same as the initial function of the per-connection thread in listing 11.21. The threads in the pool then dispatch the handlers on their own schedule. The number of threads represented by max_threads can be tweaked easily based on the number of processors in the system.

While using the thread pool limits the number of threads, it does little to improve the responsiveness of the server. In the event of a large influx of new connections, handlers of the newer connections would form a big backlog in the queue, and these clients would be kept waiting while the server services earlier connections. We have already addressed similar concerns in our UDP server by using asynchronous I/O. In the next section, we will use the same strategy to scale our TCP servers better.

Asynchronous TCP server

The synchronous TCP server is inefficient mainly because the read and write operations on the sockets block for a finite amount of time, waiting for the operations to complete. During this time, even with thread pools around, the thread serving the connection just waits idly for an I/O operation to go through, before it can proceed to handle the next available connection.

We can eliminate these idle waits using asynchronous I/O. Just as we saw with the asynchronous UDP server, we could either use chains of handlers or coroutines to write the asynchronous TCP server. While handler chains make the code complex, and therefore error-prone, coroutines make it far more readable and intuitive. We will first write an asynchronous TCP server using coroutines, and then use the more traditional handler-chaining, just to put the difference between the two approaches in perspective. You can skip the handler-chaining implementations on first reading.

Asynchronous TCP server using coroutines

The following is the complete code for a TCP server employing asynchronous I/O via coroutines:

Listing 11.22: Asynchronous TCP server using coroutines

```
 1 #include <boost/asio.hpp>
 2 #include <boost/asio/spawn.hpp>
 3 #include <boost/thread.hpp>
 4 #include <boost/shared_ptr.hpp>
 5 #include <boost/make_shared.hpp>
 6 #include <boost/bind.hpp>
 7 #include <boost/array.hpp>
 8 #include <iostream>
 9 #include <cstring>
10
11 namespace asio = boost::asio;
12 typedef boost::shared_ptr<asio::ip::tcp::socket> socketptr;
13
14 void handle_connection(asio::yield_context yield,
15                        socketptr socket)
16 {
17   asio::io_service& service = socket->get_io_service();
18   char msg[BUFSIZ];
19   msg[0] = '\0';
20   boost::system::error_code ec;
21   const char *resp = "Hello from server";
22
```

```
23   size_t size = asio::async_read(*socket,
24                     asio::buffer(msg, BUFSIZ), yield[ec]);
25
26   if (!ec || ec == asio::error::eof) {
27     msg[size] = '\0';
28     boost::array<asio::const_buffer, 2> bufseq;
29     bufseq[0] = asio::const_buffer(resp, ::strlen(resp));
30     bufseq[1] = asio::const_buffer(msg, size);
31
32     asio::async_write(*socket, bufseq, yield[ec]);
33     if (ec) {
34       std::cerr << "Error sending response to client: "
35               << ec.message() << '\n';
36     }
37   } else {
38     std::cout << ec.message() << '\n';
39   }
40 }
41
42 void accept_connections(asio::yield_context yield,
43                         asio::io_service& service,
44                         unsigned short port)
45 {
46   asio::ip::tcp::endpoint server_endpoint(asio::ip::tcp::v4(),
47                                           port);
48   asio::ip::tcp::acceptor acceptor(service, server_endpoint);
49
50   while (true) {
51     auto socket =
52         boost::make_shared<asio::ip::tcp::socket>(service);
53     acceptor.async_accept(*socket, yield);
54
55     std::cout << "Handling request from client\n";
56     spawn(service, boost::bind(handle_connection, ::_1,
57                                socket));
58   }
59 }
60
61 int main() {
62   asio::io_service service;
63   spawn(service, boost::bind(accept_connections, ::_1,
64                              boost::ref(service), 56000));
65   service.run();
66 }
```

We use two coroutines: `accept_connections` handles incoming connection requests (line 42), while `handle_connection` performs I/O on each new connection (line 14). The `main` function calls the `spawn` function template to add the `accept_connections` task to the `io_service` queue, to be run as a coroutine (line 63). The spawn function template is available through the header `boost/asio/spawn.hpp` (line 2). The call to the `run` member function of the `io_service` invokes the `accept_connections` coroutine, which spins in a loop awaiting new connection requests (line 65).

The `accept_connections` function takes two arguments in addition to the obligatory `yield_context`. These are a reference to the `io_service` instance, and the port to listen on for new connections—values bound by the `main` function when it spawns this coroutine (lines 63-64). The `accept_connections` function creates an endpoint for the unspecified IPv4 address and the specific port it is passed (lines 46-47), and creates an acceptor for that endpoint (line 48). It then calls the `async_accept` member function of the acceptor in each iteration of the loop, passing a reference to a TCP socket, and the local `yield_context` as the completion handler (line 53). This suspends the `accept_connections` coroutine until a new connection is accepted. Once a new connection request is received, `async_accept` accepts it, sets the socket reference passed to it to the server-side socket for the new connection, and resumes the `accept_connections` coroutine. The `accept_connections` coroutine adds the `handle_connection` coroutine to the `io_service` queue for handling the I/O on this specific connection (lines 56-57). In the next iteration of the loop, it again waits for new incoming connections.

The `handle_connection` coroutine takes a TCP socket wrapped in a `shared_ptr`, as a parameter in addition to `yield_context`. The `accept_connections` coroutine creates this socket, and passes it to `handle_connection`, wrapped in the `shared_ptr`. The `handle_connection` function receives any data sent by the client using `async_read` (lines 23-24). If the receive is successful, it sends back a response string `Hello from server`, and then echoes back the received data, using a buffer sequence of length 2 (lines 28-30).

Asynchronous TCP server without coroutines

We now look at how to write an asynchronous TCP server without coroutines. This involves a more complex handshake between handlers, and hence, we want to split the code into appropriate classes. We define two classes in two separate header files. The class `TCPAsyncServer` (listing 11.23) represents the server instance that listens for incoming connections. It goes in the `asyncsvr.hpp` header file. The class `TCPAsyncConnection` (listing 11.25) represents the processing context of a single connection. It goes in the `asyncconn.hpp` header file.

TCPAsyncServer creates a new instance of TCPAsyncConnection for each new incoming connection. The TCPAsyncConnection instance reads incoming data from the client and sends back messages to the client until the client closes the connection to the server.

To start the server, you create an instance of TCPAsyncServer, passing the instance of io_service and a port number, and then call the run member function of the io_service to start processing new connections:

Listing 11.23: Asynchronous TCP server (asyncsvr.hpp)

```
 1 #ifndef ASYNCSVR_HPP
 2 #define ASYNCSVR_HPP
 3 #include <boost/asio.hpp>
 4 #include <boost/shared_ptr.hpp>
 5 #include <boost/make_shared.hpp>
 6 #include <iostream>
 7 #include "asyncconn.hpp"
 8
 9 namespace asio = boost::asio;
10 namespace sys = boost::system;
11 typedef boost::shared_ptr<TCPAsyncConnection>
12                 TCPAsyncConnectionPtr;
13
14 class TCPAsyncServer {
15 public:
16   TCPAsyncServer(asio::io_service& service, unsigned short p)
17         : acceptor(service,
18                   asio::ip::tcp::endpoint(
19                       asio::ip::tcp::v4(), p)) {
20     waitForConnection();
21   }
22
23   void waitForConnection() {
24     TCPAsyncConnectionPtr connectionPtr = boost::make_shared
25         <TCPAsyncConnection>(acceptor.get_io_service());
26     acceptor.async_accept(connectionPtr->getSocket(),
27         [this, connectionPtr](const sys::error_code& ec) {
28             if (ec) {
29               std::cerr << "Failed to accept connection: "
30                       << ec.message() << "\n";
31             } else {
32               connectionPtr->waitForReceive();
33               waitForConnection();
```

```
34                    }
35                });
36    }
37
38 private:
39    asio::ip::tcp::acceptor acceptor;
40 };
41
42 #endif /* ASYNCSVR_HPP */
```

The TCPAsyncServer class has an acceptor member variable of type boost::asio::ip::tcp::acceptor, which is used to listen for and accept incoming connections (line 39). The constructor initializes the acceptor with a local TCP endpoint on the unspecified IPv4 address and a specific port (lines 17-19), and then calls the waitForConnection member function (line 20).

The waitForConnection function creates a new instance of TCPAsyncConnection wrapped in a shared_ptr called connectionPtr (lines 24-25) to handle each new connection from a client. We have included our own header file asynconn.hpp to access the definition of TCPAsyncConnection (line 7), which we will look at shortly. It then calls the async_accept member function on the acceptor to listen for new incoming connections and accept them (line 26-27). We pass to async_accept, a non-const reference to a tcp::socket object that is a member of TCPAsyncConnection, and a completion handler that is called each time a new connection is established (lines 27-35). It is an asynchronous call and returns immediately. But each time a new connection is established, the socket reference is set to the server-side socket for serving that connection, and the completion handler gets called.

The completion handler for async_accept is written as a lambda, and it captures the this pointer pointing to the TCPAsyncServer instance and the connectionPtr (line 27). This allows the lambda to call member functions on both the TCPAsyncServer instance, and on the TCPAsyncConnection instance serving this specific connection.

> The lambda expression generates a function object and the captured connectionPtr is copied to a member of it. Since connectionPtr is a shared_ptr, its reference count is bumped up in the process. The async_accept function pushes this function object into the task handler queue of io_service, so the underlying instance of TCPAsyncConnection survives, even after waitForConnection returns.

Upon connection establishment, when the completion handler is called, it does two things. If there were no errors, it initiates I/O on the new connection by calling the waitForReceive function on the TCPAsyncConnection object (line 32). It then restarts the wait for the next connection by calling waitForConnection on the TCPAsyncServer object, via the captured this pointer (line 33). In case of an error, it prints a message (lines 29-30). The waitForConnection call is asynchronous, and we will soon find out that so is the waitForReceive call because both call asynchronous Asio functions. Once the handler returns, the server proceeds to handle I/O on existing connections or accepts new connections:

Listing 11.24: Running the async server

```
 1 #include <boost/asio.hpp>
 2 #include <boost/thread.hpp>
 3 #include <boost/shared_ptr.hpp>
 4 #include <iostream>
 5 #include "asyncsvr.hpp"
 6 #define MAXBUF 1024
 7 namespace asio = boost::asio;
 8
 9 int main() {
10   try {
11     asio::io_service service;
12     TCPAsyncServer server(service, 56000);
13     service.run();
14   } catch (std::exception& e) {
15     std::cout << e.what() << '\n';
16   }
17 }
```

To run the server, we simply instantiate it with the io_service and port number (line 12), and then call the run method on io_service (line 13). The server we are building will be thread-safe, so we can as well call run from each of the pool of threads to introduce some concurrency in the processing of incoming connections. We will now see how I/O on each connection is handled:

Listing 11.25: Per-connection I/O Handler class (asyncconn.hpp)

```
 1 #ifndef ASYNCONN_HPP
 2 #define ASYNCONN_HPP
 3
 4 #include <boost/asio.hpp>
 5 #include <boost/thread.hpp>
 6 #include <boost/shared_ptr.hpp>
```

```
 7 #include <iostream>
 8 #define MAXBUF 1024
 9
10 namespace asio = boost::asio;
11 namespace sys = boost::system;
12
13 class TCPAsyncConnection
14   : public boost::enable_shared_from_this<TCPAsyncConnection> {
15 public:
16   TCPAsyncConnection(asio::io_service& service) :
17       socket(service) {}
18
19   asio::ip::tcp::socket& getSocket() {
20     return socket;
21   }
22
23   void waitForReceive() {
24     auto thisPtr = shared_from_this();
25     async_read(socket, asio::buffer(buf, sizeof(buf)),
26         [thisPtr](const sys::error_code& ec, size_t sz) {
27           if (!ec || ec == asio::error::eof) {
28             thisPtr->startSend();
29             thisPtr->buf[sz] = '\0';
30             std::cout << thisPtr->buf << '\n';
31
32             if (!ec) { thisPtr->waitForReceive(); }
33           } else {
34             std::cerr << "Error receiving data from "
35                       "client: " << ec.message() << "\n";
36           }
37         });
38   }
39
40   void startSend() {
41     const char *msg = "Hello from server";
42     auto thisPtr = shared_from_this();
43     async_write(socket, asio::buffer(msg, strlen(msg)),
44         [thisPtr](const sys::error_code& ec, size_t sz) {
45           if (ec) {
46             if (ec == asio::error::eof) {
47               thisPtr->socket.close();
48             }
49             std::cerr << "Failed to send response to "
```

```
50                            "client: " << ec.message() << '\n';
51            }
52         });
53    }
54
55 private:
56    asio::ip::tcp::socket socket;
57    char buf[MAXBUF];
58 };
59
60 #endif /* ASYNCONN_HPP */
```

We saw in listing 11.23 how an instance of TCPAsyncConnection gets created, wrapped in a shared_ptr, to handle each new connection, and I/O is initiated on it by a call to the waitForReceive member function. Let us now understand its implementation. TCPAsyncConnection has two public members for performing asynchronous I/O on the connection: waitForReceive to perform asynchronous receives (line 23) and startSend to perform asynchronous sends (line 40).

The waitForReceive function initiates a receive by calling the async_read function on the socket (line 25). The data is received into the buf member (line 57). The completion handler for this call (line 26-37) is invoked when the data is completely received. If there were no errors, it calls startSend, which asynchronously sends a message to the client (line 28), and then calls waitForReceive again, provided an end-of-file was not encountered by the previous receive (line 32). Thus, as long as there was no read error, the server keeps waiting to read more data on the connection. If there was an error, it prints a diagnostic message (lines 34-35).

The startSend function uses the function async_write to send the text Hello from server to the client. Its handler does not do anything on success but prints a diagnostic message on failure (lines 49-50). For EOF write errors, it closes the socket (line 47).

Lifetime of TCPAsyncConnection

Each instance of TCPAsyncConnection needs to survive as long as the client remains connected to the server. This makes it difficult to bind the scope of this object to any function in the server. This is the reason we create the TCPAsyncConnection object wrapped in a shared_ptr, and then capture it in handler lambdas. The TCPAsyncConnection member functions for performing I/O on the connection, waitForReceive and startSend, are both asynchronous. So they push a handler into the io_service's task queue before returning. These handlers capture the shared_ptr wrapped instance of TCPAsyncConnection to keep the instance alive across calls.

In order for the handlers to have access to the `shared_ptr`-wrapped instance of the `TCPAsyncConnection` object from within `waitForReceive` and `startSend`, it is required that these member functions of `TCPAsyncConnection` have access to the `shared_ptr` wrapped instance on which they are called. The *enable shared from this* idiom, which we learned in *Chapter 3, Memory Management and Exception Safety*, is tailor-made for such purposes. This is the reason we derive `TCPAsyncConnection` from `enable_shared_from_this<TCPAsyncConnection>`. By virtue of this, `TCPAsyncConnection` inherits the `shared_from_this` member function, which returns the `shared_ptr`-wrapped instance we need. This means that `TCPAsyncConnection` should always be allocated dynamically and wrapped in a `shared_ptr`, and any other way would result in undefined behavior.

This is the reason we call `shared_from_this` in both `waitForReceive` (line 24) and `startSend` (line 42), and it is captured by the respective handlers (lines 26, 44). As long as the `waitForReceive` member function keeps getting called from the completion handler for `async_read` (line 32), the `TCPAsyncConnection` instance survives. If an error is encountered in receive, either because the remote endpoint closed the connection or for another reason, then this cycle breaks. The `shared_ptr` wrapping the `TCPAsyncConnection` object is no longer captured by any handler and is destroyed at the end of the scope, closing the connection.

Performance and concurrency

Notice that both implementations of TCP asynchronous server, with and without coroutines, are single-threaded. However, there are no thread-safety issues in either implementation, so we could have as well employed a thread pool, each of whose threads would call `run` on the `io_service`.

Inversion of control flow

The most significant difficulty with programming asynchronous systems is the inversion of control flow. To write the code for a synchronous server, we know we have to call the operations in the following sequence:

1. Call `accept` on the acceptor.
2. Call `read` on the socket.
3. Call `write` on the socket.

We know that `accept` returns only when the connection has been established, so it is safe to call `read`. Also, `read` returns only after it has read the number of bytes asked for, or encountered an end-of-file. So it is safe for a `write` call to follow. This made writing code incredibly easy compared to the asynchronous model, but introduced waits that affected our ability to handle other waiting connections, while our requests were being serviced.

We eliminated that wait with asynchronous I/O, but lost the simplicity of the model when we used handler chaining. As we cannot deterministically tell at which point an asynchronous I/O operation is completed, we ask the io_service to run specific handlers on completion of our requests. We still know which operation to perform after which, but we no longer know when. So we tell the io_service *what* to run, and it uses the appropriate notifications from the OS to know *when* to run them. The biggest challenge in this model is to maintain object states and managing object lifetimes across handlers.

Coroutines eliminate this *inversion of control flow* by allowing the sequence of asynchronous I/O operations to be written in a single coroutine, which is *suspended* instead of waiting for an asynchronous operation to complete, and *resumed* when the operation is completed. This allows for wait-free logic without the inherent complexities of handler chaining.

 Always prefer coroutines over handler chaining when writing asynchronous servers.

Self-test questions

For multiple choice questions, choose all options that apply:

1. What is the difference between io_service::dispatch and io_service::post?

    a. dispatch returns immediately while post runs the handler before returning

    b. post returns immediately while dispatch may run the handler on the current thread if it can, or it behaves like post

    c. post is thread-safe while dispatch is not

    d. post returns immediately while dispatch runs the handler

2. What happens if a handler throws an exception when it is dispatched?

    a. It is undefined behavior

    b. It terminates the program with a call to std::terminate

    c. The call to run, on the io_service that dispatched the handler, will throw

    d. The io_service is stopped

3. What is the role of the unspecified address 0.0.0.0 (IPv4) or ::/1 (IPv6)?

   a. It is used to communicate with local services on a system

   b. Packets sent to this address are echoed back to the sender

   c. It is used to broadcast to all connected hosts in the network

   d. It is used to bind to all available interfaces without the need to know addresses

4. Which of the following statements about TCP are true?

   a. TCP is faster than UDP

   b. TCP detects data corruption but not data loss

   c. TCP is more reliable than UDP

   d. TCP retransmits lost or corrupted data

5. What do we mean when we say that a particular function, for example, `async_read`, is asynchronous?

   a. The function returns before the requested action is complete

   b. The function starts the operation on a different thread and returns immediately

   c. The requested action is queued for processing by the same or another thread

   d. The function performs the action if it immediately can, or returns an error if it cannot immediately perform the action

6. How can we ensure that an object created just before calling an asynchronous function would still be available in the handler?

   a. Make the object global.

   b. Copy/capture the object wrapped in a `shared_ptr` in the handler.

   c. Allocate the object dynamically and wrap it in a `shared_ptr`.

   d. Make the object a member of the class.

Summary

Asio is a well-designed library that can be used to write fast, nimble network servers that utilize the most optimal mechanisms for asynchronous I/O available on a system. It is an evolving library and is the basis for a Technical Specification that proposes to add a networking library to a future revision of the C++ Standard.

In this chapter, we learned how to use the Boost Asio library as a task queue manager and leverage Asio's TCP and UDP interfaces to write programs that communicate over the network. Using Boost Asio, we were able to highlight some of the general concerns of network programming, the challenges to scaling for a large number of concurrent connections, and the advantages and complexity of asynchronous I/O. In particular, we saw how using stackful coroutines makes writing asynchronous servers a breeze, compared to the older model of chaining handlers. While we did not cover stackless coroutines, the ICMP protocol, and serial port communications among other things, the topics covered in this chapter should provide you with a solid foundation for understanding these areas.

References

* *Thinking Asynchronously in C++* (blog), *Christopher Kohlhoff*: http://blog.think-async.com/

* *Networking Library Proposal, Christopher Kohlhoff*: http://www.open-std.org/jtc1/sc22/wg21/docs/papers/2014/n4332.html

C++11 Language Features Emulation

In this section, we will review some concepts from C++ programming that will be conceptually important in understanding several topics covered in this book. Many of these concepts have been introduced relatively recently as part of C++11. We will look at: RAII, copy- and move-semantics, `auto`, range-based for-loops, and C++11 exception handling enhancements. We will look at how these features can be emulated under a pre-C++11 compiler using parts of the Boost libraries.

RAII

C++ programs frequently deal with system resources like memory, file and socket handles, shared memory segments, mutexes, and so on. There are well-defined primitives, some from the C Standard Library and many more from the native systems programming interfaces, which are used to request and relinquish these resources. Failing to guarantee the release of acquired resources can cause grave problems to an application's performance and correctness.

The destructor of a C++ object *on the stack* is automatically invoked during stack unwinding. The unwinding happens when a scope is exited due to control reaching the end of the scope, or by executing `return`, `goto`, `break`, or `continue`. A scope is also exited as a result of an exception being thrown. In either case, the destructor is guaranteed to be called. This guarantee is limited to C++ objects on the stack. It does not apply to C++ objects on the heap because they are not associated with a lexical scope. Furthermore, it does not apply to the aforementioned resources like memory and file descriptors, which are objects of Plain Old Data types (POD-types) and therefore do not have a destructor.

Consider the following C++ code using the
`new[]` and `delete[]` operators:

```
char *buffer = new char[BUFSIZ];
... ...
delete [] buffer;
```

The programmer was careful to release the buffer allocated. However, if another
programmer came and flippantly wrote code to exit the scope somewhere between
the calls to `new` and `delete`, then `buffer` would never be released and you would
leak memory. Exceptions could arise in the intervening code too with the same
result. This is true not just of memory but of any resource which requires a manual
step to release, like `delete[]` in this case.

This is where we can utilize the guaranteed invocation of a destructor when exiting
a scope to guarantee the clean-up of resources. We can create a wrapper class whose
constructor acquires ownership of the resource and whose destructor releases the
resource. A few lines of code can explain this technique that usually goes by the
name **Resource Acquisition is Initialization** or **RAII**.

Listing A.1: RAII in action

```
 1 class String
 2 {
 3 public:
 4   String(const char *str = 0)
 5   { buffer_ = dupstr(str, len_); }
 6
 7   ~String() { delete [] buffer_; }
 8
 9 private:
10   char *buffer_;
11   size_t len_;
12 };
13
14 // dupstr returns a copy of s, allocated dynamically.
15 //   Sets len to the length of s.
16 char *dupstr(const char *str, size_t& len) {
17   char *ret = nullptr;
18
19   if (!str) {
20     len = 0;
```

```
21    return ret;
22  }
23  len = strlen(str);
24  ret = new char[len + 1];
25  strncpy(ret, str, len + 1);
26
27  return ret;
28  }
```

The `String` class encapsulates a C-style string. We pass it a C-style string during construction, and it creates a copy of the passed string on the free store if it is not null. The helper function `dupstr` allocates memory for the `String` object on the free store using the the `new[]` operator (line 24). If allocation fails, `operator new[]` throws `std::bad_alloc`, and the `String` object never comes into being. In other words, resource acquisition must succeed for initialization to succeed. This is the other key aspect of RAII.

We use the `String` class in code as shown here:

```
{
  String favBand("Led Zeppelin");
...    ...
} // end of scope. favBand.~String() called.
```

We create an instance of `String` called `favBand`, which internally allocates a character buffer dynamically. When `favBand` goes out of scope normally or due to an exception, its destructor is called and it releases this buffer. You can apply this technique to all forms of resources that require manual release, and it will never let a resource leak creep in. The `String` class is said to own the buffer resource, that is, it has *unique ownership semantics*.

Copy semantics

An object keeps state information in its data members, which can themselves be of POD-types or class types. If you do not define a copy constructor for your class, then the compiler implicitly defines one for you. This implicitly-defined copy constructor copies each member in turn, invoking the copy constructor of members of class type and performing a bitwise copy of POD-type members. The same is true of the assignment operator. The compiler generates one if you do not define your own, and it performs member-wise assignment, invoking the assignment operators of member objects of class-type, and performing bitwise copies of POD-type members.

The following example illustrates this:

Listing A.2: Implicit destructor, copy constructor, and assignment operator

```
1 #include <iostream>
2
3 class Foo {
4 public:
5   Foo() {}
6
7   Foo(const Foo&) {
8     std::cout << "Foo(const Foo&)\n";
9   }
10
11   ~Foo() {
12     std::cout << "~Foo()\n";
13   }
14
15   Foo& operator=(const Foo&) {
16     std::cout << "operator=(const Foo&)\n";
17     return *this;
18   }
19 };
20
21 class Bar {
22 public:
23   Bar() {}
24
25 private:
26   Foo f;
27 };
28
29 int main() {
30   std::cout << "Creating b1\n";
31   Bar b1;
32   std::cout << "Creating b2 as a copy of b1\n";
33   Bar b2(b1);
34
35   std::cout << "Assigning b1 to b2\n";
36   b2 = b1;
37 }
```

Class `Bar` contains an instance of class `Foo` as a member (line 25). Class `Foo` defines a destructor (line 11), a copy constructor (line 7), and an assignment operator, (line 15) each of which prints some message. Class `Bar` does not define any of these special functions. We create an instance of `Bar` called `b1` (line 30) and a copy of `b1` called `b2` (line 33). We then assign `b1` to `b2` (line 36). Here is the output when the program is run:

```
Creating b1
Creating b2 as a copy of b1
Foo(const Foo&)
Assigning b1 to b2
operator=(const Foo&)
~Foo()
~Foo()
```

Through the messages printed, we can trace the calls made to `Foo`'s special functions from `Bar`'s implicitly generated special functions.

This works adequately for all cases except when you encapsulate a pointer or non-class type handle to some resource in your class. The implicitly-defined copy constructor or assignment operator will copy the pointer or handle but not the underlying resources, generating an object which is a **shallow copy** of another. This is rarely what is needed and this is where a user-defined copy constructor and assignment operator are needed to define the correct copy semantics. If such copy semantics do not make sense for the class, the copy constructor and assignment operator ought to be disabled. In addition, you would also need to manage resource lifetimes using RAII, and therefore define a destructor rather than relying on the compiler-generated one.

There is a well-known rule called the **Rule of Three** that regularizes this common idiom. It says that if you need to define your own destructor for a class, you should also define your own copy constructor and assignment operator or disable them. The `String` class we defined in listing A.1 is such a candidate and we will add the remaining two of the three canonical methods shortly. As we noted, not all classes need to define these functions, only those that encapsulate resources. In fact, it is recommended that a class using these resources should be different from the class managing the lifetime of these resources. Thus, we should create a wrapper around each resource for managing that resource using specialized types like smart pointers (*Chapter 3, Memory Management and Exception Safety*), `boost::ptr_container` (*Chapter 5, Effective Data Structures beyond STL*), `std::vector`, and so on. The class using the resources should have the wrappers rather than the raw resources as members. This way, the class using the resource does not have to also bother about managing the resource life cycles, and the implicitly-defined destructor, copy constructor, and assignment operator would be adequate for its purposes. This has come to be called the **Rule of Zero**.

The nothrow swap

Thanks to Rule of Zero, you should rarely need to bother about the Rule of Three. But when you do have to use the Rule of Three, there are a few nitty-gritties to take care of. Let us first understand how you would define a copy operation for the `String` class in listing A.1:

Listing A.1a: Copy constructor

```
1 String::String(const String &str) : buffer_(0), len_(0)
2 {
3   buffer_ = dupstr(str.buffer_, len_);
4 }
```

The implementation of copy constructor is no different than that of the constructor in listing A.1. The assignment operator requires more care. Consider how `String` objects are assigned to in the following example:

```
1 String band1("Deep Purple");
2 String band2("Rainbow");
3 band1 = band2;
```

On line 3, we assign `band2` to `band1`. As part of this, `band1`'s old state should be deallocated and then overwritten with a copy of `band2`'s internal state. The problem is that copying `band2`'s internal state might fail, and so `band1`'s old state should not be destroyed until `band2`'s state has been copied successfully. Here is a succinct way to achieve this:

Listing A.1b: Assignment operator

```
1 String& String::operator=(const String& rhs)
2 {
3   String tmp(rhs);    // copy the rhs in a temp variable
4   swap(tmp);          // swap tmp's state with this' state.
5   return *this;       // tmp goes out of scope, releases this'
6                       // old state
7 }
```

We create `tmp` as a copy of `rhs` (line 3) and if this copying fails, it should throw an exception and the assignment operation would fail. The internal state of the assignee, `this`, should not change. The call to `swap` (line 4) executes only if the copying succeeded (line 3). The call to `swap` exchanges the internal states of `this` and the `tmp` object. As a result, `this` now contains the copy of `rhs` and `tmp` contains the older state of `this`. At the end of this function, `tmp` goes out of scope and releases the old state of `this`.

It is possible to optimize this implementation further by considering special cases. If the assignee (left-hand side) already has storage that is at least as large as needed to contain the contents of rhs, then we can simply copy the contents of rhs into the assignee, without the need for extra allocation and deallocation.

Here is the implementation of the swap member function:

Listing A.1c: nothrow swap

```
1 void String::swap(String&rhs) noexcept
2 {
3   using std::swap;
3   swap(buffer_, rhs.buffer_);
4   swap(len_, rhs.len_);
5 }
```

Exchanging variables of primitive types (integers, pointers, and so on) should not cause any exceptions to be thrown, a fact we advertise using the C++11 keyword noexcept. We could have written throw() instead of noexcept, but exception specifications are deprecated in C++11 and noexcept is more efficient than a throw() clause. This swap function, written entirely in terms of exchanging primitive data types, is guaranteed to succeed and would never leave the assignee in an inconsistent state.

Move semantics and rvalue references

Copy semantics are for creating clones of objects. It is useful sometimes, but not always needed or even meaningful. Consider the following class that encapsulates a TCP client socket. A TCP socket is an integer that represents one endpoint of a TCP connection and through which data can be sent or received to the other endpoint. The TCP socket class can have the following interface:

```
class TCPSocket
{
public:
  TCPSocket(const std::string& host, const std::string& port);
  ~TCPSocket();

  bool is_open();
  vector<char> read(size_t to_read);
  size_t write(vector<char> payload);

private:
```

```
    int socket_fd_;

    TCPSocket(const TCPSocket&);
    TCPSocket& operator = (const TCPSocket&);
};
```

The constructor opens a connection to a host on a specified port and initializes the `socket_fd_` member variable. The destructor closes the connection. TCP does not define a way to make clones of open sockets (unlike file descriptors with `dup`/ `dup2`) and therefore cloning `TCPSocket` would not be meaningful either. Therefore, we disable copy semantics by declaring the copy constructor and copy assignment operators private. In C++11, the preferred way to do this is to declare these members as deleted:

```
    TCPSocket(const TCPSocket&) = delete;
    TCPSocket& operator = (const TCPSocket&) = delete;
```

Although not copyable, it would make perfect sense to create a `TCPSocket` object in one function and then return it to a calling function. Consider a factory function that creates connections to some remote TCP service:

```
    TCPSocket connectToService()
    {
      TCPSocket socket(get_service_host(),   // function gets hostname
                       get_service_port()); // function gets port
      return socket;
    }
```

Such a function would encapsulate the details about which host and port to connect to, and would create an object of `TCPSocket` to be returned to the caller. This would not really call for copy semantics at all, but move semantics, in which the contents of the `TCPSocket` object created in the `connectToService` function would be transferred to another `TCPSocket` object at the call site:

```
    TCPSocket socket = connectToService();
```

In C++03, this would not be possible to write without enabling the copy constructor. We could subvert the copy constructor to provide move semantics, but there are many problems with this approach:

```
    TCPSocket::TCPSocket(TCPSocket& that) {
      socket_fd_ = that.socket_fd_;
      that.socket_fd_ = -1;
    }
```

Note that this version of the "copy" constructor actually moves the contents out of its argument, which is why the argument is non-const. With this definition, we can actually implement the `connectToService` function, and use it as shown earlier. But nothing would prevent situations like the following:

```
1 void performIO(TCPSocket socket)
2 {
3   socket.write(...);
4   socket.read(...);
5   // etc.
6 }
7
8 TCPSocket socket = connectToService();
9 performIO(socket);    // moves TCPSocket into performIO
10 // now socket.socket_fd_ == -1
11 performIO(socket);    // OOPs: not a valid socket
```

We obtain an instance of `TCPSocket` called `socket` by calling `connectToService` (line 8) and pass this instance to `performIO` (line 9). But the copy constructor used to pass `socket` by value to `performIO` moves its contents out, and when `performIO` returns, `socket` no longer encapsulates a valid TCP socket. By disguising a move as a copy, we have created an unintuitive and error-prone interface; if you are familiar with `std::auto_ptr`, you would have seen this before.

rvalue references

In order to support move semantics better, we must first answer the question: which objects can be moved from? Consider the `TCPSocket` example again. In the function `connectToService`, the expression `TCPSocket(get_service_host()`, `get_service_port())` is an *unnamed temporary* object of `TCPSocket` whose sole purpose is to be transferred to the caller's context. There is no way for anyone to refer to this object beyond the statement where it gets created. It makes perfect sense to move the contents out of such an object. But in the following snippet:

```
TCPSocket socket = connectToService();
performIO(socket);
```

It would be dangerous to move out the contents of `socket` object because in the calling context, the object is still bound to the name `socket` and can be used in further operations. The expression `socket` is called an **lvalue expression**—one that has an identity and whose address can be taken by prefixing the &-operator to the expression. Non-lvalue expressions are referred to as **rvalue expressions**. These are unnamed expressions whose address cannot be computed using the &-operator on the expression. An expression, such as `TCPSocket(get_service_host()`, `get_service_port())` is an rvalue expression.

We can say that, in general, it is dangerous to move contents from an lvalue expression but safe to move contents from rvalue expressions. Thus, the following is dangerous:

```
TCPSocket socket = connectToService();
performIO(socket);
```

But the following is alright:

```
performIO(connectToService());
```

Note here that the expression `connectToService()` is not an lvalue expression and therefore qualifies as an rvalue expression. In order to distinguish between lvalue and rvalue expressions, C++11 introduced a new class of references called **rvalue references** that can refer to rvalue-expressions but not lvalue-expressions. Such references are declared using a new syntax involving double ampersands as shown below:

```
socket&& socketref = TCPSocket(get_service_host(),
                               get_service_port());
```

The other class of references that were earlier simply called *references* are now called **lvalue references**. A non-const lvalue reference can only refer to an lvalue expression, while a const lvalue reference can also refer to an rvalue expression:

```
/* ill-formed */
socket& socketref = TCPSocket(get_service_host(),
                              get_service_port());

/* well-formed */
const socket& socketref = TCPSocket(get_service_host(),
                                    get_service_port());
```

An rvalue reference can be, and usually is, non-const:

```
socket&& socketref = TCPSocket(...);
socketref.read(...);
```

In the preceding snippet, the expression `socketref` itself is an lvalue-expression because you can compute its address using &-operator. But it is bound to an rvalue-expression, and object referred to by the non-const rvalue reference can be modified through it.

rvalue-reference overloads

We can create overloads of a function based on whether they take lvalue expressions or rvalue expressions. In particular, we can overload the copy constructor to take rvalue expressions. For the TCPSocket class, we can write the following:

```
TCPSocket(const TCPSocket&) = delete;

TCPSocket(TCPSocket&& rvref) : socket_fd_(-1)
{
    std::swap(socket_fd_, rvref.socket_fd_);
}
```

While the lvalue overload is the deleted copy constructor, rvalue overload is called the move constructor because this is implemented to usurp or "steal" the contents of the rvalue expression passed to it. It moves the contents of the source to the target, leaving the source (rvref) in some unspecified state that is safe to destruct. In this case, this amounts to setting the socket_fd_ member of the rvref to -1.

With this definition of the move constructor, TCPSocket becomes movable but not copyable. The connectToService implementation would work correctly:

```
TCPSocket connectToService()
{
    return TCPSocket(get_service_host(),get_service_port());
}
```

This would move the temporary object back to the caller. But the following call to performIO would be ill-formed because socket is an lvalue expression and TCPSocket only defines move semantics for which an rvalue expression was necessary:

```
TCPSocket socket = connectToService();
performIO(socket);
```

This is a good thing because you cannot move contents out of an object like socket that you could potentially use later. An rvalue-expression of a movable type can be passed by value and thus the following will be well-formed:

```
performIO(connectToService());
```

Note that the expression connectToService() is an rvalue expression because it is not bound to a name and its address cannot be taken.

A type can be both copyable and movable. For example, we could implement a move constructor for the String class in addition to its copy constructor:

```
1  // move-constructor
2  String::String(String&& source) noexcept
3         : buffer_(0), len_(0)
4  {
5    swap(source); // See listing A.1c
6  }
```

The nothrow swap plays a central role in the implementation of move semantics. The contents of the source and target objects are exchanged. So when the source object goes out of scope in the calling scope, it releases its new contents (the target object's old state). The target object lives on with its new state (the source object's original state). The move is implemented in terms of the nothrow swap, which just swaps pointers and values of primitive types, and it is guaranteed to succeed; hence, the noexcept specification. In fact, moving objects usually requires less work involving swapping pointers and other data bits, while copying often requires new allocations that could potentially fail.

Move assignment

Just as we can construct an object by stealing the contents of another object, we can also move the contents of one object to another after both have been constructed. To do this, we can define a **move assignment operator**, an rvalue-overload of the copy assignment operator:

```
1  // move assignment
2  String& String::operator=(String&& rhs) noexcept
3  {
4    swap(rhs);
5    return *this;
6  }
```

Alternatively, we can define a **universal assignment operator** that works for both lvalue and rvalue expressions:

```
1  // move assignment
2  String& String::operator=(String rhs)
3  {
4    swap(rhs);
5    return *this;
6  }
```

Note that the universal assignment operator cannot coexist with either the lvalue or the rvalue overload, else there would be ambiguity in overload resolution.

xvalues

When you call a function with an rvalue expression, the compiler resolves function calls to an rvalue-overload of the function if one is available. But if you call the function with a named variable, it gets resolved to an lvalue overload if one is available or the program is ill-formed. Now you might have a named variable that you can move from because you have no use for it later:

```
void performIO(TCPSocket socket);

TCPSocket socket = connectToService();
// do stuff on socket
performIO(socket);   // ill-formed because socket is lvalue
```

The preceding example will fail to compile because `performIO` takes its sole parameter by value and `socket` is of a move-only type but it is not an rvalue expression. By using `std::move`, you can cast an lvalue expression to an rvalue expression, and pass it to a function that expects an rvalue expression. The `std::move` function template is defined in the standard header `utility`.

```
#include <utility> // for std::moves
performIO(std::move(socket));
```

The call to `std::move(socket)` gives us an rvalue reference to `socket`; it does not cause any data to be moved out of `socket`. When we pass this expression of rvalue-reference type to the function `performIO`, which takes its parameter by value, a new `TCPSocket` object is created in the `performIO` function, corresponding to its by-value parameter. It is **move initialized** from `socket`, that is, its move constructor steals the contents of `socket`. Following the call to `performIO`, the variable `socket` loses its contents and therefore should not be used in further operations. If the move constructor of `TCPSocket` is correctly implemented, then `socket` should still be safe to destruct.

The expression `std::move(socket)` shares the identity of `socket`, but it would *potentially* be moved from within the function it is passed to. Such expressions are called **xvalues**, the *x* standing for *expired*.

 xvalues have a well-defined identity like lvalues, but can be moved from like rvalues. **xvalues** bind to rvalue reference parameters of a function.

If `performIO` did not take its parameter by value but as an rvalue-reference then one thing would change:

```
void performIO(TCPSocket&& socket);
performIO(std::move(socket));
```

The call to `performIO(std::move(socket))` would still be well-formed, but would not automatically move out the contents of `socket`. This is because we pass a reference to an existing object here, whereas we create a new object that is move initialized from `socket` when we pass by value. In this case, unless the `performIO` function implementation explicitly moves out the contents of `socket`, it would still remain valid in the calling context after the call to `performIO`.

> In general, if you have cast your object to an rvalue-expression and passed it to a function that expects an rvalue-reference, you should just assume that it has been moved from and not use it beyond the call.

An object of type T that is *local to a function* can be returned by value from that function if T has an accessible move or copy constructor. If a move constructor is available, the returned value will be move-initialized, else it would be copy-initialized. If however, the object is not local to the function, then it must have an accessible copy constructor to be returned by value. Additionally, compilers, whenever they can, optimize away copies and moves.

Consider the implementation of `connectToService` and how it is used:

```
1 TCPSocket connectToService()
2 {
3    return TCPSocket(get_service_host(),get_service_port());
4 }
5
6 TCPSocket socket = connectToService();
```

In this case, the compiler will actually construct the temporary (line 3) directly in the storage for the `socket` object (line 6) where the return value of `connectToService` was meant to be moved to. This way, it would simply optimize away the move initialization of `socket` (line 6). This optimization is effected even if the move constructor has side effects, which means that those side effects may not take effect as a result of this optimization. In the same way, the compiler can optimize away copy initialization and directly construct the returned object at the target site. This is referred to as **Return Value Optimization (RVO)** and has been the norm for all major compilers since C++03, when it optimized away only copies. Although the copy or move constructors are not invoked when RVO takes effect, they must nevertheless be defined and accessible for RVO to work.

While RVO applies when rvalue expressions are returned, the compiler can sometimes optimize away a copy or move, even when a named *local* object on the stack is returned from a function. This is known as **Named Return Value Optimization (NRVO)**.

Return Value Optimization is a specific case of **Copy Elision**, in which the compiler optimizes away a move or copy of an rvalue expression to construct it directly in the target storage:

```
std::string reverse(std::string input);

std::string a = "Hello";
std::string b = "World";
reverse(a + b);
```

In the preceding example, the expression a + b is an rvalue expression that generates a temporary object of type std::string. This object will not be copied into the function reverse instead the copy would be *elided*, and the object resulting from the expression a + b would be constructed directly in the storage for reverse's parameter.

Passing and returning an object of type T by value requires either move or copy semantics to be defined for T. If a move constructor is available, it is used, otherwise the copy constructor is used. Whenever possible, the compiler optimizes away copy or move operations and constructs the object directly at the target site in the calling or called function.

Move emulation using Boost.Move

In this section, we look at how, with relative ease, you can actually retrofit much of the move semantics for your own legacy classes using the Boost.Move library. First, consider the interface of the String class in C++ 11 syntax:

```
1 class String
2 {
3 public:
4    // Constructor
5    String(const char *str = 0);
6
7    // Destructor
8    ~String();
9
10   // Copy constructor
11   String(const String& that);
12
13   // Copy assignment operator
14   String& operator=(const String& rhs);
15
16   // Move constructor
```

```
17   String(String&& that);
18
19   // Move assignment
20   String& operator=(String&& rhs);
21   ...
22 };
```

Let us now see how you would define an equivalent interface using Boost's facilities:

Listing A.2a: Move emulation with Boost.Move

```
1 #include <boost/move/move.hpp>
2 #include <boost/swap.hpp>
3
4 class String {
5 private:
6   BOOST_COPYABLE_AND_MOVABLE(String);
7
8 public:
9   // Constructor
10   String(const char *str = 0);
11
12   // Destructor
13   ~String();
14
15   // Copy constructor
16   String(const String& that);
17
18   // Copy assignment operator
19   String& operator=(BOOST_COPY_ASSIGN_REF(String) rhs);
20
21   // Move constructor
22   String(BOOST_RV_REF(String) that);
23
24   // Move assignment
25   String& operator=(BOOST_RV_REF(String) rhs);
26
27   void swap(String& rhs);
28
29 private:
30   char *buffer_;
31   size_t size_;
32 };
```

The key changes are as follows:

- Line 6: The macro BOOST_COPYABLE_AND_MOVABLE(String) defines some internal infrastructure to support copy and move semantics, and distinguish between lvalues and rvalues of type String. This is declared as private.

- Line 19: A copy assignment operator that takes the type BOOST_COPY_ ASSIGN_REF(String). This is a wrapper type for String to which String lvalues can be implicitly converted.

- Line 22 and 25: A move constructor and a move-assignment operator that take the wrapper type BOOST_RV_REF(String). String rvalues implicitly convert to this type.

- Note that on line 16, the copy constructor does not change.

Under a C++ 03 compiler, the emulation of move-semantics is provided without any special support from the language or the compiler. With a C++ 11 compiler, the macros automatically use C++ 11 native constructs for supporting move-semantics.

The implementation is pretty much the same as the C++ 11 version except for the parameter types.

Listing A.2b: Move emulation with Boost Move

```
 1 // Copy constructor
 2 String::String(const String& that) : buffer_(0), len_(0)
 3 {
 4   buffer_ = dupstr(that.buffer_, len_);
 5 }
 6
 7 // Copy assignment operator
 8 String& String::operator=(BOOST_COPY_ASSIGN_REF(String)rhs)
 9 {
10   String tmp(rhs);
11   swap(tmp);        // calls String::swap member
12   return *this;
13 }
14
15 // Move constructor
16 String::String(BOOST_RV_REF(String) that) : buffer_(0),
17                                             size_(0)
18 {
19   swap(that);       // calls String::swap member
20 }
```

```
21 // Move assignment operator
22 String& String::operator=(BOOST_RV_REF(String)rhs)
23 {
24    swap(rhs);
25    String tmp;
26    rhs.swap(tmp);
27
28    return *this;
29 }
30
31 void String::swap(String& that)
32 {
33    boost::swap(buffer_, that.buffer_);
34    boost::swap(size_, that.size_);
35 }
```

If we wanted to make our class only support move semantics but not copy semantics, then we should have used the macro BOOST_MOVABLE_NOT_COPYABLE in place of BOOST_COPYABLE_AND_MOVABLE and should not have defined the copy constructor and copy assignment operator.

In the copy/move assignment operators, we could check for self-assignment if we wanted by putting the code that does the swapping/copying inside an if-block like this:

```
if (this != &rhs) {
   ...
}
```

This will not change the correctness of the code as long the implementation of copy/move is exception-safe. But it would help to improve the performance by avoiding further operations in case of assignment to the self.

So in summary, the following macros help us emulate move-semantics in C++ 03:

```
#include <boost/move/move.hpp>

BOOST_COPYABLE_AND_MOVABLE(classname)
BOOST_MOVABLE_BUT_NOT_COPYABLE(classname)
BOOST_COPY_ASSIGN_REF(classname)
BOOST_RV_REF(classname)
```

You can also use BOOST_RV_REF(...) encapsulated types for parameters of other member methods, besides the move constructors and assignment operators.

If you want to move from an lvalue, you would naturally have to cast it to an "rvalue-emulating" expression. You do this using boost::move, which corresponds to std::move in C++ 11. Here are some examples of invoking different copy and move operations on String objects using the Boost move emulation:

```
 1 String getName();                        // return by value
 2 void setName(BOOST_RV_REF(String) str); // rvalue ref overload
 3 void setName(const String&str);          // lvalue ref overload
 4
 5 String str1("Hello");
 6 String str2(str1);                        // copy ctor
 7 str2 = getName();                         // move assignment
 8 String str3(boost::move(str2));           // move ctor
 9 String str4;
10 str4 = boost::move(str1);                 // move assignment
11 setName(String("Hello"));                 // rvalue ref overload
12 setName(str4);                            // lvalue ref overload
13 setName(boost::move(str4));               // rvalue ref overload
```

C++11 auto and Boost.Auto

Consider how you declare an iterator to a vector of strings:

```
std::vector<std::string> names;
std::vector<std::string>::iterator iter = vec.begin();
```

The declared type of iter is big and unwieldy and it is a pain to write it explicitly every time. Given that the compiler knows the type of the initializing expression on the right-hand side, that is, vec.begin(), this is also superfluous. Starting with C++11, you can use the auto keyword to ask the compiler to deduce the type of a declared variable using the type of the expression it is initialized with. Thus, the preceding tedium is replaced by the following:

```
std::vector<std::string> names;
auto iter = vec.begin();
```

Consider the following statement:

```
auto var = expr;
```

The deduced type of var is the same as the deduced type T, when the following function template is called with the argument expr:

```
template <typename T>
void foo(T);

foo(expr);
```

Type deduction rules

There are a few rules to keep in mind. First, if the initializing expression is a reference, the reference is stripped in the deduced type:

```
int x = 5;
int& y = x;
auto z = y;   // deduced type of z is int, not int&
```

If you want to declare an lvalue-reference, you must explicitly adorn the `auto` keyword with an ampersand (&), as shown here:

```
int x = 5;
auto& y = x;      // deduced type of y is int&
```

If the initializing expression is not copyable, you must make the assignee a reference in this way.

The second rule is that `const` and `volatile` qualifiers of the initializing expression are stripped in the deduced type, unless the variable declared with `auto` is explicitly declared as a reference:

```
int constx = 5;
auto y = x;      // deduced type of y is int
auto& z = x;     // deduced type of z is constint
```

Again, if you want to add a `const` or `volatile` qualifier, you must do so explicitly, as shown:

```
intconst x = 5;
auto const y = x;     // deduced type of y is constint
```

Common uses

The `auto` keyword is very convenient to use in a lot of situations. It lets you get away from having to type long template IDs, in particular when the initializing expression is a function call. Here are a couple of examples to illustrate the advantages:

```
auto strptr = boost::make_shared<std::string>("Hello");
// type of strptr is boost::shared_ptr<std::string>

auto coords(boost::make_tuple(1.0, 2.0, 3.0));
// type of coords is boost::tuple<double, double, double>
```

Note the savings in the type names achieved through the use of `auto`. Also, note that while creating the `tuple` called `coords` using `boost::make_tuple`, we do not use the assignment syntax for initialization.

Boost.Auto

If you are on a pre-C++11 compiler, you can emulate this effect using the `BOOST_AUTO` and `BOOST_AUTO_TPL` macros. Thus, you can write the last snippet as follows:

```
#include <boost/typeof/typeof.hpp>

BOOST_AUTO(strptr, boost::make_shared<std::string>("Hello"));
// type of strptr is boost::shared_ptr<std::string>

BOOST_AUTO(coords, boost::make_tuple(1.0, 2.0, 3.0));
// type of coords is boost::tuple<double, double, double>
```

Note the header file `boost/typeof/typeof.hpp` that needs to be included to use the macro.

If you want to declare a reference type, you can adorn the variable with a leading ampersand (&). Likewise, to qualify your variable with `const` or `volatile`, you should add the `const` or `volatile` qualifier before the variable name. Here is an example:

```
BOOST_AUTO(const& strptr, boost::make_shared<std::string>("Hello"));
// type of strptr is boost::shared_ptr<std::string>
```

Range-based for-loops

Range-based for-loops are another syntactic convenience introduced in C++11. Range-based for-loops allow you to iterate through a sequence of values like arrays, containers, iterator ranges, and so on, without having to explicitly specify boundary conditions. It makes iterating less error-prone by obviating the need to specify boundary conditions.

The general syntax for range-based for-loop is:

```
for (range-declaration : sequence-expression) {
  statements;
}
```

The **sequence expression** identifies a sequence of values like an array or a container, that is to be iterated through. The **range declaration** identifies a variable that would represent each element from the sequence in successive iterations of the loop. Range-based for-loops automatically recognize arrays, brace-enclosed sequences of expressions, and containers with `begin` and `end` member functions that return forward iterators. To iterate through all elements in an array, you write this:

```
T arr[N];
...
for (const auto& elem : arr) {
  // do something on each elem
}
```

You can also iterate through a sequence of expressions enclosed in braces:

```
for (const auto& elem: {"Aragorn", "Gandalf", "Frodo Baggins"}) {
  // do something on each elem
}
```

Iterating through elements in a container that exposes forward iterators through `begin` and `end` member functions is not all that different:

```
std::vector<T> vector;
...
for (const auto& elem: vector) {
  // do something on each elem
}
```

The range expression declares a loop variable called `elem` using `auto` to deduce its type. This use of `auto` in range-based for-loops is idiomatic and common. To traverse sequences encapsulated within other kinds of objects, range-based for-loops require that two namespace-level methods, `begin` and `end`, be available and be resolved via *Argument Dependent Lookup* (see *Chapter 2*, *The First Brush with Boost's Utilities*). Range-based for-loops are great for traversing sequences whose lengths remain fixed during traversal.

Boost.Foreach

You can use the `BOOST_FOREACH` macro to emulate the basic uses of C++11's range-based for-loops:

```
#include <boost/foreach.hpp>
```

```
std::vector<std::string> names;
...
BOOST_FOREACH(std::string& name, names) {
  // process each elem
}
```

In the preceding example, we use the BOOST_FOREACH macro to iterate through the elements of a vector of strings called names, using a loop variable called name of type string. Using BOOST_FOREACH, you can iterate over arrays, containers with member functions begin and end that return forward iterators, iterator pairs, and null-terminated character arrays. Note that C++11 range-based for-loops do not readily support the last two types of sequences. On the other hand, with BOOST_FOREACH, you cannot deduce the type of the loop variable using the auto keyword.

C++11 exception-handling improvements

C++11 introduced the ability to capture and store an exception that can be passed around and rethrown later. This is particularly useful for propagating exceptions across threads.

Storing and rethrowing exceptions

To store an exception, the type std::exception_ptr is used. std::exception_ptr is a smart pointer type with shared ownership semantics, not unlike std::shared_ptr (see *Chapter 3, Memory Management and Exception Safety*). An instance of std::exception_ptr is copyable and movable and can be passed to other functions potentially across threads. A default-constructed std::exception_ptr is a null object that does not point to any exception. Copying a std::exception_ptr object creates two instances that manage the same underlying exception object. The underlying exception object continues to exist as long as the last exception_ptr instance containing it exists.

The function std::current_exception, when called inside a catch-block, returns the active exception for which the catch-block was executed, wrapped in an instance of std::exception_ptr. When called outside a catch-block, it returns a null std::exception_ptr instance.

The function std::rethrow_exception is passed an instance of std::exception_ptr (which must not be null) and throws the exception contained in the std::exception_ptr instance.

Listing A.3: Using std::exception_ptr

```cpp
1 #include <stdexcept>
2 #include <iostream>
3 #include <string>
4 #include <vector>
5
6 void do_work()
7 {
8   throw std::runtime_error("Exception in do_work");
9 }
10
11 std::vector<std::exception_ptr> exceptions;
12
13 void do_more_work()
14 {
15   std::exception_ptr eptr;
16
17   try {
18     do_work();
19   } catch (...) {
20     eptr = std::current_exception();
21   }
22
23   std::exception_ptr eptr2(eptr);
24   exceptions.push_back(eptr);
25   exceptions.push_back(eptr2);
26 }
27
28 int main()
29 {
30   do_more_work();
31
32   for (auto& eptr: exceptions) try {
33     std::rethrow_exception(eptr);
34   } catch (std::exception& e) {
35     std::cout << e.what() << '\n';
36   }
37 }
```

Running the preceding example prints the following:

```
Exception in do_work
Exception in do_work
```

The main function calls do_more_work (line 30), which in turn calls do_work (line 18), which simply throws a runtime_error exception (line 8) that finds its way down to a catch-block in do_more_work (line 19). We declare an object eptr of type std::exception_ptr in do_more_work (line 15) and inside the catch-block, we call std::current_exception and assign the result to eptr. Later, we create a copy of eptr (line 23), and push both instances into a global vector of exception_ptrs (lines 24-25).

In the main function, we run through the exception_ptr instances in the global vector, throw each using std::rethrow_exception (line 33), catch it and print its message. Note that in the process, we print the message from the same exception twice because we have two instances of exception_ptr containing the same exception.

Storing and rethrowing exception using Boost

In pre-C++11 environments, you can use the boost::exception_ptr type to store exceptions and boost::rethrow_exception to throw the exception stored in boost::exception_ptr. There is also the boost::current_exception function which works akin to std::current_exception. But without underlying language support, it requires help from the programmer to function.

In order for boost::current_exception to return the currently active exception wrapped in boost::exception_ptr, we must modify the exception before throwing it to make it amenable to be handled using this mechanism. To do this, we call boost::enable_current_exception on the exception to be thrown. The following snippet illustrates this:

Listing A.4: Using boost::exception_ptr

```
 1 #include <boost/exception_ptr.hpp>
 2 #include <iostream>
 3
 4 void do_work()
 5 {
 6   throw boost::enable_current_exception(
 7             std::runtime_error("Exception in do_work"));
 8 }
 9
10 void do_more_work()
11 {
12   boost::exception_ptr eptr;
13
14   try {
15     do_work();
```

```
16   } catch (...) {
17     eptr = boost::current_exception();
18   }
19
20   boost::rethrow_exception(eptr);
21 }
22
23 int main() {
24   try {
25     do_more_work();
26   } catch (std::exception& e) {
27     std::cout << e.what() << '\n';
28   }
29 }
```

Self-test questions

1. The Rule of Three states that if you define your own destructor for a class, you should also define:

    a. Your own copy constructor

    b. Your own assignment operator

    c. Both a and b

    d. Either a or b

2. Assuming the class String has both copy and move constructors, which of the following does not invoke a move constructor:

    a. String s1(getName());

    b. String s2(s1);

    c. String s2(std::move(s1));

    d. String s3("Hello");

3. The purpose of std::move function is to:

    a. Move contents of its argument out

    b. Create an lvalue reference from an rvalue reference

    c. Create an xvalue from an lvalue expression

    d. Swap contents of its argument with another object

4. In which of the following cases does Return Value Optimization apply?:

    a. `return std::string("Hello");`

    b. `string reverse(string);`
    `string a, b;`
    `reverse(a + b);`

    c. `std::string s("Hello");`
    `return s;`

    d. `std::string a, b;`
    `return a + b.`

References

- *Effective Modern C++: 42 Specific Ways to Improve Your Use of C++11 and C++14, Scott Meyers, O'Reilly Media*

- *A Tour of C++, Bjarne Stroustrup, Addison Wesley Professional*

- *The C++ Programming Language (4/e), Bjarne Stroustrup, Addison Wesley Professional*

Index

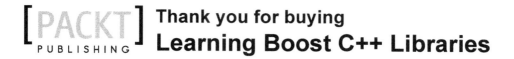

Thank you for buying
Learning Boost C++ Libraries

About Packt Publishing

Packt, pronounced 'packed', published its first book, *Mastering phpMyAdmin for Effective MySQL Management*, in April 2004, and subsequently continued to specialize in publishing highly focused books on specific technologies and solutions.

Our books and publications share the experiences of your fellow IT professionals in adapting and customizing today's systems, applications, and frameworks. Our solution-based books give you the knowledge and power to customize the software and technologies you're using to get the job done. Packt books are more specific and less general than the IT books you have seen in the past. Our unique business model allows us to bring you more focused information, giving you more of what you need to know, and less of what you don't.

Packt is a modern yet unique publishing company that focuses on producing quality, cutting-edge books for communities of developers, administrators, and newbies alike. For more information, please visit our website at www.packtpub.com.

Writing for Packt

We welcome all inquiries from people who are interested in authoring. Book proposals should be sent to author@packtpub.com. If your book idea is still at an early stage and you would like to discuss it first before writing a formal book proposal, then please contact us; one of our commissioning editors will get in touch with you.

We're not just looking for published authors; if you have strong technical skills but no writing experience, our experienced editors can help you develop a writing career, or simply get some additional reward for your expertise.

Boost C++ Application Development Cookbook

ISBN: 978-1-84951-488-0 Paperback: 348 pages

Over 80 practical, task-based recipes to create applications using Boost libraries

1. Explores how to write a program once and then use it on Linux, Windows, MacOS, and Android operating systems.

2. Take advantage of the real power of Boost and C++ to get a good grounding in using it in any project.

Boost.Asio C++ Network Programming

ISBN: 978-1-78216-326-8 Paperback: 156 pages

Enhance your skills with practical examples for C++ network programming

1. Augment your C++ network programming using Boost.Asio.

2. Discover how Boost.Asio handles synchronous and asynchronous programming models.

3. Practical examples of client/server applications.

4. Learn how to deal with threading when writing network applications.

Please check **www.PacktPub.com** for information on our titles

C++ Multithreading Cookbook

ISBN: 978-1-78328-979-0   Paperback: 422 pages

Over 60 recipes to help you create ultra-fast
multithreaded applications using C++ with
rules, guidelines, and best practices

1. Create multithreaded applications using
   the power of C++.

2. Upgrade your applications with parallel
   execution in easy-to-understand steps.

3. Stay up to date with new Windows 8
   concurrent tasks.

4. Avoid classical synchronization problems.

Getting Started with C++ Audio Programming for Game Development

ISBN: 978-1-84969-909-9   Paperback: 116 pages

A hands-on guide to audio programming in
game development with the FMOD audio library
and toolkit

1. Add audio to your game using FMOD
   and wrap it in your own code.

2. Understand the core concepts of audio
   programming and work with audio at
   different levels of abstraction.

3. Work with a technology that is widely
   considered to be the industry standard
   in audio middleware.

Please check **www.PacktPub.com** for information on our titles